CENTERS ~ INFLUENCES FROM WITHIN

The Essential Wisdom of Mindfulness and the Fourth Way

Cheryl Shrode-Noble

ISBN: 1974034062
ISBN 13: 9781974034062
Library of Congress Control Number: 2017911978
CreateSpace Independent Publishing Platform
North Charleston, South Carolina

TABLE OF CONTENTS

PREFACE

There are many paths which one can follow to develop enhanced self-awareness to achieve higher states of consciousness. These different paths may lead one to distinctive ways which can potentially help one to discover previously unknown areas within one self. On each path, there are various concepts, methods and practices which one can utilize to help develop enhanced self-awareness. But, we are all unique, so finding the right methods and tools which will work best for oneself is vital. Each of us has inherent possibilities which we may not be aware of, have not yet understood, or have not yet sincerely embraced. While many paths may exist, the most important path to follow is the one which speaks most directly and authentically to your true essential nature. Therefore, it is best to follow a path which is the most natural way for you in your normal daily life, and can be easily implemented efficiently in a practical manner.

Many of the paths that lead to self-knowledge, are complimentary to one another, primarily because at their innermost core they do not contradict one another. I have journeyed upon multiple paths studying various ways of knowledge in my personal quest for enhanced self-awareness. While traveling the world, I sought to gain a broader comprehension of the diverse cultural origins of many wisdom traditions. Perhaps because of my own essential nature and my desire to learn, numerous opportunities opened up before me. All the paths which I have encountered and studied have been uniquely beneficial, and I discovered they were also quite similar. Each way has increased the scope of my understanding and the depth of my perceptions. We live in an extraordinary world of opportunities, with endless potential to experience our personal growth. But, real growth is only available to those who are honestly willing to step outside their comfort zone of illusion, negativity, false personality, identification and attachment.

My aim with this book is to present key elements of the Fourth Way, a transformational esoteric system which I have studied, practiced and incorporated into my life since 1975, This unique system was originally taught in the early 20th century by Georges Gurdjieff, and brilliantly elucidated by Peter D. Ouspensky. The Fourth Way system of knowledge, and the extraordinary men who expounded its wisdom, have left an indelible mark on the world of self-discovery and higher consciousness. The Fourth Way abounds with insightful wisdom, guidance and effective practical methods which can help one develop enriched personal self-awareness. It encompasses a massive body of knowledge from which I have selected a small portion to elaborate, that focuses on understanding and knowing oneself deeply to the core of one's truest inner being. My primary goal is to elucidate the information about our internal centers of influence, but I have included other essential esoteric concepts to supplement and flesh out these brilliant ideas more effectively. My writings are based on my personal studies and verifications while implementing Fourth Way disciplines in my life. Thus, my understandings are derived from my own personal practice and application, direct experience, and verifications whilst studying and living with the profound concepts and practical methods of this remarkable esoteric system. The transformational psychological wisdom of the Fourth Way, has had a significant influence on my life. I have repeatedly verified that these insightful ideas and methodologies have the potential to assist sincere individuals on their personal journey to attain enhanced self-awareness.

The distinctive elements of the Fourth Way regarding our internal centers of influence within, provides a practical view of how and why we manifest as we do. These internal centers have an influence on virtually everything in our life; how we feel, think, move, sense, and, basically how we survive physically. Keep in mind, the concept about our centers of influence within, is extraordinarily unique to the Fourth Way system of esoteric knowledge. Although I have verified that many wisdom traditions share great similarities in the general body of their teachings, I have not found this exact concept about the human centers of influence explained in the other wisdom teachings, whether they were metaphysical, spiritual, psychological, or scientific. In this regard, the Fourth Way teachings about our centers of influence within are of unique significance. Learning about the centers within yourself will help you gain greater personal knowledge while you work to attain enhanced self-awareness. Recognizing the centers of influence within will assist you in comprehending yourself and other people, with much greater clarity and depth.

These unique ideas and methods can be effectively incorporated into your normal daily life in a highly practical manner. With consistent sincere mindful self-observation, you will gradually begin to harness and harmonize your internal influences, as you gain increased self-knowledge and enhanced self-awareness. The only real requirement is your sincere willingness to be present in the moment as you observe yourself impartially and honestly, so you can truly begin to know yourself. Practicing mindful self-observation regularly with the sincere desire to minimize and discard that which is false within you, will help encourage your submerged essential nature to emerge into the reality of your personal potential. You can begin to observe yourself right now in this moment, as you are and without judgment. Please always remember, no one can awaken you, but you yourself by your own efforts. We cannot depend on anyone else to elevate our self-awareness. Knowledge is power, but self-knowledge is personal empowerment.

My sincere wish is to present these ideas in a concise, direct manner to help you understand, recognize and become aware of the true inner dynamic of your essential natural self. While the external influences of life often discourage us from being true to our self, this is always counterproductive to living a more fulfilling existence. The key question in one's life should begin with, "Who am I really, at the core of my being?" Incorporating these practical concepts and methodologies into your life can help demystify the complex, elusive elements about your inner self and your true nature within in your essence. This is a practical method of self-development. Owing to the unique nature of this esoteric system of knowledge, these ideas, methods and disciplines must be put into practical use in your normal daily life to be effective and produce results.

You are your own best teacher in your personal quest to reach the higher states of your true self-awareness. Remember, only you can awaken your slumbering essential natural self within. While mentors, guides and teachers may be helpful at certain points, ultimately your personal awakening is your own responsibility. Following another person or teacher is not necessarily the most direct, or the shortest route to your personal self-realization and awakening. Keep in mind, any potential guide, teacher or school must be verified prior to embarking into their unknown realm. Establishing trust, with an honest open line of communication is a vital factor before you can realistically determine whether someone might be helpful to your personal aim, or not. Whatever you decide, my best advice is to trust your own sincere instincts. It is solely up to you to awaken by your own personal efforts. Self-knowledge, personal awareness and higher consciousness is your birthright, but there is no one on earth who can ever give you these precious treasures.

To clarify this point, Gurdjieff made it explicitly clear that one can gain self-awareness without joining a particular group or school. He emphasized that one's own life becomes one's personal path, and he called this, the objective way. Further, he said the various ways are simply help, which is given to people based on their personal individual type; however, he emphasized that one can most certainly work independently. With regards esoteric schools, Peter Ouspensky stated, there are no obligations, and, that one is certainly free to leave whenever one wishes. While many people are led to believe that a teacher, an esoteric school, or a monastery, is an absolute necessity, please understand, this is simply not true. You do not need a school, nor a teacher, and it is not necessary to go into seclusion, or enter a monastery to successfully begin working on yourself. Developing your self-awareness by employing mindful self-observation, with what Gurdjieff and Ouspensky called, "self-remembering," will greatly assist your personal efforts.

The Fourth Way terms, self-remembering and self-observation, are synonymous with the Buddhist term, mindfulness, which has been in use for millennia in the ancient Asian wisdom traditions. It may be helpful to realize the Buddhist term, mindfulness, originates in the Pali language as *sati,* and in Sanskrit as *smrti,* and both terms translate as, "to remember." This is, of course, the essential meaning and message in Gurdjieff's use of the term, "self-remembering," which he utilized in his Fourth Way directives. In this sense, Gurdjieff's terminology is quite similar to Buddhist concepts, and are employed in the same context, and for the same purposes and aims. It is reasonable to assume that many of Gurdjieff's teachings, were appropriated from the Asian ideas he encountered, and, from Buddhism in particular; as he had travelled, studied, and lived in various regions of Central Asia, including China and Tibet. It is apparent that these timeless Eastern traditions had a massive influence on his Fourth Way system, and, may well have been the inspiration for various elements of Gurdjieff's teachings. Certainly, the term, mindfulness, resonates clearly and rather distinctively with the Fourth Way concept, self-remembering to attain enhanced self-awareness.

The transformational validity of mindfulness practice is recognized and respected around the world, and is taught in many accredited academic institutions. The University of San Diego Center for Mindfulness in Southern California offers courses and retreat programs. Oxford University in England has established the Oxford Mindfulness Center which promotes training and research programs to encourage human potential, build inner strength, and reduce suffering. These are just two of the many accredited institutions for higher learning around the world offering mindfulness training to propel self-knowledge forward with a powerful practical modality. There are countless credible mindfulness meditation groups available locally as well as globally. I mention this intentionally to establish clear guidelines, so you will understand the numerous options available as you embark on your quest for self-knowledge.

Yet, your personal awakening can never be dependent upon other people, teachers, schools, or institutions. Awakening and enlightenment are the result of the dedicated individual making consistent sincere efforts. Please do not doubt your potential at any time, and do not let anyone limit your possibilities with rigid ideas or with obsolete rules and outmoded regulations. These concepts are practical methods intended to increase your self-knowledge, enhance your self-awareness and elevate your consciousness. But, there is no need to ritualize esoteric ideas in mysterious obscure hierarchical doctrines, or disguise them in dogmatic expensive elitist agendas. Please remember, there can be no restrictive dogma surrounding your personal growth and transformation. Also, these ideas are not attached to any specific religious doctrine; therefore, your belief, or faith is not required, and you are free to maintain your own personal spiritual, or religious preferences. The only requirements are your sincere efforts with attentive mindful self-observation in the moment while living with intentional presence in your normal daily life. Your awakening and enlightenment are truly your own personal responsibility.

My personal goal is to share the ideas in this book with those who recognize their unique, significant value. This practical esoteric wisdom can assist those who possess a sincere desire to gain self-knowledge. These ideas can help you, whether you are just beginning your personal path of self-study, or have been working on yourself for many years. My aim is to present these ideas and methods in a direct and lucid manner, to avoid trivializing this masterful body of wisdom and knowledge. Ouspensky encouraged us to reconstruct this system for ourselves. Hence, this book represents my sincere personal offering of timeless Fourth Way ideas, which I have studied, practiced, verified and treasured for more than 40 years. Although at this time, I have no desire to personally teach or give lectures about this system, my hope is that this book will serve as inspiration and assistance to individuals on their path to self-awareness. I simply wish to present these timeless ideas for others to explore, experience, and employ in their normal daily life.

The larger aim of this book is to inform, empower and encourage you to awaken to your natural essential self within. You are your own best teacher in your personal quest to reach the divine states of your innate higher awareness. My hope is that these ideas will inspire your aspirations to discover your true inner self, to live harmoniously in your essential nature as your guide. With sincere self-study, you can achieve enhanced self-awareness, higher states of consciousness, and personal fulfillment. My greatest wish is that these remarkable ideas will help illuminate your personal path, leading directly to your own miraculous inner self. Only you can awaken your true essential self, as no one can ever do it for you. We are each like the caterpillar that ultimately realizes its own essential nature only after it evolves into a beautiful butterfly. So too can you become what you truly are within, but only by your own consistent sincere personal efforts. I wish you timeless moments of pure self-awareness, higher consciousness and good fortune.

Your path is within you.

C. S-N.

INTRODUCTION

Throughout history mankind has sought to attain a more rewarding, joyous and meaningful life with deeper understanding. Today we continue to strive for these same ideals along with enhanced personal happiness, loving relationships, successful careers, increased prosperity and greater personal freedom. But, in our yearning to achieve a better and richer life we continually reach outside of ourselves. Despite having an abundance of everything we discover that "more" simply does not fulfill us, nor provide the answers which we seek. Relationships, money, objects, activities and endless distractions ultimately cannot fulfill our deepest needs, or our most sincere desires. In our quest to have more of everything, we often feel confused, stressed, and unfulfilled, as we become even more dissatisfied.

There is much we do not understand and many elements of life remain a mystery. At birth, we are not given technical advice or instructions on how to understand the experience of living our life as a human being. Life continues to mystify the individual striving for a more meaningful reality. We consult with doctors, priests, psychologists, psychics, fortune tellers, or search for spiritual leaders in the quest to satisfy our perennial longing for fulfillment. But, the deeper personal meaning and satisfaction we seek in life remains elusive. Instead of getting closer to our goal of living the more rewarding and meaningful life we desperately seek, we may simply end up feeling thwarted, inadequate, insecure, and perhaps somewhat alienated. We often hear people say, “There must be more to life than this;” or, at least more than they are personally experiencing. Many people seem to endure this perplexing dilemma.

Despite our vast technological achievements, we as individuals remain puzzled about our own existence in the overall scheme of life, the world and reality. But, the keys to understanding our unique personal mystery are not actually out of our reach. Philosophers throughout history have advised us to seek our answers within ourselves. Hence, the ultimate goal is to know one self. But, self-knowledge can be a mysterious realm of exploration, and where does one begin? While our personal answers may reside within us, individually we may simply not know where to look, or, more precisely, what to look for, and how to look. Self-discovery requires new methods of looking at one self in order to see one self clearly, impartially, objectively, and optimistically. It is a matter of adjusting ones focus inward with practical user-friendly guidance, methods and direction.

For the past 40 years, my aim has been to enhance my personal self-awareness by implementing esoteric sciences and psychological systems which I have studied in depth. This book focuses on some of the unique teachings from one particular esoteric system, which elucidates and demystifies the innate motivational tendencies born within us, which emanate from our inherent internal centers of influence. These internal centers act as organs of influence, stimulation, sensitivity, and perception. They can be regarded as separate brains, which predispose humans to feel, think, move, and physically sense. The four primary centers govern all our functions which include our emotions, thoughts, physical actions, and internal chemistry as physiological processes. The esoteric science regarding our internal centers of influence forms an essential component of the Fourth Way system, which was eloquently elucidated by Peter D. Ouspensky.

Having a basic comprehension of the four primary centers of influence gives one the advantage of approaching self-knowledge as an impartial science to study one self. Learning about the centers within inspires greater self-acceptance and understanding, which leads to enhanced self-knowledge. You will begin to see the influences as they affect how you feel, think, behave and sense as you do. Within this body of knowledge are effective ideas and tools to help one see one self with clarity and depth. The wisdom of this system provides essential information as to how we function as human beings. These concepts are profound in their elegant simplicity, yet lend powerful insight into the study of one self. The basic reality that we can understand our personal tendencies and traits, helps demystify the confusion of why we are the way we are. This system methodically instructs the individual to gain objective self-knowledge to achieve heightened awareness by employing mindful self-observation while being present in the moment.

My intention in writing about and detailing the internal centers of influence within all of us, along with other essential esoteric concepts, is to simplify these enlightening ideas for practical use in your normal daily life. This book is for all sincere individuals who are genuinely striving to attain more clarity, and gain enhanced self-awareness. These ideas are practical tools which can assist you to discover and unravel your own personal internal mysteries, and learn how and why your life has unfolded as it has thus far. This knowledge is powerful and can be extraordinarily self-empowering. Your personal self-knowledge is the most important knowledge you will ever acquire in your life.

The innate centers of influence described in this book are derived from the Fourth Way esoteric system of knowledge, which focuses on increasing self-awareness through one's personal efforts. Please understand, the centers of influence, as described in this book are not a reference to chakras, which are from a different wisdom tradition and are defined quite differently. From my personal studies, I have verified that chakras, as referenced in yoga, meditation, Reiki, Tibetan healing and other holistic healing sciences, are taught and utilized in a different context. The distinction between centers and chakras is quite evident. The Fourth Way system of knowledge elaborates the practical concept of our internal centers of influence to assist us in gaining enhanced self-awareness with self-knowledge. Your self-knowledge will assist your personal work as you strive to develop your inherent potential to achieve the higher states of conscious awareness.

I became interested in the esoteric ideas of the Fourth Way system during the 1970's while living in London, England, where I met Richard Gardiner, the renowned philosopher and Tarot scholar. I had been studying Taoism and Buddhism, and was interested to learn more about other ancient wisdom traditions. I traveled the world for many years for my career, but also sought greater understanding in my quest to have a more meaningful life purpose. After eight years living in Europe I returned to America to study the Fourth Way in depth, ultimately spending more than ten years in several uniquely different schools. While I studied this system in somewhat secluded schools similar to monasteries, clearly this is not possible, practical, or necessary for everyone. I wish to be clear, an esoteric school is not an absolute necessity for personal work. You can certainly develop higher awareness independently, by living your life intentionally with mindful self-observation, whilst being present in the moment. Moreover, the Fourth Way system emphasizes that one must develop self-awareness and higher consciousness in the ordinary conditions of one's normal life.

The brilliant Russian author Peter Demianovich Ouspensky gave the Fourth Way its precise and distinctive voice. He taught and wrote extensively in the first half of the 20th century as a scholar who probed the depths of knowledge, from the physical world to the mystical. Ouspensky articulated, refined and compiled the fragmentary esoteric teachings of the Greek Armenian, Georges Gurdjieff, thus elevating the ideas to the precision of mathematics. When he first met Gurdjieff in Moscow, prior to the Russian Revolution, Ouspensky was a well-regarded author with an international following, and a member of intellectual circles. It is evident that Gurdjieff actively sought out Ouspensky, reaching out to him through his own students. They initially approached Ouspensky after he returned from his travels to the Orient and India. Upon meeting Gurdjieff, Ouspensky was intrigued and wanted to learn more about his system. At that time, Gurdjieff was presenting his Fourth Way ideas as fragments.

Ultimately, it was Ouspensky who interpreted, articulated and organized the Fourth Way ideas into a cohesive system of study, as a comprehensive body of practical esoteric knowledge. His articulate voice elucidates the Fourth Way with the clarity of an enlightened scholar. But, keep in mind, these were extremely turbulent times in history, and Ouspensky's work, teachings and writings were processed through the lens of harsh suffering, amidst the difficulties of a chaotic world at war. Forced to flee his home to escape the volatile Russian Revolution, Ouspensky lived in exile while enduring hardship. He courageously prevailed through the stress of revolution, and the subsequent heinous wars that plagued Europe and the world. Like the extraordinary Peter Ouspensky, we are each influenced by the stressors of the era in which we are born. Our current generation lives with many different wars being waged, while we are enveloped in a massive technological surge forward to an unknown destination into the unforeseeable future.

Yet, our personal difficulties can help shape our character and raise our awareness if we sincerely strive to gain mastery over the negative effects they might have on us. All eras are uncertain, but we must aspire to a higher possibility, even if it appears as though the cards are stacked against us. Despite uncertainties, the inspiration to attain personal self-knowledge and develop self-awareness must continually evolve to survive in all eras. Over time the ancient truths and gems of esoteric knowledge reemerge in fresh interpretations. Timeless ideas presented in fresh ways serve new generations of sincere seekers in contemporary cultures, and breathes new life into remarkable concepts that might otherwise be considered a bit old fashioned, or out of step with the times, or the technology. While transformational ideas are timeless, virtually everything, including the profound knowledge of wisdom traditions are subject to innovation, and revitalization to render them current and fresh. The way must fit within and adapt to the times.

My aim is to present these extraordinary esoteric ideas in a direct and easy to understand manner, as simply as possible for clarity. I believe that these valuable esoteric concepts can be presented to new audiences in a user-friendly manner, aligned with and in context with our own era, as a new version of the incredible universe within us. With this as my focus I have documented the esoteric wisdom about our internal centers of influence within, to be used as a practical guide in one's normal everyday life. I have included additional essential esoteric ideas to assist you and to facilitate your understanding. These supplemental concepts can easily be incorporated into your life in a practical manner and you can begin where you are at this moment. This book has been written for those who possess a sincere desire to develop enhanced self-awareness with self-knowledge to reach higher states of consciousness. Awakening is clearly no longer reserved for monks, disciples and students living in remote monasteries or obscure esoteric schools.

As my own inner work evolves I feel a greater need to inspire others to explore the secrets which mystify and intrigue us, but with more transparent revelations. My honest aim is to reveal the primary essential elements of this miraculous esoteric system. I originally wrote the initial outline for this book in 1985, shortly after leaving a Fourth Way school. During this rather lengthy cycle I have developed a clearer sense of my personal goals, and a more precise direction for what I wish to accomplish. This book is inspired by my original outline, but has been written with enhanced objectivity, a fresh perspective and inspired rationale. Over the years my personal appreciation for this great esoteric wisdom has grown immeasurably, while my comprehension has deepened proportionately. I have worked diligently on this book for the past two years to include the essential elements of this unique system, while focusing on my personal verifications to expand and imbue the ideas with a greater sense of meaningful authenticity.

All descriptions of centers are based on my personal studies, drawn from over 40 years of work on myself; experiences and verifications with friendships, acquaintances, and from observing others. I have included personalized examples detailing how each center manifests based on people I have known, studied with, interacted with, and observed. Realistic examples drawn from life are practical and help to illustrate manifestations of the different centers within us. I wish to elucidate the centers of influence by revealing them as personally relatable, thus, clearly knowable. Individually, each of us tends to personify the general characteristics of our primary dominant influencing center. The descriptions will clarify the range of influences from the numerous centers, to help you observe them in yourself, and in the people around you. In some segments, I have combined characteristics of more than one individual into a center's description for illustrative purposes. Often, people who emanate from the same center are quite similar to each other. We can recognize familiar manifestations from various individuals who tend to exhibit similar traits, as they are being influenced by the same center within. The examples given span more than 40 years of my personal observations, experiences, interactions and verifications. Some center descriptions also include examples of historical figures, or celebrities, whose distinctive characteristics and unique traits which are commonly known. The world we live in provides us with a parade of caricatures and characters to observe as the centers of influence manifest, and this is especially true when we honestly observe our self.

We are each individually the instrument of our own observation and study for psychological growth and transformation. The only requirements are mindful self-observation and verification in your normal daily life. Regarding personal transformation, please understand you are not trying to become something, or someone, which is not natural to your true essential nature. Anything which is false in one self is a hindrance to one's development. Self-doubts, negativity, personal misconceptions, and artificially acquired traits are limitations which mislead us, and create confusion and unnecessary barriers within. When we begin to recognize, address and eradicate that which is false and unnatural in ourselves, we can finally begin to move forward successfully to achieve our higher possibilities and reach our true natural potential. One must strive to observe, learn, know, and become that which one truly is, at the core of one's essential nature. Always remember, the hidden source of your talents and abilities, natural inclinations, cherished longings, and most sincere personal desires resides within your own true essential nature.

As you become familiar with the ideas, concepts, methods, and tools in this book, the obscured mysteries about your natural inner self will gradually become more clarified. As you practice mindful self-observation you will become more transparent to yourself which assists personal growth. As you gain understanding of how centers function and process, you will begin to notice the distinctive centers manifesting in others. You will become better equipped to comprehend why people feel, think, behave, sense, act, or react as they do. This allows greater tolerance and compassion for people in your personal life, and for those you will meet.

There are no secrets, and the unknown can certainly become known. As we delve into the transformational esoteric realm, our deep inner potential begins to awaken. The aim to expand one's personal awareness has become a major force in the burgeoning consciousness movement. Awakening and enlightenment may be quite realistic, practical and realizable goals for those of us who make consistent efforts. You do not need to go anywhere and you do not need to find anyone to help you begin. You can start right now by observing yourself where you are, as you are at this moment in time in your normal daily life. You truly only need a sincere desire to be self-aware to become more consciously evolved.

Obviously not everyone on the path of consciousness has a lifestyle, or the financial means which would afford them the opportunity to study in remote lands, or secluded monasteries; and this is not necessary. There is nothing to stop you from incorporating these practical ideas independently in your life right now to facilitate and enhance your self-awareness. You can begin to work on yourself and awaken exactly as you are, and where you are now at this moment in time. Please know, you can proceed at your own suitable personal pace and desire. It is a healthy impulse to feel the need to strive for your true essential nature, to acquire real self-knowledge, and gain enhanced self-awareness. We each have an opportunity to awaken and start fresh in every moment that occurs, starting right now with mindful self-observation.

Gaining enhanced self-awareness is an equal opportunity for every sincere seeker. Please do not discount your potential to gain self-knowledge, and to actually achieve your own enlightenment. It is not impossible, and may be more within your personal grasp than you might realize at this particular moment. The fact is, we are quite often discouraged by the very systems, teachers, schools or methodologies we study. Please do not discount your true personal potential, or your innate possibilities to awaken to your own illuminated enlightenment. Your awakening and enlightenment are truly your personal natural inherent birthright.

My wish is to share these ideas with those who aspire to discover their true essential nature, to gain enhanced self-awareness and higher states of consciousness with purity and integrity.

To those who seek to awaken to their true essential nature and become enlightened, I wish you good fortune.

Your path is within you.

CHAPTER 1

ESOTERIC WISDOM OF THE CENTERS

The esoteric wisdom about centers approaches the study of the human being as an objective science. This human science advises that we can begin to understand our self if we observe our self impartially, while monitoring our innate functions and processes. Essentially there are four primary centers and their subdivisions which serve as our internal centers of influence. Each specific center is like a separate brain which governs each particular function and its processes within us. In this book, we will explore our innate centers in depth as they influence our emotions, thoughts, actions and physical senses. As you start to observe yourself you will begin to recognize the different centers as they function with their diverse, and distinct nuances. By implementing the practical tool of mindful self-observation, you will gradually become more familiar with the different centers, and the influences they have in your life. With objective practice, you will begin to gain greater control over these influences and their manifestations. Rather than simply being controlled by our centers, we can become aware of them. This encourages us to exercise intentionality to gain more conscious control over our feelings, thoughts, physical actions and senses.

One can certainly begin to take greater command of one's unique personal destiny. This is an extraordinarily wise, yet user friendly body of knowledge. Traditionally these unique esoteric concepts have been handed down orally from teacher to student; however, this is not possible for every person who has a sincere desire to gain self-knowledge to experience higher states of awareness. Yet one can commence self-study and begin to learn about and understand these beneficial ideas independently. These distinctive ideas are highly practical for personal use and can be implemented and incorporated into your life right now, as you are this moment. You have all the centers within you; you merely need to observe yourself to begin to see them.

As you embark on your journey of self-study it is important to understand that you alone are responsible for your personal awareness and developing your potential for enlightenment. Awakening, or enlightenment is only possible individually through one's consistent sincere personal efforts. Others may help you initially, however, you cannot become enlightened in masse with a group. It is simply not possible to awaken simultaneously or artificially with other people. This is a critical point that you must remember. If you are ever pressured, or feel overwhelmed by any person, group or teacher that insists that you cannot do it alone, remember to return to this vital point. While you may wish to spend a bit of time studying with a mentor, or with other people in a group, temple or monastery, ultimately you must understand that you alone are responsible for your personal awakening and enlightenment. Monasteries or esoteric schools may teach, but they cannot grant or guarantee your personal awakening or enlightenment. Self-awareness is a personal task, and can only be acquired through one's own consistent sincere efforts. This is the reality of the situation for everyone, and it always will be. Awakening is your personal work. No one can ever awaken you, but you yourself. Enlightenment is solely your personal responsibility.

Strive to remain tranquil and impartial as you mindfully observe yourself, to recognize your feelings, thoughts, physical actions and senses. It is with personal verification that these enlightening ideas come alive and become part of your own inner wisdom. Throughout his teachings, Ouspensky insists on the empirical need to verify everything. Perhaps because of his personal experiences, he reminds us of the necessity for verification. He advises us to make consistent and tenacious personal efforts to self-observe, while being present in the moment. Remember, you can awaken by your own sincere, consistent personal efforts; but, no one can do it for you. It is my strong belief that many individuals can become more conscious than they realize, and they have the potential to awaken to become enlightened. Begin to practice mindful self-observation, paying attention with intentional presence in the moment. Your consistent personal efforts to become self-aware are essential for personal growth. Thus, you commence your journey of self-study in this moment, and in each moment, that follows. It is your consistent moment to moment efforts that will yield real verifiable results. Practice mindful self-observation whilst being present in the moment to increase your self-awareness. Everything is possible for those who make these practical conscientious efforts. Please know, you have the potential to awaken to higher states of consciousness, and you can become enlightened.

It is by our own sincere personal efforts, that we gain limitless possibilities to awaken. This is your personal journey of self-exploration to discover your vast deep inner spaces. From this unique inward perspective, you will gain a firm grasp on the essential reasons of why you feel, think, move, sense and experience life as you do. You are only limited by your personal cloud of self-doubt, illusory self-perceptions, negative imagination, artificially acquired traits, and unnecessary attachments. Your natural potential to become enlightened is already within you. It waits patiently for you to realize your true essential nature and to explore your own personal universe within as you journey on your path to self-awareness and enlightenment

The history of Esotericism and timeless wisdom teachings: Extraordinary people have left a vast legacy of timeless esoteric teachings to guide us on our path to become self-aware. The heroic beings who preceded us achieved enlightenment and bequeathed their astonishing wisdom to inspire us, but also, to put into practical use. As we seek to understand our true deep inner nature it is vital to use the revealing knowledge they have left for us. Understanding the unique esoteric science of centers helps us achieve enhanced knowledge of our personal inner dynamic with much greater insight into our own authentic essential nature. The eternal knowledge and timeless teachings which have prevailed through the ages were realized by and manifested through the greatest minds of history. To this day, we continue to study and benefit from their miraculous legacies. These great beings reached beyond the summit of consciousness bequeathing massive volumes of knowledge and expanded wisdom to posterity, each in their respective areas of expertise and mediums of expression. Piercing the walls of ignorance and distorted illusions they broke free of their own limitations, elevating and liberating their consciousness from the ordinary pervasive realms of delusion.

Many of the monumental beings from recorded history continue to educate us, and to elevate our minds. Among these immortal greats are Pythagoras, Socrates, Plato, Buddha, Lao Tzu, Wu Men, Copernicus, Galileo, Leonardo Da Vinci, William Shakespeare, Johann Goethe and many others. Their astonishing efforts have given us timeless treasures which encompass a vast range of subjects including philosophy, psychology, mathematics, science, theology, architecture, engineering, art, literature, nature, spirituality, mysticism, and progressive thought which continues to inspire our personal aspirations. Entire kingdoms would later be shaped along the lines of their elegant themes and ideologies, such as the ancient Greek classical influences on the mighty Roman Empire.

These beings reached the pinnacle of awareness to realize great enlightening truths, while simultaneously attracting opposition and often imperiling their own lives. Their brilliant works shook the foundations of convention and threatened the status quo which governed with an iron fist. For some their massive efforts caused them personal conflict and suffering within their own lives. Socrates was condemned to death for influencing the young minds of ancient Greece. Others met with similar fates, harsh judgments and imprisonment, with extreme suffering and death as their reward. Many enlightened beings whose lives, ideals and teachings raised controversy or suspicion faced extreme adversity. The greatest minds and souls of history were often penalized by the very civilizations they sought to help enlighten. It became vital for these philosophers, artists, scientists, astronomers, and others, to shield their work, their wisdom and enlightened teachings from ruling bodies and rigid government policies. Forging a path to awakening, many went underground for self-preservation and protection. Flying below the radar of conventional thought and dogma, their powerful wisdom and teachings were obscured or camouflaged for their personal survival. Their vast and immeasurably powerful bodies of knowledge were often passed down in oral traditions, from teacher to student in esoteric monasteries and secret societies. Others veiled their teachings in mathematical equations, diagrams, symbols, poetry, art, and architecture which has endured through time.

Great knowledge has power and endurance, leaving a perpetual legacy in diverse forms. Classical literature endows us with powerful stories whose deeper meaning may be veiled, but can be uncovered with increased effort. One must penetrate beneath the surface to grasp treasure troves of insight, knowledge and wisdom. However, one thing is constant, despite adversity and obfuscation, real knowledge endures through the cycles of time, emerging from suppression to become immortalized and live on for newer generations to encounter, investigate, unravel and decipher. Through the ages, great systems of esoteric knowledge evolve, reemerge and are rediscovered in fresh interpretations which trickle into the cultural consciousness to inspire new seekers who aspire for self-knowledge. Timeless wisdom must be presented in a manner that speaks directly to the contemporary culture.

Each individual who encounters these precious gems of wisdom tends to comprehend it through the lens of their own life and personal experience. Those of us who take it upon ourselves to breathe new life and fresh energy into these precious concepts do so with the greatest respect and the purest hopes, so they will not be overlooked or forgotten. Great knowledge is not predicated upon trends or style; however, to discover it one must be able to recognize it in one's life. But, we can only recognize what we need to know when we have sufficiently prepared our self with an open heart and a willing mind. Truth is alive for those who possess a sincere desire to discover it.

Timeless knowledge and wisdom inspire us to raise our level of awareness, to refine our thinking, and to strive to reach our goals even if they feel impossibly difficult to achieve. These ideals implore us to look within to become in harmony with our true essential nature. As we strive to develop, we fortify our character with self-awareness, consciousness, compassion, conscience, humility, humanitarianism, tolerance, and respect for others. Let us also remember to honor and respect our dear earthly environment.

The Esoteric, Mythical and Mystical:
While studying the esoteric concepts of the Fourth Way system of knowledge I came to learn about certain hidden deeper meanings within the mystical teachings of many ancient mysteries. In his writings, Peter Ouspensky makes references to the veiled messages and deeper knowledge underlying the symbolism of the Tarot, Astrology, and other mystical systems of symbolic esoteric wisdom. He emphasizes that certain symbols represent quite exact truths and have very specific meanings. He advises us to explore these mystical concepts, encouraging us to interpret the hidden meanings and penetrate to the deeper knowledge hidden beneath and within these shadowy secretive vaults.

Mystical concepts have been alluded to throughout history in legends, mythologies, fables, and folklore, preserved intact cloaked in symbolism. Beloved childhood fairy tales such as, "Alice in Wonderland," kept us enthralled with magical misadventures and strange creatures. Our favorite fantasy stories are filled with bizarre characters we laughed at, admired, or shuddered in fear, or disdain. Most people regard these odd characters as purely fictional. But, what if these distinctive caricatures with their peculiar attributes and strange traits actually do exist? And, what if they are readily observable in our own normal daily life? Yet, how is this possible, and what exactly should one be looking for? Often, we see and experience diverse qualities and puzzling traits in others that perplex or confuse us. Certainly, it would be very helpful to understand others with greater clarity and insight. I will go into depth addressing these questions and many others with practical answers that can help define the hidden meanings. Most importantly the answers will help you to see and observe yourself in new ways.

Fairy tales are typically characterized by strange people and creatures with distinctive and exaggerated personalities. But, is it possible that some of these features and characteristics might be visible in one self, or in others? This becomes quite apparent as we peek through the layers of accumulated personality traits to observe our self and others with enhanced perspective and objectivity. You may begin to notice features or patterns of behavior in yourself, or, in others that are somewhat reminiscent of fairy tale caricatures. Take a moment to think about your personal friends, your family and yourself. Is there anyone you know who reminds you a particular character, or type? Consider the melodramatic and volatile Queen of Hearts from Alice in Wonderland. Does her extremely unpredictable and turbulent nature remind you of anyone? Or, perhaps someone you know is more like the pensive King of Hearts, who solemnly endures the Queen's outlandish temper tantrums. Though exaggerated, many caricatures from fairy tales seem to illustrate vivid patterns of human behavioral traits quite explicitly. These observable behavioral traits are characteristic of the specific centers of influence which exist and function within each of us, although, certainly, with varying degrees of influence. Some influences have greater impact on us, while others much less; however, these influences are present in all of us to some degree.

Lewis Carroll had a vast comprehensive grasp of our human behavioral traits which we clearly recognize in his monumental, phenomenal story, Alice in Wonderland. His knowledge of how the centers work within us is clearly evidenced in each character as portrayed by different playing cards. He paints a vivid picture of how the numerous centers manifest as they each perform their various unique functions. We can see the Queen of Hearts depicted as a highly explosive character, acting and reacting almost uncontrollably, with her volatile bursts of emotional energy. Whereas the quiet King of Hearts remains dignified and thoughtful as he ponders more equitable diplomatic solutions to problems, pressures and demands. The Jacks are depicted as utilitarian and mechanically useful, while, trying to get their work done, perhaps haphazardly, in an automatic manner amidst terribly chaotic circumstances. They are fast paced, and energetic as they frenetically paint the roses red without a single question, and perhaps with very little thought being given to the rather bizarre task at hand. The Jacks function somewhat like automatons in this regard.

Many great mysteries are visible in our daily life if we simply know how to look for them. Cloaked within a deck of playing cards is the esoteric system of knowledge about our innate internal centers of influence. The ancient wisdom symbolized within the playing cards belies its depth and complexity. The unique symbols represent the complex internal workings of our emotional, intellectual, physical, physiological, and, our more conscious and refined self, which we have the potential to become. Each card depicts one of the primary centers and its subdivisions which influence and govern all the functions and processes within us. The iconography of each card represents one of our human functions which are the result of internal influences from a particular center. However, it is important to understand that no specific center has an advantage over another, regards working on oneself to become self-aware and more conscious.

Influences from the four primary centers predispose us to feel, think, physically move, sense and survive. This system proposes that our internal centers stimulate and activate much of our behavior, functions and manifestations. These internal influences emanate from the centers which exist within each one of us. Just like a deck of cards, there are at least 52 different centers within us. Each card in the deck is a symbolic representation of one of the centers that govern each of our functions. These symbols represent each center functioning within us which are directing our feelings, thoughts, movements and our physical survival. The four primary centers, through which we live and experience our lives, exert their continuous influence over how we feel, think, move, and sense. This esoteric wisdom within playing cards has remained relatively invisible throughout history, almost as though it was hidden in plain sight. We will uncover the influences of each card in the deck as we explore our own innate functions, processes, manifestations and sensations.

Understanding our human behavior as a function of centers helps us to see our self with greater facility and objectivity. This system is based on the esoteric concept that within the human being the many different centers perform their functions just like separate brains, or motors which influence our emotions, thoughts, movements, and physical sensations; hence, most of our manifestations. Typically, one center predominates in each person and it is around this particular center that one's life tends to revolve. This dominant center which is one's primary influence in life is known as one's center of gravity. This center of gravity tends to influence and determine what one is interested in, what one is attracted to and how one lives one's life, with regards to personal preferences and behaviors, and also, with regards to one's relationships with others. Understanding that each person has a specific center of gravity influencing their actions and their behavior helps us recognize certain repetitive traits, characteristics, and habitual manifestations. We have all of the centers within us, but are relatively unaware of them until malfunctions occur, such as with illness or injury. As we are not generally cognizant of the functioning of our centers, some of their qualities and abilities are somewhat diminished; hence our lives may be slightly out of balance. Learning about, observing and recognizing how the centers function within us, helps us to gain more control over habitual patterns and tendencies. Ideally you will learn to recognize and become aware of your centers, in order to achieve balance and harmonious equilibrium. Studying the centers becomes a valuable transformative tool that can assist one in developing greater self-awareness with enhanced self-acceptance and personal understanding.

The transformational wisdom about centers permeates Peter Ouspensky's Fourth Way writings and lectures. I studied the symbolism of the playing cards as a representation of our internal centers of influence in all the Fourth Way schools which I participated with for more than ten years. However, each school had a slightly different approach to how they presented the ideas, each with their own perspective of the teachings. With a few of the schools, their approach to Fourth Way concepts and methodologies were dependent upon whose line of thought had influenced them the most; whether it was Ouspensky's massive intellectual genius, or Gurdjieff's sly man approach. Nevertheless, each school I studied and participated with, added another dimension to my knowledge. So, I was able to develop my own empirically objective overview of the ideas from various different angles of thought, with slightly different approaches to the methodologies.

When I began to study the system regarding the centers of influence more than 40 years ago, it was taught primarily as an oral tradition. There was not a lot of detailed written information available about the specific components of this unique methodology. Therefore, I took it upon myself to document my personal studies, with an emphasis on the symbolism of playing cards for understanding our human psychology, influences and behavior. While studying in these schools, one is advised not to speak of the ideas to other people, nor to speak about the school. This simple directive is to mitigate inarticulate transmission of information which can result in distortion and confusion, and may also attract opposition or negativity. Over the years, I have verified the futility of speaking about esotericism to people who are not interested. And, I have also experienced the opposite phenomenon of others becoming negative when I chose not to discuss, nor reveal my personal studies. However, informal discussions about esoteric psychological concepts and methods is discouraged for practical purposes, as it may confuse, or discourage others.

The main elements in this book are derived from the Fourth Way esoteric system of knowledge. My intention is to document these ideas in an objective conscientious manner to help preserve them honorably. With this as my primary aim, I have focused my attention on a straight forward presentation with details and descriptions based on my lengthy studies, observations and my personal verifications. I have worked diligently to eliminate unnecessary trivia which might detract from this substantial body of timeless knowledge. My intention in writing this book is to elucidate the wisdom of our internal centers of influence which are depicted as a coded symbolic formula for self-knowledge embedded in a deck of playing cards. This symbolic code illustrates the internal centers which function within each human being. To begin we simply need to know how to interpret this symbolic esoteric code in order to apply it to our self as we commence with mindful self-observation.

For over 40 years, I have consistently verified the extraordinary value of this remarkable system of knowledge. I have primarily focused my descriptions, definitions and characterizations on the concepts, methods and practical applications which I studied in Fourth Way schools. This elegant esoteric system about our centers of influence within can help you to recognize and to observe yourself from a much larger perspective, as it helps to reveal why you are the way that you are. There are also additional supplemental esoteric concepts included to help you gain a more comprehensive understanding to assimilate and utilize the information about the centers of influence that are within us all. This unique system can help you discover essential truths about yourself in an efficient manner as you make consistent efforts to practice mindful self-observation with attention and intentionality. I have followed Ouspensky's directive, and in this regard, I have reconstructed the system as he encouraged.

CHAPTER 2

CARD ELUCIDATION PART ONE

The symbolic hidden meaning within a deck of playing cards represents the different centers of influence within the human being. These centers function as separate brains for different purposes and processes. The primary centers stimulate and influence our feelings, thoughts, movements and sensory functions. As we begin to differentiate these various components within us, we will gradually separate our true self more distinctly from that which we usually consider our identity, and see the parts from which we are composed. This gives us tremendous insight into our authentic human nature. By acquiring this objectivity, we can drop the illusion that we are a cohesive being. We will see we have many components as influencing elements which need to work together harmoniously to serve our best interests and greater aspirations.

The idea of different centers operating within us becomes more obvious when we need to make important or difficult decisions. At these times, we tend to feel the straining pull of contradicting thoughts or conflicting emotions more sharply, suggesting we are a complex, multi-minded being. Sometimes, we make poor decisions which become the mistakes we regrettably realize later were not in our best interests. Perhaps you can begin to understand that a decision made at a given moment of time is based upon which center is manifesting at that particular moment. Certainly, it becomes a bit more complex as we delve into the depths of our psychological and physiological composition regarding heredity, endocrinology, socio-economic factors, education, planetary influences, and every influence we have experienced since birth, positive, negative, or neutral. The influences we live under affect the decisions we make on a daily basis. We cannot control every influence in life, but we can be more aware of them. As you study the centers, you will learn which centers are primarily influencing your life and the decisions you make on a regular daily basis.

Playing cards are a symbolic wisdom tradition which illustrates the various influencing sources of our human functions and processes for motivation and behavior. Within its symbolism is a key to a more complete approach to self-knowledge. This key can help unlock the door to an esoteric vault of valuable wisdom to help you discover yourself as a more authentic version of you. With a fundamental grasp of the centers, we begin to get a glimpse into the mysteries that comprise our numerous different functions, processes and manifestations as human beings.

We can begin to observe and verify the basic reality that:

1. We feel and emote. Feelings are a function of the Emotional Center
2. We think. Thinking is a function of the Intellectual Center
3. We move. Movement is a function of the Moving Center
4. We sense with the physical body. Our physical body is the Instinctive Center

We easily recognize that the heart suit represents the emotional center, while the diamond suit represents the intellectual center, the spades suit represents the moving center, and the clubs suit represents the instinctive center. Within the distinct iconography of the suits there exist varying levels that influence manifestations which will become apparent as we explore the relevancy of each card.

The King, Queen and Jack cards are each further broken down into three smaller units as levels of influence which are represented by the numeric cards. For example, the King of a suit represents the intellectual part of a center and the numeric cards, 10, 9 and 8 correspond to the three divisions within the King. This continues in a descending numeric pattern with the Queen, and with the Jack. We will explore the different levels within each iconic suit that further defines, refines and clarifies the individual influences and unique characteristics of each center. The aim of this book is to provide practical information to help you gain insight into your own natural psychological and physical predomination, as well as other motivations, tendencies, talents and abilities. By focusing on the four primary influencing centers that govern our human functions, you will gain greater knowledge and understanding about your life and your personal wellbeing.

Gaining self-understanding will enhance your relationship with yourself, and your relationships with others. Having a clear picture and understanding of oneself facilitates one's growth within. Achieving heightened awareness and inner harmony does not happen instantaneously; however, as you begin to make consistent efforts to observe yourself moment to moment you will gradually become more attuned to your true inner self and become more in tune with your authentic essential nature. As we observe our centers manifesting, we begin to see ourselves more clearly as we really are naturally. Please remember, it is essential to be impartial about what you see in yourself as you begin to practice mindful self-observation. Remember, it is not necessary to change anything in yourself in the beginning. Simply observe yourself as you are and where you are in your normal daily life. Obviously, it will be relatively easy to observe your ordinary habits, such as how you wear your hair, which newspaper you read and other routines that are part of your daily activities; however, these habits may have their origin in the influences of your personal center of gravity. Observing our habitual patterns of behavior, which occur almost automatically, requires that we make increased efforts with self-observation so that we may witness these habits as they manifest.

Knowledge is power, and self-knowledge is personal empowerment. To know one self begins with small, yet sincere efforts. By observing yourself you will begin to recognize your personal dominant motivator as your center of gravity. There are of course numerous other external influences we live under, and many which we have no control over; however, we can begin to understand and recognize the internal influences which our centers have directly on our life in every moment. By observing centers, we begin to see more clearly why we feel, think, move, respond, act or react in a certain manner. Understanding that we are comprised of centers that govern particular workings within us will help us in discovering our true inner self on a much deeper level. Gaining self-knowledge, even in small measure will help you to feel more at ease with yourself so that you begin to experience greater self-acceptance and self-confidence. As we develop self-awareness we may attract situations, people and opportunities that are more attuned to our true essential nature. Perhaps you will develop new life goals that are more in line with what you truly want or need. With enhanced self-knowledge and honest self-observation, one can surpass one's prior limitations.

Embarking on your path of self-discovery by observing the centers at work in yourself, will greatly assist you in becoming more fully self-aware, self-realized, and quite possibly, even becoming enlightened. But, please keep in mind that developing self-awareness is a growth process and certain things you observe about yourself may initially make you feel somewhat uncomfortable. Remember, it is vital not to judge yourself or what you see. It is best to observe yourself impartially, without self-deprecation or negative criticism. Gaining self-knowledge requires consistent efforts and ongoing attempts to see yourself more clearly. Developing awareness through mindful self-observation will bring you closer to self-knowledge. In time, your inner self will become your best guide and counselor for living your life more attuned to your true essential nature. Ultimately the most important relationship you have is with yourself.

Applying the ideas of centers facilitates your ability to see your personal natural inclinations. We generally develop preferences and tendencies based on predispositions in our dominant center of gravity. You may discover the habits which you see often, are rooted in a tendency of a specific center. Our dominant center predisposes us to feel, think, move and sense in a certain manner. Gaining insight into our internal workings with mindful self-observation ultimately gives us much more control over our emotions, thoughts, actions and manifestations. Applying the wisdom of centers in a practical manner will assist you in seeing yourself with enhanced objectivity. Implementing this knowledge will help you recognize and understand your inner world with more clarity and less confusion. This naturally affects all the areas of your life, including your relationships. Self-knowledge will help you to understand your relationship needs and may encourage more harmonious experiences with others. Overall you will gain a broader perspective of the possibilities for your personal growth and self-awareness. Gaining increased self-knowledge with mindful self-observation is an organic fulfilling exploration into your inner self. Self-knowledge and self-awareness are keys that open the doors to enhance your perceptions of the world around you and your unique personal part in it. We all fit in the world we inhabit, but we must each seek our essential part with mindful self-observation, increased awareness and self-knowledge. Practicing mindful of self-observation facilitates the discovery of our true inner essence to become who we really are deep within our natural self. The more we become what we truly are, the more we will attract and experience that which we truly desire and yearn for in our life.

I will unveil the deeper symbolic meaning of playing cards which can help you to understand your natural self as you begin to observe your personal manifestations with enhanced clarity. We each have inherent tendencies, but we are generally unaware of the separate internal motivators which influence our lives so powerfully. As you practice mindful self-observation, you can gradually incorporate these transformational concepts into your normal daily life. This is an eminently practical method to help you gain self-knowledge. For simplicity, this book is based on the symbolism of a regular deck of playing cards. The esoteric references within playing cards can be viewed on many levels. To learn about these concepts and to apply them effectively it is helpful to have an open mind and a willingness to be receptive to previously unknown information. It may feel somewhat like learning a new language. While these ideas are not really new, you may be hearing them in a different manner than you are accustomed. We often prejudge new ideas, or distort them with our own emotions or personal thoughts, which can alter their meaning. To learn about these ideas and concepts, it is best to have an open heart and a neutral receptive mental attitude. Be impartial as you verify the ideas.

Initially it is important to understand how these ideas come together in order to apply them effectively. At the present time, your personal life may feel rather complicated, your emotions may feel confusing, and your thoughts may seem out of your control. However, with mindful self-observation your confusion will gently subside to reveal a discernible pattern. As with all new psychological concepts, it is wise to take these ideas one step at a time. Start by learning the basics about centers, so you can apply them practically. Slowly you will perceive yourself more clearly, particularly in the context of the world you live in. Keep in mind, you did not just suddenly arrive where you are at this point in your life. Your life consists of many layers and many facets which you have spent all your years acquiring. Like the layers of an onion, we have multiple layers which comprise our being. Learning about centers will help you see through the many layers to recognize your more authentic self. Ideally, you will gradually peel away unnecessary layers to arrive at your true essential nature within. As you embark on your journey of self-discovery, it is vital to understand that it is really not necessary to make any drastic or sudden changes to your life.

It is helpful to realize that while you may be making incremental increases and adjustments to your awareness as you practice mindful self-observation, it may not be apparent to other people. One does not necessarily change visibly by one's efforts to become more self-aware. Becoming self-aware is an invisible process of self-improvement. However, some individuals may become quieter as they monitor themselves and their awareness, and this is perfectly normal. The optimal ideal is that one is becoming truer to one self, and in the process of developing self-knowledge and self-awareness one may discover that, "less is more," with regards one's outward energy expenditures. Gaining self-awareness is a personal and organic process of self-conservation, and, this process will help to minimize your energy leaks and harmonize imbalances.

It is vital to begin your journey of self-exploration where you are right now by simply observing yourself impartially. As you learn more about centers you will slowly begin to recognize which center or centers manifest most distinctly and most frequently in your life. You may observe that some of the centers in this book are instantly recognizable in your life, while other centers seem rather unfamiliar; perhaps they have been ignored and have remained undeveloped, but yearn for expression. Our life is often a combination of what we need to do to get by on a daily basis, in contrast to what we deeply yearn for while hoping to fulfill our dearest wishes and most cherished dreams. As you begin to see yourself as you truly are in your essential nature, it will help you to actualize your hopes and achieve your dreams. Living in one's essential nature brings one closer to reality as it is happening moment to moment. Living in the present is the beginning step to attaining a realizable enlightened future. Remember, your path is within you.

CHAPTER 3

CARD ELUCIDATION PART TWO

A simple deck of playing cards can be used as a powerful tool that will help you gain greater insight into your personal internal influences. Virtually all of our behaviors and manifestations, how and why we feel, think, move and sense, are influenced by our personal center of gravity. Using the system of centers for guidance along with a deck of regular playing cards will provide a solid foundation for understanding your innate qualities and inherent dispositions. From this perspective, you will begin to recognize the symbolic centers portrayed in playing cards, as an esoteric psychological system about our inherent human potential. Incorporating these ideas with consistent mindful self-observation will help you to understand yourself in an objective and impartial manner that is conducive to healthy self-confidence and enhanced self-esteem. Ideally you will become more self-aware to attain balance in your centers for optimal internal equilibrium. As you will discover, a deck of playing cards can be used as a valuable tool for your self-development. With practical application, you will get a glimpse into your inner psychological dimension, including your emotions, thoughts, actions, impulses, and your physiological and sensory nature. Each card in the deck represents a center corresponding to the functions within the human being. The functions of the four centers manifest as the emotional, intellectual, moving and instinctive centers within us. The centers represent the feelings, thoughts, actions or movements, and sensory physiology inherent in a healthy human being. As implemented herein, these centers correspond to the hearts, diamonds, spades and clubs that we recognize in playing cards. These centers are referred to as the emotional, intellectual, moving and instinctive centers.

Playing cards as we know them today, appear to be of European influence, especially in the style of the royalty cards. But, it is quite likely that playing cards originated in China. History reveals that the Imperial Chinese had playing cards as far back as the 9th century, during the Tang dynasty (618-907 CE). Just prior to this era woodblock printing began in China, flourishing as it promoted Buddhism throughout Asia. Chinese pictograms and calligraphy express ideas and knowledge. The massive volume of ancient Chinese wisdom regarding human physiology, psychology, and philosophy has prevailed for more than 2,500 years, influencing almost every element of Chinese culture. Taoism, Confucianism, Buddhism, the wisdom of nature, music and the arts intermingle fluidly in Chinese traditions. Playing cards travelled the ancient Silk Road, with knowledge and merchandise, but in a very different early style, gaining popularity throughout Asia, and later, in Persia, India, and Egypt, while appearing in Europe by 1377. The Tarot Deck originated in Italy, circa 1440, at the time of the Renaissance, during the Visconti-Sforza duchy, and later gained favor in France. The Renaissance was a time of innovative creative genius from artists like Leonardo da Vinci, and, perhaps, a source of masterful hidden esoteric knowledge. The Renaissance was also a time of religious oppression, and those who questioned the church were branded as heretics, targets for harsh treatment, and even death. Many cloaked their personal ideals, vast knowledge and massive wisdom in creative mediums.

Exactly where, when and who introduced the distinctive iconic symbolism of the centers into the cards is unknown. Decks of cards have evolved over the centuries, through turbulent times, different countries, cultures, and customs to prevail to modern times. And the history of both decks is interwoven, yet often misinterpreted. There are distinct similarities between a deck of playing cards which consists of 52 cards and the Tarot Deck which has 78 cards. Some say playing cards were derived from the Tarot as a streamlined version of the hidden esoteric and psychological concepts. Yet it is possible that each deck influenced the other as both decks appear embedded with similar symbolic esoteric knowledge. Looking at the cards we recognize a constant in both decks, the royal court cards, the suits and the numbers. Both decks have evolved over time and both decks continue to be increasingly popular today, yet perhaps for very different reasons. As with any system based in symbolism, there are multitudinous interpretations and suggested usages for decks of cards. Today the most common use of the Tarot deck is divination, or fortune telling as an oracle of consultation, while decks of playing cards are synonymous with gambling and sleight of hand magic tricks. Glamorous cities, such as Las Vegas and Monte Carlo, have flourished because of mankind's intrigue with the element of chance. Cards beckon with the excitement of winning, and the mystique of magic. Playing cards carry an eternal mystic promise of magic possibilities by their very nature. Human beings seem to have an affinity for cards, a deep yearning, and we never tire of the magical potential they hint at. But, esoteric evidence suggests that playing cards are much more than a game. Playing cards were possibly designed and altered with conscious intention to create a storehouse of vital information about our most essential human nature. Human beings are the embodiment of what playing cards symbolize.

It is helpful to take into consideration that the original purpose of the cards was possibly more than fortune telling or games. Playing cards are an ideal medium to preserve specific ideas and symbolic knowledge regarding human functions, processes and behavioral patterns. The Tarot and playing cards read like ancient databases containing information to be consulted for the purpose of gaining deeper understandings of our human psychology, emotions, thought, behavior and physiology. These repositories of hidden knowledge and wisdom continue to yield life enriching potentialities, if we simply learn how to tap into their source. We have consulted cards for answers since their inception, whether intrigued by mystical questions, financial concerns, an identity crisis, or romantic inquiries. Cards are emblematic of our search for answers and meaning in life. Centuries of humanity have utilized cards as an oracle to address our deepest mysteries. Humans have always sought comfort for their burning questions, and the answers which cards provide help enlighten and enrich our human experience. Cards can help us understand why we feel, think, behave and react as we do. Both the tarot deck and playing cards have survived to our modern times in various forms and designs with the basic symbolism intact. We can look at this lineage as having an important historic purpose and esoteric intention, yielding a continuum of diverse interpretations and methodologies. Cards have perpetuated a hidden symbolic vault of wisdom whose inner meaning can be applied practically to gain self-knowledge and enhanced self-awareness.

Playing cards serve a unique purpose as a means of gaining direct access to specific areas of inquiry with simplicity and clarity. This system aims to decipher our complex human psychology and physiology by focusing on the work of the four primary centers within each human being, and how these centers with their various subdivisions work together, creating our functions and processes. The centers represent the emotional, intellectual, moving and instinctive centers as they influence our life in every moment. Playing cards symbolize our most basic internal influences which determine how and why we function as we do. Gaining understanding about the functions and workings of our internal centers, will enhance your efforts to increase your personal self-awareness. By understanding how centers influence and affect us, we gain deeper insight into what naturally motivates us from within. As you learn about centers you can apply each card to a specific area of study within yourself. Understanding how the centers work within yourself will enhance your awareness and self-knowledge. The emphasis on self-knowledge to attain a grasp of reality is the basis for all further work in developing awareness and gaining a lucid comprehension of life. As you examine the elements of the different centers, you will see how each center exerts its distinct influence on us as we feel, think, move, sense and express ourselves on a moment to moment basis. Thus, how our own centers function, is a vital key to understand why we feel, think, move, sense and live our lives as we do.

As you begin to observe the centers in yourself a more expansive internal world will open for you. With continued sincere self-observation, you will recognize the manifestation of the centers at work in yourself, and in your life. You will more clearly understand why you or someone else behaves or reacts in a certain manner. With an objective perspective and self-awareness, you will gain a healthier understanding of your personal world as you attain greater insight and clarity into what is most important for your wellbeing. By initially studying all the cards as centers you will acquire a fundamental comprehension of the overall concept of how they manifest. You can explore each center to see which feels most familiar to you as you live your life on a daily basis. As you observe how you process emotions, ideas, movement and sensations you will begin to recognize patterns.

Watching your personal patterns will help you to recognize that you are centered in a particular card, and that particular card significantly affects your life and all that you do. We have all the centers within us, but one center, or card will predominate. By paying close attention to your natural tendencies you will begin to recognize your true essential being, your innate inclinations, tendencies, talents and capabilities. Each one of us has multiple natural abilities which we were born with. But, they often lay dormant in our life as we act out of character and stray from our true essential nature. It is vital to have practical tools to help us on our journey of self-discovery. Remember, your essential nature has the potential to create and attract what you truly need in your life. As we elevate our being through consistent mindful self-observation we attract a different level of response to meet our heightened self-awareness. The greatest reward is becoming your true self. Self-knowledge is the key. Knowledge is power, and self-knowledge is personal empowerment.

As you look at a deck of playing cards from this new perspective you will begin to see a massive volume of psychological, emotional, intellectual, physical, and physiological wisdom. As you study the different primary centers, you will notice certain elements that may feel familiar to you. Applying these elements to your life will help you to understand your personal inclinations which emanate from your essential nature. This will give you a clearer perspective and direction for your life path. Personal growth and transformation begins from within. Learning about the centers and how they influence us will help you to study their manifestation. It is important to understand each of the centers has its own distinctive characteristics and tendencies. Observing the centers in yourself is the ideal way to recognize and understand the complex being that you are. These ideas will help clear the way as you venture onto your journey of self-exploration.

Each one of us is an individual with vast possibilities. By respecting our natural inclinations, propensities, abilities and talents we can become more than we are at present. Do not discount your possibilities or marginalize your self-worth. You are a valuable human being. What is more miraculous than simply looking through your eyes and being present in the moment? Our lives become even more miraculous as we observe the world around us. Fortunately for us on planet earth the voyeuristic Hubble Space Telescope has revealed that we live in an incredibly spectacular universe. By studying the ideas cloaked within a deck of playing cards, you will acquire a more realizable grasp of the miniature, yet infinite universe contained within the human being. When we begin to understand the parallel similarities between the human being and the universe, we start to realize there is no separation, and that we are part of the limitless expanding universe. Knowing this is empowering for us as individuals

We will begin with essential defining information to prepare you for your journey of self-discovery to reach your highest natural potential. The following elucidation chapters will provide descriptive definitions of characteristics inherent with each center, which lend insight into specific functions within the human being. It is vital to have a solid foundation to build upon to reach your aim to achieve enhanced self-awareness. These ideas will help serve as your map to navigate the way to your true essential self. Each one of us has unique assets that we can tap into with enhanced self-knowledge. When we focus our attention inward we can see the world around us with greater awareness.

Living our lives with genuine self-awareness and enhanced self-knowledge complemented with dignity, integrity and compassion is probably the closest thing we have to real magic.

Always remember, your path is within you.

CHAPTER 4

CENTERS WITHIN US

To understand how centers, work within a human being it is helpful to learn certain fundamental concepts.

We each have all of the centers within, hence all the cards, or a full deck. Each of the internal centers serve a definite function for a particular purpose and manifests with a specific process. Ideally each center would work in harmony with the other centers to create a smoothly functioning human being, but this may not always be the case. Each center has its unique place within the structure and overall running of the human being for maximum levels of performance. This is their ideal purpose. However, due to endless external stimuli, multitudinous extraneous diversions, acquired traits, habits, and the incessant distractions in our life, the average human being simply does not function harmoniously. Quite often we malfunction due to wrong work occurring in our centers. Being attentive to your life as it is happening, while being more intentional in each moment and mindfully observing yourself in the present, will help restore balance to the different functions of each unique center and will help harmonize your energies and your life in general.

Having a clear understanding of the centers will help you to recognize and pay attention to their properties and manifestations as they operate. This unique knowledge can help restore optimal functionality. When our centers work together harmoniously we can accomplish our aims with greater proficiency. Remember, we each have all the centers within and all of the centers are equally useful in living our life to our fullest potential. Each center has its own essential defining qualities and each has unique inherent abilities. This will become much more apparent as you explore the various card descriptions. Keep in mind, despite their unique predispositions and tendencies, no center has a particular advantage over another regarding the development of self-knowledge, self-awareness or higher consciousness. These qualities are solely derived from your personal efforts to be present in the moment as you work intentionally to harmonize your centers.

Understanding the different functions of each center will help clarify the many mysterious and marvelous reasons why each person has certain distinctive traits. With consistent mindful self-observation, you will begin to see the specific traits and characteristics of each different center within yourself. You will become more self-aware by conscientiously making efforts to observe the centers as they function. Gradually you will become familiar with their distinctive tendencies and will recognize their manifestations in yourself and in others. This will give you the opportunity to learn why you habitually behave in certain repetitive manners. With consistent mindful self-observation, you will begin to recognize your repetitive and perhaps somewhat automatic inclinations and habitual patterns of behavior. Sincere mindful self-observation is the best method to monitor your behaviors to witness your centers as they function. As you elevate your attention you will notice when your centers are out of balance. These moments may be quiet epiphanies, but continued mindful self-observation will yield greater self-awareness for your transformation to achieve optimal balance within.

As we begin to understand the numerous internal influences, as well as the ongoing external influences we live under, it becomes easier to understand why certain energies manifest. As your comprehension of the centers increases you will begin to notice and recognize that many events seem to occur because of your personal internal influences from your centers, and not necessarily because of external events. Gaining this understanding helps one to process events which transpire with enhanced clarity, and allows us to put things into their proper perspective. While this clarity greatly assists one in the present moment, it also allows one to more fully understand past events that have occurred, along with lingering unresolved painful issues which may be holding one back from reaching one's potential. People often feel limited by memories of past events or trauma, which can create unnecessary hurdles that might stifle their personal growth. As you gain more understanding of your life in this moment it becomes easier to understand and dismiss old attachments so you can move forward with much greater freedom. Certainly, we can take greater command of situations which are occurring in our life, and begin to understand people and events as they unfold with greater lucidity than we have at the present time.

The concept, "Know thy self" has long been quoted, yet perhaps not fully understood in the context of making it a specific area of study in one's life. Learning about the different centers within will help you see how certain mechanics of human life work with elevated clarity and insight. This can propel you forward to attain enhanced self-knowledge and increased self-awareness. Used in this sense, self-awareness, does not imply self-consciousness that manifests as shyness, or embarrassment. And, it is not self-absorption or arrogance, which may be a property of other features which cause wrong work of centers, imbalances, lopsided development, or harmful psychological behaviors and attachment. Overall, it is highly beneficial to truly understand the various reasons why this wrong work might occur within us. We will explore some of the causes that result in wrong work of centers further along as we investigate other essential esoteric concepts that complement the remarkable wisdom about the centers.

How our centers function is how we feel, think, move, and sense as we live our lives. Our centers affect what we attract in our life, and how we interact in relationships with family, friends, and others. We will start by learning about the centers and how they manifest within us. In the following chapters I will describe each card regarding its function, manifestation, and purpose. Keep in mind, each card in the deck is based on a particular center which has a specific influence in the human being. Perhaps, you will notice how certain cards remind you of someone you know. Recognizing this familiarity will help illustrate how each center influences and determines an individual's tendencies, potential, their habitual behavior and their manifestations. Observing others can be a useful exercise, but, ultimately, it is primarily your personal self which you need to observe. With a bit of practice, you will begin to recognize and understand how the centers affect you, and others, and how they predispose you to certain mannerisms, behaviors, actions and reactions. This will assist you as you continue mindful self-observation to achieve enhanced self-awareness.

Learning about the centers within, will assist and inform you as you observe yourself to gain greater clarity. The key to finding your personal center of gravity is mindful self-observation. Mindful self-observation is the activity of maintaining your awareness in the moment as you objectively watch and monitor yourself. It is being present in the moment while intentionally observing oneself without judgment, deprecation, analysis or comparison. This remarkably simple practice will assist you with gaining insight into how and why you feel, think, move, and sense as you experience your life. Becoming familiar with the different centers, each with their specific traits and characteristics will advance your practice of mindful self-observation. The centers comprise a complex group of different brains like motors, which influence all our functions from within. Most likely you will begin to recognize familiar feelings, thoughts, actions, responses and sensations as you learn about centers. Remember, it is best to refrain from self-judgment or self-criticism, particularly if you see something that comes as a surprise to you, or as a disappointment. Each of us has preconceived imaginary and psychological notions of how we need improvement. Perhaps these notions need to be vanquished to eliminate the barriers which block our heightened awareness and personal transformation. There is no need to be hard on yourself or anyone else. Certainly, nearly every one can use a bit of fine tuning refinement to become our highest self.

Begin mindful self-observation with an open mind and impartial attitude. Please allow yourself to break free from the invisible barriers which have been blocking your progress and self-acceptance. The ultimate goal is to balance your own centers so they work more harmoniously. With mindful self-observation, our personal self-awareness increases as does our level of conscientiousness. Developing our conscience helps guide us to more thoughtful behavior towards our self and towards others. You can begin to view others in a different light with more attention to their situation, and with more compassion. Compassion evokes humility and greater respect for each person we encounter. With mindful self-observation, you will recognize the manifestation of the centers in yourself and in others, hopefully with greater compassion. Consistent mindful self-observation will help clarify why you feel, think, behave and react in a certain manner, day after day. Each one of us is influenced by our primary center of gravity in everything we feel, think, experience and sense. As we become more familiar with our primary center of gravity, we may begin to attract energies, people or situations to our life, that are more in harmony with in our essential nature. Perhaps, what we thought were our true needs in the past may have actually been counterproductive to our life goals, and are no longer necessary. As we become more self-aware we begin to recognize what we genuinely need, rather than seeking misguided fulfillments. Keep in mind, as we emote, think, speak, behave and sense, our life will unfold and manifest.

With enhanced self-awareness and an objective perspective, we can develop a healthier attitude to achieve a more desirable, and appropriate result. As you elevate your awareness with mindful self-observation and self-understanding you may attract a different level of response to meet your increased self-knowledge. As you consistently practice mindful self-observation you will also minimize unnecessary energy leaks which will help conserve your energy expenditures. This can assist in bringing enhanced harmony to your inner being and will steadily restore harmonious balance to your life overall. By learning about and observing the centers you will begin to recognize them as they function within you. As you sincerely observe yourself it is vital to avoid negative self-criticism. Honorably respect the authentic person you see in yourself and your vast potential. In the beginning, simply observe yourself. Then, with consistent efforts you will slowly begin to transform certain aspects of yourself which you wish to improve upon. As you observe the centers within yourself you will gradually begin to understand how they function in their processes, and a more expansive view of yourself will open up for you. "Know thyself," will become a much more realizable goal as you begin to understand the centers of influence within yourself.

The following descriptions will help you to achieve more clarity about your innate personal influences, along with your natural talents, abilities and tendencies. By observing yourself you will begin to see your personal influences with greater clarity. Practicing consistent mindful self-observation, you will grow to truly know yourself as you become awakened to your essential nature. The greatest treasure in the universe is to become your true self. Living with self-awareness and self-knowledge, while being true to our essential nature is probably the closest thing we have to real magic.

Your path is within you.

CHAPTER 5

GENERAL OVERVIEW OF THE FOUR PRIMARY CENTERS

The four primary centers are represented by the four familiar symbolic icons on playing cards as the Hearts, Diamonds, Spades and Clubs. These icons symbolize the four primary centers which govern basic functions within us. Each center function is defined and further clarified by the different Royalty cards, as the Kings, Queens and Jacks. The Royalty cards are then defined by subdivisions descending sequentially through the numeric cards, starting with number Ten, on down through to the Two of each suit, which characterize the different influencing elements of the centers. The four primary centers and their subdivisions govern the essential functions of the emotional, intellectual, moving and physiological processes in the human being.

Each center represents an element of influence over our emotions, thoughts, movements and our physical body. As you consistently observe your own particular tendencies and predispositions you will begin to understand how each of the centers functions within you, and affects your life. Keep in mind that while we each have all the centers within us, we are essentially centered in one particular dominant part which is our center of gravity. By intentionally observing your emotions, thoughts, actions, and physical functions from the four centers you will begin to notice which center tends to react, respond or manifest most frequently. As you observe functions of centers you will become aware of their tendencies to manifest in particular behaviors and habits. With consistent mindful self-observation, you will become more aware of which center predominates in your life. As you observe your inherent tendencies, predominant natural inclinations and interests, you will be able to make an assessment of which center may be your personal center of gravity. Mindful self-observation is the key to discovering your particular influencing center of gravity.

Learning about and studying the centers in our self gives us vital information which enables us to access their unique properties intentionally. The practice of mindful self-observation is an empowerment method for gaining self-awareness to increase and expand self-knowledge. When you begin to notice that the four primary centers tend to operate without your conscious participation it can motivate you to make more consistent efforts to observe yourself. To increase your personal self-awareness, it is beneficial to methodically and impartially observe the four primary centers as they function within your life as you go through your normal daily activities. You will begin to notice when you feel emotional about other people, or feel strong emotions about events occurring, such as political issues. You will notice when you need intellectual clarity, mental stimulation or more information. You will notice when you have an impulse to dance, run, or exercise. You will notice when your body needs nourishment, rest and more healthy attention.

It is an empowering initiative to bring your attention and awareness to the functioning of your centers. Simply observe yourself with attentiveness to become aware of the elements and influences in your life that you do not usually notice or pay much attention to. There is a great deal that occurs in life which just slips right past us, quite unnoticed. Mindful self-observation assists us in being more present in the moment, but it requires consistent efforts to bring our self-awareness and attention to all that we feel, think. do and sense. Bringing your awareness to the diverse functioning processes of the different centers with self-observation will help you see which specific center manifests most prominently and regularly in your life. Keep in mind, all the other centers will continue to function in their normal capacities, though some may be less noticeable or observable than other centers. As we raise our level of awareness with mindful self-observation we can experience each moment more intentionally which helps balance all of our centers. This has a normalizing and harmonizing effect on our life overall. This harmonizing influence allows many aspects of our life to be more under our direct control with our active participation, rather than everything just happening to us.

For example, quite often we multi-task while juggling our emotions, thoughts, actions and physical needs. Our centers get over loaded and we do not function optimally, nor efficiently. This causes our centers to be out of balance as the wrong center is trying to do the work of another center. When wrong work occurs in our centers it can result in energy loss, confusion, imbalance, unhappiness and general disharmony. Mindful self-observation helps us to maintain our true inner balance and restore optimal functioning to our centers.

In the following segments, you will discover what the iconic Hearts, Diamonds, Spades and Clubs suits symbolize and the varying influences they exert on us as we live our lives. It helpful to understand that each center lends certain characteristics and contributes specific factors which influence how and why we feel, think, move, or physically respond to our life. I will begin with an overview of what the Hearts, Diamonds, Spades and

Clubs iconography represents to elucidate the general characteristics of each of the iconic suits. The following segments provide characteristic descriptions of the four iconic suits and how they represent the four primary centers. In subsequent chapters I will go into greater detail regards functions, processes, tendencies, manifestations, and inherent behavior patterns of each center from their different numeric parts.

As you explore each of the various distinctions and defining clarifications you may begin to get a general sense of which suit, and perhaps, which cards seem the most familiar to you as applied to your own life. With ongoing mindful self-observation, you will be able to make an informed determination of your personal center of gravity. This may take some time to evaluate, but with sincere mindful self-observation and patience, you will be able recognize your own specific influencing traits with much greater clarity. Again, it is important be as impartial as possible about what you observe. As you get more familiar with the different centers, you will begin to truly understand why people are so very different from one another, and also, why they are sometimes quite similar to one another.

Please understand, in the beginning it does not matter which card you are centered in as you can utilize the powerful strengths of all the centers. Eventually, you can incorporate all the centers into your life more fully by accessing them intentionally with mindful attentiveness. This enables you to consciously direct the energy of the centers to their necessary purpose, rather than being habitually controlled by your center of gravity. At this point it will be useful to make notations of your observations for reference later. Your notes will help you to recognize your repetitive and habitual patterns of emotion, thought, movement and sensing.

Knowledge of the centers used as an objective tool helps give you the necessary overview to know yourself more honestly and to live your life with heightened attention and mindful presence. It is highly beneficial to attentively observe our internal influences in order to live our lives more intentionally and consciously. Without gaining knowledge of the essential components and basic workings of the complex human being, it is difficult to understand the numerous complications that arise in our daily life. With consistent mindful self-observation and increased self-awareness, one will gain more conscious control of the centers within.

We can actively participate in gaining more control over functions of our centers, rather than allowing our functions to control us. When we observe ourselves clearly with objectivity, we can see where we are losing energy on a moment to moment basis. If we do not pay attention we slip into habitual patterns that manifest in unmonitored energy drains, creating stress or strains which deplete our valuable life energies. Using the technique of mindful self-observation allows one to be more attentive to the centers while conserving one's energy. Developing intentional attentiveness will help bring elevated self-awareness to all your centers. Increasing your self-awareness with mindful self-observation allows you to gradually gain control over your centers and over your life. Please remember, it is not necessary to change anything in the beginning. Simply observe yourself with attention, and what you shine light on may actually begin to change naturally.

As we acquire more understanding of how the centers function, influence and manifest, perhaps we will also gain a bit more compassion and tolerance for our differences. By observing different people in various situations, whether adults or children, we begin to notice certain specific characteristics in each of them. Watch a group of children playing a game of baseball. Some will be lean and athletic, hitting every ball as they effortless score home-runs. Other children may giggle and laugh in merriment as they miss the high, flying baseballs that zoom right past them. This is a simple comparison of the differences between a moving centered child and an emotionally centered child. Keep in mind, no center is better or worse than another and each person has the potential to excel within their personal center of gravity. Watch your favorite emotionally centered Auntie as she brings family, friends and others together for the holidays. Watch your clever accountant as he calculates your taxes, his glasses sliding down his intellectually centered nose. Watch your favorite basketball player make every hoop, as he effortlessly scores points with his coordinated moving centered body. Watch the gourmet chef at your favorite restaurant preparing sumptuous foods with his keen instinctive sensory knowledge, while everyone awaits their delicious plate.

In the beginning, you may not recognize the subtle nuances and variances of each card, but keep observing, as the distinctive differences of the centers will soon become more apparent. Used as a method to observe one self and others, study of the centers allows for a deeper penetration into the mysterious realm of human behavior. Understanding our unique differences and familiar similarities gives us immeasurable guidance and knowledge. As you begin to understand yourself with greater clarity, your personal self-awareness will increase. Consequently, your relationships, direction and general life decisions will become less challenging and more comprehensible. The knowledge of centers is a transformational tool to help you gain enhanced self-awareness and higher consciousness. Working with mindful self-observation and the knowledge of centers will help you achieve a healthier psychological environment for yourself and others in your life.

Keep in mind, metaphorically each normal individual has a "full deck," within, with all of the cards of every iconic suit and number that exist in a deck of playing cards. As you begin to practice the art of mindful self-observation you will soon recognize manifestations of the different centers as they function within yourself. As with most new experiences, mindful self-observation may feel a bit awkward initially, but continue to make sincere efforts. Consistent, impartial self-observation is recommended. Please remember, you do not need to change anything in the beginning, simply observe yourself impartially without judgment or criticism. It is helpful to treat this as an experiential human science to gain enhanced human knowledge. Please allow yourself sufficient experimentation in the beginning to become familiar with the process. Consistent efforts to observe yourself will naturally yield increased self-awareness. As you gradually build your personal self-knowledge base with conscientious mindful self-observation, you will naturally attain enhanced self-awareness, ultimately gaining higher states of consciousness.

The following overview of the four primary centers will introduce you to the realm of the individual centers. There are fifty-two cards in a deck of playing cards, which suggests there is the possibility of fifty-two different influencing centers within us. We will commence with the four primary centers so you can familiarize yourself with the attributes, processes, traits and the general characteristics of the symbolic suits. Remember, each card represents a different function within the human being. After the primary overview, we will explore the Royalty cards and the numeric subdivisions within each symbolic suit. This will refine and clarify nuances, variances and tendencies of the parts within the iconic royalty suits. As you learn how the centers manifest, you will begin to recognize their distinctive elements in yourself and in others. Some of the descriptive traits and characteristics may inspire you laugh, or cry. Or, you may find yourself thinking about intellectual matters while analyzing ideas. Other descriptions may make you want to dance, jump or move about, while other examples may quite possibly, make you feel rather hungry, or a bit sleepy.

Please understand that any reaction you have, positive or negative, may indicate that the very center you are reading about is being activated by this new information and your mental stimulation about it, and this is perfectly natural. Continue with impartial mindful self-observation and monitor what occurs within.

Your path in within you.

CHAPTER 6

THE FOUR PRIMARY CENTER'S ICONOGRAPHY

Regarding the Hearts:

The Hearts correspond to the Emotional Center within the human being. Our emotions are generally what we refer to as our "feelings," which influence our emotional needs, responses and reactions to emotional stimuli. Emotions can range from the simple joys of life, to the depths of sorrow, and the emotional feelings we experience such as love, happiness, anger or hatred. Keep in mind, the depth to which one experiences emotions will depend on one's center of gravity. However, we are all equipped with an emotional center, to a greater or lesser degree. Emotion is the sensation we feel within the realm of the chest and heart, and sometimes the solar plexus, when the stimulation of an emotional nature triggers a response, attraction, action or reaction. Emotions are felt almost instantaneously as the emotional center is the fastest organ of perception in the human being.

An emotionally centered individual will experience their life primarily through their emotional impressions, stimulations, and emotional perceptions. Their personal emotional feelings are of paramount importance, whether positive, negative or neutral. The emotional center is attuned to emotional stimuli.

Depending upon a person's placement within the emotional center, the stimuli may consist chiefly of interactions with other people, but may also be stimulated by experiential impressions such as art, literature, and music. Where one is centered in the emotional center determines how one will respond to emotional stimuli. The level of emotional impression one responds to depends on one's personal center of gravity, or which part of the emotional center one is influenced by. The range of emotional stimuli will vary from friends and family, babies and puppies, soap operas on television to the theater or opera, comic books to fine art museums, greeting cards to Rembrandt paintings, and so on, depending on the person's emotional requirements.

The emotional center is a receiver and storehouse of energy, like a wonderful battery that we can tap into, whether we are emotionally centered or not. We all have an emotional center and by harnessing this energy we can utilize it to our advantage. The emotional center receives, processes, manages and responds to our experiences of emotions and feelings about virtually everything in our life. This includes other people, our preferences for socializing, art, music and essentially anything we feel emotional about. The emotional center serves as an organ of perception for emotions, feelings, responses and reactions to emotional stimuli. Again, the emotional center is the fastest of the four primary centers. With the emotional center, we experience emotions in varying degrees depending on which particular subdivision center predominates. The emotional center has the ability to assess situations and emotional climates immediately when working correctly. The emotional center, as with all centers, works best when we employ mindful self-observation and attentive intentionality to normalize, maintain balance and minimize energy loss.

As the emotional center works at a speed faster than any other center it is an excellent organ of perception capable of almost instantly assessing a person, or a situation. Whether or not this perception is utilized depends upon many factors, including one's insecurities and self-doubts. For example, one may meet a new person at an event or through one's friends, but the emotional center may sense this is a difficult person as a warning. However, we often ignore our powerful emotional insights and perceptions, which may cause us to feel self-doubt. This is an example of how we may not always make proper use of the important messages we receive from the emotional center. Learning to trust the instantaneous perceptions of the emotional center may provide vital clues which you can learn to pay attention to. Also, the depth and manner to which a person experiences these perceptions, depends on where they are centered in the hearts. Of course, how they act out and respond to their perceptions is also based on this placement. The depth of the perceptions and the responses which the individual experiences to emotional stimuli depends upon whether they are centered in the King, Queen or the Jack of Hearts. Each part of the emotional center influences the degree to which emotions are felt or perceived, how emotions manifest, or how one reacts and responds. And each part accordingly affects the speed with which this occurs.

For example, the emotional center is stimulated by emotional input as energy. A person who is centered in the King of Hearts will respond and experience the stimuli or emotions in a slightly slower, more subdued or restrained manner. The emotional emanation of a Queen will be fast, robust, effusive, volatile and audible depending on the nature of the stimuli, positive or negative. While, the Jack of Hearts tends to have an instantaneous habitual or automatic response from the emotional database stored in their memory banks. Thus, the King of Hearts may be stimulated by fine art, literature and music. The Queen may be stimulated by other people, flattery, lavish gifts and a lot of attention. The Jack of Hearts may be stimulated by simple fun, melancholy and sentimentality, such as elicited by birthday parties and greeting cards. Keep in mind, these are highly simplified examples to illustrate the diverse emotional responses from the different parts of the heart suit. Generally, people are somewhat more complex than this. We can gain more understanding about our emotions by carefully monitoring them as we mindfully self-observe.

One can also learn to discern the differences between the emotional center and what may be the emanations of the other centers. For example, the sensation of hunger is not a property of the emotional center, but of the instinctive center. However, if one becomes excessively hungry, the emotional center may get involved to express its physical discomfort. Reading a mystery novel can stimulate the intellectual center, but it is the emotional center which enjoys a heart wrenching romantic love story. When you feel elated after a physical workout it is a result of the moving center stimulating endorphins, rather than the emotional center. We work with our emotional center to develop loving emotional relationships. However, certain physical attractions may be attributed to the instinctive center. It is beneficial to observe different emotional feelings and the various physical sensations you experience to accurately attribute them to the proper center. As we learn and discern the difference between emotions and what are sensations emanating from other centers, we can begin to experience our emotional center more directly and distinctly.

Our preferences, loves, likes and dislikes are determined by our emotional center. Certainly, our personal relationships stimulate and require a large amount of emotional energy. By gaining an understanding of the emotional center we begin to get more control over the emotions we might feel for another person. Learning about and understanding the emotional center will help to determine more clearly the emotions which one is feeling. Emotionally centered types are drawn to interests and activities that keep their emotional energies activated, enlivened and fulfilled. The actual placement within the Hearts depends which card, or part that one is centered in. This card will influence the range of emotional interests, attractions, interactions, responses and reactions; whether it is fine art impressions or birthday parties. We will explore each card within the Heart suit individually in subsequent segments.

General Physical characteristics of the Hearts:
Physical features and characteristics of the emotionally centered individual will depend upon where they are centered in the Hearts suit; however, they have a tendency to be somewhat soft or fleshy. This fleshiness can range from having a slightly soft appearance to being quite overweight; however, body weight will be further influenced by the placement within the hierarchy of the suit. By comparison, the King of Hearts as the intellectual part of the emotional center tends to be much slenderer than the emotionally voluptuous and excessive Queen of Hearts. But, the Queen of Hearts will have more abundant and lavish appetites than the rather moderate King of Hearts. Due to their moving element, the Jack of Hearts tends to be slenderer than the highly emotional, fleshy Queen of Hearts who has big appetites. Emotionally centered individuals may tend to gain weight and experiment with dieting more often than the other centers. Yet, this may simply be attributed to their social interactions with others, which often revolve around festivities and celebrations. Parties, lunch dates, dinners and social gatherings are second nature to emotionally centered types, as other people stimulate their emotions. The appetites of the emotional center correspond to the characteristics of the predominating part, whether the King, Queen or the Jack, and which numeric part one is centered in.

The different parts of the iconic Hearts suit will be further clarified in subsequent descriptive segments.

Regarding the Diamonds:
The Diamonds iconography represents the Intellectual Center. The Diamonds are employed in all thinking processes in everything we take in intellectually when we learn and study. We use the intellectual center when we process information we have learned and to recall data. The intellectual center is located in the head, or brain. The brain is where intellectual data is taken in and processed and where the thinking functions take place. When we are in the process of learning new subjects the intellectual center must focus and concentrate in order to process and store the information. The Diamonds take in data, assimilate and process information, similar to a computer database. Afterwards the intellectual center needs to be able to access the information stored in the memory banks effectively to retrieve the data.

The Diamonds, as the intellectual center govern all of our thinking and learning processes. All intellectual information is initially taken in by the intellectual center, processed, sometimes memorized and stored. When we learn, or study information, the job of the intellectual center is to process data, whereupon it is able to utilize and disseminate the information appropriately as needed. Many factors will determine how well, accurately or inaccurately one processes and utilizes information in the intellectual center. All the parts within the Diamonds, from the King down to the Two of Diamonds, have their unique job to perform, each with specific processes and functions. The different parts of the intellectual center organize learned information and disseminate it to the appropriate center accordingly when needed. It is important to note that the intellectual center is the slowest functioning of all the centers. The intellectual center works more slowly than the other centers as information must first be taken in, evaluated, analyzed or comprehended, and then stored in the memory banks. It is similar to a database file wherein information can be recalled when required. The intellectual center operates slowly for the purpose of analysis, memorization and storage. As an organ of perception, it is the slowest to respond as thinking and retrieving information takes time to process. The emotional center receives and processes impressions almost instantaneously, but the intellectual center is slower as it processes and evaluates information for retrieval and response.

Someone who is centered in the intellectual center may tend to approach life in a somewhat methodical manner, may be slower to react or to respond. An emotionally centered person may react and respond too quickly, whereas an intellectually centered person will think before they react. They ponder and evaluate their actions, reactions and responses to the stimuli which will affect reaction time considerably, slowing down the response mechanism. Remember, initially, one must pay attention to take in new information to learn and gain understanding. The information will then be stored in the memory banks as data. Our memory banks allow for efficient access to information. They operate in an automatic manner to recall data which has been memorized and stored. The intellectual center is the slowest functioning of all the centers. Which card of the Diamonds suit an individual is centered in will determine their retrieval pace, response and speed of manifestation.

Individuals centered in the Diamonds tend to be somewhat slower in all their functions compared to the other primary centers. All parts of the Diamonds suit are attracted to and stimulated by ideas, information, data and thinking. The massively intellectual Albert Einstein types are actually the slowest of all the centers as they take a great deal of time to arrive at their precise theories through complex investigation, careful analysis, calculation, comparison and methodical evaluation. However, the different subdivision parts within the intellectual center all function at slightly different speeds, depending upon which influencing element is present. For example, someone centered in the Queen of Diamonds has an emotional element which tends to process information more swiftly, although perhaps rather hastily. Intellectually centered people are activated, energized and enlivened by information, data, analysis, and calculation as they arrive at their intellectual understandings. Each person has the Diamonds intellectual center, thus we can remember our name, where we live, what we learn in school, or information we have memorized, depending upon its relevance in our life. The degree to which we use information may be influenced by energy from the other centers; however, we access our intellectual center constantly throughout our life for reference. At this point, please be aware that the information about centers may be new to you, and there is a natural learning curve. Realizing this you can easily observe your own intellectual center as it processes the new information and data. Although some of these ideas may sound complicated or a bit confusing, this is quite normal when new information enters the intellectual center. It takes time to learn new and unfamiliar information, to process and then comprehend it. All the centers will be described in detail and they will become more apparent to you. Personal verification can help you during this learning process. As you read about each center try to observe it within yourself. This can facilitate verification.

The Diamonds intellectual suit also has a unique part which functions as the database memory banks for virtually all information which we all take in. These memory banks in the Jack of Diamonds are called the "formatory apparatus." Information kept in this storage database, is available for instant use and can be retrieved automatically. However, we tend to habitually rely on this storage database of the intellectual center as we can access it automatically. We can become overly dependent on this part of the intellectual center which has minimal powers of objective discernment. It functions chiefly as stored information, but not of articulate selection. This is the part people draw from to have common conversations, to recall details, people's names, clichés, and basic information for ordinary functioning in everyday life. However, this is not intentional thought. I will provide a detailed description of this part in subsequent intellectual segments.

General Physical characteristics of the Diamonds:
Intellectually centered types are often relatively slender as they are stimulated by information and learning. They may not have physical appetites like other centers as they are attracted to information, and acquisition of data which fuels their needs. Intellectually centered individuals may not be particularly gregarious or outgoing as they typically prefer to study, read, work on computers, do analytical exercises and so on, rather than socialize. They may appear aloof due to their slower reaction time, as they tend to ponder and reason while thinking thoughts through. The stereotypical book worm, librarian, scientist, or computer nerd fits the physical description characteristics of intellectually centered types. However, specific physical traits are influenced by the subdivisions within the intellectual center. This will be further clarified in subsequent segments.

Regarding the Spades:
The Spades as the Moving Center governs all of our external physical movement. The moving center is located within and throughout our physical body and influences all the movement of the physical body. Keep in mind, although located in the physical body our moving center functions differently from our internal functions, such as our organs and glandular secretions. All the moving centered actions must initially be learned, such as walking, talking, and so on. The moving center requires training to initially learn and direct all learned movement to develop movement skills. A baby must learn to walk, feed itself, and learn

to talk. We engage the moving center when we learn a new dance, learn a new sport, and when we learn to drive. As we observe the skills of an Olympic gymnast doing complex maneuvers, we witness a well-trained moving center at work. This is an example of the different levels a center can operate from.

The moving center is the mechanism in the human being through which all external movement is learned. Again, a baby must first learn to crawl before learning to walk, and also must learn to put food in its mouth to feed itself. These early efforts begin to teach the moving center how to function properly with coordination in concert with the other centers. This learned movement information is stored in our moving center memory banks. Thus, after the baby has learnt to walk and to hold a spoon, their actions eventually become more graceful, fluid, agile, and ultimately, they become habitual. However, all movements must first be learned for the moving center to have the basic knowledge to develop movement skills so one may function correctly and naturally with ease and coordination.

The moving center is incorporated into virtually all of our normal daily activities; however, all movement must first be learned. At birth, we enter the world with an untrained moving center that requires education and training. We spend our lives learning new movements as we begin to walk, talk, feed our self, take up dancing, tennis, skiing, golf, and other activities to engage or challenge our moving center. While not everyone is interested in participating in sports, most healthy individuals have a moving center with the potential to walk, talk and perhaps waltz through life. We all use the moving center constantly throughout our daily life, unless one has a physical impairment that limits their mobility. The moving center moves us through life. However, when someone is moving centered, movement takes on greater significance.

Regardless of one's center of gravity, the moving center serves all the other centers quite well by getting us where we need to go, by moving us through our life in every way. The moving center takes us to meet friends, drives us to work, rakes leaves in the garden, goes for a hike, goes on a bike ride or roller-skating, does the dishes and housework, enjoys skiing and snowboarding, and performs all our physical activities. The majority of professional dancers, athletes, and musicians are moving centered. The level of skill acquired, developed and exhibited in an activity will be determined by which particular card an individual is centered in. It is useful to note that speaking is a combination of centers working together, the moving center working with the intellectual center. Healing practices such as yoga and meditation are helpful holistic disciplines that utilize the intellectual center in concert with the moving center and the instinctive center to achieve physical wellness, and to attain higher states of awareness. Activities such as ballroom dancing and competitive sports, stimulate the emotional and instinctive centers due to the socializing which is involved. These are examples of how the different centers may work together harmoniously.

Moving centered types are innately propelled to move physically throughout their life. They naturally tend to gravitate toward physical action and activities, such as sports that enliven and activate their moving function, allowing them to keep their body in motion. It is likely that they will prefer playing basketball, or any other sport, while their emotionally centered friends and family cheer them on. When you see, a graceful lean individual running track, jogging on the beach, playing volley ball, playing tennis, golfing, swimming, bicycling, or roller-skating along the promenade, you are most likely observing a moving centered individual in motion. But please keep in mind, physical exercise is beneficial and healthy for everyone, whether one is moving centered or not.

General Physical characteristics of the Spades:
Moving centered types tend to be relatively slender, and they usually exhibit supple muscular tone. They use their physical bodies as an instrument through which they experience movement throughout their life. Generally, they are active bodies in motion which contributes to their muscle tone and slender physique. Moving centered types are those people who dominate in sports and athletics, dancing, playing musical instruments and most activities that involve physical movements with physical participation. These are the folks who seem to glide through life, as they are naturally motivated to exercise their moving center. They efficiently burn the food they consume as fuel in their natural impulse to move. Also, some moving centered people I have known over the years were keen on consuming the right types of food to meet their energy requirements for peak performance in sports, and other activities.

I feel it is important to mention that it is the moving centered individuals who are naturally slim and slender. But, this is not necessarily true for all centers, and people often experiment with unhealthy dieting trends. For example, thin models in the fashion industry, especially those who walk in runway fashion shows are moving centered. This is evident with their naturally slim slender bodies. However, on this note, please be aware that the physical look which predominates in the fashion industry is not natural for everyone. Trying to look like a moving centered slender body type may be impractical or impossible, particularly if one is centered elsewhere. Being perpetually thin is an unrealistic and unhealthy goal for many people. Please keep in mind, your personal center of gravity effects your natural physical traits and characteristics.

Regarding the Clubs:
The Clubs suit represent the Instinctive Center which is our physical body and all of our internal functions, organs, glandular

secretions, digestion of food, and so on. The instinctive center is born fully functioning and operational in a healthy individual. Inner workings of the human body are all governed by the instinctive center. For example, the physical heart beats, our lungs breathe taking in the oxygen we need to survive, our stomach digests the food we eat for fuel, and the elimination of waste occurs. All of these processes take place automatically and naturally in our instinctive center as inherent internal functions in a healthy physical body. It is the instinctive center that miraculously heals our injuries and illnesses. The instinctive center is our physical body with all its sensory capabilities and internal functions. A properly functioning healthy instinctive center ensures that the heart beats and blood flows. The instinctive center is innately conscious of itself, so that it monitors efficient operation in a healthy human body. It is within our instinctive center that all other centers exist. It is highly beneficial to treat one's instinctive center with respect, to provide healthy nourishment and adequate rest. It is because we possess an instinctive center that we have the potential to gain self-awareness and achieve enlightenment.

The instinctive center governs the five senses within the human body, and all our sensory perceptions. The instinctive center is second only to the emotional center in speed, and operates swiftly at an accelerated rate of perception and response. It is the instinctive center that alerts us to danger with its acute sensory abilities. For example, the instinctive center can often sense when someone is watching us. When you walk into a strange place the instinctive center instantly comes to attention, sensing the atmosphere to perceive any potential danger. This center probes the environment for security and self-protection. The next time you get an eerily suspicious chill down your spine, possibly warning you of danger, remember this is the instinctive center doing its job to protect you by activating its unique sensory radar to monitor the environment. It is the instinctive center which is responsible for sensitivity to the occurrence of coincidental phenomenon, such as when we sense something before it happens. This may account for the sensing of déjà vu when you feel you have experienced an event prior to the moment it is happening. Our intuitive thoughts may be attributed to the perceptivity of the instinctive center. When one experiences a tingling sensation at the back of the neck, or shivers down the spine, it is caused by the instinctive center sensitively responding to events, people or stimuli. Sometimes we get a chill or goose bumps if we sense weird energy in the environment. Our sensory perceptions alert us with the instinctive center's acute antennae, cautioning us to be aware.

When you look at any human being initially you see them as their physical instinctive center. How they emanate as a person depends on where they are actually centered, their level of being, their psychological predisposition, their evolutionary path and their level of conscious awareness. But, our human existence depends upon having an instinctive center. To some extent each one of us is under the direct influence of our instinctive center's sensitivities, needs, and demands. If an individual is instinctively centered their physical body's needs and senses will have a more pronounced influence. Each part in the Clubs suit lends characteristics to the appearance and functioning of the instinctive center. People who are instinctively centered may exhibit a charismatic presence or energy. They may unwittingly command attention when they enter a room because of their energy emanations and physical presence. The Clubs may also have the ability to detect subtler sensory stimuli, psychic impressions or intuitions owing to their acute sensitivities.

We each have an instinctive center which performs its functions almost automatically, depending on our personal center of gravity and health. Each one of us experiences our instinctive center's physical body on a personal level. It is likely we have developed certain preferences for what is comfortable or uncomfortable for ourselves. As you begin to observe yourself and your centers at work, you will recognize when your body is making too many demands. We do not want to upset the delicate balance between all the centers. Keep in mind, all the centers play a part in maintaining the instinctive center to stay healthy. So, it is essential to be mindful that you eat well, sleep well and avoid excesses in general. Remember, balance is important within all the centers, but with the instinctive center it is vital for optimal health.

General Physical characteristics of the Clubs:

The different parts of the Clubs suit will ultimately determine how one's physical appearance manifests. Someone centered in the Clubs suit will be fairly consistent in maintaining their physical wellbeing, as their primary concern is the preservation of their physical body. Both women and men centered in the Clubs may exhibit a degree of sensuality. Men may tend to be muscular and women may tend to be curvaceous. If they have an intellectual element they may exhibit a somewhat commanding presence that can be felt, sensed or perceived by others when they enter a room. The emotional part of the Clubs may be rather voluptuous and fleshy, whether a man or woman, as their appetites can be somewhat excessive. The physical sensory appetites of the Clubs centered individual will vary depending on which part is dominant. However, all those who are centered in the Clubs suit require their instinctive needs be met in a timely manner to maintain optimal functioning of the physical body.

An important note regards the Instinctive Center:

It is helpful to be impartial and realistic when you look at your own physical body as you begin to determine your potential center of gravity. Try to be neutral and remain objective in order to avoid judging yourself. People typically regard their physical body as their total identity; however, this is simply not the case. We are made up of the many centers and their parts which are all vital to our human existence. Naturally, the human body plays a major role in our life, and gives us our human form which contains our true essential nature. The instinctive center houses all of the centers which together compose our personal human tendencies, predispositions, natural abilities, talents, proclivities and our dynamic potential. While I will give some general physical tendencies of the different centers, it is important to understand that there are other contributing factors which determine our personal physical appearance and our physical tendencies.

Just as there are different centers of function within the human being, there are also different glandular predomination's that affect our specific physicality. Perhaps we can observe this more readily with different types and breeds of animals. For illustrative purposes, a Chihuahua and a German Shepard are both dogs, however, they have very different physical appearances. The same can be said of human beings. While one person may be quite petite and very slender, another person will be larger and have a muscular physique. Another person will be quite tall, skinny and angular, while someone else might be of average height and have an ample, fleshy full-figured body. Our physical type and tendencies are determined by our glandular predomination and our center of gravity. However, the study and science of body types is too complex to cover in this book. I mention it primarily to help you understand we are the way we are for a specific reason. Acceptance of one's physical body is a healthier attitude than the prevalent tendency to criticize one's personal appearance. Keep in mind, body shaming and self-persecution are harmful to one's wellbeing.

Remember, it is vital to do what is best for your overall health. Regardless of your personal center of gravity, your human body is a complex magnificent organism that you must treat with respect. Our physical body is our instinctive center and serves all of our other centers. Developing healthy habits is essential to your wellbeing. For example, physically moving your body will help activate your moving center and can also enhance your emotional state. Many of our disharmonious emotional issues are exacerbated because we have low energy from unhealthy eating and sedentary habits which cause illness. Physical exercise may elevate and balance emotional moods and negativity. Physical activity can help minimize excessive intellectual concerns, unnecessary thoughts, self-doubts and prevent weight issues. Getting adequate exercise, sufficient sleep and developing healthy eating habits will help you keep your instinctive center in good working order.

It is great wisdom to treat your physical body well with healthy intentionality, compassion and self-respect. Be kind to yourself and to your instinctive center as you treat your body with respect and develop healthy living habits. Balance is the key in harmonizing all your centers.

CHAPTER 7

REGARDING THE ROYALTY CARDS

The iconic royalty cards represent the different elements within the four primary centers. The royalty cards are comprised of the Kings which represent the intellectual parts of a suit, the Queens which represent the emotional parts of a suit, and the Jacks which represent the moving parts of a suit. The Jacks also serve as memory banks where acquired data and learned information is stored. Keep in mind, we each have all the cards within us, and therefore we have all the royalty cards to access in our living experience. Thus, we each have the potential to emanate from the King, the Queen or the Jack of the centers on occasion. Gaining clarity that your personal center of gravity might a King, Queen or Jack will add depth and dimension to understanding your personal tendencies, abilities, preferences, manifestations, and behavior. Recognizing the different centers within yourself as they function will help you to identify your center of gravity. The ability to recognize and harmonize your centers with mindful self-observation will enable you to experience clearer perceptions of all that is occurring in your life. This will help you achieve enhanced self-awareness.

As you learn about and observe the various royal attributes you will discover certain innate tendencies which each suit has a proclivity toward. The Kings of centers emote, think, speak and act with intentional rationale. They methodically evaluate and make consistent intentional efforts with analytical thinking. The Kings have succeeded in sending astronauts to the moon in a rocket ship. This requires intentional precise thought. Whereas, the Queens tend to emote, think, speak and behave in dramatic emotional absolutes, such as never, forever and always. Queens seem to dramatically fall in and out of love. She might fly into a rage over a trifling incident, and with her abrupt change of heart she gives someone a tongue lashing. She may say she loves you or hates you, perhaps forever, but these emotions can change quite suddenly. The Jacks of centers tend to feel, think, speak, move and act in habitual patterns. They go along with the status quo and prefer doing what everyone else is doing without giving it a lot of thought or analysis. They habitually mimic others and often adopt popular trends, as they naturally gravitate toward the path of least resistance.

Initially, it is helpful to learn to differentiate the manifestations of the various centers, in order to recognize each suit clearly. For example, you will begin to recognize emanations of the Hearts as the emotional center, the Diamonds as the intellectual center, the Spades as the Moving center, and the Clubs as the Instinctive center. As you gain understanding of how each suit functions you will notice subtler nuances and degrees of variance. Certainly, in the beginning it is incredibly powerful to simply recognize when you, or another person is manifesting from the emotional, intellectual, moving or instinctive centers. Developing the ability to discern tendencies and qualities in yourself and others gives you tremendous insight into our human functions, processes, or habits, and why we are all somewhat different in our preferences, behaviors and manifestations.

Remember, while each one of us is centered in one of the four iconic royal suits, we have all of the centers within us. However, the dominant center that manifests regularly is our personal center of gravity, and affects everything we feel, think, do and sense in our life. Mindful self-observation is key to recognizing the centers and building self-knowledge to enhance awareness. Self-knowledge is available by mindfully observing what we feel, think, do, or sense in each moment. Becoming familiar with the royal suit that seems to have the most influence on you in your life, will help you to identify your personal strong points. With sincere mindful self-observation, gradually you will recognize your personal center of gravity.

It is helpful to understand that all of the cards of each royal suit are elementally connected to one another across the royal suits. For example, all of the Kings of the different suits are connected to one another owing to the intellectual element. The Queens are all connected owing to the shared emotional element. The Jacks are all connected owing to the shared moving element. The numeric cards represent the further division and clarification of the key influences within each of the royalty cards. From this perspective, all the cards of the deck are essentially royalty cards, and the numeric cards serve as the defining and refining influences of the Kings, the Queens and the Jacks. The numeric cards clarify the distinctive functions, tendencies and characteristics of each center within the royalty cards. Again, please keep in mind that each iconic member of the different royalty suits is connected across the iconic suits to their royal counterparts within each suit.

The Kings of centers are all connected, the Queens of centers are all connected, and the Jacks of centers are all connected. To clarify, the King of Hearts has direct connected access to the Kings of the Diamonds, the King of Spades and the King of Clubs. Likewise, the Queen of Hearts has connected access to the Queens of the Diamonds, the Spades and the Clubs suits. And, the Jack of Hearts has a direct connected access to the Jacks of the Diamonds, the Spades and the Clubs suits. All the iconic royal centers are connected across the iconic royal suits. Each particular influencing element, whether Emotional, Intellectual, Moving or Instinctive will always have a natural affinity for it's like counterparts across the four iconic royalty suits.

It is unlikely that someone centered in a King of one of the royal suits would directly access the Queens, or the Jacks, as their energies are inconsistent with the King's normal tendencies. This also applies to the other royal suits. Queens would not naturally access the Kings or the Jacks, and this also is true of the Jacks. But, there are exceptions when one may gravitate toward the other iconic royal suits. For example, regardless of where one is centered, one may experience sentimentality or melancholy during the holiday season, though this is normally attributed to the Jack of Hearts. If one is very hungry, it is possible one will experience the Queen of Clubs, as the instinctive center would demand attention from the physical duress. However, under normal conditions, each royal suit would tend to naturally access their royal counterparts across the suits. I have listed the "Keywords," and "Key behavior traits," associated with each royal iconic suit below and in each subsequent segment for your convenient reference.

Reference overview of the Royalty Cards general attributes:
Keywords associated with the Kings: thoughtful, methodical, analytical, objective, diplomatic, intentional, thorough, deliberate, pensive, dignified, reserved, calculating, detached and exacting.

Key behavior traits of the Kings: Kings think, speak and act with enhanced rational objectivity examining potential outcomes to determine what is possible to achieve with consistent efforts. Slow to act or react.

Keywords associated with the Queens: dramatic, temperamental, expansive, gregarious, controlling, lavish, extravagant, passionate, indulgent, vain, excessive, volatile, enthusiastic, exuberant, and moody.

Key behavior traits of the Queens: Queens think, speak, and behave in dramatic emotional emphatic absolutes, emphasizing who they will never ever speak to again, or what they will never do again!

Keywords associated with the Jacks: habitual, imitative, mechanical, automatic, superficial, simplistic, repetitive, conventional, common, spontaneous, routine, formulaic, and subjective.

Key behavior traits of the Jacks: Jacks function, feel, think, speak and act from pre-learned programming in general, often mimicking what others feel, think, say or do without analysis or verification.

Keywords and behavior traits references are included with each corresponding royalty segment to assist as you gain a comprehensive overview. Also, identifying characteristics of different centers will manifest in an individual's physical appearance. Inherent physical traits exhibit specifically, corresponding to different parts of the centers. These traits are consistent within the different iconic suits and their numeric parts.

For example, emotionally centered people, or those who have the emotional influence whether in the Hearts, the Diamonds, the Spades or the Clubs have a tendency to be a bit fleshy and may gain weight rather easily. They often appear rather animated when they are with friends and may speak excitedly, or talk more than other people. Their emotions tend to enliven their energy and others, and may be visible and audible.

Intellectually centered people, or those with the intellectual influence whether in the Hearts, the Diamonds, the Spades or the Clubs tend to be somewhat angular and may have a rather slight physique. They tend to respond more slowly than others as they ponder their thoughts while measuring their words. They may appear somewhat awkward physically and may have a tendency to move less, or more slowly, as they are intellectually preoccupied and typically think their way through life with mental deliberation.

Moving centered people, or those who have the moving influence whether in the Hearts, the Diamonds, the Spades or the Clubs possess a natural physical tendency to be rather slender and trim, agile and coordinated. They have a more streamlined physique due to their innate tendency to move and be physically active. You will recognize their distinctive moving element in how they function with coordination and skill as they dance, design buildings, hike, play competitive sports, and glide through life. They tend to move skillfully.

Instinctively centered people, or those who have the instinctive influence whether in the Hearts, the Diamonds, the Spades or the Clubs will have a more sensual physical appearance. The women may be more naturally curvaceous and the men may be more muscular. Those with the instinctive influence will have a more sensuous appearance generally as they are activated by the senses. They can be quite charismatic, and may exhibit psychic abilities, or sensitivity to subtle energies, as they tend to have enhanced intuitiveness.

The Kings of Centers:

The Kings of the Hearts, Diamonds, Spades and Clubs represents the intellectual element as it functions within each suit. These are the parts of centers governed with intellect, reasoning, rationale, contemplation and mental cogitation. Although an overview, the main influence of the Kings of centers is their intellectual thinking processes. Utilizing thought processes to understand, evaluate and determine, they think matters over which is slower and more time consuming than an automatic instant reflex response. The mental cognitive element influencing the Kings slows their speed of action considerably. The Kings perform their functions the slowest of all the parts of centers as they operate with analytical thought processes. The Kings of centers tend to feel, think, speak and act with enhanced intellectual objectivity. They direct their thoughts with deliberate analysis as they slowly and methodically think and consider variables and options. Because of this they may appear to be more aware than the other parts of centers, but, they are also much slower. Their objectivity is attributed to the intellectual influences that give them an analytical approach to gaining understanding, which takes time. The enhanced thinking element sufficiently slows down the speed of whichever center they occupy, hence they appear quite intentional. However, even if one is not centered in a King, one can still access and utilize their enhanced intellectual objectivity. Intellectual objectivity helps to balance all the centers which can help one gain heightened self-awareness. When we intentionally access our Kings, we can experience their innate attentive reasoning characteristics and qualities.

The elements of analysis, objective thought and rationale are distinguishing characteristic of Kings of centers. These are the centers that evaluate and assess a situation or issue to gain an objective intellectual perception prior to responding, reacting or manifesting. In this sense, they tend to be the voice of reason and rational sensibility in critical situations and can lend much needed balance to tense heated exchanges. The Kings of centers operate with focused attention, as required for mental comprehension and precise calculation. But, most often, people manifest from less intentional parts of centers, and the memory banks. So, we recognize thoughts and works that arise from an attentive intellectual analytical nature as the Kings of centers, and which possess a singular uniqueness. The element of attentive intentionally required to access the King of a center can certainly give one enhanced potential to ultimately reach higher states of awareness. Attempting intentional behavior will help you to be more present in a moment, more self-aware and more alert. Employing mindful self-observation with attention and intentionality gives one the ability to access all the centers more readily. Regardless of one's inherent center of gravity, one can gain access to experience the Kings of centers by bringing more attention with intentionality to the present moment. The Kings of centers are slower to take action in a situation, which gives them the opportunity to be more concise, articulate, and precise. Decisions the King's make tend to be reasonable and well thought. The Kings of centers are reserved and do not jump to hasty conclusions that may result in unnecessary energy expenditures. Contemplation is beneficial for making assessments and decisions of an important nature.

As you gradually recognize and comprehend the functioning of Kings of centers, you will observe the process of how they manifest. The Kings think before they act or react. The thinking process effectively slows down the speed of centers to actuate precise emotion, thought, movement and sensory factors. Yet, their slowness in processing information, ideas, opinions, other people, events and so on, can also create delays as they may potentially take too long to arrive at decisions. Their propensity to slowly think things over in order to understand a person or a situation may seem stubborn or obstinate to those who are centered elsewhere. Other people may become impatient with the slow pace of the King who simply cannot make quick decisions. They are the individuals who do not jump to conclusions, or make hasty choices which they regret later. The expression, "haste makes waste," might be the King's words of caution to others.

The Kings of Centers are naturally predisposed to step into the roles which are suited to their pensive nature and they seem to be born leaders. The Kings of centers may be regarded as the intellectual over seers of life who often guide others, owing to their enhanced ability to intellectually arrive at understandings. As youths, they most likely do well in their scholastic endeavors and may go on to management or executive positions, or become teachers, professors, or serve as team leaders. As one develops the desire to be more aware one will discover that by intentionally accessing the King one can begin to attain more presence in the moment, a requisite for becoming more self-aware. Remember, the Kings of each suit are all connected to one another across the suits. As you observe yourself you will begin to be more aware of the similar interconnectedness of the centers as they manifest. Perhaps you will recognize certain distinct characteristics that are familiar to you, either within yourself, or which you see manifesting in other people. Try to notice the particular character traits that you feel an affinity for and make notes of these. Also, make a note of patterns or traits that do not feel particularly familiar to you as this will assist you in determining your own center of gravity. Let us explore the world of the Kings.

Keywords associated with the Kings: thoughtful, methodical, analytical, objective, diplomatic, intentional, thorough, deliberate, pensive, dignified, reserved, calculating, detached and exacting.

Key behavior traits of the Kings: Kings think, speak and act with enhanced rational objectivity examining potential outcomes to determine what is possible to achieve with consistent efforts. Slow to act or react.

The King of Hearts:

The King of Hearts is the intellectual part of the emotional center. The King of Hearts is responsible for the intelligent emotions that are methodically analyzed with reason and rationale prior to expression. These are the emotions which are monitored and directed with thought, and sense of discernment to help determine appropriate emotional responses. The King of Hearts also exhibits consistency and steadfastness in their emotional connections with others. As we become more intellectually aware of emotions we conserve energy and access clearer perceptions which optimize and accelerate our psychological growth. While the emotional center is the fastest organ of perception, the King of Hearts has a slower response mechanism due to the intellectual element. The King of Hearts demonstrates that being emotional does not imply losing one's composure. Conserving energy and minimizing leaks enhances our ability to manage our emotional center. The King of Hearts serves another unique function as it represents our intimate connection to unlock, enter and access our innate higher centers of awareness. The King of Hearts is said to be the doorway to higher states of consciousness; however, this door requires your consistent sincere efforts to open and enter.

By becoming more attentive, intentional and discerning about one's personal emotional feelings, one gains greater access into the King of Hearts experience. This can be a valuable tool to enhance your emotional wellbeing and to maximize your emotional energy for personal growth. Keep in mind, we all have the King of Hearts within to assist us to evaluate, understand and express intelligent composed emotions. As the intellectual part of the emotional center the King of Hearts helps clarify emotions, and is uniquely equipped to monitor our emotional attitudes and emotional expenditures. The King of Hearts slows down emotional reactions and response time by introducing the element of thought to emotional feelings, states and attitudes.

This can lend vital intellectual strength to our emotional self-awareness. Experimenting with the King of Hearts will help you to develop emotional energy conservation skills. Certainly, it is not wrong to cry when watching a sad movie, nor to laugh while playing with a cute puppy. These emotions may even be connected to your more authentic essential nature. But, some emotional responses cause us to lose excessive energy.

Loss of energy through lack of emotional control, or through the expression of negative emotions, results in wasting one's precious life energy. For this reason, it is helpful to become more aware of inappropriate emotional energy losses and expenditures. This is not to imply that you should be unfeeling, uncaring or insensitive, but rather, suggests that you bring attentive awareness to emotional attitudes and situations to help conserve your energy. The King of Hearts is the organ of perception that has the ability to evaluate emotional situations through its process of intellectual emotional analysis. This is the heart that thinks, while feeling with the mind. The King of Hearts helps us to develop healthier emotional attitudes for right action with proper understanding. This allows us to make intelligent emotional responses which helps conserve our vital life energy. Conserving emotional energy can help advance our efforts to become more self-aware. And, though you may be centered in another card, you also have the King of Hearts to access for your best interests by employing attention and intentionality.

As we become more emotional about our personal work on our self, we may also feel more sensitive to the needs of others, which is the beginning stage of compassion. True compassion, as opposed to sentimentality, is a property of the King of Hearts. By compassion I mean a sense of emotionally knowing what another person is feeling, or experiencing, and having the emotional awareness to respond to their needs in an appropriate manner. Putting oneself in the position of recognizing and understanding the pain of others, helps put our personal pain into perspective, with scale and relativity. As we begin to experience a stronger sense of compassion for others we enter the King of Hearts domain. We are able to see our own situation with more clarity, as we acknowledge the needs of others with compassion.

Enhanced emotional clarity is a property of the King of Hearts which enables a compassionate overview of oneself and others, but without the sentimental overtones that keep us attached to an illusion. Compassion also allows us to cut the ties of any unhealthy relationships so that each person can be released to their higher possibilities.

The King of Hearts employs intellectual discernment to evaluate the emotional climate and retain calmness. This generates understanding, which results from emotional analysis of what is most important. The King of Hearts has an objective emotional overview that helps one see another person, or a heated situation more rationally. This helps slow down emotional processes and reactions, while retaining pensive detachment. For example, one can visualize the quiet King of Hearts in Alice in Wonderland who carefully assesses the situation and pardons wrongfully accused criminals who are condemned by the volatile Queen of Hearts. With kindhearted compassion, he averts the unjust and unnecessary melodrama. The ability to evaluate and assess a situation with intelligent emotional compassion lends calm detachment which restores balance. The King of Hearts helps us detach from our personal identifications, to understand others and situations with the use of intellectual analysis. Detachment enhances our ability to understand our emotional bonds and issues with increased clarity and objectivity, which generates healthy respect for the needs of others, and enhances our own self-esteem. As we begin to be freed from our mechanical emotional responses we may experience that we have more energy, are more effective and can see a situation with greater insight. As we increase our emotional intentionality, we can conserve energy, which is accumulated as fuel. With attentively conserved emotional energy, we have resources to arrive at clearer perceptions more naturally.

The King of Hearts has an appreciation for what might be a better course of emotional action, what is more appropriate for others and for them self. They are often the voice of reason in an unreasonable world, and are naturally diplomatic and tactful. There may appear to be an air of aloofness to the King of Hearts person owing to a pensive demeanor. Engaging with others or participating in activities, they assess the situation. Emotional mannerisms tend toward the rational because of the enhanced intellectuality. The King of Hearts ponders and deliberates what is suitable or required in the moment and has the ability to act appropriately. The King of Hearts person may seem a bit detached or aloof until they reach their emotional comfort level. They tend to take their time to evaluate whether to be outwardly friendly, or whether it is more advantageous to remain detached or reserved. However, the slow methodical emotional thinking processes of the King of Hearts may also be a hindrance in their life as they can be too slow to react, or respond to what they feel. They have a tendency to wait for the right time to make emotional decisions, rather than make spontaneous choices, especially concerning matters of emotional significance. These are the late bloomers who may spend their entire life waiting to find the right person to marry, if they marry at all. Although, the King of Hearts may not wear their heart on their sleeve, they do feel that the person who is right is worth waiting for. But, it is possible that people centered elsewhere may lose patience with the slow deliberate King of Hearts. The Queens of centers may become fascinated or mesmerized with the King of Hearts; however, she can also abruptly lose interest and flip if the King is too emotionally slow, reserved, aloof or detached.

Less effusive, the King of Hearts may quietly take in impressions, whether a painting, a poem, or a musical performance. This individual feels it necessary to have their emotional center nurtured in a certain manner, perhaps with fine art or music. They may prefer impressions that are refined which nurture their emotional depth. To understand more about the King of Hearts, refer to artistic works that reflect intelligent emotion. Fine literature, such as Shakespeare or Hermann Hesse require thought, but, nurture compassionate understanding of humanity with insightful observations of the human condition. You may also experience the King of Hearts when viewing fine art impressions in museums. Listening to refined classical music may help you to experience the King of Hearts, regardless of your own center of gravity. Depending on the individual, the King of Hearts may prefer art and music created in the context of their own generation during their personal era. It would not be out of character for a King of Hearts individual to relate to contemporary art and music trends that make sympathetic social commentaries, and speaks directly to the compassionate individual who grapples with social injustice and senseless inequalities in the world.

King of Hearts individuals may be drawn to careers or professions that bring them into proximity with other people. Their emotional needs can be met in their working relationships with others. Because of their ability to think rationally, they make effective leaders in the workplace. Their compassionate nature gives them an ability for analysis which may lead them to psychological work where intelligent emotions help others reach healthier understandings. They can be impartial counselors who are able to see all sides of an issue. Tact and diplomacy are natural to the King of Hearts, so they make peaceful diplomats, and gracious talk show hosts. Remember, each center has specific needs for certain fuel that is most appropriate for the center. The King of Hearts primary emphasis is to fuel their emotional center appropriately, intelligently and to understand the emotions they are experiencing, expressing and living on a moment to moment basis. So, it is ironic that some King of Hearts individuals may regularly find themselves spending time alone, despite being emotionally centered. I've known many artists, writers and film makers who create dynamic and inspirational works of art, yet they are often alone and relatively isolated while creating their artworks. These King of Hearts artists need to express their creative and emotional energies through their particular personal medium, which frequently requires solitude. They personify a strong sense of purpose to create meaningful art to enrich the world. Whatever path they travel there will be a marked element of intelligent emotion. They may choose to spend time with others, or they may be equally satisfied reading or writing a literary work of artistic merit. Remember, there are certain predispositions inherent in every center, yet other influences will also help determine how a person will manifest overall.

Regarding physical characteristics of a King of Hearts, they may exhibit softness or slight fleshiness in their appearance. But, the intellectual element of the King of Hearts can moderate a tendency to gain weight as their thought processes discern what best serves their physical needs. Also, the intellectual element slows down impulsive desires, so they may not give in to excessive cravings that are not be suitable for their health and wellbeing. While they may exhibit some physical softness, this is tempered by their intellectual ability to discern which foods are most beneficial for them. They may also prefer to be healthy role models, which encourages selective dining habits. For them, discernment is the emotional and the mental aptitude to determine what is the most objective decision, the best action or most appropriate response in a situation. This objective rationale aptly describes the King of Hearts thinking processes. Their acute discriminating faculty allows proper discernment to do right action for others as well. Theirs is an innate ability to recognize the higher right in a situation and act accordingly in the best interests for everyone. The King of Hearts centered individual is unlikely to feed negative weaknesses in another person, as it would be contradictory to their inherent rational discernment, and they often have a desire to help others. Their aims may be based on compassion and intellectual discretion fused with their keen emotional perceptions and insightful reasoning. The King of Hearts influences one to emote and act based on careful discernment and to make decisions with an overview of the objective benefit and ultimate good for those involved.

The King of Hearts intellectual emotional approach with its inherent capacity for compassion and reasoning, makes it a worthy goal to access this King within oneself. Experiencing the King of Hearts as part of one's psychological makeup can be a valuable tool to help one reach higher levels of conscious awareness. Enhanced conscious awareness brings expanded levels of perception to employ appropriate emotional behavior. By accessing and utilizing the intelligence of the King of Hearts intentionally you will be able to look into your heart for answers to realize what is the right and the best action in an emotional situation. Patience and compassion are required in order to act in the best interests of all people when a situation calls for it. The King of Hearts can help guide you to evaluate people and situations with careful deliberate consideration in order to take the right action. As you begin to access and experience this center on a more consistent basis it will benefit and enrich your personal relationships as well. As you consistently observe yourself you will begin to notice when your own life requires focus and attention to achieve better solutions for your personal issues. The highest aim is to work on oneself intentionally to reach comprehensive understanding and balance within. When we are balanced within, we can offer the world our more genuinely self-aware presence. As you investigate the thoughtful emotional realm of the King of Hearts you enter a domain that will help nurture your own emotional center, regardless of your personal center of gravity.

As we intentionally develop more rarified and pure emotions within ourselves, it helps us to experience higher states of personal self-awareness. The King of Hearts is said to be the doorway to the higher centers of consciousness. As one consciously cultivates and experiences the King of Hearts within, one gets closer to attaining greater self-awareness and compassion, which fosters an enlightened heart and mind.

Keywords associated with the Kings: thoughtful, methodical, analytical, objective, diplomatic, intentional, thorough, deliberate, pensive, dignified, reserved, calculating, detached and exacting.

Key behavior traits of the Kings: Kings think, speak and act with enhanced rational objectivity examining potential outcomes to determine what is possible to achieve with consistent efforts. Slow to act or react.

The King of Diamonds:

The King of Diamonds is considered a rare center which may manifest or appear somewhat infrequently. It is not typically accessed in one's ordinary daily routine, unless one is a true genius. The Intellectual part of the intellectual center it is attributed to the unique intellectual geniuses that occasionally manifest in the world. If you consider the brilliant work and achievements of Albert Einstein, Nikola Tesla, Madame Curie, and Stephen Hawking, you will begin to comprehend the rarity of this center. These unique individuals exhibit King of Diamonds characteristics which one can recognize in their brilliant research and scientific revelations. These few examples may help you comprehend the uniqueness of the rare King of Diamonds.

The Kings of all the centers utilize the intellectual element which slows the speed of their functions to allow sufficient time for contemplative intellectual analysis or investigation. Therefore, the intellectual part of any center will considerably slow down the speed of their function. The King of Diamonds is the intellectual part of the intellectual center; therefore, by its nature it slows down the thinking process to allow for in depth inquiry, analysis, processing, or calculation of information pertaining to the subject being examined. As mentioned in a previous segment, simply introducing the thinking element to a negative emotion will greatly inhibit its speed of escalation. By incorporating the slow King energy with intentional thought, one can conserve energy which might be wasted if expended impulsively or combatively in the expression of negative emotions, or other negative habits. The intellectual center works slowly because of its necessity to examine, evaluate and classify as it processes information as data. This is its primary function.

Having suggested earlier that information can be stored for later use illustrates the manner in which different parts of the centers work. The King of Diamonds is the slowest of all the centers, and calls forth data with methodical detailed precision in a meticulous manner as needed; so, information is recalled slowly with deliberation. The Kings require time to methodically recall any appropriate information, as intellectual parts of centers work much more slowly than other centers. As you begin to observe the different speeds of centers you will notice that your emotions happen very quickly, and almost instantaneously. The moving center is slower as it needs to engage the physical body to run and retrieve a ball flying to the outfield. The instinctive center works faster as it experiences sudden gut feelings as intuition, or may sense danger, at which time it becomes necessary to protect itself. However, the intellectual center is the slowest function.

It may be easier to understand the slow speed of the King of Diamonds heightened intellectual capability by understanding what it is not. It is not instant total recall played back like a tape recorder, as imprinted on the brain cells of our memory banks. It is not some facts one has memorized to pass a school exam. It is not the clever person on television game shows who rapidly spews forth answers instantaneously in response to questions from a game show host. It is not automatically recalling your parent's anniversary, your best friend's birthday or any other general information which has been stored as data in your memory banks. The Kings operate slowly to think. The King of Diamonds individual functions in a precise, exacting manner at a deliberate slow-pace. Also, this allows them to conserve energy for contemplative analysis in their thought processes. All intellectual parts of centers share this trait. The King of Diamonds centered individual is not well adapted to be a speed reading whiz kid, as they operate slowly.

The thinking processes of the King of Diamonds may be approached rather differently from what we ordinarily refer to as thinking. Ideas are formulated, theories are speculated upon, information is weighed and calculated, evidence and analysis of data is considered, and conclusions are arrived at only after careful investigation of the facts has been fully evaluated. This center does not arbitrarily jump to conclusions impulsively. In their thorough examination of a subject, pertinent information would be considered so they can arrive at an articulate conclusion for their comprehension. By comparison, a person who functions primarily from the memory banks, or the automatic parts of centers, is able to recall data at a fast speed. Certainly, what is often viewed as genius level in our world may be the mechanical part of the intellectual center simply spewing forth recorded information from its own memory banks. In reality, this type of memorization is not the work of a genius. Memorized data is comparable to a document stored on a disk or in a computer data base. Information about the Jack of Diamonds will follow in a subsequent chapter.

A friend utilized her King of Diamonds center to develop a theory regarding certain aspects of cosmology. She selected a starting point for her investigation, an idea relevant to the subject about which she wished to gain greater comprehension.

Beginning with a seed of an idea, she pondered concepts significant to the development of her theorem. During the course of a year she contemplated her subject from many different angles. Employing the King of Diamonds, she was able to process well developed lines of thought in a manner that led to new revelations. Each answer evoked a new question, and so on. After one year of intentional thought, she was satisfied she had reached a more complete understanding. Shortly thereafter, she discovered a book written in 1935 containing a lecture regarding cosmology. She had arrived at the same theoretical comprehension as another scholar years many prior, by utilizing her King of Diamonds.

The King of Diamonds has potential for achieving intelligence of the highest level, developing theoretical concepts along strategic parallels to reach new paradigms. It was believed that King of Diamonds people are rare; yet, upon review of great achievements in human history, we recognize the King of Diamonds has played a major role in shaping our world, perhaps rather quietly. The accelerating world of technology is also calling forth individuals whose intelligence excels in brilliant technological realms. The increasing emphasis on technology reminds us that it required the intentional thinking processes of the King of Diamonds to create, invent and assist in developing computers. These smart devices are capable of processing data swiftly and accurately. When doing inventive work, which requires precision with exactness, such as designing technical systems, writing computer code and programming, the King of Diamonds is called upon to think with meticulous accuracy. The King of Diamonds, like all intellectual parts of centers, works slowly and precisely. But, intellectual parts of centers have the ability to invent machines that work faster, calculate with accuracy, and work 24 hours a day. It is impossible for humans to work like the marvelous computers and other technological devices the King of Diamonds has invented and continues to improve upon.

Here we can draw a comparison to the other parts of centers which serve as our memory banks. Most information stored in our memory banks can be recalled rather quickly; however, not by the King. For example, a friend who is centered in the King of Diamonds has difficulty in swiftly remembering people's names when he has a chance encounter. If he sees someone out of his usual environment, he needs time to recall their name. He told me about one rather striking incident while out shopping when he noticed someone approaching him who seemed familiar. But, he was so deeply engrossed in reading the product labels and analyzing the ingredients, that he simply did not instantly place the man. It was quite a jolt when the person said, "Hello son," and he suddenly realized the person in the market was his very own father! Although he is a meticulously slow and methodical thinker, he is a highly intelligent King of Diamonds.

The King of Diamonds objective is to think and investigate details with scrutiny in a methodical, and thorough manner. There is no rush as all perspectives must be examined, calculated and analyzed with the aim to understand, while developing consistent themes. Theories arrived at will be refined and revised in an organized manner as they are calculated, proved or disproved, until a comprehensive understanding is reached. The King of Diamonds intends to attain in depth comprehension of the subjects which they focus upon. Perhaps in moments when learning a new language, studying a mathematical concept, or doing science experiments in chemistry class, you might have had a personal experience of the King of Diamonds. When the intellectual center is learning something new, the King is called upon to take in the information. Ideas are evaluated and analyzed for their potential value to arrive at heightened understanding. The King of Diamonds functions with concentration and intentionality for precise answers, which is a slow process. However, it is rather difficult to maintain this intense focused attention for long periods of time, unless one is actually centered here. Young students in school cannot be forced to learn in the King of Diamonds if it is not natural for them.

To know what it feels like to experience the King of Diamonds in yourself you can try the following experiment. This is intended to put you in an intentional space intellectually and to be mentally focused with attention and presence. This experiment is an attempt to think like the King of Diamonds thinks. Select from the library shelf a book of an intellectual nature and about a subject with which you are unfamiliar. It could be a Shakespearean play, a Mathematics book, a foreign language you wish to learn, a science book, or any other book that requires your complete attention in order to absorb its content. Now focus your attention on the words. Take in each word with deliberation and intentionality. Do not speed read and do not skim the page. Read each word on the page with focused attention. If at any time your attention waivers and you notice that you have not been aware of what you were reading, go back and begin where you last remember paying attention. Begin reading each word again, but with more intentionality. Every time you notice that you have lost yourself and are not paying total attention go back and begin again. It is important to pay close attention to every detail that you are reading. Focus your mind on each word on the page. Take in the impression with your eyes and your intellectual center. It is also useful to observe the frequency at which you drift off and are no longer aware of the subject in front of you. This will become more apparent if have chosen a subject with which you are unfamiliar. Please keep in mind that this exercise is a practical experiment to intentionally experience your King of Diamonds and to think objectively with attention. Doing this experiment on more than one occasion can provide insight into what it is like to be intellectually centered, and how the King of Diamonds functions slowly, with attention and intentionality. Incidentally, it is quite all right if you find this experiment rather difficult. The concentration required may be too intense for many people. However, this is a skill we can develop to help us access and utilize the King of Diamonds for more efficient learning and enhanced intellectual growth. As you read about the King of Diamonds, and begin to process the information mentally, you will directly experience the intellectual center. By experiencing each of the centers as you read each segment you will begin to comprehend how all of our remarkable centers function within us.

Learning new facts about a subject requires our attention; however, after the facts have been committed to memory we can access memorized data from our memory banks in the Jack of Diamonds, which is similar to a computer hard drive. By understanding this simple comparison, you can verify how different parts of centers work, witness their differences in response time and how they manifest. The King of Diamonds operates slowly with attention, while, the Jack of Diamonds can function more rapidly as memory banks. Both centers operate within us, as they each serve us in our life as useful centers with specific functions. The King of Diamonds has the ability to reason and use rationale, but operates slowly with deliberation, while giving considerable thought to possible conclusions, while the Jacks can work more quickly as the memory banks. This comparison between the King of Diamonds and the Jack of Diamonds may hint that people rely on the memory banks rather than intentionally engaging deliberate analytical intellectual processes. However, our centers function more efficiently when we pay attention and employ intentionality.

The King of Diamonds is able to intentionally evaluate potential answers and options. Thinking on a higher level requires consistent concentrated mental focus which requires energy. It takes an enormous amount of intellectual energy to maintain focused concentration. This may explain why we use such a small percentage of our mental potential, as Einstein suggested. We have the King of Diamonds center within us, but we might not access it due to the level of attention which is required. The intellectual center is the slowest functioning of all the centers, and owing to its slowness, one is afforded the opportunity to refine and revise one's thoughts and ideas as more understanding is reached. As mentioned earlier, a friend spent one year developing her theory about cosmology, only to discover the same theory had been reached by another individual several decades earlier. This evidence helped verify her meticulous use of the King of Diamonds.

Someone who is centered in the King of Diamonds may have the physical appearance of being intelligent. Interestingly, typecasting in the film industry has done much to corroborate the ideas about certain specific physical characteristics of the centers. The typical librarian stereotype, and the myopic bookworm with his eyeglasses slipping down his nose may well fit the description of an intellectually centered person. Certain general traits vary, but there exist distinguishing characteristics in each of the centers. You can observe the King of Diamonds individual as being rather slow to react. The thinking element predisposes them to slower reactions as they tend to think about their responses slowly. Their enhanced attention with directed focus affords the King of Diamonds the time required to do in depth studies along theoretical lines. They may take many years to complete their intellectual studies, theoretical work, doctrines or their scientific treatises. These unique people might be more difficult to observe in daily life as they may be occupied doing research, developing intellectual theories and documenting discoveries. Picture the King of Diamonds individual deep in thought contemplating intellectual concepts and theoretical ideas. Thinking and analysis is fuel which nourishes their unique intellectual center needs. If you visit a science library or a science university, such as Cal

Tech, you will probably encounter individuals who are centered in the lofty King of Diamonds.

Albert Einstein was most likely centered in the King of Diamonds. Einstein made remarkable observations about our intellectual potential determining that we use only a portion of our intellectual ability, perhaps as little as ten percent. Einstein also whimsically suggested, imagination is more important than intelligence. Perhaps, by employing creative visualization you can picture the possibilities and transformational potential which exists within your magnificent intellectual center. Hopefully, as you learn and utilize this information about the centers of influence within, you will recognize the potential for experiencing the vast untapped resources within yourself. Start by simply observing yourself regularly. Mindful self-observation is your key to gaining self-awareness. As we become more self-aware we begin to grow into our fullest potential. By experiencing the King of Diamonds directly you will know whether it feels familiar or unfamiliar, comfortable or uncomfortable to you. Keep in mind, the King of Diamonds requires intentionality and thoughtful participation with attention. Attempting to think in an intentional manner will help you recognize and examine intellectual traits in yourself, and in others. Mindfully observe what feels familiar to you and what resonates with your inner being. Remember, one particular center generally predominates, and this is likely to be your center of gravity. It will become apparent as you observe and verify which of the primary centers resonate with you. As we become increasingly aware of our centers and how they function within us an immense world of possibilities opens up to us. We each have almost unlimited potential for growth and self-development. Perhaps we will begin to tap into and access the unused portion of our intellectual capacity. Imagine all that you could accomplish simply by using more of what you already have.

Keywords associated with the Kings: thoughtful, methodical, analytical, objective, diplomatic, intentional, thorough, deliberate, pensive, dignified, reserved, calculating, detached and exacting.

Key behavior traits of the Kings: Kings think, speak and act with enhanced rational objectivity examining potential outcomes to determine what is possible to achieve with consistent efforts. Slow to act or react.

The King of Spades:

The King of Spades is the intellectual part of the moving center, which imparts deliberate physical action with attention to the execution of physical movements. The King of Spades possesses an enhanced dimension of intentionality owing to the thinking element which brings enhanced focus to movements. The intellectual part of the moving center directs intentional movement to enable precision in physical activity. This attentive thinking process facilitates precise execution in physical actions, such as professional athletics, art, architecture and all areas of design. The ability to conceive structural design and spatial relationships in multiple dimensional spaces requires the focused attention, coordination and intentionality of the King of Spades. The King of Spades individual is influenced by the intellectual element and may be inclined to careers dealing with spatial relationships such as architecture, art, and graphic design. As you observe the King of Spades, you will recognize their unique ability to incorporate their innate intentionality into their design. The architect uses precision to accurately calculate spatial relationships for a multi-dimensional structure on several levels. This necessity calls upon the intellectual part of the moving center for implementation and coordination in their design.

The King of Spades individual would most likely be interested in careers and jobs which require focused attention for intentional movement. Artists, architects, inventors, and musicians utilize the King of Spades to master moving centered skills to create their works of art. Yet, many other professions necessitate being centered in this card. These careers would include aerospace engineers and designers, carpenters, landscape architects, fashion designers, and other creative professionals. Vocations which require that one utilize shape, space, design, measurement, and coordination in an intentional manner, draw upon the King of Spades for attentive intelligent direction of the moving center. This innate ability manifests in outstanding architectural accomplishments such as the Taj Mahal, Notre Dame and other Gothic Cathedrals, as well as the Pyramids of Egypt, which some believe were divined by gods. It should be apparent that the architects and builders of historic cathedrals of Europe, such as Chartres in France, or Rosalyn Chapel in Scotland, utilized innovative intentional design concepts inherent to the King of Spades to create stylized monuments of architectural genius. The mystery surrounding the Pyramids of Egypt might be better understood if we pondered the presence of heightened awareness fused with attentive intentionality in the design process. This intentional methodology surpasses our ordinary patterns of thinking. It seems likely that an enhanced awareness directed these complex designs and is a reasonable explanation for these remarkable timeless structures, imbued with the King of Spades attention to complex fine detail. While being centered in the King of Spades does not necessarily imply one is in a higher state of consciousness; however, experiencing the intentionality of the intellectual parts of centers can help one to attain enhanced awareness.

We have all been in awe of the athletic skill and proficiency of professional athletes and Olympians whose precision and agility propels them to achieve almost supernatural physical feats. Yet, the skills which they exhibit, initially had to be learned step by step, practiced to achieve proficiency and trained in the King of Spades. Precision maneuvers require the intellectual process for coordination and accuracy. Intentional movement is accessed through the intellectual element of the King of Spades. The skilled professional athlete needs the focused attention of their mind and body working harmoniously together. The ability of a King of Spades athlete to execute precision movements helps them excel in sports incorporating calculated coordination and dexterity. Many professional athletes were recognized for their innate skills while quite young in high school. They often become recipients of sports scholarships for universities and colleges. As you observe you may notice that professional athletes seem to be intentional King of Spades individuals.

Remember, each center has its own distinctive natural talents, affinities and abilities that one can implement in one's daily life. This would be the right use of our natural inherent predispositions. It is ideal for each person to put their own personal inherent talents and abilities to use. To understand the King of Spades you can observe your moving center in yourself. Begin by thinking about raising your left arm, and then follow through while thinking intentionally as you execute the movement. By bringing your focused attention to this simple movement experiment, you will consciously experience the King of Spades for a few moments.

When one is learning new movements, such as driving an automobile, or playing an instrument, it is necessary to access one's King of Spades. There may be a feeling of disorientation or awkwardness as one strives to pay attention to a new moving centered activity. When the King is activated there is a general slowing down process which you will experience because of the focused slower intellectual element. It may feel somewhat peculiar as you are learning new movements. Also, it may take years of training to become skillful and precise in an activity, such as playing the guitar with fluidity and grace. All precise movement must initially be learned by the King of Spades.

After any movement has been memorized it will be stored in the memory banks for convenient swift access. Keep in mind, it would be tedious to be in the King of Spades to execute all previously learned movement. For example, "I am opening my car door. I am sitting in the driver's seat. I am putting my key in the ignition. I am turning the key to start the car's engine. I am looking in the rearview mirror for safety. I am looking both ways for oncoming traffic. I am now shifting the gears. I am now pushing the gas pedal with my foot," and, so on. Certainly, here we can understand how efficiently the memory banks work to facilitate expediency and efficiency in executing our daily routine actions.

There are times when one must access the King of Spades and come to attention at once. We may suddenly find our self in a traffic incident, and we are abruptly brought to attention in the King of Spades. If you are cut off by another driver on a busy freeway you must instantly come to attention to the moment to avoid an accident. At these particular moments, time may feel as though it is slowing down as we intentionally access the King of Spades to execute vital movements in an emergency. The slowing down sensation can be an important clue as to how the Kings of centers operate with deliberation. The intellectual parts of centers are the slowest functioning. The intellectual part of the intellectual Center, the King of Diamonds, is the slowest functioning of all the centers. The King of Spades would be next in order of speed. One simply must think clearly and methodically in order to prevent an accident, by bringing intentionality to the moving center.

There is an interesting aphorism, "Haste makes waste." We can all verify the inefficiency of rushing through life. This will help you understand how slower functioning of the Kings contributes to their effectiveness. To achieve greater efficiency, one can employ mindful self-observation, attention and intentionality in the moment to execute movements. Meticulous intentional movement is a property of the King of Spades which is articulated with precise action. The Kings of centers are utilized to maximize thinking with right action as the occasion or situation necessitates. Keep in mind, merely being centered in a King of a center, does not imply one will automatically become self-aware, or that one is more conscious. Self-awareness and higher states of consciousness are not automatic or mechanical tendencies in anyone, regardless of their center of gravity. The Kings of centers appear more aware, because of their attentive behavior. Picture the skilled athleticism of LeBron James.

The Kings of Spades physical characteristics tend to be slender and streamlined. The added intellectual element will also contribute to their trim physique. A moving centered individual utilizes food efficiently to fuel their movements. They tend to burn off calories in their quest to move through life. I have observed moving centered friends consume large quantities of food at mealtime, while maintaining a slim silhouette. An automobile requires adequate gasoline for it to continue moving as you drive. Likewise, the moving centered person requires sufficient fuel to maintain movement. In the realm of athletic competition, it has become somewhat of a science to determine what is the best food or fuel to reach their peak performance. There is much speculation about carbohydrate loading and amino acid intake to maximize performance levels. In this regard, we can understand why moving centered types need to fuel their body adequately.

The lean King of Spades individual may display a rather unusual gait or unique manner of movement. This trait is due to deliberation in the execution of their movement. Theirs is a world of precise, articulate action, and they appear to have a destination to arrive at, as they think and move toward it. Accessing this card intentionally may provide you with rather interesting, although perhaps awkward moments of clumsiness. You can observe yourself trying a new unfamiliar dance step, where you will experience the King of Spades, which tends to move slowly, step by step. When you try to perform a new dance maneuver, or any other unfamiliar movements which require coordination, you might actually look and feel rather uncoordinated while doing the preliminary steps. Yet, these observations can be quite valuable in your process of mindful self-observation. Your efforts will help you to recognize and understand which center feels comfortable, or uncomfortable, especially when determining your center of gravity. By bringing attention to the Kings we have the opportunity to experience new sensitivity to unfamiliar areas within our self.

As we balance our centers with intentionality by paying attention we accelerate the momentum of our work to gain self-awareness. The King of Spades is ideal to study as it is readily observable and easy to begin experimentation with. You can also make valuable observations about how you may have developed energy draining habits in your centers. The added benefit of observing any wrong work of centers will help bring scale and relativity into the equation. This ultimately allows you to correct the wrong work in your centers to help you to function more fluidly in harmony and with balance.

Even if it is not your personal center of gravity, try to access the King of Spades intentionally to move you forward on your life enhancing journey of self-discovery.

Keywords associated with the Kings: thoughtful, methodical, analytical, objective, diplomatic, intentional, thorough, deliberate, pensive, dignified, reserved, calculating, detached and exacting.

Key behavior traits of the Kings: Kings think, speak and act with enhanced rational objectivity examining potential outcomes to determine what is possible to achieve with consistent efforts. Slow to act or react.

The King of Clubs:

The King of Clubs is the intellectual part of the instinctive center. This is the finely tuned center that governs our senses and sensory perceptions in the psychological and physical realm. It is this center that monitors the environment for subtle energies that may indicate the general atmosphere, mood, safety and security. This is the center that mysteriously cautions us in a moment and leads us away from danger. The King of Clubs also receives and perceives slight energies that arise when one is being observed by another person. It functions as the antennae of our complex sensing center which processes subtle sensory impressions. It receives and analyzes all the data from our sensory perceptions. The King of Clubs detects and determines sensory impressions with its exquisite sensing mechanisms. This unique world of sensory perceptions is so rarefied that its gives the King of Clubs individual the ability to have what is called a sixth sense. These are perceptions attuned to matter so very fine as exist in thought forms or electronic wavelengths. When you encounter a King of Clubs Centered person you will immediately sense their presence. Though they may not wish to draw attention to themselves, their very presence may unintentionally attract attention. Look for their intense, charismatic eyes peering at you from the intellectual part of the instinctive center. This is also the center that perceives the mystical electronic impulses that notify him or her when they are being observed by others. This person will turn toward you and gaze cautiously upon you, with a glance that acknowledges your mortal existence and inquisitiveness. The King of Clubs is not one to suffer fools gladly, particularly when someone is overzealous or behaving inappropriately. They tend to apply the brakes if too much energy is being spent unnecessarily through lavish displays, either from personality or zealotry. It would be out of character for the Kings to behave with excessive zeal in a foolhardy manner. They may appear rather aloof, but are quite aware of what is going on around them as they navigate life.

The King of Clubs can be effectively intimidating as their intense presence monitors the environment. As they sense their way through life, their emanations may be felt by others. This is the King of Clubs way of signaling to others that they are there, possibly as a means of securing their territory. Certainly, many eyes will turn in their direction as the intellectual part of the instinctive center enters a room, so commanding is its presence. This center governs internal functions of the physical body and makes its presence felt. The King of Clubs is an extraordinarily well-developed organ of perception. This is the part of our consciousness within which resides the mysterious attributes of the sixth sense. Psychics and clairvoyants can credit the King of Clubs for their ability to sense subtle matter that may warn them of approaching danger, or to sense events in motion to occur. As the intellectual part of the instinctive center, the King of Clubs has unique sensing abilities for detecting subtle impressions of a rarefied matter that enter their sensitive domain. Certainly, we have all had intense moments while experiencing a sudden sense of danger. At that moment, the King of Clubs was aroused and ready to take precautionary action to protect itself. One may feel the chill of goose bumps as one's sensory antennae suddenly become alert.

The King of Clubs is the brain responsible for keeping the human body safe while functioning optimally, as it governs the sensitive inner workings and maintenance of the physical body. It also brings attention to malfunctions, such as with illness or when one accidentally hurts oneself. The King of Clubs intervenes by focusing the attention on the physical body in its need to attend to the illness or heal the injury. The King of Clubs brings attention to an injury through the physical sensation of pain, which is right work of the instinctive center as it functions as a warning to immobilize the body to repair and heal. All parts of the instinctive center are involved when one is ill or injured; however, it is the King that determines the action to be taken for preservation of the physical body. We can probably all recall a time of illness or an accident that caused us to experience the King of Clubs. Try to remember the experience and in particular your awareness during the incident. When we are ill, or injured, we typically have minimal energy to talk, eat, or think. This is the King of Clubs doing its duty of keeping the physical body still and quiet so it can work to heal and become well. By intentionally conserving physical energy expenditure the body may then direct its focus on putting all available energy into the healing process. Most likely, at this time you were more physically aware of your body, your surroundings and your personal energy conservation.

You may remember intense moments of heightened physical awareness during which you had a glimpse into the King of Clubs experience. During such times, you may have been aware of the need to conserve your energy with minimal outward expression; this is the King of Clubs signaling one to remain still. Many King of Clubs individuals are drawn to work in the health fields. Their calm, cool demeanor would be of great assurance to an accident victim and would help instill confidence as they are being treated in an emergency situation. The King of Clubs has an intelligent take charge attitude that can remain calmly detached while assessing and treating injury to another's physical body.

Obviously, it is easy to see that one has a physical body; however, the instinctive center as the brain of the body may prefer not to be looked at with scrutiny. This could be regarded as the correct working of the King of Clubs in its effort to protect its domain. By sitting quite still and focusing your attention on the body, you can begin to sense the internal workings of your body. You can touch your wrist and feel your pulse, or put a hand on your chest to feel your heart beat. But to feel your internal functions working with their precise processes is a different sensation. Slowly, you may come to notice the various impulses and sensations that travel throughout your body as it performs its remarkable duty of keeping you alive and running efficiently in every moment. As an experiment, sit in a quiet space, knowing that you are quite safe from intrusion, and focus your attention on your breathing. Remain very relaxed as you impartially observe the rhythmic pattern of air being inhaled, then slowly exhaled. After a few minutes, you will sense the rhythm of your body as it miraculously takes air into the lungs. This simple experiment can assist you to observe the King of Clubs watching itself. From this perspective, you can verify that it has a consciousness of its own. This consciousness is focused in the physical body, its protection, care and survival. Each of us experiences our own King of Clubs at various times as it is the brain behind the physical body we inhabit.

Observing our physical body as it functions helps us to recognize the instinctive center as one of the four primary centers. We can readily observe our own physicality moment to moment as we gain greater insight and understanding about our centers. With enhanced understanding, we can go further in our aim to be more aware to increase our self-knowledge. To add a bit of relativity, without our instinctive center, there would be no absolutely no possibility of awakening to our own higher states of awareness or consciousness.

One can easily observe a cat manifesting from its instinctive center. The cat appears almost totally conscious in its actions, and perhaps a cat is conscious in its own feline world. Regards attaining higher psychological states, we believe humans have a far greater opportunity for conscious evolution than animals. Yet, our pets seem to have a finely attuned conscious presence and awareness about their physical domain, and, they probably possess a more acutely developed sensory awareness than human beings. In this regard, the King of Clubs individual may possess a somewhat noticeable animal grace about their physical presence. They will be intensely aware of the environment as they move their physical body through life, always on the alert for the unknown or the unexpected. Their eyes bespeak their physical awareness as they take in the surrounding impressions and subtler energy vibrations. Theirs is a world of rarefied sensations that keep them alerted to changes in the immediate environment and in the vicinity which they occupy. This gives the King of Clubs individual the appearance of consciousness, or that they are being present to the moment. From one perspective, they are more present; however, this is due to their attentive ultra-sensory nature, an automatic process of self-preservation. Because of this, the King of Clubs may appear unapproachable with their laser focused commanding appearance. This is their inherent self-protective mechanism which also serves as a powerful deterrent to anyone thinking about approaching them. In this regard, the King of Clubs can give the appearance of being slightly intimidating, especially to avoid interactions with others whom they do not know, or have never met.

I wish to reiterate that the Kings of all the centers operate with attention from their intellectual element. This attentiveness may make them appear to be more aware than others; however, becoming self-aware requires intentional work on oneself with consistent intentional self-observation. The Kings possess a natural ability to be attentive, but this does not necessarily endow them with higher states of consciousness. Remember, attentiveness is a natural characteristic of the intellectual parts of centers which employs the thinking process, but does not automatically invoke higher consciousness. Knowing this will help you gain understanding of the innate awareness within your own physical body as the miraculous instinctive center.

When experiencing the King of Clubs, one may be less inclined to exhibit unnecessary behaviors. Certainly, the King of Clubs is inclined to deter energy waste. This King has a sense of economy, especially regarding its own precious life energy, which it would prefer to direct to maintaining a healthy, safe environment for its personal protection and preservation. Of course, this is the right action for each of us to exercise in our own life daily and at certain specific moments. It is crucial to the King of Clubs that you have a body to dwell in, and it is in your best interests to keep your body safe and healthy. When you are ill, injured or endangered the King of Clubs will ascend in order to calm down your energy expenditures. Also, someone who is centered in this King may tend to be a rather cool character and can appear fairly calm, detached and unemotional to people around him or her. Their need to be aware of their physical safety and their environment will elicit their calm exterior, which may appear rather aloof to the more emotional types.

The King of Clubs may have an intense alluring manifestation which magnetically attracts people and many actors and movie stars are centered in this card. They radiate an enigmatic, charismatic presence that draws others to them. Powerful religious leaders and spiritual types are often centered in this card. They have a natural ability to mesmerize the crowd and encourage people to follow their preaching. The charisma of the King of Clubs is quite ominous in its strong presence. This magnetic charisma may be why charlatans are able to dupe innocent people into giving them large sums of money. Keep in mind, this charismatic powerful presence is merely one center functioning. Appearances can be deceptive in this regard. It is possible that psychics and clairvoyants who claim to see the future may be intriguing King of Clubs individuals. With their acutely attuned sensitive antennae they seem to pull answers out of the air magically. To add a bit of relativity, it is prudent to carefully consider what a psychic tells you, rather than base your life on their predictions. In this particular field, there may be clever charlatans who deceive innocent people out of their hard-earned money. Remember, people generally consult with a psychic or fortune teller during a time of need, precisely when they are having difficulties. Perhaps these psychics know in advance why people are coming to consult with them. If they are an altruistic type who genuinely wishes to help people that may be a different matter. One should use caution and employ one's own King of Clubs to make careful character assessments to discern whether a clairvoyant is genuine or not.

By simply being more attentive to the moment at hand, perhaps you can begin to rely on your own powers of divination, answer your own questions and carefully guide your own life. Rather than depend on another to guide us, we might simply employ our own Kings to gain more insight into a situation. You already have all the centers within you to utilize in your life. By accessing your own Kings of centers, you can seize the power that is available through the intentional use of these masterful centers. In so doing you can maximize the strength you already have within to skillfully navigate your personal direction. Bringing attentiveness to the intellectual parts of centers will help you gain understanding to enhance your life with greater success. The long-range benefits will prove to be invaluable to your personal transformation and growth. By intentionally accessing the King of Clubs, you develop a clear sense of your personal physical presence. This sense of presence will help you understand how the Kings of centers bring attention and intentionality to your living experience. This is available to you on a moment to moment basis. Putting the centers into proper perspective helps us to understand how each center serves a necessary function in our life. We can observe how we habitually access certain centers more frequently than other centers. This is a vital step in recognizing your personal center of gravity. As you study the Kings of Centers you will begin to notice how little attention we normally pay to the small details in our daily life. Remember, we have all the centers within us, and no particular center is significantly better, or worse than another center. This lends valuable relativity which helps you to be more objective in your overview and understanding of yourself.

Keywords associated with the Kings: thoughtful, methodical, analytical, objective, diplomatic, intentional, thorough, deliberate, pensive, dignified, reserved, calculating, detached and exacting.

Key behavior traits of the Kings: Kings think, speak and act with enhanced rational objectivity examining potential outcomes to determine what is possible to achieve with consistent efforts. Slow to act or react.

The Queens of Centers:

The Queens of the respective Hearts, Diamonds, Spades and Clubs represent the emotional influence within these iconic suits. The enhanced element of emotionality in these parts of centers increases their speed of function and manifestation. This predisposes the Queens to exhibit a palpable heightened energy, which is observable in her instantaneous reactions, responses, behaviors and overall manifestation. The Queens have a unique character trait that predisposes them have a surprisingly abrupt Queen flip. The distinctive Queen flip may appear extremely positive one moment, then suddenly become negative in a proverbial heartbeat. Their distinctive flipping trait can make them highly unpredictable as they can suddenly become volatile or explosive. The Queens of centers are extremely passionate and are not at all vague about their likes and dislikes. Keep in mind that each center with its respective parts are all uniquely different and equipped to handle life situations in their own particular manner. However, the sudden, and often melodramatic Queen flip can be very confusing to other people, yet, it is a distinguishing characteristic unique to the Queens of centers. Perhaps the most infamous example of the notorious Queen flip is described in Lewis Carroll's fairy tale, Alice in Wonderland. In one moment, the flamboyantly boisterous and melodramatic Queen of Hearts absolutely adores dear Alice, and in the next moment it is, "Off with her head!" Such volatility is observable in the Queen's reactions and responses to situations, people and stimuli. The Queen of each royal suit responds to the type of stimuli that distinctly affects that particular suit. I will go into detail in each of the description segments for the different Queens of the four iconic suits in subsequent chapters. It is important to note, that Queens are not subject to a particular gender, but are generally referred to as she, or her. All the centers are always gender neutral and both men and women possess the Queens of centers.

It is invigorating to spend time with a Queen who adores everything, at least in this moment. She can infuse our life with her enthusiastic emotional energy. You will receive a great deal of energy from a person who is centered in the Queens, whether the Hearts, Diamonds, Spades or Clubs. The Queens can also evoke strong emotions in others and may induce powerful reactions. The Queens have a rather tempestuous demeanor, which tends to be somewhat unpredictable. The Queens lavish attention on whomever or whatever she is attracted to and obsessed with in the moment. But, she may suddenly lose interest with her unpredictable Queen flip. Though baffling to most of us, the Queen often abruptly changes her mind, whether it is a love interest, a belief or opinion, an athletic activity, or an ice cream flavor.

This can happen instantaneously, before the rest of us have had a chance to understand what is occurring. The Queens of centers are stimulated by attraction to external stimuli and that which can satisfy her intense cravings. Whatever she is currently interested in, or pouring her energy into, is what she is attracted to at this specific moment. Keep in mind, what she is strongly attracted to in this moment, she may suddenly be repulsed by the next moment. The Queens of centers exhibit compulsive and obsessive tendencies which can be quite confusing for others who are not inclined to extremes. Fabulously energetic one moment, but completely exhausted the next moment, the Queens are somewhat indiscriminate about how, when, where and upon whom they may lavish their exuberant emotion fueled energy. Remember, whomever, or whatever attracts her in the moment is what she becomes compulsively magnetized to; becoming the object of her obsession, craving and desire, at least in this moment.

You may notice the Queens as they surround themselves with others who support their desires, causes, and their demands. The Queens of centers expect a great deal from their interactions, which can put them in the position of being disappointed when expectations are not met. We have all experienced the disappointment of the Queen within us feeling disappointed, but also, flattered or manipulated. Yet, the Queens can easily overwhelm other people with their seemingly inordinate demands, which they seem to feel entitled to exercise. It is the Queens of centers hold onto to bitter resentments after an ordeal has passed. The Queens of centers tend to experience a great deal more moodiness than other centers, but the cause of their extreme mood swings is rooted in their sudden Queen flip. Lacking the slow steady pace of the Kings, the Queens crave instant fulfillment and gratification. By observing attractions, she can monitor energy expenditures to slow the speed of her actions and reactions. Self-observation can bring attention and intentionality to the moment which slows down the momentum of her strong energies to help control the outcome of events.

The Queens of centers often set high goals for themselves, but she may lack the structured discipline which is necessary to reach their lofty aims. They are easily overwhelmed and can become distressed; thus, they may experience imaginary symptoms of failure before they have attempted to begin a project. Daunted or overwhelmed by their personal goals, they may quit before even starting. They may erroneously feel like a failure and blame it on lack of talent or knowledge, which may be entirely unfounded. However, the Queens quite fortunately tend to attract a support group around them to turn to during their emotional down times, who they turn to regularly. But, the Queens can also exhibit an inordinately defeated disposition when they are disappointed or wronged by another person. This behavior is the negative half of the Queen flip that occurs when things are not going their way. An example of this is the evil Queen in the fairy tale Snow White who repeatedly inquires of her closest confidante, "Mirror, mirror on the wall, who is the fairest of them all?" When the mirror suddenly responds that, Snow White is the fairest maiden in the land, the selfish Queen goes berserk with jealousy and vows to kill the innocent girl who has surpassed her beauty. While this is an exaggerated Queen flip, it offers insight into the Queen's potentially volatile temperament. We have each experienced intense Queen reactions on the occasion when you felt a sudden rush of combustible emotional energy. You may notice, the Queens who are depicted in most fairy tales tend to have exaggerated characteristics and personality traits. This also supports the possibility that the knowledge of centers was known to the authors of these stories.

The Queens of centers are typically the larger than life, abundantly ample, full figured individuals we often encounter in life. Their exterior tends to mirror their internal world which is likewise ample and abundantly lavish. While they may strive for a slender silhouette, their inherent natural tendency is to be quite fleshy. The Queens can personally benefit by acknowledging that not everyone is naturally predisposed to have a slender silhouette. She is fleshier and has a softer, rounder physique because of her Queen center of gravity. Please remember, psychological damage is often caused by having an unrealistic body image and unhealthy eating habits. Moreover, one's metabolism can be adversely affected when one starves the body of healthy nutritious food. The Queens can work themselves into a dieting frenzy and frazzle themselves into illness. Keep in mind, eating healthy foods in a mindful healthy manner is always the best directive for everyone. However, Queens of centers may focus on satisfying dramatic desires, urges, cravings and possibly their addictions. What they crave may cause them to experience its opposite effect, and with it the abrupt flip manifestation. Each one of us has probably experienced the after effects of over indulgence on occasion.

We each have the Queens of centers within us, but people who are centered in a Queen will tend to exhibit her more dramatic and expansive traits to a greater degree. If you recognize these traits in yourself, remain impartial and continue to self-observe. Learning about centers and being impartial about what you see, can help you gain vital understanding of what you can realistically expect from yourself, and from others. While the Queens may be subject to excessive expectations due to their abundant desires, each one of us has also experienced the failure of having unrealistic expectations within our self. As one begins to self-observe regularly, one becomes better equipped to monitor and assuage the accumulation of unrealistic desires or goals. This can help minimize disappointments we might experience from our own unrealistic expectations and the illusions they foster. Observe what feels familiar to you or what you may have experienced regards the Queens in your own personal life. As you read about the Queens you may recognize familiar traits, either in yourself or in other people. It is useful to take notes of your observations to help you determine your center of gravity. There is an abundance of information and examples for the Queens as they command more attention in life than the other centers. Let us explore the flamboyant world of the Queens of centers.

Keywords associated with the Queens: dramatic, temperamental, expansive, gregarious, controlling, lavish, extravagant, passionate, indulgent, vain, excessive, volatile, enthusiastic, exuberant, and moody.

Key behavior traits of the Queens: Queens think, speak, and behave in dramatic emotional emphatic absolutes and contradictions, such as who they will never speak to again, or what they will never do again!

The Queen of Hearts:

The Queen of Hearts is the emotional part of the emotional center. The enhanced emotional element makes her a powerful force to be reckoned with. The Queen of Hearts is a uniquely robust center that infuses the world she inhabits with abundant energy. Her pronounced and often slightly domineering effusive energy fills the atmosphere. People who are centered in this card can often be observed gushing and obsessing over others in dramatic bursts of emotional energy. She can also be rather overbearing, temperamental, and smothering. She has a tendency to be impulsive, and may also have obsessive compulsive inclinations. She can be excessively cheerful, loving, lavish, expansive, and generous, but, she might suddenly flip to the opposite extremes of remorse, hate, sorrow, spite, or grief. The Queen of Hearts has the dramatic dilemma of suddenly flipping as she abruptly changes her mind about someone or something.

Everyone vividly remembers the notoriously abrupt Queen flip so explosively characterized in the fairy tale, "Alice in Wonderland." One minute, the Queen adores dear Alice, and in the next minute she condemns Alice to death. This example gives a clear image of the impulsive volatility which the Queen of Hearts frequently exhibits in her emotional life and in her often times turbulent world. She may abruptly flip and exude the polar opposite emotion of that which she had just been audibly gushing. The double emotional influence increases the hyper speed of the Queen of Hearts reflexes, reacting as an extremely fast organ of perception. Rightly or wrongly she makes instantaneous emotional assessments of a situation or a person at lightning speed. Some of her perceptions are indeed too fast and she can appear quite rash to others who are less inclined to jump to emotional conclusions. Think of the turbulent behavior of the Queen of Hearts in Alice in Wonderland. Almost no one can comprehend her volatile actions and extreme reactions. The current American political climate is governed by the audaciously turbulent and disruptive Queen energies.

The Queen of Hearts can sway people and may boldly influence their thoughts and actions. She is uniquely equipped to be inordinately gracious, and generous, but her emotions may simultaneously smother and stifle others, as she is domineering and sometimes overbearing. The Queen of Hearts exhibits emotional extremes because she feels intensely about everyone and everything that affects her. She seeks to fuel her massive emotional needs with other people, but she can stifle others with her excessively needy, controlling nature. She is a presence who controls with a commanding voice that demands you to pay attention to her. The Queen of Hearts is definitely not a wallflower and will not tolerate being ignored in any manner. The strong emotions and the powerful feelings we may experience about the people and things we are passionate about, quite likely emanate from our own Queen of Hearts within. A person who is centered in this card will be strongly opinionated and may be intensely motivated. The Queen of Hearts needs to feel adored and be the center of attention, which she considers her birthright. She is outgoing, effusive, expressive, entertaining, generous, lavish, and socially desirable for her ebullient personality. Her company is courted for the lively energy she brings to the dullest party. She lights up a room with exuberance, but she can unpredictably flip for any reason. She may suddenly storm out of the room if she feels the least bit annoyed, or slighted by an unknowing offender. She is temperamental and easily provoked, though we may never understand why.

The Queen of Hearts can be a powerful motivational speaker to inspire others to reach for the stars and achieve their wildest dreams. She can be highly persuasive and will convince others to join her cause and help raise money to benefit her current favorite charity, fund raiser, or politician. She may devote much of her already busy schedule to worthy causes that she feels passionate about. She may not give you a choice whether to believe in whatever she says, or not. She expends extreme emotional energy, as she exhibits a pronounced martyr alter-ego, as she gives so much from her larger than life self. She is the image of sainthood when it comes to helping the charities she is currently lavishing her attention on. She will spend hours helping and advising friends about their personal problems that she believes she alone can solve. Her emotional center is a vast storehouse of energy to spend on those she cares about. She will quite happily offer to help manage your life if she considers you worthy, despite your personal ideas, or your reluctance. She will help whether you want it or not. It is vital to her existence that she gives emotional energy in abundance to those in her close circle. But remember, this is the Queen of Hearts on a good day.

She can of course suddenly become the exact opposite of the above description. She can turn on a proverbial dime, become cold as ice, give wicked tongue lashings to unsuspecting victims, and devastate others with her wild temper tantrums. She is quite capable of making life very difficult for anyone and everyone with her sudden abrupt Queen flip. As much as we love her positive attention, we loathe her negative attention. She has the capacity to flip over the slightest provocation. I knew a woman who was centered in the Queen of Hearts and she had a highly volatile and aggressive nature. She was extremely ruthless in her business dealings, and gave little thought of how her actions affected other people. Ironically, she often spoke of her devout religious beliefs which totally contradicted her brash and heartless business dealings. I suggested that she give more thought to how she treated people as her behavior was neither compassionate nor spiritual. She told me in no uncertain terms that she was "a chosen person" and that her deity pardoned her unequivocally. Her Queen of Hearts always felt she was right, no matter how wrong she was.

Perhaps the term, "Hell hath no fury like a woman scorned," may be attributed to the Queen of Hearts when she is having a bad experience. Unfortunately, no one knows what might provoke her wrathful Queen flip in any given moment. So, beware, for whoever incurs her wrath over whatever trifling matter it may be, this Queen can suddenly explode into a raging and abusive temper tantrum. It may be difficult to know exactly who is really in the wrong or why, as this Queen feels that any injustice to her is the worst possible crime that could ever be committed. She may suffer visibly with combustible displays of crying and uncontrollable sobbing, as she simply cannot tolerate anything or anyone that does not favor her. Regardless of the actual truth in a situation, she always believes she is right. Keep in mind, the word restraint is not part of the Queen of Hearts vocabulary. She is undaunted in her quest to dominate her personal emotional world. And, though flattery can win favor with the Queen of Hearts, it can also be her ultimate downfall. She fully believes all the flattery that comes her way, and accepts it as her birthright. But, her volatile nature has a tendency to be her unravelling if she feels slighted. She can lose her composure rather dramatically when upset about someone, or something. Whatever, or whomever has adversely affected her mood, she can manifest with abruptly flaring emotions and tantrums. The Queen flip can be clearly recognized in a sudden display of extreme mood swings and bi-polar depression. She is highly melodramatic.

By observing her emotions, the Queen of Hearts could use her sudden bursts of emotional energy to her own advantage for personal growth. Mindful self-observation, attention and intentionality will help the Queen of Hearts gain control over her wide range of intense emotions. While the Queen of Hearts can be moody, temperamental, tempestuous, and egocentric it is important to understand we all have this center. Each of us has experienced the positive and negative sides of her rather tumultuous disposition. However, someone who is centered in the Queen of Hearts will exhibit these character traits to a much greater degree. While emotions are generally fast, by paying attention with self-observation one can begin to slow down the speed of the Queen. If the Queen of Hearts centered individual begins to work to develop self-awareness, and exercise more self-control, they will be able to experience the more rewarding elements of this center.

The Queen of Hearts is not a pragmatic black and white person. She is a vibrantly colorful character with a spectacular presence that demands attention. When she calls you on the telephone, be prepared to devote a considerable amount of time listening to her emotional adventures. The scenarios of her life are quite melodramatic as she is very theatrical. Dressed in suitable attire to match her vibrant psychological predisposition, whether a man or woman, the Queens of Hearts will grab your attention as she makes her appearance in bold, colorful attire. The Queen of Hearts needs to be noticed as this robust emotional part of the emotional center requires your undivided attention. She feeds her abundant appetite for attention with her emotional conquests over other people. She thrives on attention from others just as much as she lavishes her own attention on them. If she does not receive the attention she desires she will spend inordinate amounts of time and energy to rectify the situation in her quest to win you over. She can be insistent that you join her special circle. As a sensitive emotional being she seems to have an uncanny ability to see directly into a person or an emotional situation, provided it does not affect her personally. But, everything does eventually affect her personally, particularly if it is happening to one of her nearest and dearest. Meaning well, she takes on a great deal of everyone else's emotional baggage or relationship problems with the best intentions to magically fix everything. The Queen of Hearts pours a great deal of her emotional energy into the people who are part of her circle or within her personal domain. She firmly believes that she has your best intentions at heart when she takes on your burdens and tries to solve your problems.

The Queen of Hearts is an exaggerated personality with very complex overtones. She is not subtle, she is intrusive. She does not ask, she demands. She feels it is her right to dominate others and will make every effort to this end. She feels that she knows best, about everyone and everything. The Queen of Hearts is stimulated by the world around her, and her response is observable in her attractions and her repulsions. She is attracted to external stimuli that can trigger her complex range of emotions; however, her attractions may abruptly change, and on a rather frequent basis. It is simply a matter of whom, or what relationships attract her in this moment that keeps her interested. However, due to her tendency to flip she may suddenly lose interest in a person as quickly as she was initially attracted. Even-tempered individuals find her extreme moods and behavior too erratic and unreliable, but she will oppose anyone who blocks her.

The Queen of Hearts exhibits ample fleshy body mass which requires adequate space in her environment, and in everyone else's environment. She has a tendency to gain weight rather easily due to her large appetite for all that she craves. She indulges in sumptuous foods to fuel her vast emotional center. Food can help energize her as she emotes on whatever person, subject, object, or interest that has currently captured her attention and possessed her heart. When she is enraptured the Queen of Hearts will feel on top of the world. Conversely, when she is heartbroken, she feels devastated and may behave as if she is on the verge of heart failure. And, she is certain that her heart will never recover. The Queen of Hearts is impulsive, compulsive and possessive. Obsessing over love interests causes her much suffering. It is the Queen of Hearts within all of us that suffers the most from the impact of a broken heart in relationships that do not work out well.

The Queen of Hearts is a larger than life presence that is neither subtle nor subdued. Someone who is centered in this card could do well in the theatrical world of the stage or screen. Flamboyant and influential, this center does well in careers that involve being with other people or managing their affairs. The Queen of Hearts prefers professions where she can be outgoing and aggressive. Careers that suit her well are real estate, interior decorating, consulting, theater management, and professional match making. The Queen of Hearts infuses life with passion and fire as she sets our hearts ablaze with her abundant emotional energy. You can easily envision her effusive outgoing personality closing the deal on an expensive yacht, or selling a magnificent mansion in Beverly Hills. This is not a passive bystander, but, someone who gets intrigued by and becomes involved with everything and everyone around her. She is a rather visible and audible social creature who will go out of her way to get your attention, with hopes that you will soon adore her. The Queen of Hearts is simultaneously exciting and exhausting as she feels, thinks, acts and reacts so rashly. She sets a brisk pace that may be quite difficult for anyone to keep up with; that is, until she completely burns herself out emotionally, and theatrically collapses in total exhaustion.

The Queen of Hearts is a unique and dynamic center that infuses the world she inhabits with her abundant emotional energy. She can be observed gushing over others with enthusiastic bursts of emotional energy, or throwing a temper tantrum if she is not given enough attention. The Queen of Hearts is tumultuous, temperamental, overbearing, and smothering, but she is also, energizing, entertaining, gracious, loving and caring, and she loves to give advice on everything in the world. Remember, this Queen may quite suddenly flip, and abruptly abandon you and everyone else. But, just as quickly and dramatically she may try to win you back to her emotional kingdom. Do you recognize this melodramatic center in yourself or others?

Keywords associated with the Queens: dramatic, temperamental, expansive, gregarious, controlling, lavish, extravagant, passionate, indulgent, vain, excessive, volatile, enthusiastic, exuberant, and moody.

Key behavior traits of the Queens: Queens think, speak, and behave in dramatic emotional emphatic absolutes and contradictions, such as who they will never speak to again, or what they will never do again!

The Queen of Diamonds:

The Queen of Diamonds is the Emotional part of the intellectual center. This motivates the person who is centered in this card to be attracted to and stimulated by information, knowledge and data. This Queen has a passionate desire to learn about everything and anything that captures her attention. She may study massive volumes of research to satisfy her voracious appetite for information, data, or knowledge. This person collects information and might thoroughly investigate subjects which attract her attention, until she suddenly loses all interest. As a Queen, she operates and manifests by attraction to whatever intrigues and triggers her interest to learn; at least until a new subject of inquiry appears. Her attraction to ideas may change frequently, unexpectedly and quite abruptly. The "Queen of data," might be a more appropriate name for the inquisitive Queen of Diamonds. She is endlessly in search of the latest, brightest, or newest information that might provide answers to the relentless questions that besot her mind. Her treasure trove is a diverse and eclectic body of information to be called upon at any given moment to answer questions on virtually every subject. This is a Queen who has a massive collection of intellectual tidbits, assorted trivia, handy hints, computer code, technical jargon, and reams of miscellaneous information. Owing to the Queen element she functions at enhanced speed to collect data rather swiftly. The mind is alert, quick and quite adept at hopping onto a new information bandwagon almost instantaneously.

The various interests of the Queen of Diamonds change at an accelerated pace, so it can be rather difficult to keep up with what is going on in her eclectic, but interesting life. The curiosity of the Queen of Diamonds may lead one to study mystical ideas, or search for hidden knowledge. This is apparent when a new subject, idea, concept, theory or philosophy has captured her attention, at least in this moment. But, remember, her interests change swiftly as she thrives on new information and instant mental stimulation. Speed is a manifestation of the Queens and she changes subjects faster than is customary with the intellectual center. Of all the Queens of centers the Queen of Diamonds is the slowest, which is due to the intellectual element which has the need to think and process new data. However, the Queen of Diamonds may not seem slow at all, at least to those of us who are centered elsewhere. Keep in mind, the Queens are typically quite robust.

The Queen of Diamonds is curious and attracted to, while fascinated by information on various topics and diverse subject matter. One week she may be studying ancient languages, but may suddenly drop it to study astronomy, or something else. Hers is an eclectic collection of data as varied as a warehouse of memorabilia. The Queen of Diamonds will often go to great lengths to study a particular subject. She will purchase volumes of information about her new intrigue, but she might suddenly lose interest. It is not that she cannot complete a study, but rather there exists so much to learn about, and so little time to investigate it all. This center will acquire as much information about a subject as possible, until a new interest attracts her active mind. She may not specialize in an area of study if it takes her away from her other interests. The Queen of Diamonds prides herself on knowing something about almost everything, as her interests are so varied and diverse. Owing to her Queen flip she may not become an expert in one particular subject as she is eager to move on to new topics that stimulate her mind. While she frequently changes her field of study she amasses assorted gems of knowledge that make for lively conversation. One Queen of Diamonds friend of mine seems to entertain with her rather eclectic collection of information and knowledge. Although she attended college for many years, she does not have a degree because she changed her field of study too many times. She also has a massive collection of unusual and phenomenal books that could probably fill a small public library. Her eccentric home is stacked with reference books she simply cannot live without. And, her books share space with her ever-growing collection of computer equipment and technical gadgets.

Due to her insatiable curiosity, The Queen of Diamonds individual collects information and data on various subjects, and perhaps not surprisingly, whether it is useful or not. An intense need to satisfy their curiosity contributes to the ability to speak on diverse subjects, and with bravado. The Queen of Diamonds may be somewhat vain about the information she has amassed and often has a tendency to lecture others whenever an opportunity arises, whether they are interested or not. A certain Queen of Diamonds friend frequently and abruptly changes the subject whenever we are speaking. Although it is immensely interesting to talk with him, we rarely arrive at a mutually shared understanding due our different manner of processing ideas, philosophies and information. His agile mind jumps from subject to subject and in mid-sentence he may go off on a tangent to introduce a different idea. However, he has repeatedly introduced me to new concepts which I might not normally look into. He is always eager to share interesting ideas and information that sometimes proves to be quite useful. It is the insatiable inquisitiveness of the Queen of Diamonds that seeks out unique information that may help others gain new knowledge or enhanced understanding.

Queen of Diamonds individuals tend to have a passion for computers and cutting-edge technology. They are absolutely enraptured and enthralled with the latest cyber-technological gadgets, software, hardware, gaming, programming and so on. While online, the Queen of Diamonds centered person will visit all the social networks to check the status of everything and everyone. They are addicted to information, ideas and opinions and seem to have endless tidbits of data and advice which they willingly expound upon, even when no one else agrees. The Queen of Diamonds is impulsive and compulsive about information. Whatever attracts her in this moment becomes her latest subject or object of obsession. This obsession may change tomorrow, but right now she has an urgent need to explore her latest obsession with driving passion and fervor. Witty and intellectually energetic, these gymnasts of the mind leap from idea to idea with adept eclecticism. While they often lack the gracious elements of tact and diplomacy, they can be most interesting and highly informative. But, keep in mind the Queen of Diamonds is subject to the unpredictable and abrupt Queen flip. The flip may manifest as topic hopping from one idea or subject to another, or making a sudden decision to change their field of study in college or university. However, the Queen of Diamonds will just declare that she simply changed her mind, which does occur rather frequently.

The Queen of Diamonds can be attracted to vast philosophical ideas and concepts, but may lack the interest to commit to one ideology or school of thought. One fellow I know frequently attends lectures of a metaphysical nature that capture his attention. While he is intellectually eclectic and eager to probe diverse topics and philosophies, he cannot seem to alight on one particular ideology. The Queen of Diamonds has the potential to be captivated by metaphysical concepts, philosophies and psychologies that could help them manage and navigate their own intelligence. It would be beneficial for them to develop more discipline, which is vital to help them harness their intellectual potential. Information appeals to them, but a negative attribute of the Queen of Diamonds is a tendency to indulge in gossip about other people. Gossiping is a harmful character trait that one should make efforts to avoid. Indulging in gossip is always harmful as it emanates from false personality and lack of compassion. Speaking or hearing negative information about another person is never helpful. Gossip is a habitual pattern of negative behavior that people indulge in to make them feel superior, which is an illusion. Remember, only harm is borne of gossip.

The Queen of Diamonds individual will generally appear fleshier than other intellectually centered people. Because of their emotional element, they have a tendency to put on weight rather easily. They may also collect cookbooks and exotic recipes to experiment with, hoping to satisfy their eclectic tastes and unique ideas about food. They are also drawn to gatherings to share information with their intellectually stimulating friends. Food is often implemented as an intoxicating lure to entice others to come and chat, and perhaps to learn, teach or give a lively lecture. The Queen of Diamonds emotional intellectuality will take them where there are people to share ideas with. They can be found in coffee houses and restaurants talking excitedly over cappuccino whilst sharing their latest discovery. They attend science lectures to learn of breakthrough technology, and will quickly post the discussion on their social network. With friends or colleagues, the room will echo with their exhilarating and often eclectic discussions and robust conversations.

Lecturers, college professors, teachers, writers, news reporters, and librarians are some careers which may attract the intellectual diversity and facility of the Queen of Diamonds individual. A career as a journalist with the opportunity to cover unique and interesting subjects would be an excellent choice for the insatiably curious Queen of Diamonds. Investigative research fields where they can explore concepts and variables might give satisfaction to this lively inquisitive mind. The Queen of Diamonds is an animated speaker who voices dazzling thoughts punctuated with dramatic facial expressions. One can picture a college professor giving a lively animated lecture in his slightly unkempt attire with his eye glasses sliding down his nose. All the while he is busy shuffling his rumpled papers, which he refers to often when he strays off the subject.

Listen carefully when you are in the presence of the Queen of Diamonds centered person. Initially so you can track their line of thought, but also because you will most likely pick up an interesting bit of information that may never have occurred to you. The Queen of Diamonds individual is intrigued by new ideas and concepts in a never-ending palette of colorful topics. One week they may study UFO phenomenon, and the next will study how to raise Macaws in an apartment in the city. This center stimulates us all to seek information and knowledge to satisfy our thirsty minds and souls.

Your own Queen of Diamonds may be attracted to esoteric sciences, metaphysical information and mystical knowledge that may also potentially help to bring you to a higher awareness of yourself and the miraculous world which you are part of. Allow the emotional part of the intellectual center to introduce you to the deepest mysteries that might just answer your puzzling questions while they intrigue and mystify your spirit. Always plumbing the depths of new data, the Queen of Diamonds will probe bizarre mysteries and is quite willing to share the information with anyone who will listen. For yourself, follow your intellectual heart as it leads your mind to explore and discover the miraculous undiscovered universe that dwells within you.

Keywords associated with the Queens: dramatic, temperamental, expansive, gregarious, controlling, lavish, extravagant, passionate, indulgent, vain, excessive, volatile, enthusiastic, exuberant, and moody.

Key behavior traits of the Queens: Queens think, speak, and behave in dramatic emotional emphatic absolutes and contradictions, such as who they will never speak to again, or what they will never do again!

The Queen of Spades:

The Queen of Spades is the emotional part of the moving center and operates with fascination and attraction to movement and activity. She moves for the sheer joy of movement itself, and is always ready for adventure. Forever seeking her emotional fulfillment through movement, this Queen is on a quest to satisfy her compulsive inner need that compels her to dance, run, jog, golf, ski, bicycle or rollerblade through life. The Queen of Spades centered person operates and moves at a brisk pace because of the enhanced emotional element; hence the attraction to energetic, exciting and often frenetic activities. This Queen has a lust for movement that needs fulfillment, preferably with a heavy dose of thrill factor. This is the center that craves the excitement of amusement parks and a frightening, white-knuckle rollercoaster ride might just qualify as her idea of fun! Certainly, moderation is never a strong point for the Queen of Spades.

The Queen of Spades moves relentlessly through life in search of new ways to excite her moving center, but she may not consider possible risks or potential consequences. The symptoms of burn-out may befall these active Queens who often ignore common sense in their quest for a thrill. The Queen of Spades may not be aware of the need for discipline or pacing oneself in activities to mitigate hazards. The Queen of Spades craves action packed movement and the rush of a rollercoaster, driving a fast car, running a marathon, or flying a hang glider off a cliff are all experiences she might really enjoy. The Queen of Spades has an emotional attraction to what she is interested in. She moves towards what she is attracted to, and often responds excitedly to external stimuli with flamboyant gestures to emphasize and accompany her movements as she indulges in a new activity. For example, one day she may be wildly attracted to jazz dancing, but may suddenly decide she wants learn how to play tennis. The Queen of Spades thrives on excitement and variety that satisfies her need for movement. But, she tends to habitually over exert herself physically, only to wilt in exhaustion after an exciting episode. She is a combustible whirlwind of energy in motion. The Queen of Spades is a lot of fun to be with until she exhausts her energy supply, or ours. She may dance until dawn until she depletes her energy; but, when she recoups her physical strength she goes off on a new adventure. For example, the Queen of Spades individual may be an avid racquetball player, but may get bored with it and suddenly switch to golf, skiing, or rock climbing. She indulges in her activities to the ultimate degree, but frequently overdoes it, and then she may abruptly lose interest, or simply exhaust herself. This is when her Queen suddenly flips; hence, she is abruptly done with this activity! At least for this moment, as she often changes her mind; thus, it is quite possible she will flip back to her prior passions.

I have a Queen of Spades friend who is a successful ballroom dancer. She is highly skilled and has won many dance competitions. She has also taught ballroom dancing to many people. As a child, she was trained in the ballet, but as she got older she found it difficult to achieve success as a ballerina. She was a naturally gifted dancer, so she moved on to other forms of dance as a career. Her repertoire includes ballroom, jazz, tap, belly dancing, jazz dance and calisthenics, all of which she has taught over the years. For recreation, she goes ice skating, running, bicycling and skiing. It was no surprise that when Salsa dancing became very popular she quickly became one of its leading competitors and teachers. After a competition, she would complain of being completely drained and totally worn out. Not knowing how to pace herself, she also frequently suffered from muscle strain. Over the years, she has often cancelled our luncheons or social plans to visit her physical therapist, or chiropractor. She is a Queen of Spades who does not see the need to pace herself. This is the natural order for the Queen's experience, and the reason why she experiences her sudden flip. Her devotion to so many moving centered activities takes a toll on her body and her energy.

Queen of Spades individuals might have mighty aims, but may be quite unrealistic about how to achieve them. For example, one Queen of Spades fellow often said he wanted to be a millionaire; however, he did not have a business plan to follow, or a strategy for how to get rich. He simply did not realistically consider all the steps that were necessary to fulfill his millionaire desires. Queens of centers can lack the necessary scale and relativity which would help them bring their desires to fruition in a realistic way with discipline at an achievable level. The tendency to overwhelm them self emanates from the Queen's vast hopes and desires, but they may simply lack a realistic plan to attain their goal. The Queen of Spades in all of us have probably become overwhelmed at certain times, perhaps when learning a new skill such as skiing, or playing an instrument. To become proficient in athletics or with playing a musical instrument one must devote the appropriate time and energy to acquire the necessary skills. But, the Queen of Spades wants to become the best skier or greatest violinist in the world before she has even begun to learn. This can set the Queen of Spades up for a gloomy defeat, before an attempt has even been made. This gloomy attitude is simply another version of the Queen's flip. The Queens within all of us may inflate illusions about our true capabilities or talents, but on the flip side of this, they can also deflate our hopes and wishes. For a Queen, the speed of mastering an activity is proportionate to her intrigue. Although the Queen of Spades will throw herself fervently into her passions, she may become disillusioned when proficiency does not occur rapidly. If the desired results do not come quickly the Queen of Spades can experience distress, or may simply abandon the goal altogether.

I knew a Queen of Spades musician who was quite talented, but he was extremely moody about his guitar playing abilities.

He wished to be recognized as a virtuoso, and worked hard in his pursuit of fame and fortune. But, it was not easy to achieve the level of fame which he so desperately wanted. Fame may have been an unrealistic goal tied to his passion for the guitar. Perhaps it was his Queen that craved worldwide success, recognition and the financial rewards. Although he played guitar in recording sessions and with various bands, the massive fame and adulation he craved did not occur. His desire for great success remained elusive, and it caused him chronic depression with severe mood swings. In this sense, he reminded me of the passionate artist, Vincent Van Gogh, who unfortunately was not successful during his lifetime. Van Gogh also suffered from severe depression and extreme mood swings which prevailed throughout his tumultuous career. Yet now, his exuberant paintings with their radiant color and vibrant brushstrokes are greatly admired for their uniquely masterful artistry. Perhaps Van Gogh was a Queen of Spades, as his lavish artwork commands our attention, which belies his intense, massive artistic temperamental talent. The Queens of centers have a great yearning to be recognized for their talent, much more than the other centers.

Yet, I have known other rather similar Queens of Spades centered individuals who were more attentive to their psychological wellbeing. They worked consciously with intentionality to minimize their potential for mood swings and depression by engaging in healthy energetic physical activity. One friend in particular attends as many yoga classes as possible as soon as she begins to notice any gloomy negative thoughts of depression which might cause her to experience mood swings. As you observe your own personal behavior regularly you will begin to recognize certain attitudes and habitual thought patterns that may trigger certain feelings of negativity within yourself. If your changeable moods seem to be a manifestation of the Queen of Spades, or any other Queen, try to remember to make consistent efforts to mindfully observe yourself, and engage in healing holistic movement activities which can help assuage the moodiness. Oftentimes simply moving and engaging your body actively will help ward off negative thoughts. Keep in mind, most people experience mood swings and bouts of depression occasionally. Gaining awareness with mindful self-observation can help modify negative thought patterns and can also help control impulsive reactions.

Competitive sports with a risk factor, such as automobile racing, may attract the Queen of Spades. The element of danger and excitement could certainly entice the Queen of Spades need for speed, glory and the potential rewards. High risk extreme sports seem to magnetically attract Queen of Spades centered athletes seeking the exhilaration that accompanies dangerous adventures. Several years ago, I knew a professional skier who prided herself on having skied almost every mountain on planet Earth. She was famous for her extreme cliff jumps and appeared in adventure films. Eventually her bold skiing stunts took a toll and she experienced severe tendonitis, an acute inflammation of the tendons. Although it was apparent that her extreme skiing caused the tendonitis, she had a blind spot about the adverse effect it had on her body. We spoke about it, but she refused to believe that skiing had anything to do with her pain. The Queen of Spades individual may lack sufficient relativity and scale to understand the consequences of their extraordinary physical activities, stunts and behavior. The trend for extreme sports are clearly a Queen of Spades activity. But, these sports require well developed skills and instant reflexes to execute exaggerated precise moves. Yet, the inherent risk factor is part of the allure. The world of the Queen of Spades may appear incredibly exciting and thrilling; however, their fast-paced energy and habits can be rather overwhelming for others. Remember, Queen of Spades individuals are subject to extremes of behavior in almost all areas of their life. Many years ago, I had an interesting conversation with a champion snowboarder friend who is centered in the King of Spades. We spoke about some of the risky dangers with extreme winter sports. His reasonably moderate observation was, "People who jump off steep 100-foot snow cliffs for fun are crazy."

There is another potentially hazardous element of risk a Queen of Spades may exhibit by taking unlawful chances that can harm others in rather devious way. Long ago I knew a successful career woman who had a disturbing experience with a family member who was centered in the Queen of Spades. My friend was transferred to Japan for her marketing job with an international company, but flew home to visit her family for a few weeks each year. During one annual visit, her sister drove her to her American bank before she caught her return flight to Japan. The Queen of Spades sister accompanied her while she did her bank transaction, and then drove her to the airport. Several months later my friend was transferred back to Los Angeles from the Japanese corporate offices. Soon after arriving home she went to her bank to withdraw funds, but she discovered that all of her money was gone! The bank informed her that her sister had made withdrawals, but they could do nothing as she told them she was acting on her behalf and had the account access numbers. The bank advised her the only recourse was to go to the police and file criminal charges against her sister. Her family pleaded with her to drop it as her sister had just gotten a good job after being unemployed for a long time. Using my friend's bank account, the sister bought herself a new car, new clothing, leased an apartment and bought beautiful expensive furniture. My friend said she felt victimized and sabotaged by her sister. Although she tried to cope to with the expensive betrayal, she recently told me she has never gotten over it.

Certainly, not all Queen of Spades individuals are criminally motivated. However, they may be motivated by their own needs for fulfillment which may present an element of risk. This element of risk may result in gambling, recklessness, pranks, or doing anything for excitement, whether their actions are positive or negative. Acting as a Queen they tend to exhibit an attitude of entitlement, though it may be unearned, or undeserved. Perhaps they do not consider the negative impact their irresponsible actions can have on others. In their adventures, or misadventures, they can exhibit extreme behavior. They may lack critical thinking, which would encourage them to evaluate potential consequences of their actions. This is an example of the Queen's flip as they fail to foresee negative outcomes of their behavior which may adversely affect others. Following ethical guidelines and honest protocols would be beneficial to help them achieve worthier goals.

Rather than take risky chances which might backfire on them, the Queen of Spades can strive to be cautious and more intentionally careful.

It would not be out of character for the Queen of Spades to forego precaution in their rush for excitement. Jumping off a boat dock into an icy cold lake without a life jacket is a Queen of Spades maneuver. Road rage in heavy traffic may emanate from the negative half of the Queen of Spades. But, serious accidents or other mishaps can occur which they will later regret. They often act without thinking of the potential consequences and also, without proper preparation. They tend to be in a rush and might skip over the important details. Certainly, being moving centered they have a natural ability for picking up sports, but, many sports necessitate in depth instruction and consistent practice to develop vital skills. I have often heard people say they would love to learn to ski, surf, or other sports, but it takes too much time and effort. This type of comment may be expressed from the negative part of the Queen of Spades, who can overwhelm herself with the enormity of a task. The Queen of Spades individual may not appreciate the need to take the necessary steps to truly master a precise skill, in order to be more self-protective.

In their passionate quest to move, the Queen of Spades person tends to be relatively trim and slim. Owing to their enhanced emotional element they may also be passionate about food and dining with friends. I have known several Queens of Spades individuals who regularly went on very restricted eating regimes to lose a few pounds quickly. Quite often they endured severe fasting in hopes of becoming slim and trim again. Keep in mind the emotional element of the Queen of Spades tends to be a bit fleshier than other moving enters. A common problem many dancers experience is the need to be extremely slender. I have heard about ballerinas suffering from eating disorders and body image issues because of the professional requirements to be slim. The Queen of Spades centered ballerinas with their enhanced emotional element tend to endure the most stress from the rigorous physical demands to be slender in the world of professional dance.

But, do not confuse the Queen of Spades obsessive need for activity with individuals who are hyper-active due to a medical condition, such as overactive glands or a nervous condition. Many individuals have thyroid problems, or other glandular disorders which predispose them to being highly energetic and frenetic, which is different from the Queen of Spades eclectic moving centered energy. Glandular influences relate to endocrinology and are not necessarily a function of the centers, but rather of body types. The study of endocrinology has shown that there exist various different body types and combinations of types; however, this is a complex subject which requires further reading and study to understand. Rodney Collin's book, "The Theory of Celestial Influence," explores this concept and discusses the theory of body types.

The energetic Queen of Spades may seem hyper-active, but it is useful to realize that we all have this center. We can each observe our Queen of Spades becoming energized, but, someone centered in this card will embody active traits to a much greater degree. We may enjoy our Queen of Spades friend's adventures, but it is helpful to point out they may be taking risks. We can encourage them to slow down, avoid gambling, mitigate unnecessary risks, use caution and vigilance, and also, to drive carefully. In their haste for adventure the Queen of Spades may not always be the most careful or cautious person.

Keywords associated with the Queens: dramatic, temperamental, expansive, gregarious, controlling, lavish, extravagant, passionate, indulgent, vain, excessive, volatile, enthusiastic, exuberant, and moody.

Key behavior traits of the Queens: Queens think, speak, and behave in dramatic emotional emphatic absolutes and contradictions, such as who they will never speak to again, or what they will never do again!

The Queen of Clubs:

The Queen of Clubs is the Emotional part of the instinctive center, and possesses heightened sensory proclivities and physical sensitivities. The acute physical senses and sensory mechanisms amplify their needs and desires, which increases their abundant physical appetites. Their sensory apparatus is attuned to their distinct likes and dislikes. She craves luscious foods and provocative adventures to appease her physical sensual desires. The Queen of Clubs responds to stimuli that activates, stimulates and enlivens her senses. She is attracted to gourmet foods, sumptuous aromas, intoxicating alcoholic beverages, and all manner of mood altering substances, or drugs that may enhance her sensory apparatus and quicken her lively pulse. She loves to experiment and may often behave rather impulsively or compulsively.

However, once the Queen of Clubs is satisfied by her highly overindulgent whims she may temporarily be out of action, at least until her sensual passions overcome her again. When her sensual appetites are aroused, she feels she needs instant gratification, which is one way this Queen flip manifests.

She can be quite a demanding Queen whom we have all seen manifest within us. Try to recall an occasion when you were particularly hungry, thirsty or over tired. Were you cranky and moody? The answer for almost everyone is yes, without a doubt. It can be somewhat difficult to control the part within us that reacts negatively when the center involved has an enormous influence over how we feel physically. The Queen of Clubs can exert a great deal of power over us when she feels hungry, tired, cold, hot, sick or generally physically out of balance. As a result, the Queen of Clubs exerts a great deal of control over how we function based on her sensory needs and demands. Certainly, our performance is adversely affected if we have not eaten well, or have not had sufficient restful sleep. It is the Queen of Clubs who ultimately throws a royal fit to make sure the instinctive center gets the nourishment she craves and sufficient sleep. The Queen of Clubs makes lavish demands that are difficult to ignore, and she will not just go away quietly.

Keep in mind, the Queen of Clubs center exists in both women and men and is gender neutral. Queens of all centers do not differentiate with regard to one's gender. The Queen of Clubs is activated in both sexes by whichever, and whatever stimuli the individual is partial to. This may manifest in different forms depending on one's preferences for food, fragrance, sex, alcohol, drugs, or whichever sensory satisfying substance the individual favors. Unhealthy addictive behaviors are often a recurring theme as an identifiable trait exhibited by the Queens of centers. As with all Queens, the Queen of Clubs is a bit of an extremist. She may happily devour an entire box of chocolates, only to suffer the consequences by becoming quite ill after her unhealthy indulgence. Having overtly satisfied her sweet tooth cravings, the Queen flips and vows she will never do that again! But, next week having forgotten she had disavowed chocolates forever, another box of candy finds its way into her craving hands. The vow is broken, and once again, the Queen of Clubs will gorge to her hearts content, only to pay the painful price later. She does not seem to possess a strong memory mechanism that has the ability to recall her suffering from previous indulgences.

We all have a Queen of Clubs we can observe, and, sensuality we can verify. Pay attention to yourself when you smell a fragrance that appeals to your sensory delight mechanism. The perfume industry was born to satisfy the Queen of Clubs desire for alluring fragrances. The sensitive noses of individuals who create fragrances in the perfume industry probably belong to the Queen of Clubs. They have the innate ability to blend fragrant oils that enchant our senses. Lovely models stroll around the fragrance section in department stores with the latest aromatic creation to intoxicate our senses into submission. It is typically our very own Queen of Clubs that will purchase the fragrant perfume that has mesmerized our senses. The Queen of Clubs is quite easy to observe in oneself and in others. When you are in a restaurant and see, someone devouring a huge plate of food, it is likely they are indulging in the emotional part of the instinctive center. Of course, when we are hungry we all seem to have the proverbial, "eyes bigger than our stomach." This is the Queen of Clubs overestimating the amount of food that she can comfortably consume while she is experiencing hunger pangs. A Queen of Clubs recurring theme might be that, she lives to eat, rather than she eats to live. Entire food philosophies and schools of thought exist based on satisfying this hungry Queen.

Cordon Bleu epicurean gourmet cooking schools cater to her very demanding food whims and wishes. Beautifully photographed food magazines feature sumptuous feasts which promise to fulfill her abundant desires for luscious foods. She is a lavish gourmand demanding the most delicious food life has to offer, and in large portions. Some of the greatest chefs in the world are Queen of Clubs centered individuals who are acutely sensitive to the delicate and subtle nuances of flavor. People often express exuberant delight from their Queen of Clubs in reaction to gastronomic delicacies. They are the devotees of famous chefs and food masters who create delicious gourmet meals. It is quite likely that most cook books, and perhaps even diet books are written by Queen of Clubs individuals. While other centers may have the discipline to realize they need a well-balanced, nourishing meal, the Queen of Clubs indulges in whatever edible delight strikes her fancy at any moment. She simply does not remember her previous painful verification that three scoops of chocolate fudge ice cream topped with melted marshmallows, whipped cream and chocolate sauce is really not very nutritious, or healthy. Food commercials on television, and at the cinema are designed to appeal to and activate the Queen of Clubs. Before the movie starts, most theatres will advertise their snack stand while the buttery aroma of freshly popped popcorn fills the air. Have you ever watched a food commercial showing a sumptuously prepared meal and suddenly felt compelled to eat, or get a snack? Notice the next time you are in the grocery store and your Queen of Clubs suddenly has a craving, recalls the food commercial and goes in search of the delicacy that inspires her sudden phantom hunger.

The Queen of Clubs will also go to great lengths to satisfy sexual appetites, and may also exhibit an alluring, sensual demeanor. Most of us have experienced this phenomenon to some degree when we have been attracted to someone and wished to get their attention. By flirting we achieve our aim to send out a signal. We hope our message will be well received and hopefully returned to us. In general, the Queen of Clubs is quite active in sending out signals to attract the person who is the object of her attraction. Sexual desire is a strong impulse with the Queen of Clubs and her sensual needs can become obsessive if unchecked. However, she radiates a magnetic sensuality that works like powerful radar to attract the person, or persons she desires. Both men and women who are centered in the Queen of Clubs tend to possess this dynamic sensual magnetism. The Queen of Clubs individual has abundant appetites for all the sensual pleasures of life, and it is vital for them to feel attractive for their potential lovers and mates.

The sensual Queen of Clubs female is generally rather fleshy and voluptuous, like Marilyn Monroe for example. The emotional element endows them with the characteristic softly rounded body mass that can easily become overweight. However, they may also have highly sensitive body issues. It is documented that Marilyn Monroe struggled with her weight, dieting and took amphetamines, which caused a sleeping disorder that necessitated taking sleeping pills at night. When the Queen of Clubs is not satisfied, she may throw a royal temper tantrum. This is an example of the negative half of the Queen of Clubs if she is experiencing sensory deprivation. Her cravings and desires can be obsessive and must be satisfied or she has the potential to become quite difficult. Members of both sexes who are centered in the Queen of Clubs tend to have ample appetites for food and drink, and will generally have to watch their weight throughout their lives. Queen of Clubs males who have a large physical presence may be slightly more immune to pop culture image pressures, as the media does not necessarily dictate impossibly slender image ideals to men as much as it does to women. But, a man centered in this card may be fleshy and muscular. I have known Queen of Clubs individuals who struggled with exercise to work off excess weight, coupled with low calorie diets bordering on starvation. But, their diet was generally sabotaged when the Queen flipped and later binged on ice cream and other treats after an aerobics class.

A Queen of Clubs friend went through a painful divorce and became addicted to alcohol. This is a common addiction, and like all addictions drinking creates an illusory effect, and the alcohol severely exacerbates problems. During her bouts of drinking she relinquished self-control and responsibility as her Queen manifested in negative self-destructive behaviors. Fortunately, she got medical treatment and therapy to help control her drinking. People have different addictions which can cause them harm, and yet they refuse to relinquish their habits, regardless if it is eating, drinking, drugs or other odd harmful physical behaviors. For example, I knew one Queen of Clubs who persistently washed her hair every day, wreaking havoc on her scalp and causing bald patches. She came to see me in great distress and I asked her what caused this condition? She claimed she took excellent care of her hair, shampooing and blow-drying it daily. However, her frequent washing and blow-drying was depleting her scalp of vital essential oils. I encouraged to stop washing her hair so often, but she refused, insisting that she had to be clean! However, her hair was brittle and falling out in clumps because as she washed and blow dried it excessively, much to her detriment. These are some examples of potentially unhealthy habits which the Queen of Clubs may exhibit.

Certainly, the media does not make it easy on Queen of Clubs centered individuals who are prone to weight gain and therefore may not fit the fashion industry's picture of perfection. But, the ideal of slim, slender perfection is usually only embodied by young moving centered models. Unfortunately, many individuals believe the media hype and suffer from a poor body image and low self-esteem due to the stereotypical ideas of beauty. This completely unrealistic ideal can have a disturbing psychological effect on the majority of people who possess a naturally fleshy body. Perhaps this false ideal of perfection adversely affects the Queens of centers most significantly, who may regard it as a personal threat to their unique individuality. The Queen of Clubs operate with the law of attraction to stimuli, and they also have an extreme need to be attractive to potential lovers or mates. Their robust instinctive physical and sensual needs must be gratified, and other people are extremely important to their need for approval, fulfillment and contentment.

The Queen of Clubs has a tendency to develop habitual compulsive cravings. These cravings can result in harmful addictions to food and alcohol, causing weight gain and other health issues. Incessant overeating and dieting often results in yo-yo syndrome, a constant battle of gaining and losing weight. Food issues often plague the Queen of Clubs, so they tend to experiment with trendy eating experiments. But, this confuses and exacerbates the obsessive-compulsive mechanisms of the Queen. Keep in mind, if the Queen of Clubs is on a diet, then she wants everyone to be on a diet with her, whether they need to or not. Many years ago, I shared a house with other people, one of whom was a Queen of Clubs. She was from Germany and often spoke of her family's tavern and the rich foods she loved to eat. Her primary interests seemed to be food and cooking, but, her menu of rich foods caused her to gain weight easily. Her weight issues were a chronic problem and she became obsessed with losing weight. Then she heard about a natural food society, and studied their diet regime which was based on healthy food combinations, which she followed, rather obsessively. Afterwards she became the consummate food expert, telling everyone what they should eat, whether they were interested or not! She was quite unaware that others were not interested in her odd food lectures. All of her conversations were focused on food, what to eat, and how to combine foods to lose weight. Her life revolved around her food rituals, cooking, eating, grocery shopping, and giving diet advice. Ironically, she also suffered from bouts of excessive binge eating, followed by purging, an unhealthy Queen addiction. Her incessant food obsessions exemplified the Queen of Clubs with her rather compulsive habits.

While Queen of Clubs individuals tend to have significant vanity about their appearance and sex appeal, this can have the potential to compromise their health if they do not gain control over excessive appetites. They have a strong impulse to satisfy physical cravings and sensual appetites, but also have a strong desire to be attractive and desirable. The Queen of Clubs individual may have impulsive sensory desires and cravings which if uncontrolled, can become unhealthy addictions. If desires create complex psychological issues and addictions, the Queen of Clubs must strive to develop healthy self-care habits to regain physical balance. The Queen of Clubs can make efforts to develop sensible eating habits and practical patterns of behavior to enhance their health and wellbeing. However, I knew a rather large Queen of Clubs female who had an abundantly healthy self-image and self-esteem. She accepted herself as a big woman and did not try to hide her full-figure plus-sized proportions. Her loving husband was quite slender and seemed slightly diminutive in her presence, but they had a very happy marriage relationship. Perhaps this was partly because she was not concerned with how the world perceived her physical presence. Her main concern in life was to be true to herself, and to her essential nature which manifested in healthy self-esteem and self-confidence. She had a successful business and a large circle of interesting friends who were assorted sizes and shapes.

The potentially harmful behavior patterns of the Queens of Clubs can shed light on the social pressures and media hype which society is subjected to, all the while promoting impossible illusions of perfection. The fundamental problem is that this concocted picture of perfection is quite unnatural, and dictated by people who lack understanding of the human physiological condition. The skinny image that has been perpetuated by the fashion industry is based on unrealistic illusions for most normal people in the world. It is absurd to have self-doubts or to suffer from low self-esteem simply because one is a bit fleshier, or heavier than the thin models in fashion magazines. It is equally ludicrous to base one's own ideal of beauty or perfection on marketing tools. Trends in the advertising media are devised to promote and sell products. Fashionable clothing needs to display well on hangers in retail stores in order to sell. Super skinny models do not detract from a garment, just as a hanger does not detract from a garment. Yet, the reality of life is that most people do not fit the fashion industry's exaggerated ideal of an ultra-slender body. If you are fleshier, curvier or heavier than fashion models, please do not despair. There is hope as the fashion world is addressing this obsolete nonsensical conundrum. They have realized the reality of life and are now actively marketing and show casing fashion trends on the runway for normal females who are curvier, heavier and also plus sized.

If you accept the possibility that you may be a Queen of Clubs, or perhaps one of the other Queens of a center, you will gain a much healthier self-perception by accepting yourself on your own natural terms. Accepting yourself as you truly are in your essential nature will most certainly help you to achieve more balance and harmony in your life. Real happiness and feeling secure about oneself can only come from within oneself by living true to one's essential nature. Gaining knowledge about your center of gravity will increase your understanding of why your life manifests as it does, emotionally, intellectually, physically and sensuously. Self-knowledge will help you gain self-acceptance to enhance your self-esteem and nurture your true essential nature.

Keywords associated with the Queens: dramatic, temperamental, expansive, gregarious, controlling, lavish, extravagant, passionate, indulgent, vain, excessive, volatile, enthusiastic, exuberant, and moody.

Key behavior traits of the Queens: Queens think, speak, and behave in dramatic emotional emphatic absolutes and contradictions, such as who they will never speak to again, or what they will never do again!

The Jacks of Centers:

The Jacks represent the moving function processes of the four centers. The moving element of the Jacks of centers works in union with the instinctive center, physical body. The Jacks of centers also serve as the memory banks which we rely on to function efficiently, automatically, and habitually. The data stored in these parts of centers is available for use almost instantaneously to provide information which is needed in a given moment. As memory banks, they are essential to our existence, as the Jacks provide information that allows all the centers to work swiftly and affectively. The Jacks of all the centers assist us in every moment to ensure that we function optimally. The Jack of Hearts stores emotional data, such as your favorite aunt's birthday. The Jack of Diamonds keeps the conversation going. The Jack of Spades enables you to walk, drive your car, or ride a bicycle. The Jack of Clubs keeps your body functioning, your heart beating and lungs breathing so you do not have to think about it. This automatic functioning and processing allows all the other centers to work smoothly. The Jacks serve as information databases that influence all your functions to work effectively, thus enabling centers to operate optimally. The Jacks do not expend vast amounts of emotional energy like the Queens. The Kings require intellectual attention, but they rely upon the Jacks to keep track of all the data for use to intellectualize and theorize.

The Jacks of centers occupy the realm of data entry, information input, data storage, memorization and also imitation and mimicry. They are less inclined to originality or inventiveness of new ideas and concepts. The Jacks of centers, when working optimally, function at a rapid speed. This speed fluctuates with each center, but the Jacks have almost instant recall when they work correctly. Essentially, if we are balanced and all of our centers are working optimally, we can experience a more harmonious living experience. When centers are out of balance, and doing the work of another center, they may not be working optimally. Because of our habitual patterns of behavior, we have a tendency to rely quite heavily on the Jacks of centers, and much of our life is spent living from our memory banks. Notice when a friend greets you with, "Hey, what's happening?" Most greetings manifest habitually and automatically from the Jack of Hearts combined with the Jack of Diamonds, and without effort. These casual cliché expressions are stored in our memory banks for instant use. But, this is a highly-simplified example of how our memory banks operate.

The Jacks are activated when we need instant answers, gestures, responses, reflexes and movements. And this occurs if we are being attentive or not, because we have stored data available. But, if the Jack is asked a question that is not in their stored repertoire of data, they may not be able to come up with an answer. They may have limited resources for problem solving if information is not already in their memory banks. We may observe the Jacks of centers malfunctioning at times when we cannot remember or recall stored information. Perhaps memory diseases, such as Alzheimer's, originate in malfunctioning Jacks of centers.

Under the best circumstances, the Jacks of centers are extremely beneficial as they allow us to live, breathe, feel, think, and move fluidly, effectively and expediently through our daily life without having to search for answers and guidance while processing every detail in each and every moment. Therefore, the smooth and instantly accessible functioning of the Jacks of centers allows us to experience our life without draining our life resources constantly trying to figure out every single detail as we go through our day. By allowing the intellectual and emotional parts of our centers to utilize the energy required for intentional thinking and emotional understanding the Jacks of centers provide us with the vital resources that allow us to feel, think, move and sense. The Jacks assist us in every moment while enabling us to seamlessly live our life. Now that you have a glimpse into the Jacks of centers, let us explore the world which they inhabit and influence.

Keywords associated with the Jacks: habitual, imitative, mechanical, automatic, superficial, simplistic, repetitive, conventional, common, spontaneous, routine, formulaic, and subjective.

Key behavior traits of the Jack: Jacks function, feel, think, speak and act from pre-learned programming in general, often mimicking what others feel, think, say or do without analysis or verification.

The Jack of Hearts:

The Jack of Hearts represents the moving physical element of the emotional center. This lends the moving influence with the instinctive sensory element to emotions. Its primary function is to store the emotional information and data to serves as memory banks for the emotional center in a general capacity. This is where previously learned emotional information is stored. This includes our feelings and memories of an emotional nature for instant response, to be recalled fondly, happily, sadly, sentimentally, regrettably, or to be experienced as melancholic moodiness. Many commonly shared emotional reactions and responses to situations arise from the stored information and memories which we hold so dear in our Jack of Hearts center. The Jack of Hearts tends to manifest almost instantly and automatically, spontaneously reacting with laughter, tears, glee, sadness, sorrow, sentimentality, melancholy, or whichever immediate emotional response is elicited from their memory banks.

One characteristic of this center is lighthearted emotions. Silly jokes, birthday parties, and simple fun are characteristic of the Jack of Hearts approach to common emotional situations. For example, a baby is born and a person centered in the Jack of Hearts reacts almost immediately with a card or a gift, probably wrapped with pink and blue ribbons, just to be sure. A darling little kitten or cute puppy will illicit squeals of delight and have one rolling around on the floor playing with the adorable critter. Their family and friends are sure to receive birthday gift and holiday cards. Melancholy is often exhibited and a sentimental Hallmark card will bring tears to their eyes. In general, their almost instantaneous emotional responses emanate automatically from their Jack of Hearts. The television and Hollywood film industry, as well as advertisers rely on the sentimentality of the Jack of Hearts to promote situation comedies, movies and to sell merchandise. During the holiday season people dash about buying gifts and send greeting cards which are examples of how this center responds to emotional events as stimuli. Sentimentality is a common trait of the Jack of Hearts centered individual. An emotional event, person, film or book will cause the Jack of Hearts to manifest with instantaneous emotional reflexes and reactions. Automatic uncontrolled giggling in response to a joke, or the stream of tears which flow when watching sentimental movies, or fond memories we reminisce about when looking at family photos are examples of how the Jack of Hearts may manifest.

The instantaneous responses and reactions of the Jack of Hearts are often endearing. We can depend on the person centered in this card to give us a moment to chat or to comfort us if we are having a bad day, or to share our joy when we have a nice victory to celebrate. The warmth that emanates from this center can be very reassuring when we need a little bit of consolation.

The Jack of Hearts individual has a light energy with others and is often quite popular, especially for the spontaneity they bring to any festive gathering. Just picture a family gathering where your Queen of Diamonds uncle is busy arguing political issues with your dad. Meanwhile gushes of laughter and fits of giggling flow in the playroom as the little kids are surrounded by your Jack of Hearts aunties and grandmas, playing and teasing and tickling toes and tummies.

Someone who is centered in this card generally has an easy time meeting people and making friends. The Jack of Hearts mingles at parties and is quite comfortable introducing themselves to complete strangers. They treat new acquaintances like old friends and excel at telling jokes. The Jack of Hearts tends to employ an abundance of silliness with their sense of humor. They typically have a vast storehouse of what they consider hilarious jokes and funny stories. Though often at the expense of another person, they may find little pranks irresistible. They remember all the corny jokes which elicit bursts of laughter as they tell their humorous stories, keeping everyone amused. The Jack of Hearts probably invented slapstick comedy which seems to be the lowest common denominator of silliness and everyone joins in for a good hearty laugh.

A friend of mine is a Jack of Hearts who has been married several times and he likes to keep in contact with his former wives and their families. He is not particularly attractive, but he often wins the favor of lovely women with his playful sense of humor. Once he held a grudge against a lady he was attracted to because she would not go on a date with him. It seemed my friend secretly enjoyed his anger as sort of a private vindictiveness. Despite their bright cheerful demeanor, the Jack of Hearts may have a gloomy spot that clings to bad memories of other people, or those who do not enjoy their silly jokes and comic witticisms. The Jack of Hearts can have a tendency to hold onto petty resentments. Remember, this center serves as the memory banks of the emotional center, so they have difficulty forgetting when someone acts unfairly or is mean spirited towards them. They may dwell on petty gripes and minor resentments, avoiding people who have offended them. However, if the offender apologizes all will be forgiven and they can be friends again. The Jack of Hearts can be your favorite confidante with whom you share emotional joys or and woes. They will commiserate your broken heart if you break off your relationship, or share in the problems you are experiencing, and they seem to know about everyone's problems. They are normally surrounded by friends at social gatherings, sharing the latest love relationships, break-up dilemmas and heartbreak doldrums. The Jack of Hearts tends to be popular, possibly because they are willing to share your mirth and your misery.

The Jack of Hearts will poke fun at those who are being too serious in order to lighten the mood. They tend to form emotional bonds, often filled with lightheartedness and silliness. They may even help you to see things in a different light, or make jokes when you are engrossed in over analyzing your problems. From this perspective, they seem to help us understand it is simply not worth the inordinate amount of energy we are spending trying to figure everyone out. Perhaps they make an interesting and valid point, as they seem to take life relatively lightly. Keep in mind, the Jack of Hearts does not want to spend time endlessly brooding over problems, so there can also be a slightly superficial element to their perspective. When it comes to analyzing large scale problems of a more significant magnitude, they may simply not want to think about it, and may prefer not to get involved. They may exhibit the attitude of the ostrich with its head in the sand at times, which prevents them from gaining deeper insights that could help assuage painful or difficult situations. As they emanate primarily from the memory banks of the emotional center, they may prefer to gloss over details that require more intense and intentional analysis.

Someone who is centered in the Jack of Hearts will quite naturally experience these tendencies as a normal response from the emotional data stored in their memory banks as their reaction to emotional stimuli. Their emotional responses tend to be relatively habitual and automatic, not requiring attention nor intentionality. Easily evoked emotions tend to function as their automatic reaction to emotional stimuli. We can readily observe the quick emotional responses of those who are centered in the Jack of Hearts, as they appear to be very sensitive and caring. However, this is not to imply the emotions which emanate from this center do not feel real to the person who is experiencing them. When we observe that we, or another individual may be automatically responding to a certain type of emotional stimuli, we may recognize that this is the pattern from our habitual emotional response mechanism. If one habitually relies on the Jack of Hearts to process emotions, then most reactions or responses will be based on automatic mechanical emotions. These stored emotions manifest without thought, and as a result do not require one to explore other options or efforts to achieve more satisfying emotional experiences. A potential problem of this center is to rely on stored emotional memories, which may not allow for more optimal solutions in complex emotional situations. The missing element of intentionality may detract from effectiveness regards emotional decision making.

It is helpful to keep in mind that the Jack of Hearts is not a deep thinker. They may not realize that their comments might sound a bit shallow, or even rather insensitive at times. Remember, they emanate quickly, reacting from the mechanical parts of the emotional center and may not give their words a lot of thought, nor consider the effect they have on others. I am acquainted with a Jack of Hearts person who often has a rather curt response to situations. She tends to sum things up very quickly and tells others her opinion of what she thinks is good for them. Some people regard her comments as heartless, despite the fact that she is emotionally centered. They are often quite offended by her comments, but she believes she is helping people. She offers her guidance to everyone, thinking she is helping them, but her advice is typically rather insensitive because it is an automatic and habitual response. Part of her manifestation is directly due to the connection between the memory banks of the emotional center and the intellectual center. Her responses seem to emanate from the stored data in her Jacks, so her remarks are not given any thought before she utters them. As a result, she tends to blurt out her advice rather thoughtlessly and insensitively. Please note, in the next segment I will clarify why responses from the Jack of Diamonds may also not be appropriate. These are examples of how the different centers work together and connect across the suits. The Jacks of centers are all connected to one another; as are the Kings of centers, and the Queens of centers. Generally, the Jack of Hearts are very quick to assess a situation and often give a quick response to others that takes the form of a ready-made pat answer, or cliché, perhaps without any consideration for the effect it might have. This does not work well for everyone or under all conditions, but especially not with complex issues.

However, there is a beneficial lesson we can learn from the Jack of Hearts which may help ease tensions in our life. Many of us who have an intellectual element in our center of gravity typically spend too much time and energy analyzing everything as we try to understand a situation, a person, or an issue. We can learn to economize our energy if we simply stop over thinking. We can benefit from the efficiency and expediency of our own Jack of Hearts, which has a natural ability to make almost instant assessments of a person, event or situation. Frankly, many issues which arise are not worth squandering our precious life energy over. By intentionally initializing our emotional memory banks we can benefit in this moment from past experiences, in order to assess and monitor new issues that arise much more efficiently. For many of us this requires effort and practice primarily because we believe every situation is completely unique or different, but there is a very real similarity and connectedness in all that we do and with all the people we meet. With practice, you can call upon what you know from past emotional experiences and effectively apply it to new situations.

Whatever relates to love, the Jack of Hearts is quick to jump on the emotional bandwagon. This center has more emotional crushes on people than other centers. When the Jack of Hearts individual reaches adulthood, they continue to fall in love like a young person. The term, "puppy love," fits this center quite appropriately and is not necessarily emotion based upon deeply shared ideals. I have a Jack of Hearts acquaintance that seems to fall in love easily and frequently. She is currently divorcing her third husband, while reuniting with her first husband. I have noticed with each marriage her new husband tends to be treated in the same manner as the last one. All of her ex-husbands seem to be very similar to one another; they all share a sentimental melancholy attitude towards birthdays, holidays and emotional situations. One Christmas she bought presents for her new husband's four dogs to put under the Christmas tree. There is a common thread that attracts her to the men she marries which is based in the Jack of Hearts, where she has her center of gravity. She insists each marriage is special to her, and she tends to be melancholy and sentimental.

Although people are quite fond of their memories and sentimental feelings about their family and their childhood, it is important to realize that these are often stored emotions, and may not actually be consciously evaluated emotions. Although it is expected that we should love our families, many people suffer painful feelings of guilt, or shame for not feeling love toward their family. This guilt or shame, may emanate from wrong work of the emotional center owing to a conflict of not feeling what supposedly should be felt, or not having the feelings that supposedly should occur naturally. This is relatively common and many people suffer from feelings of guilt, and self-doubt due to the lack of healthy, loving family bonds. Perhaps their childhood was unhappy and this carries over. Many individuals have not had a psychologically healthy childhood, and did not live in a loving home environment. Keeping this in mind, one can gain vital relativity that will help one begin to process and eliminate feeling this burden of guilt. Many individuals are simply trying to recover from the pain they endured while growing up. By re-educating your Jack of Hearts with more realistic and objective wisdom regarding the past, you can begin to understand and heal your emotions. You have the option to re-educate your emotional center with healthy ideas in the present moment that are more beneficial for your life. By taking time to carefully and reasonably re-evaluate and discard negative elements that are stored in the mechanical parts of centers, we can move forward to heal and grow into more intelligent emotions, regardless of what card we are centered in. Keep in mind, we all have memory banks that are filled with old emotional baggage in the Jack of Hearts. But, we absolutely do not have to continue being victimized by our sad memories, or old feelings of guilt. Perhaps you will gain a new understanding to help create healthy new memories free from guilt and based on a realistic evaluation of your past situation. Honesty and balance are the keys to your personal emotional health and wellbeing.

Someone centered in the Jack of Hearts may not share your high regard for Shakespeare, but they are usually a fun friend who can make you smile, and will listen to your problems. They will bake cookies, and put the kettle on to make a nice cup of tea to soothe your woes, unhappiness, or disappointment. Individuals who are centered in the Jack of Hearts tend to have slight fleshiness as they love social gatherings, and food plays an important part in these occasions. They like to host pot luck dinners, and in the warmer months they love a barbeque with all their pals. They invite their buddies over for a meal whenever they get the opportunity. I had a dear friend who was centered in the Jack of Hearts and one year for Christmas she decorated her apartment with red ribbon stripes on her walls. This created a panoramic candy cane effect, and, of course, red lights and green candles twinkled everywhere. She enjoyed the decorations so much that she left them up for the entire following year, which was quite humorous to her friends. Remember, when the office gets decorated on every holiday the Jack of Hearts employee is usually responsible for the brightly colored favors that bedeck the workplace accompanied by bowls of candy and plates of cookies everywhere.

It has been said that, "A trifle consoles us, because a trifle upsets us". This could well apply to the easy flux of the Jack of Hearts. You only have to smile at someone centered in this card and their mood is lifted. The Jack of Hearts mood range varies depending on whether they are reasonably happy, or somewhat sad. They can be uplifted by a simple joke, just as they can fall into a funk over a missed phone call from a loved one. The Jack of Hearts tends to experience life's more basic emotions, that may lack complex overtones. Theirs is a world where everything can be made better by a simple gesture such as a birthday card, a box of candy, an apology, or a postcard from a friend. The next time you see a cute kitten playing observe your reactions. Try to feel that part in yourself that just needs a sweet, cute little tug and your heart begins to sing.

The Jack of Hearts can be very lighthearted and cheerful and regardless of our personal center of gravity, it might help us to overcome our emotional dilemmas and difficulties in the moment. Watch a funny comedy and just indulge in the silliness of the Jack of Hearts. Remember, we have all the centers within us to access. By experiencing all the centers with intentionality and consistent observation you will begin to understand how they function and manifest in yourself, and in other people.

Keywords associated with the Jacks: habitual, imitative, mechanical, automatic, superficial, simplistic, repetitive, conventional, common, spontaneous, routine, formulaic, and subjective.

Key behavior traits of the Jack: Jacks function, feel, think, speak and act from pre-learned programming in general, often mimicking what others feel, think, say or do without analysis or verification.

The Jack of Diamonds:

The Jack of Diamonds represents the moving part of the intellectual center which stores all your learned information as data. Thus, the Jack of Diamonds represents the memory banks where intellectual data and information is stored. It functions as the mechanical part of the intellectual center, and it operates automatically, without attention or intentionality. The Jack of Diamonds does not necessarily generate new ideas, concepts or theories, to the degree that it stores accumulated data, information and concepts. The memory banks of the intellectual center endow this card with unique properties to store information and data. The collected information in the Jack of Diamonds has special significance for the intellectual center, storing all the bits and pieces of data so it can recall them at a later time, easily and swiftly as needed. However, this function often works mechanically in an automatic manner without necessarily utilizing discernment or making an intentional effort. For example, when we are taking in new information or learning new knowledge we need to be aware in the moment in order to record the data. But, when we have assimilated new information, our Jack of Diamonds can store it conveniently in its memory banks. This data will remain there until there is a need for it, at which time the memory banks can release it automatically. Almost all of our learning throughout our life is stored within these memory banks.

Many people who appear quite intelligent have this center functioning as their primary center of gravity. To others, the Jack of Diamonds appears to know virtually everything there is to know. However, much of what they know is merely stored data that they have memorized and kept stored in their memory banks. A person who operates from this center is generally viewed as being very intelligent in the ordinary world. However, this is not quite accurate. The memorization of data is quite different from the intentional formulation of theories and concepts, which require the attention and presence of the King of Diamonds. It is helpful to understand this clearly, as the automatic functioning of the Jack of Diamonds causes confusion regarding what is considered true genius. The Jack of Diamonds center is a repository of data; therefore, is not particularly innovative, nor discriminating about information, and someone centered in the card would not typically be characterized as an original thinker. These individuals are somewhat of the jack-of-all-data, when it comes to having almost unlimited information at their proverbial fingertips. These are the folks who are always willing to put in their "two cents," to almost any conversation.

The Jack of Diamonds individual may suggest some ideas from their memorized data base to inform us of almost anything they think we should know. If you ask a Jack of Diamonds person about the weather, the news, the rainforest, the top colleges, the ten best dressed people in the world, or the latest movie starring a famous or infamous actor, most likely they can provide you with some sort of answer, and rather quickly. Keep in mind, almost anyone can parrot information from the Jack of Diamonds, when it is working properly. However, the Jack of Diamonds does not necessarily have the requisite brain power to develop conceptual ideas along abstract theoretical lines of thought. For example, it would be quite incorrect to suggest that someone, such as the great mathematician Pythagoras, was centered in the Jack of Diamonds. Pythagoras was a master of intentional thought, conceptualization and theorization that required total mental focus and concentration, which is consistent with the King of Diamonds. But, this type of in depth concentration is not a property of the Jack of Diamonds. The function of the Jack of Diamonds is to store data, process and distribute information; however, it would not be likely to formulate abstract mathematical concepts, or to expound original philosophical doctrines.

Nonetheless, the function of the Jack of Diamonds is vital for all the centers so they can remember the data they have accumulated to use as required. The King of Diamonds makes good use of the memory banks in order to keep track of what it has theorized thus far, in order to do its advanced work of developing lofty ideas. Everything must be brought together as a whole concept. This is an example of how our memory banks can assist us to develop a line of thought. Each one of us utilizes our Jack of Diamonds memory banks daily for our basic instant recall. Without this center, we would probably not be able to even pass an elementary school class examination. Our ability to store data to readily recall later is a highly advantageous phenomenon. Putting our stored information into proper use is where the other centers make sense of what has been learned. Also, discernment and discrimination is needed to delegate data to its appropriate channel. Common sense is an excellent tool to consistently incorporate into ones thinking processes. However, as Benjamin Franklin said, "Common sense is not so common." We will explore the inherent dilemma of the Jack of Diamonds much more in following segments.

The Jack of Diamonds memory banks are remarkably well adapted to store our vital statistics. Similar to a computer it processes data automatically so we do not need to make efforts to think about the basics. Similar to a computer which stores data, the intellectual center stores information and can usually retrieve it when needed for reference. However, as with computers, this center can also malfunction. Quite often files get lost, cannot be found, become corrupted, or are simply used incorrectly. Although our intellectual center's memory banks have the necessary data filed away, there may be a glitch in our mental processes that does not allow all data to be retrieved when needed. Also, memorized responses lack the intentionality of the King, or the spontaneous inventiveness of the Queen of Diamonds. In many cases the information stored in the Jack of Diamonds is utilized mistakenly or is used at an inappropriate moment, which is a distinctive property of this center. Thus, it has been given a special title due to its mechanical tendency to operate without conscious intervention which is "the formatory apparatus." This title will become clearer as we investigate the implications of how this apparatus works automatically. The Jack of Diamonds tends to react and respond automatically, but their words may be slightly devoid of well evaluated conclusions.

The Jack of Diamonds thinks in arbitrary yes or no, and does not have the discriminating ability to fine tune their thinking, or their output. The Jack of Diamonds formatory apparatus has an uncanny knack of utilizing pre-formulated data without any critical discernment or discrimination. This is an indication that one can remain quite unaware of one's thoughts, while the formatory apparatus conducts one's life quite automatically. This unique part of the intellectual center is capable of carrying on conversations while basically spewing forth data from memory banks. Formatory thinking consists of preformed ideas which are typically basic information and data which requires no effort to evaluate or ponder. Some examples are automatic responses, which are the equivalent of yes or no, black or white. Formatory expressions are ready made pre-formulated thoughts and ideas which require virtually no intentional thought, or effort. When we are sensitive to this dialogue coming from another person, or within our self, we begin to realize how little real communication is actually taking place. It is an interesting experiment to be aware of this formulaic chatter, and observe it as it is occurring. Most clichés and slang terminology is stored in this center for immediate use as needed. We all remember common phrases such as, "roses are red and violets are blue."

Formatory expressions are abundant in every culture and society. Familiar catch phrases and slang are often employed, so that one feels that one belongs to one's peer group, or simply out of habit. This is often habitual and similar to being on automatic pilot. For example, when someone gives advice that sounds as though no thought has been given to it, most likely they are emanating from their formatory apparatus. When we are greeted by a friend with a very common phrase such as, "What's up?" we can be mindful that this is coming from the formatory apparatus. As all the Jacks are connected along suits, the formatory apparatus may also combine greetings and cliché phrases with stored sentiments from the Jack of Hearts.

The Jack of Diamonds centered individual does well in careers that require repetitive mental processes and skills. These people can speak endlessly about subjects they have an interest in, hence they can do well in jobs where talking is required. For example, they can excel in sales jobs, where they have an easy time explaining the benefits of their products. It may also be rather difficult to interrupt them, as this center tends to think it has all the answers. Teachers, who teach the same subject semester after semester may also be centered in the Jack of Diamonds. They can repeat what they know from memory with facility and ease. Secretaries who must remember details, as well as sales people who continually project their company policies may be centered in this card. News reporters, technical writers, researchers, investigators, sales people and librarians may also be centered in the Jack of Diamonds.

Someone centered in this card is energetic when speaking as they express their ideas quickly, and often repeatedly. They can chat extensively about the latest bit of information they have acquired, even though they have not yet fully grasped it meaning. Many of their conversations are based on whatever they have recently heard, although they have probably not formulated an exact opinion about it. They often speak about newly acquired information, but they typically possess only a superficial understanding. They punctuate their dialogue with common phrases or their favorite expressions which are stored for immediate use whenever they feel like chatting. People who are centered in the Jack of Diamonds have a tendency to be slight in build, as their focus is the acquisition of data. For example, they tend to be less physically active as they prefer to be mentally active, and as a result, they are less inclined to build muscle mass. Intellectually centered types tend to consume large amounts of information, rather than large amounts of food. Picture the archetypal thin bookworm, eyeglasses askew, who consumes information and data to fuel his mind.

Individuals centered in the Jack of Diamonds may tend to have a somewhat superficial grasp of knowledge. While they process a lot of information, they may not thoroughly investigate all the data they consume, and therefore, they may lack a complete comprehension of vital details. Information they convey to others may not have been examined in depth, nor sufficiently investigated for a broader understanding. Pay attention to details when conversing with intellectually centered people. If they lack the concrete facts to substantiate their ideas or concepts, it may be an indication that they are centered in the Jack of Diamonds. For example, once a county inspector come to my home to investigate some difficult neighborhood issues. He arrived late and was dressed in odd attire, as if he were impersonating an Englishman dressed for rainy weather. He asked me some standard questions, which I elaborated on; but, most of my answers he quickly dismissed as nonapplicable, or unnecessary. His behavior seemed strangely artificial for a county inspector who I felt should be more interested in neighborhood issues from a taxpayer. When he was departing, he put on his rain cap, a distinctive tweed deer-stalker hat. I was surprised to suddenly recognize he had been imitating the mannerisms of a fictional detective, Sherlock Holmes, who had great disdain for unimportant trivia. Though I rarely watch television, I appreciate Masterpiece Theater and was surprised when I recognized the inspector's Jack of Diamonds unconscious impersonation of the masterful detective, Sherlock Holmes. Thus, I followed our peculiar discussion with a letter emphasizing the importance of neighborhood safety. His odd impersonation probably emanated automatically from his admiration for a fictional character, whose mannerisms he had stored in his Jack of Diamonds, ready for instant, but ineffective, replay.

When it manifests in this manner, useful adjectives to describe this center might be dismissive, tactless, insensitive, careless and thoughtless, because they are not really thinking. However, the underlying problem is that most people have no idea they are behaving in a careless manner in their dialogues and conversations. To complicate matters, people who become involved in these day to day formatory conversations tend to respond from their own formatory center. These discourses can be compared to automatic pilot interacting with automatic pilot; very little is really shared or exchanged.

Speaking with increased intentionality can bring a higher level to conversations. For example, a few years ago, I discussed the problem of celebrity gossip with a friend. I told her that someone in our social group, who is centered in the Jack of Diamonds, was spreading gossip about a famous person. My friend made the simple, but astute observation, that gossiping is ignorant, uninformed and unsophisticated. Her insightful summary is an excellent description of how gossip emanates from unexamined and unverified data from the formatory apparatus. The Jack of Diamonds formatory apparatus is responsible for many of the blunders we make when speaking about something of which we have no real knowledge. Simply thinking in black and white without weighing the evidence, does not indicate understanding of a situation. However, people generally tend to blurt out their opinions without much thought. Typically, pre-formed negative opinions are stored in the formatory apparatus for convenience, so that people can readily speak about their favorite subjects of derision. Arguments which are based on differences of opinion, are generally based on habitual formatory thinking. The formatory apparatus does not allow for understanding, or objectivity as it works mechanically without implementing relativity and scale. Many arguments derive from superficial pre-formed conclusions that lack depth. Much of the time, when people argue, they are not thinking objectively nor thoroughly. Consequently, they are relying on the Jack of Diamonds which is simply inadequate.

Keep in mind, the formatory apparatus typically makes responses which emanate from the memory banks. These responses are not well thought out, and tend to lack an objective overview. Accuracy in thinking is necessary to make informed accurate decisions in our personal responses. For example, I recall asking someone a question regarding the whereabouts of another person. Their response was immediate, and not at all relevant to my query. His formatory apparatus had responded with random, pre-formed opinions and ideas he had about the person. However, I was not inquiring his opinion, or what he thought about the person, but simply information as to where they might be living. Often when we ask specific questions of someone, the first answer that springs forth emanates from the formatory apparatus. As the memory bank of the intellectual center, it contains virtually everything it has learned, and stored in its data banks. However, what has been learned may be based in faulty thinking, which has been acquired from listening to other people's opinions, as they emanate from their own Jack of Diamonds formatory center. The formatory apparatus has a tendency to run rampant during casual social discourse. Groups of people often congregate together, based on their similarly shared general ideas, which can be based in the Jack of Diamonds. The formatory apparatus may also make it rather difficult for us to grasp, accept and adjust to new information. The Jack of Diamonds is loaded with ideas, which are firmly rooted and fixed in the mind, so that any new helpful ideas are often unacceptable, or simply ignored. When we are unable to hear new ideas from a fresh perspective, it keeps us habitually stuck in outmoded principles and inaccurate concepts.

These deeply ingrained mechanical habits make it particularly difficult for us to change, grow, or develop self-knowledge or personal self-awareness with a fresh perspective. The Jack of Diamonds formatory apparatus encourages us to be lazy about what we think we know. To attain greater understanding, requires that one make efforts to overcome habitual mental inertia in order to open the mind to helpful new information. We cannot elevate our thought patterns if we continually allow the memory banks of pre-formulated ideas, opinions, beliefs and concepts to dictate our thinking processes. Also, there are times when a person feels that their belief system is being threatened, but this may be because they are already on rather shaky grounds with their thoughts and ideas. It may be that they have not actually verified the concepts that they believe, but have merely accepted as true without any personal verification. This is shallow thinking and does not build a firm foundation of deep thought upon which to base belief. We must continually verify ideas to gain greater comprehension. Overcoming mechanical responses from the formatory apparatus enables one to hear information in a new way for deeper understanding. This helps create a solid foundation which encourages enhanced self-awareness and personal growth.

Observe yourself when you are hearing a new idea, or being exposed to concepts that are foreign to your ordinary thinking. If you dismiss it at once, this reaction is probably coming from the Jack of Diamond's formatory apparatus. It is beneficial to try to contemplate an idea slowly before you dismiss it completely as utter nonsense, as a quick response may simply be the Jack of Diamonds. Also, there may be an inherent element of laziness in the Jack of Diamonds which can override a desire to think in a new way. Whenever you notice that you feel ambivalent, or too lazy to investigate a new subject in depth, it is probably the Jack of Diamonds influencing you. Mechanical habits can limit the acquisition of new ideas, that may actually qualitatively improve your life. New ideas require your intellectual efforts to process and understand. Habitual laziness in the intellectual center can be detrimental as it deprives us of new and different learning experiences which can help develop our minds. We need to be open and receptive to become more aware of the possibilities for us to expand our horizons and mental vistas. Watch attentively, and listen for the Jack of Diamonds to manifest as it will habitually take over, and limit new information. Try to hear ideas in a new way and at the same time try to observe the resistance of this center.

By gaining more control over the habitual functioning of the Jack of Diamonds you will begin to understand yourself and your life in greater depth. You can begin to modify or eliminate any pre-formed ideas that may have been inaccurately governing your life up to this point. There is a massively gigantic world of ideas, knowledge, wisdom and self-awareness awaiting the person who conquers this mental block. Remember, the Jack of Diamonds is an invaluable storehouse of information, but you must become aware of its limitations, and make intentional efforts to access it and use it for your best and highest interests.

Keywords associated with the Jacks: habitual, imitative, mechanical, automatic, superficial, simplistic, repetitive, conventional, common, spontaneous, routine, formulaic, and subjective.

Key behavior traits of the Jack: Jacks function, feel, think, speak and act from pre-learned programming in general, often mimicking what others feel, think, say or do without analysis or verification.

The Jack of Spades:

The Jack of Spades is the moving part of the moving center. As with all the Jacks of centers this constitutes the memory banks where learned data and information is stored. An individual centered here has a natural predisposition to move with ease and fluidity, and they move almost ceaselessly. Jack of Spades centered individuals are moving dynamos, sometimes seeming like whirlwinds of perpetual motion. The memory banks of this center store learned movement data which it has accumulated. Every moving centered activity which we learn, such as walking, riding a bicycle, dancing, painting a picture, swimming, or driving an automobile, is stored in the Jack of Spades moving center memory banks. The data can be recalled and retrieved automatically and quite spontaneously when it is necessary to perform moving centered activities.

All moving centered activities which initially required a great deal of your time and energy to learn and gain mastery of, are stored in the Jack of Spades memory banks data base. One does not need to be centered in this card to have these memory banks work efficiently. We all have this center which helps us navigate our life as we move through our day. The memory banks of the centers facilitate speed of integration by storing information which can be accessed readily when it is needed. For example, you can read a magazine while the moving center memory banks can quite automatically, but efficiently feed you your lunch.

We can readily observe the ease with which we move around during the course of our day, performing our routine tasks. One rarely needs to stop and think about detailed movement instructions such as, "put the left foot in front of the right foot, then lift the right foot off the ground, then aim the right foot forward and propel at the speed of....", and so on. If we did not have the moving center's memory banks instant recall to implement the data of how to walk, we would be quite limited in what we could accomplish. If we had to think about every single detail of how to move or perform routine tasks, it might take too much time to be efficient. Our moving center memory banks allow us to move with fluidity and grace, but, solely relying on habit can be detrimental at times. The memory banks may not be able to discriminate what might be the right action pertaining to making a decision, regarding the higher right in a given moment. The law of accident may be more prevalent if one lives habitually from the memory banks all the time.

The dilemma of living solely from our moving center memory banks, is that they are habitual. This occurs to such an extent that most people fail to pay adequate attention with intentionality. Essentially people may be spending their life on automatic pilot, relying on the memory banks to function, and to make decisions. There are many occasions where one would be better equipped to handle an action if one accessed the King of Spades and being more attentive. Rather than physically moving habitually from the memory banks, one can bring enhanced attention to the moment with mindful self-observation. However, the Jack of Spades may be quite content doing repetitive work which is already learned and programmed into their moving center memory banks of stored information. They can work almost automatically while they daydream about going skiing or snowboarding next winter. Yet, for the purpose of economizing energy expenditures, our moving center's memory banks provide the basic resources which allow us to perform most movements quite easily by employing the Jack of Spades. The memory banks provide data almost instantaneously to execute movements with facility.

You will notice that an individual who is centered in the Jack of Spades has a rather sleek, slender physique as their habitual tendency to move through life endows them with a highly efficient metabolism. These individuals move almost continually, from morning to night as this is their predisposition. The food they consume is the fuel that keeps them moving, almost constantly. Movement is their natural, mechanical tendency and habitual pattern. People who are centered in the Jack of Spades move incessantly; hence, they have a streamlined physique as they just burn off calories. They can be seen restlessly twitching if required to sit for any length of time, all the while making hand gestures and tapping their foot restlessly. In fact, restless is an excellent adjective to describe someone centered in the Jack of Spades. Another Jack of Spades male I knew put 300,000 miles on his car's odometer, whilst driving back and forth from his residence in Malibu, California where he surfs every day, to his other home at Mammoth Mountain, where he skies as often as possible. He frequently joked that he is the ideal roommate because he is rarely ever at home. Always on the go he engages in endless athletic activities and sports, which he naturally excels at. He is an avid surfer, swimmer, rock climber, skier, and runner, but, there are also other sports he engages in. He is employed as a lifeguard in Southern California, so he has endless opportunities to exercise and swim every day which is perfect for his center of gravity. He is a human being in perpetual motion.

While observing a Jack of Spades centered person, you will see that they are constantly in movement, and their mind is also quite active. They are typically engaged in movement of some sort, or working on one of their many tasks or hobbies. One lively fellow in my astronomy group was centered in the Jack of Spades. In addition to star gazing, he was a hobby inventor; however, his inventions seemed to be somewhat impractical. He spoke animatedly of how he was inventing a space ship with anti-gravity capabilities, similar to a UFO, to fly into outer space. But, he had no scientific training or knowledge about the laws of physics, and he did not seem to understand the necessity of gravity. He showed us his model space ship and spoke excitedly of how it would zoom into outer space. However, other than his creative imagination, his space ship had no means of power. Undeterred by these details he told the astronomy group he would soon have his anti-gravity space ship. Everyone joked and told him that if he knew the secret of anti-gravity he should be careful as, "the men in white coats might come to get him." They all laughed, but in reality, his anti-gravity space ship seemed quite grounded, unless of course, he knew something we were ignorant of.

Once, I nearly had a mishap which illustrates issues with unmonitored Jack of Spades movements. A friend and I had gone shopping, and when I was putting my bags into the car she got distracted and began to shut the trunk, nearly on my head! Fortunately, I had noticed her absent-minded movement and backed away to safety. This is an example the Jack of Spades not paying attention to what is occurring in the moment, and moving from an unconscious habitual impulse. The hazards of living completely from one's memory banks might manifest in unfortunate mishaps. If my friend had been intentional, rather than relying on the mechanical parts of her moving center, she would have been more attentive. Moving automatically from the Jack of Spades without paying attention is one cause of accidents. Habitual patterns of movement manifest mechanically when this center experiences an impulse to move. This illustrates of how the memory banks in the moving center may operate without intentionality and miss vital safety details in the moment. Mechanical parts of centers lack the attention span, and the intentionality required to discern and decide what is right action in a moment.

But, keep in mind, that the memory banks of centers operate habitually, instinctively and automatically, which is what they do best. However, an individual centered in the Jack of Spades may sometimes exercise unnecessary movements because of habitual patterns of behavior which predispose them to move excessively. Due to these deeply ingrained habits, the Jacks of centers do not necessarily stop to think actions through attentively for the purpose of carefully assessing what is right action, or a priority in a situation and what is not. For example, a friend confided that she had difficulty getting a good night's sleep because of her husband's restless nature. He had a habit of rocking his foot back and forth to induce sleep when he awoke during the night. But, unfortunately his sleep deprived wife was kept awake with his moving centered habits. She finally resolved the problem by purchasing a new bed with a center divider. You may notice the person centered in this card can be observed tapping their foot, swinging their legs while sitting, nodding their head while talking, or simply twitching about.

A friend who is a found-object artist, is an excellent example of the Jack of Spades being put to creative use. He moves from the time he gets up in the morning until he retires, usually late at night, as he seems to require minimal sleep. He spends the day out and about in search of abandoned objects, or, combing through junk stores, flea markets and thrift shops looking for various components to create his rather unique projects. Movement keeps him motivated throughout his day, and he always seem to be active, either working on his artistic creations or installing them in art galleries. Also, he is the drummer in a performance art band which travels to various cities to perform. Plus, he is a talented impersonator, uncannily imitating and mimicking celebrities perfectly. While he eats whatever he wishes in abundance, he maintains a slim physique. Very active, he consumes large quantities of food, but burns calories efficiently. His need for activities dominates his life as demonstrated by his constant impulse to create and to move to the beat of his own drum.

The Jack of Spades assists us in all our moving centered actions. When implemented for its remarkable reliance to execute learned movements, this center affords us the ability to instantly recall stored data to utilize in our daily life. From our memory banks in the Jack of Spades we walk, skip, swim, run, dance, or simply move our bodies to the rhythm that beckons and motivates us. Learned movements are stored in the Jack of Spades as the vital data which we can call upon as needed. The expression, "you never forget how to ride a bicycle," may be a fairly accurate description of the memory banks ability to store data. Remember, all learned movements are stored in the Jack of Spades database, the memory banks of the moving center. Most of us can observe our moving center's memory banks by paying attention to habitual patterns we have developed over the course of our lifetime. We tend to be relatively unaware of small repetitive movements which we are accustomed to as we go through our day. But, by simply putting your attention on your movements and actions, this will create a slight resistance in the Jack of Spades which can help you observe yourself. You can experiment by mindfully observing yourself as you perform small tasks. For example, if you are right handed, try to use your left hand, and vice versa. This will demonstrate the resistance of the Jack of Spades while performing routine tasks which one would normally execute easily. In this situation, you will need to be attentive to perform the task in a more intentional manner than is normally necessary. Your opposite hand may not have the manual dexterity, and this creates resistance which helps to observe. Your moving center memory banks might feel awkward, and compelled to impulsively take charge, in order to get the job done. But, your ongoing efforts to resist this impulse by not allowing mechanical, habitual patterns to take control, will provide you with an insightful look at your moving center at work.

Simply by making small experiments such as this, you will observe your centers in their habitual state. Keep in mind, you might feel rather uncomfortable initially; however, your genuine effort to override habitual patterns of behavior can yield valuable insight into how your centers function in your daily life. Your accumulated observations will ultimately assist you in determining your personal center of gravity. It is helpful to be aware, the Jack of Spades has an ability to acquire, adapt and master new methods or types of movement rather quickly. Therefore, it is beneficial to devise new moving center experiments on a regular basis to keep the resistance fresh, and not allow it to degrade into another acquired habit. This will help your efforts to observe yourself. Consistent mindful self-observation will help you to evaluate and assess your natural inclinations, and determine your own particular dominant center of gravity.

People who are centered in the Jack of Spades seem to perform movements rather swiftly, fluidly and seemingly without forethought. They tend to be the all-around proverbial jack-of-all-trades, and as such are the ultimate imitators of movement. Whether you are an expert at moving centered activities, or not, depends on your personal center of gravity which will dominate throughout your life. However, we all possess the moving center memory banks to store our learned movement data. Thus, we can activate certain movements when necessary, if we have already learned a particular activity. Of course, moving center abilities, like any other center, may be limited or impaired by injury, illness or physical disabilities. As one gets older, certain moving centered activities may be somewhat restricted by age related illnesses, such as arthritis aches and pains, which is a fairly common human malady.

Jack of Spades individuals acquire their moving centered skills quickly, and are generally able to execute some complex movements in an imitative manner rather swiftly. For example, a Queen of Spades brings a lively, emotional kinetic energy to the art of dance. Though the Jack of Spades dancer may also perform very well, they may lack the artistic temperament to deliver an innovative, star performance. Along these lines, the King of Spades individual can intentionally invent and design in spatial relationships, whereas the Jack of Spades tends to mechanically copy and imitate. Keep in mind, this is not to say that the Jack of Spades individual is not a creative type. However, the primary function and best purpose of the Jack of Spades memory banks is to store moving centered data that has been previously acquired, learned, or imitated. The data is recalled in a habitual automatic manner, and with agility. Back-up dancers in dance troupes or in the ballet may be Jack of Spades individuals. Remember, the memory banks of all the centers store all learned information, which then serves the emotional, intellectual, moving and instinctive centers more efficiently and effectively.

An individual who is centered in the Jack of Spades will connect with the Jacks of the other centers across the suits. Someone who is centered in the Jack of Spades will tend to manifest from the Jacks of the other centers as well. This is a general guideline regarding all of the centers and this connectedness applies to all centers, regardless of which royal suit is present. Each center has access across the royal suits to the other corresponding centers. But, please be aware that the innate accessing of centers across suits does not automatically create balance within an individual. It merely suggests that someone who is centered in the Jack of Spades will probably respond to emotional stimuli with assistance from their Jack of Hearts across the royalty suits. They may also retrieve information from their Jack of Diamonds memory banks, and quite likely they will respond from the Jack of Clubs, if they become injured or ill. These are simplified examples regarding the centers being connected across the iconic royal suits. However, someone who has made efforts to balance their centers would most likely be able to access the appropriate center at the appropriate time, whether it was the King, Queen, or Jack related moment.

It is beneficial to remember and be mindful that no particular center is better than any other center. Each center is enabled to perform its unique function independently, or together, when harmoniously balanced with the other centers. Regardless of one's center of gravity, it is certainly possible for individuals to possess and exhibit many abilities. One must not discount other factors and influencing elements which are at work in everyone's life. It is helpful to acknowledge that there are many external factors which may influence and inspire an individual to an activity, despite their own personal center of gravity. However, for purposes herein, I am providing a simplified overview of how each center tends to manifest. Again, please keep in mind that no center is better, or worse, than another center. From one perspective, all centers are equally mechanical unless we employ attention, intentionality and objectivity. Although I am not moving centered my description of the Jack of Spades is based on individuals I have known, and observed. My examples are what I have consistently observed with Jack of Spades individuals, as they move so fluidly, gracefully, and quite habitually from their moving center memory banks.

Being aware of your centers will help you observe when your Jack of Spades performs a routine task, perhaps habitually, but efficiently. Gaining knowledge of centers will help you gain understanding of why you feel, think, move and sense as you do. You can mindfully observe yourself with your own distinctive innate nuances and traits, as you become aware of which center influences, stimulates, and motivates your life. From this vantage point you can begin to bring more balance to your centers. By observing the centers within yourself, you can determine which center manifests most frequently as your center of gravity. Gaining clarity will help you understand your life, and will help you understand other people as well.

Watch for the Jack of Spades as you move through your life and try to monitor your actions. Are you on automatic pilot, habitually moving without thought or attention? Or are you being present to your life, living and moving intentionally in the moment?

Keywords associated with the Jacks: habitual, imitative, mechanical, automatic, superficial, simplistic, repetitive, conventional, common, spontaneous, routine, formulaic, and subjective.

Key behavior traits of the Jack: Jacks function, feel, think, speak and act from pre-learned programming in general, often mimicking what others feel, think, say or do without analysis or verification.

The Jack of Clubs:

The Jack of Clubs represents the moving physical element of the instinctive center. As with all the Jacks of centers, this particular center has the distinct qualities of functioning as the memory banks for the physical instinctive center. In a normal fully functioning healthy individual these memory banks automatically serve to perform all of the vital functions simultaneously without the need of our conscious participation. Without this unique function serving us we would probably die. These memory banks store the essential data that keeps our heart beating, our lungs breathing, blood flowing through our circulatory system, glands secreting hormones, the elimination of waste, keeps our senses operational and all our vital processes and functions working to keep our physical body instinctive center alive. For example, we do not need to consciously think about the heart for it to continue beating rhythmically. If one had to remember to think about all vital functions on a moment to moment basis in order to maintain continuous operation it would be impossible. And, it is likely that one might simply forget to breathe, digest one's food, or to make one's heartbeat.

It is incredibly fortunate for us that the Jack of Clubs efficiently manages human physical functions for us. It automatically remembers to process our vital functions, and this allows us to carry on, and live our life. The Jack of Clubs stores all pertinent sensory information that applies to physical maintenance and continuous operation of our vital organs. The essential vital data keeps us alive and is all stored within the memory banks of the instinctive center. This automatic processing ensures that our physical needs are met to perpetuate our physical life. Someone who is centered in the Jacks of Clubs may primarily be concerned with preservation of their physical body and its survival. The Jack of Clubs is directly connected to all the sensory processes which help maintain good health, and also keep the human being safe, secure and alive. Our complex network of nerves and sensory impulses work in harmony to each assist with all elements that constitute a healthy functioning instinctive center. This pertinent information is channeled to the appropriate organs through the network of nerve endings that constitute our physical senses.

The memory banks are responsible not only for the internal workings of the human machine, but, also for relaying messages to the proper organ, or the corresponding body part at the correct time. These messages are transmitted in the form of sensations, which belong to the sensing properties of the five physical senses. The instinctive center's memory banks do not actually require our conscious participation in order for these sensory messages to be sent. The Jack of Clubs database automatically remembers for us, and sends vital sensory messages efficiently, and automatically to the appropriate sense receptors and sensory apparatus. For example, when the body requires fuel in the form of food, certain sensations are produced that create the feeling of hunger within. The sensation in the form of hunger pangs acts as the sensory message that transmits signals to the brain that it is time to eat, drink, or provide nourishment as food, to fuel the physical body with nutrients. After one's physical appetite has been satisfied, the Jack of Clubs continues its work by sending impulses and sensations to the brain as a message to digest the food that is now in the stomach. The memory banks of the instinctive center take care of and manage all the inner workings and functions necessary to keep our physical body alive and well. We all possess this miraculous center which governs the vital inner functioning's of our physical body. All of us are dependent upon it to sustain the life of our physical body, but the individual who is centered in the Jack of Clubs possesses a much greater sensitivity to its own physical needs and sensations.

So, someone who is centered in the Jack of Clubs will regard physical maintenance, such as feeding the body and getting sufficient sleep, as matters of primary importance. These individuals may consider their physical needs and requirements more important than needs of other centers. Thus, the functions of their physical body usually take precedence over the other centers. One might observe a Jack of Clubs centered person as being more interested in food at an event, than being interested in the people who are there. Certainly, when hunger strikes, food is a priority for an individual who is centered here. As another example, someone centered in this card would make efforts to ensure that they had a good job or career that earned them sufficient money to guarantee a roof over their head, a comfortable bed to sleep in, and adequate food. For them, their quality of life is dependent upon meeting the essential physical needs of the instinctive center. Their primary focus in life might be to have physical requirements of life met with regular intake of food and nutrients, maintenance and overall preservation of the body. Certainly, all other centers are required for these needs to be met and are involved in the overall proper functioning and maintenance of the human physical body.

People who are centered in the Jack of Clubs can be found in any and all occupations. However, they may not be interested in a highly visible vocation in the workplace. Their essential job position may tend to place them working in the background, and possibly performing routine procedures, as is customary with all the Jacks of centers. A low-key career choice, which provides a secure salary in a stable work environment, will most likely determine their job preferences. The requirement for secure employment may lead them to pursue jobs that can provide a good steady reliable paycheck and a dependable position, such as in-service industries, which are essential to most people. These might be jobs such as a bank clerk, chef or cook, grocery clerk, security guard, plumber, janitor, gardener, or any employment that would guarantee them regular consistent paychecks. The Jack of Clubs individual may not wish to attract unnecessary attention to themselves, as they tend to be primarily concerned with preservation of their physical organism. This may not make for executive, or management career choices that require constant decision making with an intellectual overview. Their career choices may be aimed at protecting and preserving their elemental needs for the security of their overall physical wellbeing. Their primary focus would probably be safety and security and to maintain a secure home while steadily providing for their immediate family.

Someone centered in the Jack of Clubs may consider the primary requirement in their life is to provide for their physical needs, health and wellbeing. Their instinctive needs may take precedence over extracurricular hobbies, interests, studies and often times, over their social life with friends. Acquaintances who do not directly contribute to their instinctive wellbeing may not be as important. This is not to suggest that individuals centered in the Jack of Clubs are uncaring, unemotional, or unsociable; but they may prefer being at home over socializing. Their priorities seemed to be based on instinctive needs first and foremost. When these needs have been satisfied, they can then proceed to their other interests, which may certainly include other people, social events and other activities. Some cultural groups who prefer to live a simple existence, in harmony with nature, may be centered in the Jack of Clubs. Often it is their custom to live in family groups, sharing meals and accommodations. This of course, is a simple example of how the Jack of Clubs might be content with a life that satisfies their most basic instinctive center requirements. A communal residence, with an emphasis on having a family group may be indicative of instinctive center predominance. It is possible that some of the primitive tribes who live in remote exotic locations, might be Jack of Clubs instinctively centered cultures.

I have known a few Jack of Clubs individuals who were vegetarians or vegan, and they were generally very health conscious. Keep in mind, quite often disease, illness and bad health, is caused by poor eating habits or harmful habits which are cravings from other centers. For example, it is probably the Queen of Clubs that enjoys the rich indulgence in an ice cream sundae dessert which may later causes painful indigestion. When the Queen has over indulged in some rich delicacy, the memory banks automatically register the pleasant sensation of taste in the positive half of their database. But, this can cause the opposite reaction afterwards, with the negative half of the Jack of Clubs suffering the consequences of the Queen of Club's cravings and self-indulgent habits, causing discomfort, and physical duress. This is true with all bad habits which contribute to the overall poor health of the physical body. Remember, the instinctive center governs all vital physiological inner workings of our complex human body, whether we pay attention to it, or not. In the contemporary culture, an emphasis has been placed on taking more conscientiously inspired care of one's body by employing holistic eating regimes and healthy exercise routines. But, when the Jack of Clubs suffers from Queen of Clubs indulgences, it is an example of habitual cravings of these potentially harmful substances, such as rich food, cigarettes, drugs, or alcohol. These habits can become the severe addictions, which are proven to be detrimental to the health and wellbeing of the physical body. However, this is a vast subject for more study and exploration, due to the physical, as well as psychological implications of the addictive center involved. Keep in mind, the King of Clubs performs a different function than that of the Queen of Clubs; and, the King and Queen both differ in how they function in relation to the Jack of Clubs.

Regardless of one's center of gravity, all centers can strive to work together as a unity in harmony, which will prove beneficial for the optimal functioning and healthy maintenance of one's physical body. However, under adverse situations, the Jack of Clubs may become sick if it's basic primal needs are not met, and satisfied, first and foremost. On a recent airplane flight, I met a young mother, accompanied by her children, a toddler girl and infant son. She was returning to her home in Los Angeles after a visit with her family in Arizona. They had missed their original flight, so they waited for the next flight. During this time, her children's snack supply dwindled and her little ones became quite audibly cranky. On the short flight to Los Angeles she got annoyed with the flight attendant who said there was no food on board for small children. Finally, some packages of crackers were located on board, and peace was restored. Her maternal instincts of her Jack of Clubs were very stressed, until a food source was found and then she became calm.

An individual who is centered in the Jack of Clubs may appear to exhibit a pronounced sensitivity to their surroundings, which can also manifest as physical sensuality. As the memory banks of the instinctive center they tend to experience their senses directly and they radiate this sensitivity. The Jack of Clubs generally lives in the world of the senses as the primary influence in their life. However, they tend to possess a more subdued sensuality, compared to the bold sensuousness of the Queen of Clubs. Not as overpowering as the Queen of Clubs, or as charismatic as the King of Clubs, the Jack of Clubs has a natural infinity for basic sensual pleasures and desires, with a need to have their natural physical needs met. Remember, we each have all of the centers within us, and if we possess normal good health, we will have a well-functioning Jack of Clubs which monitors and regulates our vital and basic physical needs to survive. Due to the influences of our own center of gravity, we gravitate toward and make variations to suit our preferences and lifestyle. One's personal center of gravity directs and determines most of one's tendencies, along with other influences which affect one. Someone centered in the Jack of Clubs may have a dominant instinctive center which requires that physical needs are met first and foremost, over trends, fads or technologies.

As the memory banks of the instinctive center, the Jack of Clubs serves all of us to provide for the essential sensory needs and inclinations which are inherent in the human being.

Remember, it is the innate properties and propensities of this center which keep us operational, remind us when to eat, drink, sleep, heal, and simply stay alive. Listen carefully to the Jack of Clubs memory banks of your instinctive center, for they know what is naturally best for your body, regardless of where you are centered.

Keywords associated with the Jacks: habitual, imitative, mechanical, automatic, superficial, simplistic, repetitive, conventional, common, spontaneous, routine, formulaic, and subjective.

Key behavior traits of the Jack: Jacks function, feel, think, speak and act from pre-learned programming in general, often mimicking what others feel, think, say or do without analysis or verification.

Gaining a solid overview of the centers of influence within, helps us to see our fellow human beings in a different light. Understanding and acknowledging that we each have different views and needs because of our center of gravity, helps us to develop greater compassion and tolerance for another's lifestyle and life choices. Please remember, no one is superior or inferior, because of where they are centered. Whether they have an emotional, intellectual, moving, or an instinctive influence, will determine their personal qualities, preferences and choices. Each person is predisposed to have certain needs regarding their life purpose and direction through their own particular center of gravity.

Remember, no center is better or worse than another as all centers are necessary. Also, the centers are all equally mechanical if we are not living a more mindfully self-aware life. There is no particular center which can enhance our opportunity for enlightenment, unless we ourselves work for it. Each of us must make our own consistent sincere efforts individually to become self-aware with mindful self-observation. Enlightenment is an equal opportunity for each one of us in every moment, starting right now.

In the following segment, we will explore the world of the numeric cards and the defining attributes they lend to each center. I will provide an overview of each of the numeric cards characteristics, and will also give examples of various individuals whom I have known or observed, who tend to personify and embody the different numeric cards distinctively. By detailing different characteristics, I hope to render the numeric cards recognizable as you go through your normal daily life, and also relatable. Perhaps you will begin to notice some of the distinguishing traits in yourself, and in the people who you encounter and interact with.

CHAPTER 8

THE NUMERIC CARDS

The Numeric cards in a deck of playing cards represent defining clarifications of the influencing factors for the different parts of the royalty cards within each iconic suit. It is helpful to understand that all of the cards in a deck of playing cards are actually royalty cards. The specific influence of each number card generates the different nuances and characteristics of the royalty suits, such as the emotional, intellectual, moving and instinctive elements. Each of the royal suits is divided into these elemental influences, and each subgroup is further defined and refined by their respective influence. We will look more deeply into the varying shades of influence that reflect the distinctly different elements inherent with the Kings, Queens and the Jacks. We will examine their respective divisions in the Hearts, Diamonds, Spades and Clubs. The Numeric cards are the clarified subdivisions within the Kings, Queens, and the Jacks of centers which represent the intellectual, emotional, and combined moving instinctive parts of the iconic suits. Each individual numeric card provides insight into its unique predispositions, tendencies, traits or innate abilities within the iconic court cards. Please keep in mind that all the centers and all the parts of centers are always gender neutral.

The Numeric cards, beginning with the number Ten, and descending down to the Two of each suit, are the defining refinements and clarification of the royalty cards, as mentioned above. Thus, the Kings of each suit represent the intellectual element of the suit, the Queens are the emotional element of the suit, and the Jacks are the moving element of the suit. Each King, Queen and Jack is subdivided into three clarifying influences, the intellectual, emotional and combined moving instinctive parts. Each royal court card is defined by the numeric cards which represent the different elemental influencing factors within the royal suit. The numeric cards Ten, Nine and Eight represent the intellectual, emotional and moving parts of the Kings. The Seven, Six and Five again represent the intellectual, emotional and moving parts of the Queens. And, the Four, Three and Two represent the intellectual, emotional and moving parts of the Jacks.

The numeric cards give us a more detailed description and overview of the manner in which each center manifests. As we examine the individual numeric cards in the following card elucidation chapters, you will begin to get a clearer picture and sense of the distinguishing characteristics, and attributes of each particular card. Observing yourself in relation to the different cards, will help you to determine whether you are emotionally, intellectually, moving or instinctively centered. With consistent mindful self-observation, you will start to recognize certain traits within yourself that correspond to the specific suits and their parts. As you gain more insight into which center you emanate from, you will ultimately be able to determine which numeric card may have an influence over you as your personal center of gravity. Each numeric card lends a particular influence and nuance to each of the royalty cards. Learning about the numeric cards contributes another level of definition and dimension to help you see the distinctive nuances within yourself, and in others. Understanding the cards and corresponding centers as they apply to you, can assist you in gaining enhanced self-awareness with greater self-knowledge. Familiarize yourself with the functions of each card so you can begin to observe the centers at work in yourself and in others. Document what you see so you can review your notes to see patterns of the centers in yourself.

Remember, the numeric cards are clarified divisions and refining attributes within each royalty suit. And, each iconic royal suit has three subdivisions which are represented by the number cards as they descend sequentially. The three subdivisions correspond to the intellectual, emotional and combined moving instinctive parts. For simplicity, I will refer to the combined moving instinctive element as the moving part. I will provide a description of basic qualities and general attributes of each numeric card in the four suits, from the Ten in the Kings, descending to the Two in the Jacks, which define particular predispositions and characteristics. Each numeric card casts an influence which lends attributes and qualities which distinguish overall manifestations. The numeric cards accentuate subtle variations which determine distinctive responses, reactions, behaviors, and other unique nuances within, and between each of the royalty cards, whether it is in the Kings, the Queens, or the Jacks of the four iconic suits. The Kings, Queens, and Jacks are defined and refined by specific numeric cards within each suit.

For example, a person who is emotionally centered in the King of Hearts will be the Ten, Nine, or the Eight of Hearts. Someone who is emotionally centered in the Queen of Hearts will be the Seven, Six, or the Five of Hearts. A person who is emotionally centered in the Jack of Hearts will be the Four, Three, or the Two of Hearts. Each specific number assigns certain essential qualities to each card which predisposes that part of the center to have slightly different traits as well as distinctive emanations and manifestations. The defining attributes are designated by the particular number which represents the corresponding influences.

The Kings are the intellectual parts of the centers in all of the iconic royalty suits. The numbers, beginning with the Ten represent the intellectual part, the Nine represents the emotional part, and the Eight represents the moving instinctive part of the Kings. To reiterate, the Kings of centers think, speak and act influenced by the intellectual element. They tend to function with enhanced objectivity for what is possible to achieve by making consistent intellectual efforts. In writing about the Kings of centers, I will refer to a particular card being described as "he" or "him." However, please remember, each part of any suit is in reality gender neutral. Both women and men equally may be centered in the Kings, Queens or Jacks of the royal suits and all cards are gender neutral.

The Queens represent the emotional parts of a center. The Queen is further clarified by the Seven representing the intellectual part of the Queen, the Six as the emotional part of the Queen, and the Five representing the moving and instinctive part of the Queen. Again, the Queens of centers tend to think, speak and act in emphatic, dramatic emotional absolutes, which results in their opposing polarities, as their unpredictable Queen flip. They use absolute terms, such as never and always; for example, if annoyed it will be who they will never speak to again, or what they will never do again! But, this may be true only for a while, or until they flip back to the opposite pole again. When writing about the Queens of centers I will refer to the card being described as "she," or "her." Both men and women can equally be centered in the Queens of whichever suit is being described. Again, please remember every card in every iconic royal suit and number is always gender neutral.

The Jacks represent the combined moving instinctive parts of the centers and are referred to as the memory banks and the mechanical parts of centers. However, the instinctive element is always present as it is innate and concerns the inner work of the human body, working from its own intelligence. Again, from this point I will refer to the Jacks of centers simply as the moving part. Within the Jacks the Four is the intellectual part, the Three is the emotional part, and the Two represents the moving part. To reiterate, the Jacks of centers function in the more habitual behaviors, and they tend to think, speak and act in generalities. Jacks tend to go along with the status quo, and think what other people think, and may simply accept information and data without actually analyzing or verifying facts. As with the Kings, the Jacks are often referred to as "he, or "him." However, all the centers are in fact gender neutral and as you will soon learn in the descriptive segments, both men and women equally may be centered in the Jacks, the Queens, or the Kings of centers.

The specific distinctions within the numeric cards of the same royal suit, impart essential elements that create the different characteristics. The number patterns are also consistent throughout the suits, whether it is Hearts, Diamonds, Spades or Clubs. Each number designates the particular influence over the card in question, and denotes certain qualities, propensities and manifestations. Each numeric card has its own specific tendencies, abilities, as well as unique quirks. Ultimately, the detailed information of the numeric cards will help you gain deeper insight into the distinctive characteristics of each center. The numeric cards will help to clarify the subtle nuances and distinctions of your center of gravity as you begin to truly observe yourself to see your more authentic essential nature. The numeric cards will help you look at yourself more deeply as you observe your natural tendencies, proclivities, sensitivities and abilities for greater clarity. Again, please be mindful that although I may refer to a card as "she," or "her," or "he," or "him," it naturally follows that both men and women equally can be centered in any of the royalty suits. Every card in the deck is always gender neutral, whether the Kings, the Queens, or the Jacks. The characteristics of the different suits may be referred to as feminine or masculine, her or him, she or he; however, they are all gender neutral.

Gaining a fundamental grasp of the numeric cards will certainly help you to more readily recognize your own essential nature and to understand yourself better, and to understand others. With practice and consistent mindful self-observation, you will begin to recognize the subtle, and the not so subtle differences, which each numeric card imparts to a center. You will begin to see the difference between your personal natural inclinations, and also, your unnatural manifestations, which emanate from acquired traits in false personality, in yourself and other people. Remember, the numeric cards lend particular elemental influences which enhance how each center manifests, responds, behaves and functions, whether emotionally, intellectually, or physically. The numeric cards lend distinct variations of influence and manifestation. The numeric definitions of the Kings, Queens and Jacks will clarify their unique characteristics, distinctive qualities and differences.

Keep in mind, that whichever the influence, whether emotional, intellectual, moving or instinctive, the different suits share certain specific similar tendencies. For example, all the Kings of centers exhibit similar characteristics, mannerisms and behaviors. To clarify, the Kings of the four different suits all share slightly similar energies in their overall manifestation, despite their different functions and processes. The Kings operate as the intellectual part of a suit; thus, they operate at the slowest speed due to the thinking element. Their responses and reactions manifest more slowly as they think through issues and situations, while weighing options, variables and potential outcomes. They think with reasoning and rationale. Again, all the Kings of centers share a connection to one another across the suits, despite their different functions.

The Queens also share very similar behavioral traits and mannerisms in how they manifest, react, respond and behave. The Queens of all the four different royal suits exhibit comparable energies with enhanced emotional speed, as they manifest their particular functions and processes. And all the Queens of centers share a connection to one another, despite their different functions due to the emotional element. Their emotional energy endows them with swift perceptions, fast reactions and responses, and the potential for volatility, along with robust appetites. The Queens tend to be dynamic and energetic. The Queens of the centers all share a connection to one another across the suits, despite their different functions.

The Jacks of centers perform as the moving part of a suit which also serve as the memory banks of centers. We rely on the Jacks of centers to allow us to operate smoothly with efficiency after we have learned and stored the data which is required for their functioning. However, it is beneficial to bring attention to the Jacks of centers so they can operate with increased intentionality. Ordinarily, the Jacks operate within their habitual programmed patterns, which tend to become automatic, or mechanical. Paying attention to the Jacks, with intentionality, will help monitor these mechanical tendencies. The Jacks manifest swiftly, so one must be vigilant and quick to catch their automatic responses and reflexes. Again, the Jacks of centers all share a connection to one another across the four primary suits, despite their different functions.

Each center can work more efficiently if we are present in the moment, mindfully aware, paying attention with intentionality to overcome our habitual patterns of behavior. This will certainly help you to achieve greater balance within. Remember, the individual components in each of the suits influences and contributes to our psychological and physiological inclinations. They influence our inherent capabilities, tendencies, talents, strengths as well as our weaknesses, to a certain degree. Of course, there are numerous external factors which influence how our life will unfold, but our internal centers influence the specific inclinations, abilities and tendencies which we are born with. The numeric card definitions are relatively simple, but can help you to understand more specifically how each part of a center manifests. These individual parts add an enhanced element that helps to clarify identifying characteristics of how a person might manifest, from their particular center of gravity. We will examine each of the fifty-two cards with their distinctive and significant aspects and unique differences. Each part lends distinctive characteristics to a given card in a suit, which can help you see yourself as you apply the information to your personal self-observation. Learning about the defining characteristics of numeric cards will help you to gain a solid grasp on the nuances of centers as you begin to glimpse your own center of gravity. Use this book to guide your observations as you begin to witness the subtle, and, not so subtle, nuances and shades of influence within each of the centers. You will soon begin to recognize the Emotional, Intellectual, Moving and Instinctive centers as they function, which will enhance your understanding of yourself and others. As you continue to observe, you will notice the characteristic differences of the Kings, Queens and Jacks. But, keep in mind that it may take of bit of practice to recognize the various influencing traits, attributes and distinguishing characteristics.

The following segments provide descriptions for each of the centers unique characteristics. I will give descriptive examples of all the different centers drawn from real life experiences based upon many people I have known, and others who exemplify a recognizably specific center of gravity. Some illustrative examples are drawn from certain well-known people, or celebrities, who typify the center being described. As you will see, we are each very clearly a product of our own personal center of gravity.

As you gain deeper understanding of the numeric cards, you will learn how your innate and inherent natural inclinations affect how you feel, think, move and instinctively emanate as you manifest in your life. Treat this as a process of fine tuning as you begin to understand the different centers while continuing to observe yourself. This will help you gain insight into your personal center of gravity. Let us focus our attention on the miraculous centers within us all, and learn how they are refined and defined by their royal numeric counterparts. We will now explore the clarified world of the numeric cards, beginning with the King of Hearts, proceeding through all the cards of the iconic royal suits.

The Emotional Center, the King of Hearts:
Ten, Nine and Eight of Hearts

The King of Hearts is the intellectual part of the Emotional Center, which adds an enhanced element of intellectuality, and intelligence to the emotional processes. The King of Hearts has the ability to feel the depths, heights and magnitudes of human emotion with intelligent perception and carefully articulated thought. This card represents the heart which thinks deeply. The enhanced intellectual element slows downs the speed of the emotions considerably, by adding a dimension of reasoning, which provides greater rationale over the emotions. Ideally, in a perfect world, our politicians and leaders would be centered in the King of Hearts to ensure leadership with compassion, to do what is in the best interests for the community, overall. King of Hearts individuals are the natural born leaders, visionaries, artists, creators, writers, teachers and the diplomats who help make the world a more interesting, unique, expansive, beautiful and harmonious place to live. The King of Hearts displays a dignified element in their endeavors and interactions with others.

Although conscientiousness, and consciousness are not by products of habitual patterns, or of mechanical behavior, the King of hearts person appears to be more self-aware. They possess an innate dignity and inherent reserve which seems to subdue their presence as they ponder their responses or actions. The King of Hearts is said to be the doorway to higher centers of perception, awareness, cognition, and consciousness. The King of Hearts has an innate ability to discern what may be weaknesses within yourself, or in others. By intentionally accessing this King for guidance, we can gain better understanding of our self and others, and with greater depth to achieve balance and harmony. The Ten, Nine and Eight of Hearts, represent subtle variations of the processes, realizations, perceptions and manifestation of the King of Hearts, as influenced by intellectuality, emotionality, or the moving elements.

Keywords associated with the Kings: thoughtful, methodical, analytical, objective, diplomatic, intentional, thorough, deliberate, pensive, dignified, reserved, calculating, detached and exacting.

Key behavior traits of the Kings: Kings think, speak and act with enhanced rational objectivity examining potential outcomes to determine what is possible to achieve with consistent efforts.

The Ten of Hearts:

The Ten of Hearts individual has an inherent need to understand others and gives considerable thought to emotions and emotional issues. Pensive analysis and assessment will be applied to a person, or situation in question. The thinking process greatly slows down their reaction time to an emotional stimulus. Proper and thorough evaluation of the emotional climate helps to maximize effectiveness, and helps determine what may be the best response, the higher right, or right action in a situation or a moment. The Ten of hearts is typically reluctant to act hastily, and takes considerable time to carefully analyze matters to make decisions in a thoughtful, thorough, precise, and in a compassionate manner.

Emotional situations are filtered and processed with clear intellectual analysis and perception to achieve emotional balance with rationale. Their emotions are well articulated, and may be somewhat conservative. The Ten of Hearts is much more reserved than other emotionally centered individuals, such as the Queens, or the Jacks. Their emotional reactions are slowed down considerably due to the time given to their emotional thought processes. The expression of their emotions is based on the Ten's methodical inclination to evaluate emotional issues and situations. The emphasis on analysis and prudent objective thinking lends restraint to their responses, allowing for conservation of their emotional energy. They may exhibit an innate interest in helping others. This individual recognizes and articulates the need for greater diplomatic action. Former American Vice President, Al Gore, whose environmental work on climate change earned him the Nobel Prize, has inspired people around the world to make more positive efforts to protect our dear blue planet. His admirable work has the Ten of Hearts quality to inform and inspire others intelligently.

This center regards their emotional responses methodically, with an objective overview and quiet dignity. Philosophy, literature, and art, which explores and expounds the emotional psychological depths of the human heart and spirit may appeal to the Ten of Hearts. They have an ability to feel and understand human needs. Serving as a psychological counselor or political diplomat may suit the Ten of Hearts individual. An ambassador, advocacy counsellor, human rights lawyer, judge, or psychotherapist are potential careers which may appeal to someone centered in the Ten of Hearts. These choices could provide them with an emotional connection to others, while working in close proximity with others in an advisory capacity. As a political diplomat, or ambassador they would be inclined to work towards justice and equality in their endeavors to improve the world, while being impartial and compassionate.

The Nine of Hearts:

The Nine of Hearts is the emotional part of the King of Hearts and adds finely attuned emotional perceptions to the intellectual part of emotional center. An individual centered here is a person who intuitively senses the emotional needs of others with a compassionate heart. The Nine is more receptive and quicker to act than the Ten of Hearts. While somewhat less subdued than the Ten, their perceptions are filtered through the emotional center with intellectuality, and enhanced sensitivity. They may not exhibit an excessive display of emotions, but, instead they are caring and concerned for the welfare of others. This is a thoughtful individual, who thinks carefully before they express their feelings, which are processed through their sensitive and finely attuned emotional antenna. With an objective overview, they are impartial, and carefully assess the emotional climate. Their gentle demeanor can be reassuring, kind, fair and considerate. The King of Hearts embodies emotional strength with knowledge, and the Nine of hearts radiates compassion with strength. They possess an enhanced perception into the inner emotional dynamic of them self, and others, to skillfully address sensitive issues with heart felt nurturing. The Nine is a caring individual that wishes to be helpful, and they can often be found in philanthropic organizations. They are interested in serving mankind through their charitable compassionate nature. Their skill at recognizing what is needed to help and inspire others allows them to get to the core of issues.

Certain television talk show hosts who are deeply interested in the human condition are possibly centered in the Nine of Hearts. I rarely watch television shows; however, it is impossible not to be aware of the massive international impact of the celebrity talk show hostess, Oprah Winfrey. She has made a career of getting to the very heart of matters and has amassed a devoted following of loyal fans. It seems apparent she is emotionally centered and displays a high degree of intellectual energy which she has invested in her career. My sisters and many of my friends have watched her talk show, and they always speak highly of her. And they are certainly among her vast dedicated fan base. She has consistently garnered praise and admiration for her humanitarian efforts, while nurturing others with kindness, compassion, generosity and charitable good will. She would be an excellent good-will ambassador to help promote world peace.

I have a dear friend who is centered in the Nine of Hearts. She is a retired actress who is exceptionally thoughtful and caring. We share interesting and illuminated conversations about art, theater, films, literature and so on. During one conversation long ago, I recommended a film to her, called, "My Dinner with Andre." I felt she would appreciate the unique content plus its lively dialogue between two men having dinner and discussing their life. The film is about a successful New York theater director who spent a considerable amount of time traveling in search of enlightening experiences, to gain understanding. My friend had been in the New York theater, so I sensed she would feel an affinity for the film. When we met for coffee a few weeks later she surprised me with a lovely video gift of the film. She had truly enjoyed watching it and expressed her gratitude with a heartfelt gesture. She is an excellent example of the Nine of Hearts, showing gracious thoughtfulness.

The Nine of Hearts has an innate ability to sense the emotional climate of situations. They are well suited to the theater, and film industry, where cooperative creative team work is essential for creative merit. As teachers in a learning environment, they would quite likely serve as mentors to their students. They may also elect to work with others in charitable organizations that call upon their acute emotional perceptions and sensitivities, working harmoniously with others, while in a position of leadership.

The Eight of Hearts:

The Eight of Hearts is the moving part of the King of Hearts, motivating the individual to move physically, perhaps in a creative manner as an artist, writer, actor, art director, or an artistic interpreter to help others fulfill their emotional and creative needs. Their attuned sensitivities imbue their creations with profound emotional content. They have a desire to deeply understand the vast scope of the human emotional, and psychological condition, fueled by their own sympathetic humanitarian nature. They are sensitive to the needs of others, and possess a strong desire to offer and provide compassionate supportive energy. Their enhanced moving element enables this individual to creatively interpret their emotional insights to assist other people in some manner. They may wish to share their inspired feelings, thoughts and visions in a tangible art form through a medium that best suits their unique particular creative expression. Their medium of creative expression might manifest through film, the theater, art, literature, philosophy, or psychology.

With their expansive desire to understand other people, the Eight of Hearts may travel the world to experience diverse cultures. They have a heartfelt desire to gain greater insight and understanding into the more sensitive, rarefied realities of life. This might be expressed in the world of art, as an artist, or as an art consultant. They are also interested in using film, and photography as outlets for their creative expression. An art consultant clarifying the renderings of creative artistic impressions, allows them to help others understand the complex cultural motivations of the artist. A museum curator involved with fine art may be an appropriate career to accommodate their natural artistic affinity and their ability to comprehend the artistic mind. They have the capacity to convey the deeper meaning of life to others.

The Eight of Hearts has an inherent need to manifest positive impressions through their intellectual creative abilities in art, literature, and film, to lift people's spirits. With their altruistic nature, they are an active force in humanitarian efforts. They have an innate talent to be a voice of positive change for themselves and others. Improving the quality of the status quo may be an underlying element that motivates them to enrich the world with their sensitivity. This is the individual who acts on their beliefs to make the world a better place to live, while inspiring understanding to encourage compassionate action. The humanitarian work of Angelina Jolie feels like Eight of Hearts energy, as she travels the world to help the plight of refugees, immigrants and others on her personal path.

The Eight of Hearts is an individual who is interested in helping others see the beauty of life, and they may work well in altruistic fields. They possess a sensitive compassionate heart which aspires to create a more harmonious world for everyone. Any type of injustice weighs heavily upon them. They strive to help make the world a better place, to manifest harmony and balance through fairness and equality. They are deeply inspired by the need for world peace.

The Queen of Hearts: Seven, Six and Five of Hearts

The Queen of Hearts is the emotional part of the Emotional center. This effusive center commands attention with her energetic, almost combustible, emotional presence. The Queen of Hearts is far more outgoing than the reserved King of Hearts, and she tends to attract people like emotional satellites. The Queen of Hearts is a gregarious, larger than life emotional presence with explosive energy. A bit of melodrama almost certainly surrounds everything she does, and drama often seems to punctuate her emanations. She gushes forth her expressions, whether of delight or despair. The Queen of Hearts does not take her life lightly, nor anything else that may affect her personally. She is notorious for her dramatic flip, which occurs predictably after her needs are met, or her intrigue has dissipated. However, if she does not receive the adoration, praise and extravagant glorification she feels entitled to she will completely wilt in utter despair. However, just as dramatically her emotions can suddenly flip and she will swing right back. Her emotional behavior is intense, while predictably unpredictable.

This center enjoys melodrama and we all know someone who fits this description. It would be rather difficult ignore the Queen of Hearts as she tends to command attention with her flamboyant gestures, and she will often dress accordingly. She loves the changing trends of fashion, which allow her to indulge in her incessant change of heart. Remember, everything is of great importance to her, until she suddenly loses interest, or until styles change, which happens on a regular basis. Her elaborate wardrobe is filled with colorful garments usually in several sizes to accommodate her ever changing weight and girth. She dresses to make a dramatic entrance, whether in haute couture or flowery muumuus. She gets noticed, even if she does not have a keen fashion sense, as, her clothing expresses her dynamic energy. Because of her propensity for excessive behavior, some problems may arise, due to a lack of restraint or moderation. For the Queen of Hearts, if something looks, feels, or tastes good, then certainly, more must be better! The Queen of Hearts is extravagant and self-indulgent, with excessive needs, and moods. She tends to lavish attention on her current object, or person, of desire. After she has satisfied her emotional desires and needs on her obsessions, whether someone, or something, she will have a sudden change of heart and lose interest, for the moment at least. Remember, it is quite easy to recognize the Queen of Hearts, as she is generally the most visible, and often the most audible person in the room.

Keywords associated with the Queens: dramatic, temperamental, expansive, gregarious, controlling, lavish, extravagant, passionate, indulgent, vain, excessive, volatile, enthusiastic, exuberant, and moody.

Key behavior traits of the Queens: Queens think, speak, and behave in dramatic emotional emphatic absolutes, such as who they will never speak to again, or what they will never do again!

The Seven of Hearts:

The intellectual element of the Queen of Hearts gives this center a vital dose of reasoning power, along with a certain sense of intellectual rationale. Her intellectual processing helps to slow down the speed of her perceptions, reactions, attitudes and responses. The enhanced element of thought allows her thinking capability to slightly moderate her emotional intensity; she thinks before taking action. With regard to the intellectual element, there is a general slowing down of the rapid-fire Queen emotions, which helps to mitigate extreme mood swings. Thinking can help to generate a much more subdued queen flip, which is the dramatic change of heart as mentioned earlier. While her responses are still very fast, especially when compared to the other centers, the Seven of Hearts has the potential to think things over before making rash decisions or rushed judgments. This thinking process affords the Seven of Hearts the luxury to conserve emotional energy for more inspired causes, such as the arts, literature, theater, fine dining and philanthropy.

The intellectual element of this center is attracted to information and knowledge which can help to satisfy and nurture her personal emotional needs. Her interests must also give her the opportunity to be with her friends, lovers, and family. But, where ever she goes, she will have a loyal group of followers around her who are most likely devoted to her, as she is to all of them. She is attracted to expansive ideas and customs that enliven her world and lend a bit of intelligence with drama. She is magnanimous, gregarious, charitable, generous, and feels entitled to her appetites for luxury and lavish living. She is the grand dame, socialite, art patron and philanthropist with a larger than life presence.

My dear Seven of Hearts friend has a flair for literature and theatrics. She is often dressed in radiant colors and wears fabulous jewelry, mixing dazzling gemstones with bold costume jewelry. She is deeply interested in human nature, politics, art and literature. Her weekly literary groups attract uniquely diverse individuals, and she organizes eloquent guest speakers to keep the topics lively. She embraces everyone whom she greets as a dear beloved friend. She is a generous, supportive ally who nurtures friendship with praise and encouragement. Artists, writers and politicians attend her lavish parties, where her husband usually does the cooking, so she can indulge her guests with attention. I was not surprised when she told me that she collapses in exhaustion after her extravagant events, and she customarily requires the entire weekend afterward to recuperate. But, she loves the vibrant conversations and all the fascinating people, so her queen flip is done in private, where she is hidden from her many friends and admirers. After her respite and recuperation, she is ready to plan her next exciting event or party. Her intellectual element has the good sense to rest and regain her emotional energy, especially so she can do it all over again, and with a flourish!

Six of Hearts:

The enhanced emotional energy makes this center the fastest, and also, the most volatile of all the emotional cards in the deck.

Her emotional perceptions or misconceptions are almost instantaneous which renders her responses immediate and perhaps, explosive. The Six of Hearts is extremely quick to make judgments, but her decisions can be quite rash and abrupt. This center is a rapid fire reactive dynamo who does not think before speaking her mind, often giving a tongue lashing to an unsuspecting victim. She gives full vent to her opinions and to her wrath, rightly or wrongly without ever considering the consequences. When she has a temper tantrum, it is loud, and can be quite irrational.

The Six of Hearts can be tempestuous, opinionated, possessive, obsessive, jealous, compulsive, volatile and demanding. She wishes to be the center of attention, but she will also lavish attention on those whom she adores. She has a robust appetite for people with a big heart to match. She needs constant emotional stimuli and surrounds herself with adoring friends and acquaintances. However, they must be on guard not to offend her, or ignore her, as she can be extraordinarily temperamental. Her temper tends to be extreme when she is vexed, crossed or deceived, but remember, she will flip back to your side if you give her sufficient apologies, gifts, and promises of endless adoration with a lot of attention. She is an extremist, passionate and vindictive, who requires and demands nothing less than your total devotion and undying love. She also expresses her affections with overwhelming flamboyant conviction, but will be aghast if you ask for too much of her incredibly precious time. She must be the center of attention and will certainly make her presence, and her annoyance felt. If anyone should fail to notice her, which rarely happens, she may become quite loud and boisterous, if only to get more attention. For her it is simply unthinkable that anyone could possibly neglect, or dare to ignore her in any manner. The Six of Hearts has the potential for volatile temper tantrums if she does not get her need for elaborate attention satisfied.

The Six of Hearts tends to be rather large and fleshy, and she requires ample quantities of food to fuel her excessive emotional passions or obsessions. Most of her social engagements will be punctuated with substantial quantities of sumptuous food. This center does not use moderation in any sense, and can be inordinately excessive and self-indulgent. Whether it is her food indulgences, or fabulous trinkets, the Six of Hearts feels a need to have it all. A few years ago, a Six of Hearts friend was overtly admiring a beautiful, and rather expensive diamond necklace. She was gushing how she absolutely had to have it, and she wanted her fiancé to buy it for her. Without any doubt, she fully expected him to rush right out and buy it for her. She is very much an "Elizabeth Taylor" type woman, and she got her wish, although with a decidedly smaller and much less expensive jewel. The Six of Hearts individual tends to be very ego-centric. But, with so many friends, admirers, and other people hovering around her, how could she possibly think otherwise?

Good or bad, she thrives on melodrama. It seems likely that the Six of Hearts has an addiction to the extreme highs and lows, the ups and downs of excessive emotions. Her life is very much like the reality television stars she so admires, along with her TV soap operas and romance novels. Exaggerated love affairs and the mournful heartache portrayed in films and novels is her vicarious indulgence, perhaps as a validation of her own emotional roller-coaster life. The Six of Hearts attracts friends and admirers, as well as enemies and detractors. But, even in controversial situations she seems to rebound with her exuberant, but often volatile energy. She does well in careers that favor her need for adoration, along with sufficient income to satisfy her excessive indulgences. She can do quite well in real estate, interior decorating, matchmaking, wedding or party planning, film and theater as she loves melodrama. She is happiest when she gets a lot of attention from others which she craves.

The Five of Hearts:
With a moving element, this lively center is attracted to movement of an emotional nature, while also making certain her instinctive needs are met. She has massive appetite for indulgence, and may enjoy an evening at the theater followed by a luscious dinner. This part of the Queen of Hearts also wants to be involved in the action, and loves to take part in the performance whenever possible. She is the original "drama queen" and loves attention, with the spotlight shining directly on her. The Five of Hearts has an abundant appetite, which is necessary to fuel her activities with friends, family, adoring fans and followers. For her, life is a celebration of fun, food and libations. She tends to be a large fleshy type, and enjoys lavish food indulgences, often paired with alcoholic beverages.

I had a charming friend who was centered in the Five of Hearts. He was a natural born comedian and made everyone laugh with his jokes and remarkable sense of humor. As a character actor, he was perfect for comic roles with his razor-sharp wit. He added a lot of fun to social events and kept everyone laughing with his bawdy jokes. He was larger than life character and liked the attention. However, he had an ongoing weight problem which was a result of his food and alcohol addictions, and it began to interfere with his career, his friendships, his finances and his health overall. When his excessive indulgences began to take a toll on his marriage, he finally decided to get the professional help he needed in order to manage his addiction problems. He joined both Over-Eaters Anonymous, and Alcoholics Anonymous with his wife's encouragement. Ultimately, he became an outspoken champion to help others to overcome their addictions. But, he later confided that he had never realized that he had an addiction problem, and he thought his lifestyle was normal. Excessive social activities, including food and drink indulgences, seems normal to the Five of Hearts. They may disregard the need for having limits and boundaries, which can result in physical illness, extreme weight issues, emotional problems and mood disorders, as well as being drained from their obsessive-compulsive excesses. This is the typical way in which their "queen flip" manifests.

The Seven, Six and Five of Hearts are the Queens of the emotional center, and all tend to have a similar larger than life presence about them. However, the different influences of the intellectual, emotional, moving and instinctive center create noticeable differences that can clearly be observed. The ordinary world of science and psychology is not aware that someone who is a "Queen," may be predisposed to excessive indulgences, and is quite likely to have addictions. Quite often, it is the Queens who are victims of their own excessive behavior.

As we increase our perceptions of the manifestations of the different centers, we see how this knowledge can help encourage healthy balance with mindful self-observation and awareness. Gaining self-knowledge can empower the Queens to exercise greater self-control, to help them gain command over their passions, obsessions, and addictions, and to be more in control of their life.

The Jack of Hearts: Four, Three and Two of Hearts

The Jack of Hearts represents the moving part of the emotional center. As with all the Jacks of the four suits, these are the "memory banks," which store information and data that is taken in by a person. While each of us has the Jacks of centers within us, a person centered in this card processes their responses to external stimuli in a somewhat more automatic manner which is inherent with their habitually attuned nature. We all experience some habitual behaviors which become our automatic, mechanical reactions, unless we are being present in the moment, and are self-aware. However, emotions which emanate from the Jack of Hearts, are generally habitual responses which are deeply ingrained, as customary and common with most people. A person centered in the Jack of Hearts emanates with the emotions they have learned, or mimicked, which are stored within their memory banks. They tend to respond automatically as directly motivated from the memory banks. Crowd emotions are generally Jack of Hearts emotions. These are the overall feelings which infuse and enthuse a group of people at ball games, and other such large-scale events. When there are big crowds of people gathered together, their overall emotions or sentiments seem to be remarkably similar. It is almost as if they are experiencing the same feelings, as if perhaps one giant brain is governing all their emotions. This is a common occurrence that most people hardly notice. These are auto-pilot emotions, where people are swayed and almost imperceptibly influenced by what everyone else is feeling. The concept of, "herd mentality" seems to describe this type of situation.

We all have the Jack of Hearts within us, and it is this center that responds to particularly sweet or cute influences. Everyone smiles in positive response to puppies or an adorable baby. The Jack of Hearts emotions are common sentiments which advertising agencies target their ad campaigns toward. When we think of our family, or friend's birthday, we usually pick out a particular card primarily based on the sentimental feelings we are experiencing at that moment. The Jack of Hearts evokes nostalgia and sentimental emotions. These are the smiley face emoticons of the world, the warm and fuzzy feelings that almost always give us some comfort, no matter how simplistic. Jack of Hearts energy is contagious, and is not unlike the recorded laugh tracks we hear in television situation comedies. When we hear the appropriately named, "canned laughter," we will almost certainly start laughing as well. Most popular television shows rely on crowd emotions, such as sentimentality, in order to be successful. Keep in mind, it is said that "laughter is the best medicine," so this is certainly a healthy response we can all enjoy on occasion. The next time you feel a sudden impulse to giggle, it may be your Jack of Hearts responding to a simple emotional stimulus.

Keywords associated with the Jacks: habitual, imitative, mechanical, automatic, superficial, simplistic, repetitive, conventional, common, spontaneous, routine, formulaic, and subjective.

Key behavior traits of the Jack: Jacks function, feel, think, speak and act from pre-learned programming in general, often mimicking what others feel, think, say or do without analysis or verification.

The Four of Hearts:

Because of the intellectual element, the Four of Hearts is more likely to think, before automatically responding to a given stimulus. This slows down their reaction and response time ever so slightly, as the intellectual parts of centers are the slowest. Thus, the Four will enjoy reading about subjects that trigger their emotional buttons. The stimulation may come from a sentimental Hallmark card, a love story, and so on. They may enjoy cute, funny or even sad movies that allow them to swiftly satisfy their emotional hunger. Films like "Lassie Come Home," that induce tears, or a silly comedy like "Ghostbusters," that tickles their funny bone, are ideal amusements for the Four of Hearts.

Having the intellectual element in their emotional center, also gives this card the ability to write stories ranging from humorous, sentimental, to melancholy, or romantic. Someone who is centered in the Four of Hearts, might be a comedy writer for films or television, perhaps situation-comedies that reduce everyone to bouts of laughter. They are excellent story tellers, provided it has an emotional twist to make you smile, laugh or cry. This person is a practical joker who enjoys a good laugh from silly pranks, and they also attract practical jokes. They have the ability to laugh at themselves and are quick to recover from whatever prank has been played on them.

The office buddies who gather around the coffee machine chatting and sharing the latest gossip are probably manifesting from the Four of hearts. I have a Four of Hearts friend who works in human relations at a large company. She interviews prospective new employees, writes employee reviews and also writes the company newsletter. She is a real people pleaser, but she is also a good judge of character. She loves seeing all the new movies, especially romantic comedies, and she collects vintage movie memorabilia. When she is not at work she spends most of her time with family and friends. She is perpetually on her phone chatting, or texting everyone she knows.

The Three of Hearts:

This is a soft-hearted person who loves to celebrate everyone's birthday, and they will quite happily plan all the party festivities. They enjoy whatever triggers their emotional responses. Other people, friendly gatherings, parties and enjoyment are their emotional priorities. They will decorate their home or office for every holiday event, with plenty of candy for Halloween and Valentine's Day. For them any event can be a reason to laugh, be with friends, or to simply have a good time. The Three of Hearts is devoted to the cute and fun pleasures of life that tickle their fancy. They enjoy having friends, and play mates to share their ongoing celebrations with. They tend to rely on, or depend on other people to a great extent in order to be happy. Dependence on others is habitual for them, and often determine their personal associations. They may shed a tear if someone cancels a lunch date, but they might reschedule a suitable substitute in their collective memory bank of friends. They rebound quickly if they can find someone to share time with, as they are definitely not loners.

While they have many friends and acquaintances, they may not use good judgment in relationships, and might seem to lack discrimination in choosing appropriate companions. For example, I knew a Three of Hearts woman who fell in love frequently on a regular basis and got married several times. She would barely be out of one relationship, before she fell in love with someone else. She seemed absolutely unable to be alone, and appeared to need constant companionship. But, she also enjoyed orchestrating blind dates for her friends, and delighted in hearing all the details of the courtship. She had a habit of collecting gossipy tidbits, and was unable to keep them to herself. She enjoyed being occupied with everyone else's business, although her own life was problematic. She enjoyed giving advice to those in her social circle, but did not understand that often people did not always want to hear her comments. Her tendency to micromanage others alienated people. Some friends grew weary of her opinions or meddling. It was tiresome to hear her remarks about what was best for them especially as it was her own personal life that she needed to repair.

The Jack of Hearts is habitually, and sometimes detrimentally, involved with everyone's life. As the emotional part of the Jack of Hearts the Three of Hearts may need to reign in their habitual enthusiasm for fixing everyone else, and try to concentrate on their own problems to focus on their own personal growth. Keep in mind, each center and all the parts are essentially equally mechanical. It takes intentional effort to overcome these mechanical tendencies.

The Two of Hearts:

The Two of Hearts function as the memory banks of the emotional center. Emotional impressions are taken in, and basically learned and memorized. From this point, they are essentially recalled as needed for responses to stimuli. To understand this concept better, consider how the general public shares quite similar emotions, and sentiments about their birthday and holidays such as Halloween, Thanksgiving, Christmas, Hanukah or whatever it may be. In essence, most people in the world share similar sentimental feelings about common holidays and other similar events. The world of advertising depends on these commonly felt emotions to successfully promote products, goods and services to the public in their commercials and advertising campaigns. The Two of Hearts functions as the memory banks for the stored information of emotional content, which is learned, memorized, and then automatically remembered when needed. People who are centered in the Two of Hearts will primarily manifest from their emotional memory banks, as they feel, and express their emotions from this vantage point. The experiences they had as children will tend to influence and determine the development of their emotional center. Quite often children will mimic, and imitate their parent's emotional behavior as they learn and grow.

To some degree we all have stored emotions that are elicited and called upon in certain situations. However, with people who are centered in the Two, these emotions are virtually automatic responses to emotional stimuli in all situations. They can appear to be sensitive due to their quick responses which manifest as instant reactions similar to reflexes. Their emotional buttons are always ready to be pushed, as they feel more alive when they are experiencing emotional energy. They seem to make friends relatively easy, and are not too fussy about quirky character traits. A Two of Hearts friend recently drove 500 miles, with her two dogs to visit friends, and watch their favorite team play baseball. They were ecstatic when their team won and celebrated with a big party. After the party, they continued to celebrate, driving to Las Vegas to see the shows and gamble. She told me it was a really silly decision to go, but absolutely spontaneous, and she simply could not resist a quick trip to Las Vegas for the fun and gambling. She came home with a new display of bumper stickers and a trunk full of gimmicky baseball souvenirs, tee shirts, stuffed toys for nieces and nephews, and Las Vegas gambling tokens for friends.

The Two of Hearts thrives on the thrill of being involved, particularly when their friends are along for the fun and enjoyment. The Two of Hearts will cheer quite heartily for their favorite team, but, may also feel defeated if their beloved team loses. They are on the sidelines cheering, whether a family member, a friend, or favorite celebrities and athletes. These individuals enjoy having fun and instantly join in the merriment when any special event arises. They are supportive of what, and whom they love, and may boo quite loudly against their team's opponents. The Two of Hearts is emotionally dependent on those they care about. They derive the most enjoyment in life from friendly camaraderie with friends and their family groups.

This center is devoted to what they believe in, whether it is religion, politics, football, or friends and family. They are loyal supporters to their emotional ties and people that fill their hearts. They do well in careers that give them the opportunity to spend time with other people, while in fun or playful environments. They would be quite good working with young children in day care, or, as teachers in elementary schools. They could also be found working in department stores, where their interaction with customers is emphasized. They would do well in party and event planning, or, as a personal assistant. Generally, they prefer jobs where they can be involved with other people, and are able to freely express themselves emotionally.

The Intellectual Center, the King of Diamonds: Ten, Nine and Eight of Diamonds

The King of Diamonds is the intellectual part of the Intellectual center. The emphasis is on the intellectual element, which slows down the speed of function, rendering this center quite slow to act, react, or respond. They are methodical, and take a significant amount of time to formulate their ideas clearly, concisely and articulately, and in a systematic and theoretical manner. This is the thinker who is committed to attaining the most precise and definitive knowledge in their chosen field. They employ their unique intellectual inclination to investigate, understand, theorize and gain as much information and knowledge about a subject as is possible. Their intellectual abilities and potential are vast and far reaching. This is a rare mind of the highest order, in the realm of genius.

The great and unique individuals, such as Pythagoras, Isaac Newton, Albert Einstein and Stephen Hawking, are King of Diamonds types. These brilliant minds exhibit the highest realms of intellectual achievement with an innate propensity to ponder, investigate, and formulate their complex theories. They probe the mysteries of mathematics and science to address multidimensional universes of space, time and infinity. Their minds work very slowly and methodically which allows them to devote the utmost precision to arrive at their masterful mathematical extraordinary conclusions. King of Diamonds thought processes are quite slow as they function, but are thorough and precise. It is interesting to note that all people theoretically have the King of Diamonds center within them; however, it may be accurate to say that few people utilize this center to the elevated level of one who is actually centered in this card.

The King of Diamonds suit represents the true geniuses of our world, past, present and future. They are the people who know that there is more to know, and discover it with their heightened levels of intelligence. These are the brilliant minds that have made enormous contributions to the world, which creates the changes in how we all understand the origins of life, reality, nature, and the universe which we are part of. But, perhaps for them, the world within their vast intelligence is the real world. King of Diamonds examples are the outstanding intellectual giants who amaze us with their multi-dimensional brilliance as mathematicians, scientists, theorists, and inventors, and astonishing geniuses like Marie Curie and Nicola Tesla.

Keywords associated with the Kings: thoughtful, methodical, analytical, objective, diplomatic, intentional, thorough, deliberate, pensive, dignified, reserved, calculating, detached and exacting.

Key behavior traits of the Kings: Kings think, speak and act with enhanced rational objectivity examining potential outcomes to determine what is possible to achieve with consistent efforts. Slow to act or react.

The Ten of Diamonds:

The intellectual part of the intellectual part of the Intellectual center is the slowest of all the centers to act, formulate, calculate, theorize, react or respond. For these unique beings, it may be that time seems to stand still while they slowly and methodically contemplate ideas, formulas and quotients to arrive at their comprehensive understandings of an idea, problem or theory. Their methods and thought processes work slowly with mathematical precision. Thinking on the highest intellectual level is the innate predisposition of the Ten of Diamonds. Evidence gathered or formulated will be weighed, measured and calculated to corroborate their theories in slow meticulous detail. Speculations to be evaluated will require proof and exactitude. Innovative intellectual concepts are derived with the execution of their intense mental capability.

The time spent to develop a theory may be inconsequential to the Ten of Diamonds. Many of the greatest minds in history have spent their lifetime devoted to the pursuit of precise and particular mathematical, scientific or theoretical understanding.

They have the ability to focus all of their attention to the subject in question, perhaps at the expense of other areas of their life. Someone centered in this card may seem quite unemotional and their behavior incomprehensible to others. However, their world of thought, calculation, theorization, computation, evaluation, and so on is how the intellectual center experiences their reality. They may seem distant or aloof, but thinking is how the intellectual part of the intellectual center functions.

The Ten of Diamonds lives in the world of investigative theoretical knowledge, invention and mathematics and abstract intellectual concepts. Theirs can be a rather solitary life which may be spent in careful, precise, methodical examination of facts, figures, numbers and quotients. They pursue lines of investigation and inquiry to solve dilemmas and mysteries of existence and life beyond the visible dimensions within which we mortals dwell. Theirs is a world of abstract possibilities, multi-dimensional reasoning and vast intellectual potential seeking to fulfill itself. The Ten of Diamonds would not merely accept something to be true unless they can prove it to be true. That which they have not yet verified, from their unique intellectual perspective may remain in question until they have proved it or disproved it.

The Nine of Diamonds:

The emotional element lends a creative aspect to the concentrated intellectual predisposition of the King of Diamonds. The investigative processes of this King may exhibit a creative approach whilst seeking solutions to the highly intellectual theories that dominate their elevated thinking processes. Albert Einstein said, "Imagination is more important than intelligence." As this comment came from one of the most brilliant minds in history, perhaps we may assume that this observation emanated from his more creative, emotional thoughts. The Nine of Diamonds would recognize the value and creative potential of the imagination and the part it plays in pursuing intellectual truths.

A person centered in this card will have a slightly quicker or creative approach to arriving at their solutions. The time spent attaining a viable conclusion to understand a multi-faceted inquiry will still be slow, but the slightly enhanced emotional aspect will quicken the pace and enliven the approach to their goal. Keep in mind, the intellectual center overall is the slowest functioning of all the centers, but the Nine of Diamonds does have a somewhat livelier emotional element. Their areas of interest will also vary slightly from the Ten or the Eight of Diamonds. The Nine may be more compelled to study subjects that have intrinsic beauty that might provide them greater inspiration. A botanist researching the medicinal properties of the herbs of the rainforest, or collecting specimens of rare wildflowers that grow in the Himalayas might be centered in the Nine of Diamonds. They might have an interest in the natural beauty of our world and all the fascinating creatures on our planet. Darwin may have been centered in the Nine of Diamonds. Cultural anthropologists who study unique indigenous people around the world might be centered in the Nine of Diamonds. Studying unusual lifestyles of the diverse ethnic groups while gaining insight and understanding of the culture might appeal to the emotional element of their intellect.

A person centered in the Nine of Diamonds may have a more humanistic aim to help preserve endangered cultures and species which are becoming extinct due to consequences of deforestation and climate change. They recognize the vital need to mitigate global warming by incorporating scientific methods. The Nine of Diamonds may be the individual who is called upon to go to Congress to explain the potential detriment of fossil fuels to our environment and atmosphere. They may invent creative solutions for cleaner power and alternative energy resources, such as the use of solar panels and wind power, to minimize pollution. The Nine of Diamonds could be attracted to the scientific and emotional elements, of many diverse subjects, ranging from unusual cultures, rare species, ecological and environmental preservation. They are drawn to compelling studies which stimulate their investigative intelligence while arriving at beneficial solutions.

The Eight of Diamonds:
This endows the Eight of Diamonds with the motivation to move toward their interests, mentally and physically. Theirs is an investigative mind that is interested in studying how and why things manifest, how they come into existence, and so on. Studying and deciphering ancient knowledge would appeal to their need to understand how the past evolved and how it affects the present time. They may be the historians who investigate, decode and document unique systems of knowledge. The moving element in the Eight of Diamonds gives them an enhanced ability to learn languages, thus they may be drawn to study, travel, and understand diverse cultures. Their investigative talent gives them the potential to become translators of ancient languages and texts. Similarly, they are insightful geniuses who are able to invent new technological languages, such as computer codes. The moving element of the intellectual part of the Intellectual center enables them to understand and write complex computer languages and programs. Their inventive ability allows them to theorize, calculate and devise advanced technology and modes of communication. These are the innovative inventive pioneers of technology, such as the cutting edge, computer genius, Steve Jobs.

The Eight of Diamonds represents the type of scientific, analytical and investigative thinker that one might encounter at prestigious universities, teaching and lecturing. They have the innate capability to teach others complex ideas and information based studies such as linguistics, computer sciences, code breaking, abstract knowledge as well as scientific investigation. Certainly, many of the brilliant code breakers in WWII England were probably individuals who were centered in the Eight of Diamonds. Copernicus and Galileo were quite likely centered in the Eight of Diamonds, as they had the ability to look far into the heavens, and to see worlds that others could not possibly have imagined. Galileo invented telescopes so he could look deeper into our solar system and our galaxy. He had an inherent need to know, with the ability to think in an inventive and investigative manner. His remarkable abilities enabled him to contemplate, create, speculate and understand our solar system in its vastness.

The Queen of Diamonds: Seven, Six and Five of Diamonds
The Queen of Diamonds is the emotional part of the Intellectual center. The enhanced emotional element enables them to respond faster than other parts of the intellectual center. They thrive on intellectual stimulation and crave vast amounts of information to satisfy their excessive need-to-know appetites. As with all the Queens, they operate on fascination, attraction, desire and craving. The Queen of Diamonds is fickle about information and is subject to ideological addictions. Like all the Queens of centers, if something is good then certainly, more is better. They have a need for gathering and collecting information and can amass vast quantities of diverse and often quite controversial data. Despite all the information they have, they may not be able to access it in an organized manner. They tend to blurt out random thoughts which they are intrigued with, even if it has nothing to do with a conversation or what is occurring in the moment.

These are the absent-minded professors who are so preoccupied with their mental investigations they forget to use common sense. They may dismiss important ideas which they do not instantly understand or agree with. Abrupt dismissive behavior is one way this Queen may flip. They can change their minds swiftly and make hasty decisions as they overload their mental capacity. Their extreme curiosity may cause them to be indiscriminate about ideas. The Queen of Diamonds may be attracted to far-out concepts which compel her to investigate. They are drawn to the new, different, peculiar or weird owing to their fascination for intrigue and mystery. The Queen of Diamonds has abundant information and she is more than willing to share it with anyone who will listen, whether they are interested or not. She loves to talk and will make a convincing argument possibly just for the sake of conversation. Her opinions are quite strong, but she may be swayed if the topic is compelling enough for her taste. Her famous queen flip occurs when her interest in a subject or belief in an idea suddenly wanes, which occurs rather frequently and abruptly. Nonetheless, the Queen of Diamonds endlessly enchants and informs us with her eclectic energetic opinions and witticisms.

Keywords associated with the Queens: dramatic, temperamental, expansive, gregarious, controlling, lavish, extravagant, passionate, indulgent, vain, excessive, volatile, enthusiastic, exuberant, and moody.

Key behavior traits of the Queens: Queens think, speak, and behave in dramatic emotional emphatic absolutes, such as who they will never speak to again, or what they will never do again!

The Seven of Diamonds:

The intellectual element of the Queen of Diamonds, slows down the impulsive tendency for swift reactions. While the Seven of Diamonds will take time to study ideas and concepts, she will certainly hop from subject to subject at a more rapid pace, than the methodical King of Diamonds. While the intellectual center is the slowest functioning of centers, the Seven of Diamonds picks up the pace and thrives on it. A distinguishing characteristic of the Queen of Diamonds is that they are stimulated by their attraction to and fascination with a subject. Yet the intellectual element of the Seven of Diamonds lends focus to their investigations. It is the very uniqueness of a subject or idea that will compel the Seven of Diamonds to study with such intensity. They will always have an abundance of ideas and information to share. The Seven of Diamonds approaches ideas as an avid learner and boasts of a vast collection of books on diverse subjects. Their wide range of subjects will be varied and explored in depth, at least until they satisfy their own personal interests. My Seven of Diamonds friend is perpetually in search of new theories and exciting fields of study. At the present time, he is particularly intrigued with the numerous conspiracy theories that abound. He seems to enjoy researching slightly unorthodox subjects and borderline scientific concepts such as UFO's, aliens, and crop circles that appear so mysteriously. He holds degrees in various fields of study, but earns his living as an accountant so he can explore the diverse ideas he is attracted to.

As this is the intellectual part of the Queen of Diamonds, she will stay with a subject or idea only until she learns all that she considers relevant and will form strong opinions about what she knows. When there is nothing more to learn about a subject she may quickly switch intellectual gears and explore new lines inquiry that attracts her attention with fascination. They move ever onward to become the well-informed experts in whatever grabs their attention in their diverse fields of inquiry. But remember, what they learn is based on their Queen tendencies and may not encompass every pertinent, relevant or important element. Keep in mind the Seven of Diamonds is subject to the sudden and abrupt Queen flip and she may exhibit extreme changes in her line of thought. I know a fellow who had a long career in science, and now he dabbles in herbal remedies, natural curatives, and alternative medicine. I told him about my knee pain, and he made several recommendations for arthritic joints. Shortly thereafter, he brought various bottles of assorted herbal preparations for my issues. I am reasonably familiar with herbs and their natural benefits, so I accepted his advice and paid for the products. However, when I had an adverse reaction to one of his herbal tonics, he became highly defensive, arguing that I had not given it sufficient time to work its herbal magic. I returned the nearly full bottle, and explained its negative affect; but, he was adamant that the herb would have been a miracle cure if I had prevailed, despite my nausea. Convinced that I was in the wrong, he became argumentative, and true to his abrupt Queen flip, he stopped speaking to me. At some point, he may understand, but will act as if nothing ever happened, as this is typical Queen behavior. Remember, things change swiftly with the Queens.

Despite their self-protective attitudes about what they know intellectually, the Seven of Diamonds can be a wellspring of information. However, those of us who prefer to be somewhat more selective about the information we take in, may be in for a rude surprise if we dare to oppose, or challenge their ideas in any manner. The Queen of Diamonds is emotionally attached to mental acquisitions, and they are not easily convinced that we might know better for our personal needs. They invest a lot of their emotionally intellectual opinions and beliefs, and can have sudden mood swings when any disagreements arise about anything which they hold dear. Tread carefully, but do not relinquish your beliefs to their domineering mental caprices. They may flip back to your side, eventually. The Seven of Diamonds are lively college professors, witty lecturers, chatty lawyers, clever investigative journalists, researchers, scientists, and writers. They draft unique ideas writing their papers of journalistic merit, but the theme will be based on their strong opinions and pet subjects. Their controversial subject matter and topics will be as diverse as the mating habits of extinct reptiles to a heated debate over politicians and government, or herbal medicine and curative controversies. They definitely have a strong opinion and will deliver it with gusto. They are witty, and pride themselves on their vast and varied collection of eclectic ideas and information. The Seven of Diamonds is well informed and generally quite interesting to listen to, at least for a while.

The Six of Diamonds:
She is the queen bee of information owing to the double emotional influence that compels her to investigate everything, and anything. She has an extreme need to know and is exuberant about topics that fascinate her. She may be drawn to highly unusual or bizarre ideas, and is impulsive about gathering exotic information to satisfy her extravagant need to know thought processes. She consumes data voraciously at a much faster speed than any other part of the intellectual center. Someone centered in this card will typically change subjects frequently during a conversation. It may be quite difficult to follow their line of thought as they rarely focus on one idea or concept at a time. She has a tendency to try to monopolize conversations and can be highly opinionated. The Six of Diamonds speaks in long, run-on sentences that make it rather difficult, if not impossible for anyone else to interject a thought. We need to remind the Six of Diamonds to pause at the end of a sentence, and to extend the courtesy to others to express their thoughts as well.

She expresses herself energetically in tangential bursts, until she exhausts herself and everyone else. This Queen may tend to badger others with her rather extreme points of view and can be an insistent know it all bully. I have an acquaintance who is the Six of Diamonds, and she never fails to insult, shock, baffle and annoy everyone with her incessant, compulsive need to intellectually dominate every conversation. She punctuates her comments with emphatic, outrageous opinions, which generally sound inordinately biased. She seems to enjoy provoking others when voicing her opinions. She is stressful, so I no longer socialize with her. She leans toward the argumentative, apparently to shake people up. She has a razor-sharp tongue, is highly opinionated, rude, and is tactless. It is no surprise she was a legal advisor for several years, but, due to her disrespectful behavior in court, her license was revoked.

The Six of Diamonds will explore subjects of inquiry until she abruptly loses interest, then moves on to new topics. I had a friend who pursued numerous majors at college, but rarely took final exams, as he was unable to sustain interest long enough, so he changed to a different subject and major. After spending eight years of continuous study in several colleges, he still does not have his degree in any field. He laments not having his degree, but he is unable to complete a full area of study, in order to qualify for a specific degree. He collects books on many subjects, and proudly boasts of the numerous boxes of books stored in his garage. His interest in a subject may last only as long as his fascination; after the fascination is gone, he is off to the next stimulating idea he is attracted to. Fortunately, he loves to talk to people, so he earns a lucrative salary as a telemarketer.

They are less concerned about their appearance than other centers, and may dress in a rather peculiar fashion. I've seen my telemarketer friend wear Hawaiian shirts with plaid pants. The Six of Diamonds tends to be large, and like all Queens of centers, they may have weight issues occasionally. They are attracted to faddish diets, and may not always follow the rules. After their initial interest suddenly wanes the diet books will be added to the boxes of books in storage. The Six of Diamonds is on an eternal quest for mental stimulation and fascination. They can be wonderful lecturers, as they love to talk, particularly if they are the center of attention. They will excel in debates, and heated discussions, but they do need to be aware that others have important ideas to contribute as well. It is interesting to note that as the emotional part of the intellectual center the Queen of Diamonds enjoys being with other people, if only to talk to them. However, she may not realize that her strong opinions can be somewhat unsettling for others. Nonetheless, they are bright speakers and can do well, if they manage to temper their ideas with tact and respect.

The Five of Diamonds:

The moving influence motivates the Queen of Diamonds and stimulates her to physically move toward the subjects she is attracted to. It is helpful to remember, the influences over a center are the royal iconic suit as the main element which stimulates, activates and determines their manifestation. The moving parts of all centers have movement involved, as an essential key to their functions, processes and behaviors. I have a Five of Diamonds acquaintance, who has traveled extensively to pursue his education. He lived in England for a while, quite enamored of English Literature, but then abruptly lost interest and decided to study the rain forest, climate change and environmental sciences. The moving influence stimulates him to travel, to study the concepts he becomes intrigued with. He tends to embellish his stories with colorful anecdotes of his various and numerous studies. All of the Queens of centers are subject to the sudden flip and this is quite observable in the Five of Diamonds. One moment they are passionate about literature, and then their Queen flips, and off they go to study the environment.

The Five of Diamonds may have some limitations in fully forming their thoughts, due to their robust mental activity. They tend to blurt out ideas, which they have not thought through completely, which may be due to their rather short attention span. They appear to experience attention deficit disorder to a certain degree, and may lack focus because they have an overabundance of ideas. They can lose interest in a subject rather quickly, and may suddenly make an abrupt change in their mental direction. They have many ideas, but they are often simply unable to sustain interest long enough to follow it through, or to develop satisfactory conclusions. If their ideas do not yield swift results, they may suddenly give it up, and move on to something new, or more exciting. They crave mental stimulation and will seek out new, different, odd or bold ideas.

In one moment, the Five of Diamonds may be heard embellishing a story about an infamous person they once met, but may suddenly change topics, tangentially digressing to the mysterious pyramids of Egypt. In the next instant, they digress yet again to lecture on the various conspiracy theories around the world, or some other odd topic which they have dabbled in. They are witty lecturers, who can speak on several subjects with a bit of authority, but, they are easily bored and change the subject to enliven their discourses. The Five of Diamonds is eclectic, happily intermixing topics and ideas, so they might be difficult to follow. Remember, all the Queens operate with attraction to an object of interest, and from their fascination with ideas. The Queens are intensely attracted to unique or controversial subjects. They are eclectic, energetic, and unpredictable, but they can be quite interesting, at least for a little while.

The Jack of Diamonds: Four, Three and Two of Diamonds

The Jack of Diamonds is the moving part of the Intellectual center, and it stores the data and information which is learned or taken in. After we learn about a topic or learn new information, we process it and store it in the Jack of Diamonds for subsequent use, when needed. For example, at the times when we experience data recall, it is retrieved from the Jack of Diamonds. This is the center that memorizes information, and stores in its memory banks just like a recording device. The Jack of Diamonds functions in an automatic manner, providing us with instant access to thoughts and memories. These mechanical responses do not require intentional reasoning or calculating, but are simply thoughts which we have memorized. These mechanical responses tend to be quite automatic and are typically habitual.

Children in elementary school are taught the alphabet and multiplication tables and must commit them to memory. When a child gives a correctly memorized response to an arithmetic problem, it is probably given from the Jack of Diamonds. Not unlike a computer hard drive, data is taken in, processed and stored for later use. However, a person may not always retrieve this information appropriately and mistakes may occur. How qualitatively one has processed information will determine how one accesses the information. For example, if a person has not properly understood or assimilated ideas which they have learned and memorized, they may not be able to correctly utilize the information. While it is stored in their memory banks, it may be used incorrectly or with indiscretion. As such most of these thoughts are basically automatic responses from the memory banks for the intellectual center.

Slang words, clichés and common catch phrases emanate from the Jack of Diamonds. Most people are familiar with certain terms and phrases that are used on a daily basis. These become the preformed terms and formulaic language which is typically used and repeated, often in casual banter. Many of our common greetings come from these memory banks. "How's it going, or "What's up?" or, "Hang tight," or, "Catch you later," are examples of clichéd slang terms that people speak or hear regularly. However, typically, when someone asks, "How is it going?" in reality they do not expect a detailed answer, or any direct information related to their inquiry. Keep in mind, these are the quick and easy phrases that we habitually use on a daily basis, and which mechanically fall from our lips when we encounter another person. We all have this center and almost everyone uses it regularly to remember names, and basic ideas and to interact with others in casual exchanges. But, expressions and responses associated with the Jack of Diamonds tend to lack depth or forethought, and are referred to as pre-formed thoughts, or "formatory thinking." The Jack of Diamonds serves as an organ of intake for information, memorization and storage, and is referred to as the, "formatory apparatus." It mechanically processes our automatic thoughts and our habitual responses. It may also be referred to as, lazy mind response.

It has occurred to me that certain mental disabilities such as Alzheimer's disease might partially be a result of the Jack of Diamonds memory banks losing their ability to retain data and to distribute information when needed. While I have not heard of any specific research to this effect, nor conducted any research myself in this regard, it does seem like a credible possibility. Nonetheless, the Jack of Diamonds serves us every day in countless useful ways, helping us to perform ongoing functions and providing information for the ability to interact in our daily life.

Keywords associated with the Jacks: habitual, imitative, mechanical, automatic, superficial, simplistic, repetitive, conventional, common, spontaneous, routine, formulaic, and subjective.

Key behavior traits of the Jack: Jacks function, feel, think, speak and act from pre-learned programming in general, often mimicking what others feel, think, say or do without analysis or verification.

The Four of Diamonds:

The Four of Diamonds is the intellectual part of the Jack of Diamonds and has distinctive characteristics which serve to collect and memorize data. However, this can result in limited investigation and may lack full comprehension. Thus, it becomes referential information stored in the memory banks, primarily to be called upon as needed. This is eminently useful for everyday tasks and activities that require our immediate response. For example, when learning mathematics as young children the Four of Diamonds can memorize arithmetic tables with ease. This helps one to have reasonably swift access for computing numbers, which allows one to function better. Someone who is centered in the Four of Diamonds would probably be a good teacher, especially due to their ability to recall, and impart information to students, such as arithmetic and other subjects.

I knew a Four of Diamonds individual who was a master of the game, "Trivial Pursuit." Interestingly, most people considered him to be somewhat of a genius as he easily recalled information almost instantaneously. He told me he collected tidbits of information and other miscellaneous details, which he could refer to with ease and swiftness. His knack for calculating distances was impressive, and he was a very reliable source of information for diverse types of data, such as how to convert kilometers into miles, or centimeters into inches. As a child, he was a spelling-bee whiz kid, and he often spoke of his triumphs at various school contests. He said that, in his mind he was able to recall each of the letters in a word in order, and verbalize them without actually making much of an effort. People who are centered in the Four of Diamonds, may appear to be quite intelligent to others. While this intelligence may be looked upon as genius, in reality it might be simply an agile ability to memorize, store data, and recall information. These people may be the proverbial, "know-it-all" types, who can deliver an instant response, or quick answer, about anything and everything. However, it is important to understand that the mechanical parts of all the centers can operate without much attention, or effort. For example, if you should happen to get advice from someone who seems to know all the answers, it would be prudent to verify their information, as they may not have fully considered alternative possibilities. While they may seemingly have all the answers, they may not necessarily be experts in what it is which they are speaking about.

I had a friend who avidly watched all the popular television game shows. She eagerly competed along with the contestants on the show, trying to come up with a quicker answer. Whenever I visited her, the television was always on. However, much of the time she was not actually watching a show, but the television was still on. When I suggested that she might enjoy listening to the informative talk shows on the public broadcast networks, she eagerly reached for the remote. She typically accumulated a stack of newspapers, but would not discard them, until she had done all the crossword puzzles. I encouraged her to recycle the newspapers, so, she got a huge recycling bin just for the newspapers. When I stopped by for tea, she proudly boasted of a newly completed cross word puzzle, on display tacked to her bulletin board. She was interesting and interested in just about anything, was an avid reader, and self-proclaimed book worm and boasted that she was a television news junkie.

The Four of Diamonds thrives on information and is prone to collecting data. They may not actually be able to use all the information they gather, but this is never a deterrent. For them, a tidbit of information just might come in handy at some point. They may not be very discriminating about the information they acquire, but, nevertheless, they tend to be data hoarders, as well as data geeks. They feed on new information, which they accumulate, and are ready to dispense it instantly, no matter if it is useful, or not. They are intrigued with data, whether it is relevant, or just bizarre. As you simply observe, you will begin to recognize when the memory banks in yourself, and in others are functioning and manifesting. We all have the Four of Diamonds within us, and it helps us to remember all the details in life, when we need it.

The Three of Diamonds:

The Three of Diamonds is a bit more emotional about the data which they take in, and therefore, are slightly more protective, or perhaps, more attached to what they know. The Three of Diamonds is attracted to ideas, or information that has an emotional element; however, they may become a bit identified with these particular concepts. It is difficult for them to be impartial about the ideas which they have aligned with. They adopt campaign slogans of their favorite politicians, and will readily incorporate the politician's rhetoric into their own belief system, regardless of its merit, or lack of.

As nerdy types, they gather all the facts about the latest technological gadget, and will inform every one of its pros, and cons. They are usually the first in line, to acquire the latest tech device to add to their collection of gadgets. Novelties of various sorts attract their attention. They love trendy devices, as well as tidbits of technical jargon or information, which sparks their interest. They also have a tendency to compare one thing to another, without necessarily differentiating the varying qualities, or, distinguishing values; such as with the cliché, "comparing apples to oranges." They may not actually utilize comparative reasoning, and tend to like, or dislike something. For example, children often adopt their parent's opinions, without developing their own real preferences. A friend's young daughter told me that, she likes country music because her dad likes country music. She adopted her father's musical taste, perhaps without actually developing her own preference, which is quite common. Also, this imitative trait is fairly consistent with all the Jacks of centers.

The Three of Diamonds may readily accept information as their own personal opinion, or belief, if it appeals to them. I found an example of this is recently when I attended some lectures on Asian healing methods. The lady giving the lectures, spoke about these particular methods, as if she had received the information from a god, or mystical entity, as she sounded rather mesmerized. After I attended a few of these lectures I noticed she repeatedly referred to the man she studied with as, "a miracle healer." As I am not particularly receptive to this type of commentary, I asked her a few simple questions about the man; such as, where was he from, and was he a medical doctor? She answered by showing a video of the man amongst local people in some rural town, or farming village in a remote part of Asia. I mentioned that he appeared to be treating the people with Chinese folk medicine. But, my comments seemed to irritate her and she became visibly annoyed and defensive. I felt uncomfortable as she appeared to be brainwashed by this man, whom she so admired. After her strange responses and odd behavior, I did not return to the lectures. Later, I mentioned this event to a friend, who had heard of this "miracle healer," in question. She cautioned me that he is a cult leader, who dupes innocent sick and disabled people out of large sums of money. The woman giving the lectures had also been duped, having aligned herself to the services of a cult leader.

Three of Diamonds individuals may lack the vital discriminating faculty for cautious discernment, and may not know how to separate fact, from fiction. They develop alliances to popular trends, which can include those people who have underlying deceitful agendas. They may readily follow fads, or trending concepts dogmatically, as they align them self to ideas, pop figures or cult leaders. They often imitate trends rather than developing their own sense of style, whether it is fashion, alternative new age ideas, pop culture, pop music, or pop politics, based on influences from whatever external sources determine the popular favorites. Advertising agencies depend on this trendy favoritism to exploit trends in advertising campaigns. People will buy a brand exclusively because of a popular advertising slogan, or a catchy tune that remains stored in their handy Three of Diamonds.

These individuals can excel in sales and marketing careers, as they exude their belief in the product.

The next time you venture out to purchase a new item, take a moment to think about whether you are buying a certain brand because of an advertising campaign you have seen, or someone else's influence. We are all somewhat imitative in this way, and quite often this is the work of the Three of Diamonds. It can be beneficial to observe the situation carefully, and try to discern for yourself. You are really your own best judge of what is right for you. Developing your own personal values, taste and preferences, is an excellent method to advance self-knowledge to become more self-aware.

The Two of Diamonds:

The Two of Diamonds is the most mechanical part of the intellectual center, and serves as the main memory banks for stored information data. It has the ability to memorize information, but without any particular discrimination, whether it is important, or not. It can see or hear facts and memorize them, regardless of their significance and without verifying if they are relevant or practical. They tend to think in simplistic terms, black and white, yes or no, right or wrong, true or false. They take the path of least resistance, and often accept, or reject ideas without any credible proof or further investigation. The Two of Diamonds can be compared to a recording device that may indiscriminately record everything, and anything it hears, but without concrete practical objectivity. Keep in mind, a recording device does not have the ability to edit the information, or to understand exactly what it is recording. The Two of Diamonds seems to function in much the same manner. Basically, it records and stores information, and then more or less, it has the ability to automatically play back the recorded data. When people try to communicate to each other by using this data, it can oftentimes create misunderstandings, and lead to confusion. Try to imagine one tape recorder trying to communicate to another tape recorder; obviously, it is absolutely impossible to communicate in this manner. Yet, this is often how people interact with one another, and unfortunately, confusion results.

The Two of Diamonds relies upon their preformed ideas and beliefs, without involving intentional thinking processes to define, or refine their thoughts. Basic stored data governs their responses and decisions. They tend to lack an objective overview, or the ability to properly evaluate ideas or situations with deductive reasoning. Often their ideas, beliefs and opinions are simply what they have heard from others, or learned easily, without verifying the merit, or value. The Two of Diamonds might respond inappropriately, as they have not carefully weighed the relevant options. This can be observed when someone blurts out a comment which does not make sense, is out of context with the discussion, or, may not be true.

The Two of Diamonds has a tendency to parrot ideas, beliefs, slogans and trivial data, without intentionally thinking about it, and perhaps without understanding it. They quickly adopt ideas, but may not attain deep understandings. They might gravitate towards ideologies that promise quick fixes for their problems and issues. While some of the ideas that interest them may be based on existing philosophies, it is quite unlikely that they will probe the depths of its origins. As they chat about their newly acquired ideas, or unverified beliefs, it may sound somewhat shallow, to an informed intellectual individual. As they do not have a solid foundation in the information they collect, nor deep comprehension, their words might sound empty or meaningless. Remember, simply parroting information does not lead to understanding and cannot become real knowledge. Merely repeating recorded data can feel insensitive or superficial to others, and results in subjective transmission of ideas which lack an objective foundation.

When you hear the spokes-people who advertise the merits of a certain product, you may notice that they sound somewhat exuberant, yet disconnected. This is because they probably do not have a genuine interest in the product which they are promoting, and might merely be reading the words from a teleprompter. Although I rarely watch television, I consider most commercials to be a form of brain washing. When a commercial comes onto the television screen, I turn off the volume, and leave the room. I prefer to make informed decisions about what I hear and what I buy. I do not want the advertiser's catchy slogan in my consciousness. I carefully select what I purchase, and prefer not to be brainwashed into wanting, or buying overly advertised products for this reason.

At this point you may suspect that the memory banks are bad, or lazy. But this is truly not the case. The memory banks of our centers are simply doing their job of storing information. It is not their primary function, nor their obligation to develop deep understanding; or to gain higher knowledge. Each individual must make efforts to develop their personal knowledge base with intentionality, by paying attention, with lucid objectivity, in order to gain greater comprehension. We all have the Two of Diamonds within, and it is important to understand that it can serve our life with much greater efficiency, when we bring attention and intention to the moment. By mindfully observing yourself with attention, you will begin to notice when you emanate automatically from your memory banks. This is where the importance of balancing the centers is highly encouraged, in order to gain greater understanding to develop self-awareness in your life. This is where real growth can begin.

The Moving Center, the King of Spades: Ten, Nine and Eight of Spades

The King of Spades represents the intellectual part of the moving center. The triad of the Ten, Nine and Eight respectively comprise the intellectual element, the emotional element, and the moving instinctive element of the King of Spades. As with all of the intellectual parts of centers they are slower to react, or, to respond to stimuli. Theirs is a world of intention, attention, precision, and deliberate action. People centered in the King of Spades have enhanced motion intellectuality which predisposes them to precise articulated movement with intentionally executed actions. The King of Spades moves with thoughtful attention and intentionality and these individuals tend to employ contemplative forethought, before initiating actions. Their movements are coordinated, well-conceived and are usually strategic to achieve an aim. They display relative conservatism and economy in the execution of their movements, rather than rapid repetitive maneuvers. The King of Spades will not appear to be in a rush; and, they may move rather slowly with economical, deliberate attention.

They understand the need to align spatial relationships into harmonious arrangements, as in artistic design and architecture. They excel in professional sports and athletics that require methodical strategies. While all the component parts of the King of Spades share an intellectual element, each part will vary slightly, depending on its primary influence, whether it is intellectual, emotional or moving. People who are centered in the King of Spades have a natural affinity for precise and exacting movement. The Ten, Nine and Eight of Spades appear similar, but each has its distinct moving qualities dependent upon the influential element.

Keywords associated with the Kings: thoughtful, methodical, analytical, objective, diplomatic, intentional, thorough, deliberate, pensive, dignified, reserved, calculating, detached and exacting.

Key behavior traits of the Kings: Kings think, speak and act with enhanced rational objectivity examining potential outcomes to determine what is possible to achieve with consistent efforts. Slow to act or react.

The Ten of Spades:

A person centered in the intellectual part of the King of Spades exhibits economy of movement, while they methodically analyze the best move, direction, and the best course of action. This is the world of mentally conceived, intellectually envisioned spatial relationships, such as with architectural engineering and design, or sporting strategy. They have the inherent ability to employ conceptualized moving lines, and shapes, in multi-dimensional spaces to create well-conceived buildings and structures. Being the Intellectual part of the King of Spades, individuals may be interested to work in fields such as aerospace technical design, and architecture, where the intellectual element is activated for its precision mathematical proportion and calculations in spatial relationships. Their impressive structures have a timeless element which lies in their precisely articulated foundation and multi-dimensional cohesiveness. We witness this precision design influence in the historic architectural wonders such as the great Gothic cathedrals, ancient monuments such as Stonehenge in England, with the timeless iconic Pyramids found in Egypt, and in other countries around the world. The endurance of these massive phenomenal monuments is based on exactness. and precision, as implemented by their designers and architects. Complex architecture which incorporates and requires mathematical precision may quite possibly be a Ten of Spades creation.

There exists an inherent abstract mathematical element in the thinking of the Ten of Spades. Astronauts and the engineers who design space ships, which must exert extremely powerful force to escape the Earth's gravitational pull, might also be centered in the Ten of Spades. These individuals utilize the intellectual part of the moving center to envision, calculate, design, construct, and launch their space ships to propel them into orbit. And, there is the vital need to create an aerodynamic vehicle which has the capacity to withstand enormous pressures and vast temperature variations, ranging from the frigid cold of outer space, to the extreme heat of re-entry into Earth's atmosphere. This brilliant level of intentionally designed movement, requires someone with the intellectual ability to design on multi-dimensional levels, and who is innately predisposed to thinking in calculative equations, to accurately determine vital, precise spatial relationships.

Of course, not all people who are centered in the Ten of Spades design space ships as a vocation, nor, are they all architects of timeless, massive, historic monuments. However, these examples will give you a rather general idea of the vast possibilities of their inherent potential to create complex machines to soar through the universe, or to design mega-structures that are capable of enduring the test of time. The Ten of Spades individual would certainly be well equipped to work in aerospace engineering, designing rockets, or space shuttles to launch astronauts into orbit, to go to outer space. The Ten of Spades utilizes planning, and deliberate action with intentionality and precision.

The Nine of Spades:

The Nine is the emotional part of the King of Spades which lends an element of emotion and intellectuality, endowing the Nine of Spades with an enhanced aptitude for creative movement, design, fine artistry, musical composition, musicianship, photography, dance and choreography. Here there is elegance and economy of design, executed with intentional movement that is fused with emotional perceptivity. The Nine, as the emotional part of the King of Spades may be talented in the arts, such as fine art, film production and computer graphics. Artistic fields such as fashion design, the ballet, or playing a musical instrument, such as classical guitar or violin, all contain an emotional element in the movement which may inspire the Nine of Spades individual. We recognize their intelligent moving capability, imbued with emotional overtones, when we visit fine art museums. The great Masters, such as Rembrandt, Vermeer, Michelangelo, and other fine artists, have created ethereal timeless works of great art, that almost appear to come to life when we gaze at them. Each of these virtuoso artists exhibit well developed skills and technique, which enlivens their art with the power to evoke an emotional response from the viewer.

When we watch finely choreographed dancers in a ballet, we see the Nine of Spades displaying technically, refined movement with skill and finesse. Each dancer must move intentionally, keeping the exact tempo with one another, and with the music. The dance is artistically arranged to interact, and flow with the music which inspires the story they tell with their meticulously synchronized intentional movement. The graceful prima ballerina exemplifies the art of dance in motion, which is the result of her efforts, intentional study, practice and physical agility. A classical musician performing a precisely orchestrated concerto, is also an example of the Nine of Spades inherent talent and skill. Melodious classical symphonies which inspire us, are created by a musician's precise hand and eye coordination to achieve musical fluidity with emotional sensitivity. The Nine of spades musical skills render beautiful harmonies into soothing balm for our souls. When hearing the lovely Brandenburg Concerto, it seems quite possible that its creator, the masterful Bach, may have been centered in the emotional part of the King of Spades.

The Nine of Spades gives us refined, intelligent movement nuanced with emotional sensitivity. Art, theatre, music, and dance are examples of where the innately skilled moving centered individuals might be found.

The Eight of Spades:
The enhanced moving influence of the Eight of Spades enables this individual to think while physically moving toward their goals. We can envision an Olympic athlete in full motion, practicing regularly with diligence to move toward the goal to win with their premiere athletic skill. Theirs is innate talent, of total body moving coordination as they execute their masterful athletic ability. Talented people who work diligently to intentionally develop intricate moving centered skills are often centered in this card. The Eight of Spades can propel one to engage in sports which require precise and intentional athletic skill. But, we also witness this influence in the creative construction careers, such as finely designed carpentry, woodworking, and cabinetry. These individuals design their creative works with attention to detail, also employing skill and precision. One might also attribute these skills to a sculptor working with clay, marble or other materials. This is the skilled artist, or technician who creates with intentional and well-developed precise ability. Automotive design engineers, as well as the highly skilled technical mechanics who work on high performance racing cars may also be centered here.

The Eight of Spades has the enhanced intellectual moving element which gives them a natural affinity for artistic coordination and compilation. The fashion designs of Karl Lagerfeld, and Tom Ford exhibit this ability. Both designers display a range of creativity that imbues their work with exquisite detail, whether fashion, photography, or film. Other design work the Eight of Spades may excel at would be landscape architecture. Recently,

I added a Zen style terrace to my patio space, as a peaceful sanctuary for meditation. The contractor I hired to do the work was highly recommended, very polite and worked in an intentional manner, with ease and quiet precision, maximizing time and materials. I drew a simple design, which he improved upon with a lovely construction that is quite appealing to the eye. He accomplished his work with economic efficiency and professional courtesy. The Eight of Spades has a keen eye for detail and can be an excellent designer in many fields.

The Queen of Spades: Seven, Six and Five of Spades

The Queen of Spades is the emotional part of the moving center. The emotional element enlivens, and infuses the moving center with dramatic flair, enthusiastic gestures, and exuberant bravado. This is the Queen who dynamically waltzes robustly through life, expressing her moving centered nature in exciting activities and thrill rides. You will recognize her appetite for lively movement, and love of adventure in people who may not stop until they drop, in their attitudes and behaviors. The Queen of Spades prefers to be moving, until she exhausts her physical resources, or, depletes her budget for tennis lessons, skiing, or other activities. Whether it is exhilarating sports, or competitive dancing, she will go to extremes to satisfy her impulsive craving for expressive exciting movement. On the flip-side, this queen will absolutely wilt if she has to be stationary for too long. She lives to move, and moves to live, especially if it is thrilling with an element of risk, or adventure.

As with all Queens of centers, the Queen of Spades has somewhat of an addiction for that which she is attracted to. Hence, if an activity is action packed, then more of it is better! This might include dare-devil sports which have an inherent element of risk, like sky diving, extreme skiing, or, racing sports cars. The Queen of Spades is action oriented and is willing to go to extremes, for whatever activity allows her to indulge in moving her body, particularly if there is excitement to be had.

Keywords associated with the Queens: dramatic, temperamental, expansive, gregarious, controlling, lavish, extravagant, passionate, indulgent, vain, excessive, volatile, enthusiastic, exuberant, and moody.

Key behavior traits of the Queens: Queens think, speak, and behave in dramatic emotional emphatic absolutes, such as who they will never speak to again, or what they will never do again!

The Seven of Spades:

The intellectual element lends a thinking influence, which helps to slow down the speed of her actions, and activities, somewhat. The Seven of Spades will ponder, and perhaps even calculate the element of risk, or other possibilities, before she takes a daring leap of faith, such as parachuting from an airplane. While Queen of Spades individuals are generally attracted to thrilling sports and other adventures, the Seven of Spades is more likely to consider the potential risk involved. She will monitor the danger involved in an undertaking, perhaps proceeding with a bit more caution. Having the ability to strategize makes the Seven of Spades a logical team leader in competitive sports. She plays to win, and can use strategy to put the odds in her favor to gain the best advantage. This can be noticeably apparent, especially when she is selecting team mates, or work mates, who can help her team win, whether it is with sports, or other activities. But, be aware if your actions should cause her team to lose. She will not fail to respond, and may just dismiss you from her team. With her it is all about having the best advantage to increase the odds for winning.

The thinking element of the Seven of Spades would be quite advantageous for a rock-climber who does free climbing without ropes, while navigating a particularly steep mountain or stone wall. An athletic friend did free climbing in the mountains and told us stories of his close calls with danger. But, he insisted that he planned all his ascents and made maps to plot the climb, so he was prepared to some extent. Nevertheless, the enticing element of danger appealed to his center of gravity. His rock climbing motto was, "Have a plan, a map, and climb." I have noticed that the Seven of Spades, in spite of being a Queen, are not necessarily as effusive in their speech. Many years ago, I had an interesting conversation with two extreme skiers who did massive cliff jumps off snowy cornices and mountain peaks, hoping to break world records. They both had a very calm demeanor and quiet attitude about their absolute passion for skiing. They said it is vital to scope out the terrain, check equipment and not blindly jump off a cliff. While their skiing is certainly dangerous, both are mentally prepared as they perform their daring feats with passion and skill. It would be fair to characterize the Seven of Spades as being a bit more cautious, owing to the intellectual factor, which ever so slightly, helps to slow them down. The thinking process allows the Seven of Spades to strategize, which helps minimize excessive risks, whether it is exciting sports, speculative investments or spinning the roulette wheel in Las Vegas. The blend of intellect with emotional movement serves to literally propel them through life, albeit with a thin safety net.

The Six of Spades:

The Six of Spades lives to move with passion, doing whatever excites her in the moment. However, her double emotional element tends to accelerate her unpredictable Queen flip. Her passionate actions motivate her until she wears herself out, over-does it, and collapses in total exhaustion. Her Queen flip is triggered by challenging indulgences in her favorite activities. For example, she may rigorously play 18 holes of golf, rather than the customary 9 holes, and, afterwards, she might vow never to play golf again! As the emotional part of the Queen of Spades, she tends to be a bit fleshier than the other moving centers, which are generally somewhat slender. Subject to extremes, she indulges in large amounts of food to fuel to her robust activities. She might learn of a trendy new exercise fad, and jump in, swearing to become an expert at whatever it is, at least for the moment. A friend excitedly bought a Nordic-Track exerciser, swearing to get fit, but never used it. The Six will join yoga, aerobic, or exercise classes to help keep her weight under control, but, she may lack discipline, and swiftly lose interest. The habit of over-doing it, is consistent with the queens of centers, and the Six of Spades is no exception. She can be moody, and those who cannot keep up with her excessive pace are subject to dismissal.

Like all Queens of centers, she can be an extremist, temperamental, self-centered, and, rather vainglorious. In her mind, she considers herself to be an expert at everything she does, and she is not shy about reminding everyone of her exalted self-opinion with frequent regularity. Rightly or wrongly, she expounds her point of view somewhat overtly, whether anyone is interested or not. She tends to be effusive and enthusiastic about her own personal interests, and often makes rash decisions at a moment's notice, but, she has not carefully considering all the possible outcomes. We often see this type of erratic behavior with politicians, who go on the road in their political campaigns, and proudly boast of all their alleged virtues, while making endless empty promises.

I knew a Six of Spades fellow who was a talented musician, and travelled the world touring with a successful orchestra. He was an accomplished musician, which made him feel over qualified to be part of an orchestra. He wanted more attention, due to his queen's vanity, so he decided to strike out on his own, hoping to be recognized as the star of his own show. He simply quit his job with the orchestra and stopped touring. A few years after this, I encountered a mutual friend of ours, who told me that he ultimately regretted quitting his orchestra job, as they had gone on to record several gold records, and, unfortunately for him, the stardom he craved was simply not in the cards.

As with all the Queens, there is a tendency to be obsessive and compulsive, which can often lead to addictive behaviors and unhealthy habits. She seems to have very little control over her passionate desires, and at any opportunity she may just go off on an inspired moving tangent. There are situations when she may attempt to do something a bit too daring, but, she is restless and nervous if things become boring, or stationary. Queens tend to be the ultimate attention seekers, and in this regard, they can be very insensitive to the needs of others. Not everyone can keep up with her pace!

Keep in mind, this is the emotional part of the Queen of Spades moving center, so, she can be quite exuberant and passionate about her activities. She loves to dance and do sports that give her the rush she craves. She indulges until she over exerts herself, and, then collapses in exhaustion. She may throw caution to the wind, but this moving centered dynamo, operates from fascination with movement and action. Promise her a thrilling white-knuckle roller-coaster ride, and she is ecstatic!

The Five of Spades:

As with the Queens of the moving center, this card is motivated by action and can become addicted to movement for movement's sake. The additional moving element predisposes this center to restlessly move incessantly with intensity and passion. The Five of Spades is a natural cheer-leader who swirls and twirls with bravado for the love of her team. She can impassion a crowd with her contagious energy. Remember, the energy of each center can exert its influence on other people. The Five of Spades can be seen dramatically waltzing across the ballroom floor, probably brightly attired in a colorful gown, or a flashy tuxedo paired with a cheerful polka dot bow-tie. This belle of the ball wears herself out dancing, forgetting that the next day she will simply be too tired to go to work. As a Queen, she over does everything with gusto, but often suffers in exhaustion afterwards. The Five of Spades might dance the night away, until she completely depletes all of her energy. She tends to vow "never again!" rather frequently, but will bounce back after resting and replenishing her energy.

If the Five of Spades employs discipline to sustain an interest, she can develop and train her natural abilities with proficiency and skill. The emotional intensity of the Queen lends an enormous amount of potential energy for their passions, and interests. The moving element of the Five of Spades may help to stabilize their attention, in order to remain focused, for a while at least. Developing more focus may help delay the customary Queen flip, especially when learning new skills, such as playing an instrument. Focus would give her the staying power to develop her skills. I've known a few musicians who were centered in the Five of Spades. Each had an energetic passion for music, but also, a tendency to be moody about their talent.

The Five of Spades can also be a fun loving sporty dare-devil, who is willing to try rollerblading, surfing, bicycling, or any other sport. They implore others to join in the fun, but seem unaware that not everyone has their natural capabilities. This is the extreme skier who urges all their friends to ski down the expert black diamond run, or to jump off the precarious mountain cornice for a thrill. However, the Five of Spades may not adequately prepare, or consider all the risks involved. She is unable to monitor energies effectively and does not stop until she has had her fill of excitement.

The Queen element of the Five of Spades may also exhibit a ruthless manner that might not take other people or consequences into consideration. I knew someone who was a real estate broker with a small company and she arose very early each day, to arrive at work before everyone else. She was highly competitive and ambitious for success and wealth. But, there was a disconcerting situation she instigated, which had disastrous consequences for the innocent people involved. Apparently, being successful was not enough for her grandiose ego, so she stole the client files of the company she worked for. Armed with the stolen client files, she offered them to a large national real estate corporation, to use as a bargaining chip to be appointed an executive in their company. Her ruthless Queen flip was a complete disaster for the smaller real estate company which went bankrupt as a result of her treacherous, unanticipated, and very expensive betrayal. *Please note: I use this person as an example in a subsequent segment, about people to avoid.*

Remember, all the Queens from the Seven, Six and the Five have a tendency to be relatively self-centered, tempestuous, excitable, vain, volatile, unreliable, and therefore, quite unpredictable. They need to be the center of attention, regardless of the outcome or how it may affect others. We all have the Queens within us and we can observe this behavior manifesting on occasion. You may not be centered in a Queen, but we have all experienced her "flip" at one time or another.

The Jack of Spades: Four, Three, and Two of Spades:

Jack of Spades is the moving part of the moving center. Thus, it serves as the memory banks where all learned movement information and data is stored. These "Jacks of all trades" seem to perform moving centered actions with minimal effort or attention. Whatever they have stored in their memory banks can be instantly recalled to put to use for any and all movements. They are quite agile, adaptable and can perform an action or movement rather quickly, simply by watching. In this respect, they tend to be rather imitative, which can be quite advantageous for them in certain situations. The Jack of Spades centered person can apply what they have learned or mimicked quickly and efficiently. The data stored in their memory banks is readily available for use. This is particularly observable when they are performing learned movements such as dancing or playing most sports. The Jack of Spades picks up skills quickly, and quite naturally. These are the folks who can play piano by ear, especially after watching, or listening to someone else play. This imitative behavior can mimic actions with ease and agility. They gravitate towards the activities, and the types of careers where they can put their imitative moving abilities to use.

Because of their natural propensity for moving their bodies into action, Jack of Spades individuals tend to be naturally sleek and slender. They move almost constantly, from the time they get up in the morning, until they retire at night. They need to get enough calories every day, to replenish their energy, and they often bring snacks with them wherever they go. Their slim trim bodies are certainly not a mystery, but simply the natural result of their moving centered lifestyle. These are the skinny folks who can eat almost anything, and not gain weight. Whatever they eat serves as fuel for their motion driven life, and calories are burned quite rapidly. For them the word "diet" does not apply. When you take a look around, you will notice the Jack of Spades individual dashing past you. They are designed to move through life. Keep in mind, each center has natural tendencies, talents, and abilities to tap into when needed. The Jack of Spades person is quite literally, energy in motion.

The Jack of Spades, from the Four, Three, and down to the Two, are the memory banks which store the moving center data information, for automatic retrieval and use. We all have the Jack of Spades centers within us, and in truth we could not live our life effectively without these amazing memory data banks. They allow us to drive a car, and have a conversation, simultaneously. Or to play a tune on the piano that we have memorized, and sing along as we play. Also, we would not be able to use the computer keyboard without the handy data stored in our moving center memory banks.

Keywords associated with the Jacks: habitual, imitative, mechanical, automatic, superficial, simplistic, repetitive, conventional, common, spontaneous, routine, formulaic, and subjective.

Key behavior traits of the Jack: Jacks function, feel, think, speak and act from pre-learned programming in general, often mimicking what others feel, think, say or do without analysis or verification.

The Four of Spades:

The Four of Spades is the Intellectual part of the Jack of Spades. The Jacks serve as the memory banks for all learned movement; however, the Four of Spades is also clever, and inventive. They can assimilate movement or assemblages quickly, and might improve upon certain actions, using their readily available database of information for implementation. This is someone who can quickly adapt. Learned movements and actions which are stored in their memory banks are instantaneously recalled for immediate use. The Four of Spades is interested in gathering useful information for future reference. They can function as a virtual, "how to do it guide," and are full of useful tips. With the thinking element present, their actions will be governed with their thought processes utilizing their remarkable memory skills. Although the Four of Spades exhibits the need to move for movement's sake, their actions will have slightly more attention involved. Therefore, they may be a bit less restless in their habitual need to move, as thinking is employed.

An automobile mechanic would put the Four of Spades to good use, when dismantling an engine, and then reassembling it afterward. The information is stored quite efficiently in his memory banks so that he is able to expediently recall where each part goes. He will skillfully remember which bolt is attached to which motor part. This center has innate capabilities for developing specific skills. These individuals are quick, but they can think on their feet. Many years ago, my Four of Spades friend installed a ski rack on the back of my car. He said he had never seen such a complicated installation for what looked like a simple rack, but, he was determined to figure it out. After a bit of scrutiny looking at the parts, he figured out where each piece fit fairly swiftly. He even accessed the tire jack and other tools, from their efficient storage space in my car to utilize them in the installation process. He laid out the components, and was able to quickly determine where each part had to be placed to install, did it quite swiftly, and it seemed as if he had done it before. He said working on cars was one of his hobbies, one of the many he enjoyed, along with a long list of his favorite sports. A few weeks later I saw him at a local ski resort and he was quite adept on the slopes.

The Four of Spades individual performs movements, and actions with agility, dexterity, speed and facility. They may watch an activity, such as a dance move, or sport, observe the movements and store the data. Afterwards, they seem to have the ability to imitate and perform the actions, almost exactly. Their moving centered abilities serve to acquire useful skills, which they are able to employ swiftly, to accomplish tasks and actions effortlessly. As the intellectual part of the Jack of Spades, they are uniquely equipped to learn, and execute skills with efficiency and proficiency. They are cleverly imitative and inventive when they need to be. The Four of Spades has the ability to assess a matter, and swiftly access a solution from their memory banks. The different elements influencing the Jack of Spades help define their actions and behavior. As the intellectual part of the Jack of Spades, the

Four moves in a more intentional manner, than the Three, or the Two. Clever and imitative they perform actions swiftly with attention when needed.

The Three of Spades:

The Three of Spades is the emotional part of the Jack of Spades. These individuals seem to be in perpetual motion, and are emotionally inspired to burst into action, energized to move. The emotional element tends to keep the Three of Spades literally hopping about, while they dash from one activity to another, from hobbies to sports, or, whatever motion sparks their interest. These restless folks are involved with just about everything and they simply cannot sit still. They seem to need a constant outlet to exert themselves, physically and energetically. The Three of Spades is generally quite talkative and chatty, due to the emotional element blending with the memory banks of the moving center. They tend to know a lot of people to share moving centered activities with and typically have like-minded sporty friends.

Remember, all the Jacks are connected across suits, so the Jack of Spades person may also link up with the Jack of Hearts. They are popular, often going to participate in, or watch athletic events, or are involved with moving activities. It may be that they are popular by default, because of their need for constant activity and attention. They are naturally outgoing, but may be a poor judge of character, owing to their eagerness to participate. In this regard, they might be a bit superficial, and swiftly form attachments. However, they may not make an effort to develop deep relationship bonds. Their perennially sleek physiques, are a testament to their physical need for movement, sports, exercise and constant activity. While they like to go to the gym to work out, they seem to naturally get adequate daily exercise, by simply living their life, as they dash about, hither and yon. They are constantly on the go, invariably involved with moving centered activities, events and friends. However, quite often they skim over important details, which can annoy others, and might get them into mischief.

I knew a Three of Spades individual who was unable to stop moving throughout her day. She twitched with energy and was active from early morning, until late at night, as she only required minimal sleep. She was constantly rushing off somewhere to do errands and activities on her busy schedule. She juggled endless projects, squeezing them into her active lifestyle. But, she often over looked important details in haste, and was unable to efficiently manage her time. She was frequently late to events, owing to her calendar of events. However, on the positive side, she was usually cheerful, provided she was active and moving about in her activities. The Three of Spades is interested in moving centered activities, and may seem generally optimistic and carefree. But, they tend to consider all activities equally important. Thus, they may lack the ability to prioritize, and are unable to determine orders of importance. They often get quite involved in whatever they are doing, and lose track of time.

Once a Three of Spades athletic friend called me asking for a ride, as his car ran out of gasoline. Caught up in where he was going, he simply forgot to put gas in his car. Time management and prioritizing are not skills which come naturally to them. It would be useful for them to develop a clear sense of what is most important. They are easily distracted, and have difficulty staying focused on one activity. They have an active imagination, and enjoy silly pranks, and other funny misadventures. While intentionality is not a natural trait of the Three of Spades person, they are quite fun loving and seem to be popular, as they are always ready to drop what they are doing to go on an adventure, and to be out and about. They have a knack for knowing the best places to go for moving centered fun, whether it is hiking, bicycling, playing billiards, dancing, or amusement parks. Enjoyment of movement is their inspiration, and infuses the activities they participate in, so restlessly and relentlessly.

The Two of Spades:

The Two of Spades is the moving part of the Jack of Spades. The expression, "Jack be nimble, Jack be quick, Jack jump over the candle-stick," aptly describes the Two of Spades centered person quite effectively. The Two of Spades is somewhat comparable to a wind-up toy, that keeps on moving. They are the folks who seem to twitter and flinch, even when they are standing still. They simply cannot sit still in a chair without rocking back and forth, tapping their foot, or moving about. They are nearly always in motion, rapping on their desk like a drum, or swinging their leg to the beat of an inaudible song, perhaps a tune they cannot get out of their head, playing on the endless loop of their imagination. They have a restless physical nature with a restless imagination to match. They do not typically just sit and listen to music; instead they play air guitar or hit invisible drums, keeping the beat of the music. They gesticulate their hands when speaking, unable to be still. They are rarely inactive, as movement is virtually automatic for them. The enhanced moving element keeps these active individuals moving, even when they rest. Movement is their natural impulse and their reason for being. They live to move, and move to live. In essence, they are the most automated, or habitually mechanical of the moving center cards. They are usually quite thin, owing to their habitual restless movement. They burn off calories quickly, as fuel which propels them through their life.

After the Two of Spades has learned a skill, or movement in a certain manner, it is unlikely that they will alter how they execute it. They are excellent at performing repetitive movements, and seem to effortlessly acquire moving center skills and abilities. They can learn basic skills very quickly by imitation and perform them almost automatically. Their daily duties are accomplished swiftly, with speed and agility, and in some cases almost robotically. Hence, the Two of Spades excels at jobs which require repetitive movement. They are equipped to perform tasks efficiently, and expediently, almost as if they are on automatic pilot. They are innately very good at repetitive motion because of their excellent memory banks, which are capable of recalling stored data or information instantaneously. Repetitive movements do not seem to bore them, so they do rather well, as long as they are able to keep moving while doing their activities and tasks. However, a friend shared a problem she was having with her Two of Spades husband's strange sleep pattern. He would habitually rock his foot back and forth, in his nightly routine to fall asleep. But, during the night he would continue to move about, restlessly tossing, turning, and even talking in his sleep. This ongoing issue caused her to have many sleepless nights. She finally started taking naps during the day to compensate for her exhausting sleep deficit. She loved her husband, so taking naps were helpful for a short while, as she was desperately trying to save her marriage. Eventually they bought a bigger bed, which had a center divider as a permanent healing solution for the salvation of her marriage. Oddly, her husband was entirely unaware of how disruptive his perpetual movement had been.

The Two of Spades is excellent at imitating almost anything they see and can usually perform the movement very swiftly. They are also quite skilled at mimicking and impersonating people's behavior. But remember, they are imitative by nature rather, than innovative. This is the talented, but typical "Jack of all trades," who learns actions, and automatically stores the data, ready for instant replay. They can call upon their excellent memory banks databases to recall information instantaneously and effortlessly without much effort at all.

The Instinctive Center, the King of Clubs: Ten, Nine and Eight of Clubs

The King of Clubs is the Intellectual part of the Instinctive center, hence, the intellectual part of the physical body and senses. The Instinctive center innately governs all of our internal functions, such as glandular secretions, digestion of food, excretion, heartbeat, lungs taking in oxygen, and healing. The Instinctive center is fully functioning at birth in a normal healthy body. The heart beats, the lungs breathe, food is digested and assimilated throughout the body, and all other internal physical processes occur continuously in a healthy body and without our conscious involvement. The instinctive center processes all of the sensory functions which we are born with, as well as processing our extrasensory perceptions, and our intuition. Some may experience enhanced development of sensory abilities, perhaps, to receive psychic impressions.

The King of Clubs has an enhanced awareness of its physicality, physical domain and inner workings, plus they exhibit heightened sensitivities and intuitive faculties. Our human physical body is a miraculous and phenomenally well-orchestrated organism with the ability to automatically process vital functions to sustain life. All of our sensory apparatus and sensing mechanisms exist within the human body to process incoming sensory stimulation and information. The King of Clubs is intuitively aware of the environment and continually monitors and analyzes the energies circulating in the environment. This endows them with a powerful presence and they are enigmatically charismatic.

Keywords associated with the Kings: thoughtful, methodical, analytical, objective, diplomatic, intentional, thorough, deliberate, pensive, dignified, reserved, calculating, detached and exacting.

Key behavior traits of the Kings: Kings think, speak and act with enhanced rational objectivity examining potential outcomes to determine what is possible to achieve with consistent efforts. Slow to act or react.

The Ten of Clubs:

The Ten of Clubs is the intellectual part of the King of Clubs. It has a double-dose of intellectuality as the intellectual part of the instinctive center. As such there exists an almost other worldly characteristic about this center. The Ten of Clubs operates with enhanced elements of heightened awareness over the five senses, which enables them to process subtle sensory impressions. Our physical senses serve us continually, monitoring and evaluating the atmosphere around us. Sensory perceptions are taken in, analyzed and deciphered as sensory impressions which enable us to navigate safely through life. With the Ten of Clubs senses are inordinately sensitive to the subtle vibrations and energy emanations surrounding them. This heightened sensitivity allows the senses to be aware of any potential threats, or hazards, in order to protect the instinctive center from danger. They exhibit extraordinary sensory awareness in their vigilance for self-preservation. Their acute sensory antennae evaluate the conditions around them, and they take the appropriate precautionary measures.

Ten of Clubs perceptions are acutely intuitive as they innately sense and decode the atmosphere to detect subtle impressions which are in motion. Their sensory perceptions may take different forms, such as when interpreting sensory stimuli from their own physical body when an illness is coming on, or other elements of physical risk, or harm. The Ten of Clubs is the mind behind the body and senses, and they radiate a powerful presence which can be intimidating for others. A person centered in the Ten of Clubs emanates with a unique charisma and sensory energy, which others can sense. They have a strong presence which commands attention when they enter a room, whether they want attention or not. Their eyes may be particularly striking and with a penetrating glance, they seem to see through people, situations or any nonsense. These intense characteristics are an element of their highly-attuned sensitivity and survival mechanism.

One of my yoga acquaintances is a Ten of Clubs with a calm, yet strong presence. He practices Oriental holistic healing, follows an organic vegan regimen and practices Tai Chi. He commented that he finds it beneficial and informative to gaze directly into a person's eyes while interacting to gain deeper insight into sensing their character. When he encounters someone, who emits negative energy, he averts his gaze to avoid eye contact, or he will leave the environment if possible to limit exposure to unwanted energy. He follows his natural inclinations and aversions to maintain his equilibrium. This type of sensitive awareness is an attribute of actors and actresses who can mesmerize an audience and steal a scene simply by walking on stage. Their physical presence will often over power others in a room, even if they are rather quiet.

We each possess an incredible instinctive center and it is highly beneficial to bring attention and intention to caring for our physical body. The Ten of Clubs does this naturally, and teaches us to be more attentive to our sensitive human body, with its innate, powerful sensory capabilities. The Ten of Clubs are excellent doctors, health advisors, naturopaths, and specialists in studies of the human body, and sensory perceptions. Professors who teach knowledge of the physical body often make a strong impression on their students. Innovative researchers and biologists whose studies focus on finding cures to combat disease, may quite possibly be centered in the Ten of Clubs.

The Nine of Clubs:

The Nine of Clubs is the emotional part of the King of Clubs. A "sixth sense" is a natural characteristic of all King of Clubs centered people; however, with the Nine of Clubs person, the emotional attribute enhances their natural ability to perceive. The enhanced emotional element predisposes these highly sensitive, intuitive individuals to have strong intuition, or psychic awareness of the inner psychological and physiological conditions of other people. They innately recognize and interpret their sensory perceptions, which enable them to read other people quite skillfully. Each of us has experienced the eerie sensation of knowing about an event before it has occurred. In some instances, we may have sensed the "vibration" of a person, even before we have met them. It may be that we have simply detected the subtle electronic impulses that permeates our atmosphere, filling the space around us with a constant flow of energies. Some schools of thought suggest that our thoughts are a substance in the form of electronic matter. Thus, we emit our own frequency of electronic vibratory emanations, not unlike radio waves. We cannot see them; however, we know they exist. An individual centered in the Nine of Clubs has the enhanced emotional sensory perceptions that enable them to perceive these rarified vibrations which are circulating around them. Their very existence is governed by the world of the senses, as they interpret the nuances of sensory impressions and stimuli which enters their environment. I have a friend who makes notes of impressions she senses, sometimes just a word, or a name. Often, she hears of an event on the news or reads about it the newspaper, and sees that it is in her notes.

Emotional psychological vibrations also have a strong energy that almost everyone can feel, such as when one enters a room filled with merriment and positive energy. The same is true if one enters a room which is filled with negativity, or danger. Whether the emotional vibrations are positive or negative, most of us can sense the energy rather quickly. This is the inherent ability and protective quality of our Nine of Clubs in action, instantly detecting energies for our safety and security. Of course, one need not be a psychic empath to sense good or bad vibrations circulating in the immediate atmosphere; however, the sensitivity of the Nine of Clubs is magnified which makes them acutely aware of vibrations and energies. They inhabit a unique world of enhanced sensory impressions as they detect and decipher sensory perceptions on a moment to moment basis. The Nine of Clubs is innately sensitive and may exhibit clairvoyant abilities. Their well-adapted finely attuned antennae readily sense waves of energy and vibrations being transmitted via the electronic world of thoughts, emotions, or other emanations.

Due to the enhanced emotional element, the Nine of Clubs is particularly aware of and sensitive to the problems that other people are experiencing. They are able to analyze and interpret these energy emanations to give advice and make suggestions that may help alleviate stressful issues. People gravitate toward clairvoyants who may be able to detect or identify problems with their extra sensory perception. The Nine of Clubs has extraordinarily receptive emotionally instinctive powers of perception. Long ago I had a friend who was a successful psychic reader. Her intense blue eyes seemed to scrutinize people and situations with certainty, and cognition. She acted as an advisor to many successful professionals. One day we were having coffee and I showed her some photographs of some other friends. She grabbed a photo of one dear friend and reacted instantly with an unexpected remark. She said, "Your friend is very sick and I am concerned for her wellbeing." I was rather surprised by this comment; however, I did know that my friend had some health issues. Sadly, not long after this chilling photograph incident, my dear friend became seriously ill and died within a very short time. Afterwards, I called my psychic friend and told her what had happened. Her response was, "I knew when I looked at her photograph that she did not have long to live."

Clearly not everyone who is centered in the Nine of Clubs is a career clairvoyant; however, the professions which require strong, intuitive leadership abilities with the skills to read people and situations instantly would be a natural working atmosphere for them.

The Eight of Clubs:

The Eight of Clubs is the moving part of the King of Clubs. The moving element serves the Eight of Clubs well, enhancing their ability to move instinctively toward actions which need to be taken for personal security and other needs. They possess an uncanny instinctive sensory memory which serves as a protective function as they sense the world around them. An individual who works in an emergency room of a hospital, either in administration or as a medical advisor, would use their Eight of Clubs ability to instinctively know how to handle a medical emergency and would also have the ability to remain calm under these stressful conditions. They maintain their composure to make careful assessments and lifesaving decisions, a vital skill in a hospital situation. They respond instinctively and intuitively with the insightful ability of one who keeps their wits about them. For example, a paramedic must take command instantly to make life saving decisions. The Eight of Clubs has the ability to remain relatively detached when dealing with crisis situations, which enables them to take command during critical moments. They can take charge and bring a sense of calm to adverse circumstances.

The Eight of Clubs individual is charismatic and radiates a strong presence, as though they have an energy field surrounding them. The acting profession attracts Eight of Clubs individuals for their unique ability to embody and radiate the essence of a character. The mesmerizing and intriguing photographic models who appear on magazine covers can immediately capture your attention, and may be Eight of Clubs individuals. They magnetically attract your attention as you look at their alluring appearance, even when transmitted via a photograph. They possess a natural ability to radiate their presence and make a strong impression with their inherent sensory faculties. We each possess the Eight of Clubs to access at moments of duress to bring composure to difficult situations. As we learn to recognize, access and harness our own powers of intuition, it will allow us to calmly take command of each moment as it arises in a harmonious manner.

The Queen of Clubs: Seven, Six and Five of Clubs

The Queen of Clubs is an overtly sensual character who gushes unabashedly over the luscious foods she cannot get enough of, the fragrances that delight her, and everything else that has to do with satisfying her lavish creature comforts in every moment. She is quite vocal about her passions for everything in life that helps to satisfy her strong instinctive needs. They want it now and they want a lot of it, whether its food, sex, drugs, and quite possibly, even rock and roll. These Queens of sensual self-satisfaction have vast appetites that must be fulfilled, until they overdo it and flip. With the Queen of Clubs, this can be their physical downfall, as they tend to have massive appetites which they indulge. They seem to lack the discipline necessary to adhere to a restricted dietary regime or exercise plan, and might forego healthy or holistic practices, in favor of self-indulgences.

The Queen of Clubs often has a chronic over-indulgence habit, which can become its opposite, resulting in physical discomfort, illness, and also, potential addiction problems. When they feel a need for instant gratification for their sensual cravings and desires, they tend to easily forget they may regret the excessive indulgence afterwards. They might vow, "I will never do that again," when paying the price with a hangover, stomach ache, or head ache. But, this is their Queen flip, caused by the negative results of their own self-indulgent behavior. The Queen of Clubs may lack the ability to discern between food that tastes good, and food that is good for them; such as healthy eating in moderation. The Queens in general tend to have addictive behavioral issues. These addictions can become quite self-destructive if they cannot gain control over their bad habits. It is helpful to remember that all the Queens of centers are subject to extremes, regardless of which suit influences them. All of the Queens have strong impulsive needs, cravings and desires. Their dramatic Queen flip may occur if their needs are not met, or, from too much of a good thing, which then becomes its opposite.

Keywords associated with the Queens: dramatic, temperamental, expansive, gregarious, controlling, lavish, extravagant, passionate, indulgent, vain, excessive, volatile, enthusiastic, exuberant, and moody.

Key behavior traits of the Queens: Queens think, speak, and behave in dramatic emotional emphatic absolutes, such as who they will never speak to again, or what they will never do again!

The Seven of Clubs:

The Seven of Clubs is the intellectual part of the Queen of Clubs. The thinking element slightly slows down the impulsive, compulsive need for immediate gratification, lending vital rationale. The life of this sensual creature revolves around attractions to, and fascination with sensory impressions, sensory desires, and, in satisfying their sensory cravings. However, the Seven of Clubs has the potential to incorporate the element of forethought, as intentional thinking, for having their sensory needs met. This lends a bit of stability and balance to the Queen of Clubs, which is essential for their personal wellbeing. While they retain a vigorous appetite for sensual pleasures, they are somewhat more selective in making decisions, and choosing how they get their needs met. Choices may be moderated by the enhanced intellectual element, which lends healthier rationale to their food cravings and habits. This Queen has the need to know, regarding what might help her, or, what might harm her. She is open to learning, or being educated, about what is more beneficial, and therefore, less harmful for her physical organism. The Seven of Clubs centered individual can achieve greater personal fulfillment with an educated approach regards satisfying their sensual desires or cravings. Although they will still indulge, it may be to a lesser degree, as they are willing to use helpful means to mitigate the after effects of excess. They are able to exercise moderate self-control, which they can employ to make better health decisions.

As a gourmet chef in the world of fine dining they are innately and acutely attuned to the subtle nuances of aroma and flavor. They are in their element preparing fine foods, and they take pride and pleasure in the attention they receive from others for their culinary skills and expertise. Their finely educated palate, and well-honed taste buds serve them well in creating Cordon Bleu delicacies to impress the most cultivated gourmand. The Seven of Clubs may also have an inherent talent to become a connoisseur of fine wines and liqueurs. They can develop a discerning palate for the ever so subtle distinctions and nuances of flavor in the fine wines they love to imbibe in. They may easily acquire knowledge about the essence of fine wines, growing grapes, harvest, cultivation and quality of the vintage characteristics.

The Seven of Clubs, as a Queen, has a naturally fleshy body owing to their love of food and luscious treats. Yet, being the intellectual part of the Queen of Clubs, they possess a measure of discipline to help assuage the potential to become too overweight, and, they prefer appearing as attractive as possible. Many years ago, I knew a Seven of Clubs fashion model, who frequently endured extreme dieting. She loved food, but also had the Queen's need for attention and praise. Once a fashion designer told her she was too fat to wear his clothing on the runway. Afterwards she developed the unhealthy habit of binging and purging. Thus, bulimia became a bigger problem in her life, and eroded the enamel off her teeth. She withdrew from fashion and studied nutrition, to lose weight and to get healthy. She still craved the rich foods of her German ancestry, but found a healthy way to manage her weight without starving herself. Being a Queen, she considered herself to be a diet expert and had a tendency to lecture others on benefits of healthy food diets. But, she gave her food lectures whether someone was interested or not. Myself and others endured her endless food discourses, suffering in silence as she extolled the virtues of food combining. She tried to convince everyone of her religious food regime, which was her obsession. Often a Queen who is unable to control her personal problems will try to control others, which manifests as aggressive controlling behavior. Her diet lectures were difficult for people to endure, so they began to avoid her. Although she tried to hide it from others, she had not actually overcome her unhealthy binging and purging habits, especially when she overindulged in ice cream, cake and candy. Please keep in mind, if you or someone you know has an eating disorder, such as excessive dieting, or unhealthy binging and purging, it should be treated as an emotional psychological disorder as it can cause very serious illnesses. It is wise to seek medical help as all eating disorders can be quite harmful to one's health. Please seek medical advice and talk to your doctor. Remember, the instinctive center serves our greater desire to become enlightened.

The Seven of Clubs has the potential to understand the need for discipline to manage their large appetites and cravings, and is willing to learn how to manage their weight to maintain good health and wellbeing. For them, a little knowledge gives them a lot of power over their abundant Queen of Clubs desires which can otherwise potentially lead to addiction issues. They can do well coaching others to live a healthier lifestyle, by incorporating natural foods, and supplements into their lifestyle. One dear Seven of Clubs friend worked for a well-known national diet organization, and spoke about the benefits of healthy portions at their symposiums. She maintained a healthy diet and wanted what was naturally best for her body. She was happy to share and support others with the benefits of healthy nutrition. The Seven of Clubs can become adept at utilizing their knowledge to encourage others to develop enhanced discipline and self-control. As a Queen, they have a strong emotional element and they are naturally gregarious, so talking about food with other people is natural for them. Please take good care of your body with healthy balance.

The Six of Clubs:

The Six of Clubs is the emotional part of the Queen of Clubs and the most magnetically sensuously alluring, and perhaps the most sexual of the instinctive center's cards. The emotional part of the Queen of Clubs renders these individuals the most sensually responsive, and most reactive of the instinctive center. Being a Queen innately predisposes this center to intensely feel instinctive reactions and instinctive reflexes to sensual stimuli. She has the enhanced emotional element that sends her sensual message with lightning speed and efficiency to either respond to signals from others, or, to attract a desirable mate. She is quite passionate and fiery regards her rather tempestuous desires and needs. Her sensual requirements are rather voracious and as a queen are somewhat volatile as well. She may desire her lover compulsively, but after she is satisfied she may quickly dismiss them as an element of her volatile Queen flip. She is moody and demanding in her physical relationships and wants immediate gratification and abundant attention. This of course does not guarantee true love for her partner, but rather, is simply an attribute of the Queen's dynamic. After she gets what she wants, she tends to suddenly flip and lose interest, at least until she her cravings return, perhaps in the next moment. She is temperamental and lusty, with voracious physical appetites.

The Six of Clubs is particularly susceptible to the Queen's compulsive behavior, and may exhibit a sudden mood swing, from one extreme to the other. She may be obsessed with someone, or something, until she has had her needs met, after which she can just as impulsively flip, change her mind, change course, and perhaps move on to her next conquest, sexual or otherwise. Of all the centers, the Six of Clubs is probably the most susceptible to sexual addiction issues. She can also be extremely jealous and possessive of her lover. It is helpful to be aware of her suspicious nature, as this Queen can become vindictive. The Six of Clubs has an immediate instinctive reaction to any possible cheating, or, any overtures to one of her competitors, which she deems inappropriate. She demands all your attention and loyalty, regardless of whether or not she is willing to do the same for you.

The Six of Clubs has an addictive nature which can create difficulty controlling lusty indulgences, appetites and excesses. She has a voracious appetite for food, drink, and perhaps drugs, and is likely to experience the down side of her appetites with ongoing weight problems, illnesses, or hangovers. She is frequently on a diet of some sort, and will have a well-stocked medicine cabinet full of remedies for her excessive indulgent tendencies. The Six of Clubs may become a victim of her own pronounced neediness for food, drink, sex, drugs or whatever craving she is subject to. While the Six of Clubs is self-indulgent with large appetites, she is equally obsessive about her own physical attractiveness. The female will be quite sensually voluptuous, a Marilyn Monroe type, while the male is likely to be muscular with a layer of fleshiness covering his frame.

They may go to extremes to increase their powers of attraction. Both the female and the male Six of Clubs are both generally quite concerned about their need to satisfy their sensual cravings. They can be compulsive about their appearance to be alluring magnets to attract satisfying relationships. The Six of Clubs needs to learn to exercise discipline to gain control over their obsessive-compulsive tendencies and help them achieve healthy balance in managing their intense cravings. The Six of Clubs has an animal magnetism, and is quite adept at attracting mates and lovers. They can implement this natural magnetism to their advantage in the acting and modelling professions. As much as they are attracted to all that is desirable in the world, they are equally desirable to others, who find them quite alluring. Marilyn Monroe is still considered one of the most sensually attractive sex symbols in the world. And, as her biography states, she had her fair share of admirers and addictive traits. If the Six of Clubs develops the knowledge and ability to manage her vast appetites, she can successfully achieve better health overall.

The Five of Clubs:

The Five of Clubs is the moving part of the Queen of Clubs, and she tends to becomes intrigued with trendy exercise regimes, the latest diets and other health fads to help mitigate the effects of her indulgences. When a new health fad comes onto the market they will give it a try in an attempt to offset the downside of their indulgences. However, if they do not quickly achieve the promised results their initial interest wears off, the Queen flips, and they suddenly abandon the health regime as just another trendy fad. In actual fact, the new diet or health regime might actually work if they gave it sufficient time or if they simply made an honest effort to stick with it long enough. However, the Queens have a habit of losing interest rather rapidly and may abandon a regime if it is too demanding. When paired with discipline, the moving element of the Five of Clubs has the potential to develop good health and wellness. But, as the Queens tend to indulge in excess, she is still subject to sensual cravings, overeating, or, over imbibing. In an attempt to assuage weight gain and other potential health issues resulting from their excesses, they may engage in extreme physical exercises, or other activities such as hot saunas, and spa treatments.

I knew a Five of Clubs who became a devotee of Pilates for a short while, then suddenly switched to hatha yoga. It was difficult to keep track of her interests as she had a habit of becoming quite enthusiastic over novelties, whether it was food, exercise, or spirituality. At one point, she was extolling the virtues of an exotic Indian guru, but suddenly became quite fascinated with the Kabala. Her dining habits were equally changeable. She would speak reverently of the health benefits of macrobiotic dining, but shortly thereafter she might indulge in junk food from a fast food restaurant. Once we were at a health and wellness fair, where an abundance of healthy food options, were readily available. But, as soon as we got into the car she claimed that she was starving, and drove to the nearest fast food restaurant where she got a massive sausage sandwich accompanied by a large sugary soda. After her sandwich and soda indulgence, she announced she was exhausted and needed to go to her home to sleep. She moved from one rather extreme health trend to its absolute opposite, all the while seemingly unaware of all the contradictions.

The Five of Clubs tends to be physically involved in the pursuit of their object of desire, although they are relentless at changing their mind. As a Queen, they are quite passionate about their attractions and desires. But, it is beneficial to be aware of their opposite reactions, which are expressed in their sudden Queen flip. They are fiery and passionate about their attractions, and about satisfying their physical needs and desires. Whatever the sensory impulse, the Five of Clubs is intent upon having her sensual needs met, and may go to extremes to satisfy desires and cravings if necessary. The Five of Clubs is well suited to work in a health food store where they can extoll the virtues of all the new food trends. They might do well in a gymnasium, as a personal trainer or advisor. They may practice body building, but as a Queen, they tend to gain weight, so exercise might become obsessive. Owing to the emotional element of the Queen they gravitate towards other people; combined with the moving element, this can lead them to careers working in physical education, or becoming healthy weight loss advocates and entrepreneurs, or other trendy health fields.

Please keep in mind, we all have the Queen of Clubs within us, and we have all undoubtedly experienced her sudden passionate urges, and extreme sensory appetites on some occasions. Just take a moment and think of how you eagerly anticipate a delicious holiday feast, with all its luscious delights. But, afterwards you probably also experienced the rather uncomfortable feeling of having over indulged. Certainly, an individual who is centered in the Queen of Clubs will experience this on a rather frequent basis. However, each one of us has our own personal encounters with the emotional part of the instinctive center. Who amongst us can resist chocolate cake? The point is to bring balance to our appetites, which is vital for the hungry Queen of Clubs. By bringing mindful attention to sensory cravings and impulses, she can achieve enhanced physical wellness and better health.

The Jack of Clubs: Four, Three and Two of Clubs

The Jack of Clubs represents the moving part of the Instinctive center. It is helpful to remember that the Jacks serve as memory banks, and store all acquired information and data which is pertinent to their specific center's function. After information is input, and stored in the memory banks as data, it can be accessed for later use. But, the Jacks are also the most mechanical parts of the centers, as they tend to function habitually, and automatically, without attention or intentionality. Yet, their ability to retain vital information, and monitor functions, serves us well and helps keep our physical body in working order, so that glands and organs operate efficiently. With the Jack of Clubs, this stored data is vital in maintaining a well-balanced healthy body; provided good habits are also developed, and bad habits are avoided, or minimized.

Perhaps we can recognize that our physical bodies are similar to a finely tuned machine which has different working elements and parts, not unlike an automobile, or computer. We understand the value of keeping our car and computer in good working order, as we depend on them daily. It is highly beneficial to become a good caretaker of one's own physical body, and the Jack of Clubs alerts us when our body is in pain, or becoming ill. It is essential to take good care of your physical body with proper rest, nutrients and exercise.

Keywords associated with the Jacks: habitual, imitative, mechanical, automatic, superficial, simplistic, repetitive, conventional, common, spontaneous, routine, formulaic, and subjective.

Key behavior traits of the Jacks: Jacks think, speak and act in and with subjective generalities and superficialities, mimicking what others think, say or do without analysis or verification.

The Four of Clubs:

The Four of Clubs is the intellectual part of the Jack of Clubs. The intellectual element of the Four of Clubs predisposes this center to store information which is necessary to assist the body in maintaining good health. This is especially true when a person gets sick with a cold, cough, the flu, and other illnesses, or injuries. The Four of Clubs will automatically respond to illness with the helpful steps, such as alerting the physical body to go to bed when it has a fever, to assist with healing and recuperation. The Four of Clubs will stock the medicine cabinet with the essential items, such as aspirin, stomach medicine, a thermometer, and so on. In times of need, this center will ascend and take over, in order to care for the body to allow rest, and recuperation, to alleviate symptoms of illness, and heal. The Four of Clubs stores pertinent data that helps to keep us running efficiently, until we become ill or injured, and alerts us when our body is not working properly by reacting to pain. Pain tells us that something is wrong with our body. At times of injury or sickness, the memory banks of the instinctive center work quite well to help our body recover.

It is helpful to understand that the Instinctive Center is a remarkably intelligent center that works best when balanced harmoniously. A Four of Clubs person may possibly be rather quiet or unobtrusive, as their focus is the physical body, and its requirements. While they attend to their personal duties, it is the needs of their physical body that are of primary importance. As the intellectual part of the physical body's memory banks, the Four of Clubs is primarily concerned with maintenance and preservation of the physical body. Therefore, the Four of Clubs reminds us when it is mealtime, with sensations of hunger to alert us. Someone who is centered in the card will likely think in advance about having food prepared and readily available to ensure the body will be fed when hungry, and at the appropriate time. A Four of Clubs friend always takes her lunch to work, to be certain that she has a meal ready to eat at lunchtime. She said that it feels quite normal to bring food with her so she can take care of her needs in a timely manner. Another friend, who is centered in the Four of Clubs, works as a nurse at a medical center and she always has a first-aid remedy handy, such as an aspirin, cough drops, or a band-aid.

Unlike the Queen of Clubs, the Jack of Clubs is concerned with the most basic requirements of the physical body. The Four of Clubs is a remarkable center that reliably attends to most of our basic physical needs. We all have this center, although generally we are unaware of its functioning until we become hungry, injured or sick. There is a very practical element to the Four of Clubs with their function serving to maintain the physical body to keep it in good working order, and running efficiently, on a day to day basis, in a consistent manner.

The Three of Clubs:

The Three of Clubs is the emotional part of the Jack of Clubs. This is the card that adds an emotional element to the basic physical functioning of the Jack of Clubs. Keep in mind, the memory banks of the human organism are uniquely equipped to keep our instinctive center in good working order. This center is where many of our remembered sensory preferences, likes and dislikes are stored from past experiences. This data includes favorite foods, tastes and flavors that remind us of childhood, or other experiences we associate with feeling good. People centered in the Three of Clubs may tend to focus their attention on personal comforts and satisfying the most basic primal instinctive urges to fulfill their physical needs. Their pantries will be well stocked with their favorite foods and beverages, while their homes will reflect their need to maintain preferred creature comforts. We all experience the Three of Clubs when we have a sudden flash back to our childhood, or other past event, when we smell, or taste something that evokes that particular moment in our life. It may happen unexpectedly, but we are transported back in time.

A family member has a friend whom I remember quite well from my childhood. She always said her goal in life was to get married, have children and live on a farm, like her parents did. This represented comfort and security and all that she really wanted in life. She married quite young to her high school sweetheart, and shortly thereafter had a child. Over the years, she stayed in touch and occasionally I heard about her growing family and life on their farm. Many years later, when I learned about centers, it was clear to me that she was the perfect example of the Three of Clubs. Since that time, so long ago I've met other people centered in this card, but she stands out quite definitively as someone whose life choices were decided early, based in the Three of Clubs.

People centered in the Three of Clubs may have specific tastes, likes and dislikes that they favor, and, in fact, which they rely on to help them keep their focus. They have learned what they prefer and what works for them, and they do not necessarily feel the need to venture into unknown territory with their diet or any other element of their lifestyle. Their tastes and preferences may be somewhat simplified, but their choices are based on what feels physically natural to their center of gravity. We all have the Three of Clubs within serving our instinctive center's needs. We can observe it rather clearly, when we taste something delicious that reminds of a good, or happy experience from our past. These memories and preferences, are recorded and stored in our Three of Clubs physical memory banks, as sensations, which we may recall on occasion.

The Two of Clubs:

The Two of Clubs is the moving part of the Jack of Clubs and represents our most primal center regarding the physical needs and functions of the human organism. This is the center that is responsible for the most basic and essential functioning, which is necessary to maintain the health and operation of our physical body. The Two of Clubs is the center that serves as the memory banks for our basic daily physical wellbeing, and the survival of the human organism. Under ideal conditions it works efficiently to maintain physical health. For the most part this center works mechanically, more or less on automatic pilot, and with good reason. The Two of Clubs is connected to the smooth functioning of our physical body, life energy and addressing our physical needs. For example, when we are tired, the Two of Clubs works correctly and we go to sleep, quite naturally. When we are hungry, we eat. Hence the Two of Clubs working optimally helps us stay healthy, and it keeps our body in good working order. The Two of Clubs works exceptionally well to address our most basic physical needs in life. Most of the natural functions of our physical body are automatically managed by this center. A person centered in the Two of Clubs will most likely be an individual whose main focus in life is to maintain physical health, have a secure home and enough food to eat. Their primary concerns may be food, shelter, sex and procreation, and simply living their life. Of course, these are the common and most basic needs which we all share in our physical realm. Someone who is centered in the Two of Clubs might be attracted to jobs which are involved with elements of a physical nature, such as farming, cooking and baking. Careers they may be attracted to could involve physical needs, and products that are essential for maintaining health of the body. Over the years I have met many people who were centered in the Two of Clubs. They were all interested in health and physical fitness. One worked as a masseuse in physical therapy, and another worked in a health spa. Another worked with the food preparation at a hotel restaurant, and another was a successful tomato farmer. All of them seemed to derive great satisfaction from their work.

People who choose to live close to nature and who prefer to be unencumbered by the ambitions of the ordinary commercial world may be centered in the Two of Clubs. Possibly some of the more primitive people who inhabit the remote places on planet Earth, may be centered in this card, and they follow their natural instincts for their survival. Remember, the Two of Clubs within everyone helps maintain human existence to populate the planet and perpetuate humanity with this essential instinct for survival. And, it is helpful to understand that the vast numbers of people who constitute the masses are motivated by this most basic instinct for survival. Quite fortunately we each have the Two of Clubs within us to keep our physical human organism functioning. This center helps us every minute of each day to stay alive by automatically utilizing the data stored in its memory banks. For example, we get hungry so we eat, we get tired we go to sleep. The Two of Clubs has the amazing ability to help us simply stay alive, and it is not really necessary for us to think about this, as the Two of Clubs memory banks do it for us.

Understanding that we each contain all of the centers within, from the King of Hearts to the Two of Clubs, helps to lend relativity to the concept of centers. We can appreciate that each center is vital for our existence.

CHAPTER 9

THE ACES AND JOKERS: SELF AWARENESS, HIGHER CONSCIOUSNESS AND HIGHER CENTERS

In a deck of playing cards, the Aces, and the Jokers represent a unique category of their own. These cards symbolize an elevated state of consciousness and enlightenment. This heightened state of consciousness is usually thought to be rare in ordinary realms of human awareness. However, accessing higher centers is certainly well within our realm of possibility. Yet, higher centers do not automatically function within us, nor do we experience them in ordinary states of awareness, which we generally experience in our day to day life. This is primarily because we tend to live, and experience our lives, while immersed in chronic habitual and mechanical patterns of behavior. Ordinarily, we are unaware of our vast potential to experience these higher centers as they must be accessed in a conscious state of self-awareness. We are born with higher centers, but because of acquired traits and habitual patterns of behavior, we do not utilize them. These higher centers are innate, but are not automatically activated, and must be developed with attentive mindful self-observation and objective intentionality.

Buddha attained enlightenment, and there is an abundance of evidence that many others have also. In most esoteric and mystical teachings, there is a reference to those who have reached the higher levels of being. As we make efforts to become more aware we have the potential to raise our personal level of being. In the Fourth Way system of knowledge, it is said that the functioning of the higher centers would be a permanent property of one who has worked intentionally to raise their level of being. These higher levels are the realms of the Buddha's, and the other conscious beings who made efforts to reach permanent states of higher conscious awareness and enlightenment.

Addressing the highest levels of awareness may be beyond the scope of a book; however, I wish to mention it with hopes to inspire you. We each have within us the potential to awaken, to live our life consciously, and, to experience the elevated awareness of the higher centers. One teacher advised, to awaken and become enlightened one must act as if one is already awake and conscious. This unique statement opened a door to enhanced possibilities within my personal work. And, to live in this more conscious manner, became my new directive to reach my own miraculous universe within.

It becomes more apparent that awakening and becoming enlightened is well within our natural potential. The essential key to awaken, is first to realize that one is usually quite asleep. However, awakening and experiencing higher states of consciousness is our birthright. What is required is the relinquishment of illusionary internal barriers and elimination of self-doubt, which hinders and prevents personal growth and self-transformation. To awaken to higher centers also requires the absence of negativity, the absence of identification, the absence of imagination, the absence of false personality, and the absence of chief features. We will look into these matters in subsequent chapters. But, Ouspensky and Gurdjieff both advised that one must recognize the need to reduce one's energy expenditures in unnecessary actions, and in habitual patterns of behavior. One may also enhance, and attain higher states of awareness by implementing simplicity, honesty, purity, compassion, internal balance, moderation, self-discipline, and mindfulness presence in one's daily life activities, and in one's interactions with others. Mindful self-observation with presence is the starting point.

Be assured that gaining increased self-awareness and activating higher centers is possible for you. It is well within your personal destiny to master and govern your life with enlightened self-awareness, by observing your centers, and being intentional with feelings, thoughts, actions, while consistently monitoring your physical sensory experiences. Awakening is an equal opportunity for everyone. Always know, you have the absolute right and the inherent ability to awaken to a more enlightened awareness, and to activate and experience your innate higher centers. Remember, no other person and no group can ever awaken you. You can only awaken yourself, with your own personal efforts. We begin self-study with our consistent efforts of mindful self-observation in the moment.

To commence, it is essential to gain personal insight into the basic esoteric premises of the centers. The previous segments gave you a foundation, upon which to build your understanding of the centers. Again, we are born with the four primary centers, Hearts, Diamonds, Spades and Clubs, which generally function normally in most healthy individuals. While experiencing ordinary states of awareness, we can become more aware of centers as they function, by observing our self attentively as we live our life. By working intentionally, we begin to witness our life as it is happening, which gives more control to manage our life, and help us arrive at our essential potential to awaken. Remember, we have the ability to activate higher centers and to achieve a more conscious psychological evolution. This was the focus of

Peter Ouspensky's work and teaching, and has become my humble aim.

The following descriptions are a brief overview of the immense possibilities of the higher centers. Though we do not normally access these centers, we can begin to make efforts to experience them with greater frequency. Once you have an understanding of their limitless potential, you will begin to realize your true potential to have a more enlightened destiny, to awaken and become conscious.

Regarding the Aces

The Aces represent the elevated awareness of higher centers, which one can attain with consistent efforts. The higher centers can be accessed with our conscious efforts based on understanding. Here the Aces will be discussed as a group rather than breaking down the individual suits. This is due to the nature of their elevated stature, and connectedness serving as the Higher Emotional Center, the Higher Intellectual Center and the combined Higher Sex Center. The Aces essentially represent the higher centers which are available to us as higher functions that can be accessed with consistent conscious efforts. Although the Aces are innate, we are not born with them activated. We can access their higher realm, by making consistent sincere efforts. To activate the Aces, one must initially gain control over the four primary centers, and over one's habitual behaviors, to achieve balance within.

There are rare moments in life, when we experience the higher centers in an instant, as a brief flash of consciousness. This is usually caused by a startling event, or a sudden accident, which causes one to instantly come to full attention, with total awareness. Though it may not last, afterwards you will remember these unique moments with unusual lucidity, and crystal clarity. Developing the heightened level of conscious awareness to experience the Aces, requires consistent intentional work on oneself with sincere and impartial self-observation. The higher centers can function within us if we make ongoing intentional efforts to self-observe, as we also stop energy drains, which emanate from our false personality, negative emotions, imagination, and identification. I will go into more detail about these particular limiting ideas and issues in the following chapters.

The Aces represent higher centers, and the cards below the Aces, are referred to as the four primary centers. The four primary centers are generally functioning in most healthy humans at birth, although they need training to develop. However, it is helpful to understand that these basic functions and processes do not normally require intentionality, or our conscious efforts. Understanding the functions of our primary centers helps one to recognize how rarely the Aces are activated in our ordinary awareness. With discipline and consistent mindful self-observation, activating higher centers is possible. Ouspensky said that man is like an airplane that doesn't know it can fly. This analogy applies well to the Aces. You are limited only by your personal self-doubt, and lack of effort.

Occasionally, one may experience the Aces in an altered state of consciousness or awareness, such as serenity, or tranquility; but, this is usually transient, and impermanent. By working on yourself with mindful self-observation to gain enhanced self-knowledge and self-awareness, you will begin to activate the heightened state to evoke and awaken your higher centers. By activating the Aces, one may experience the feeling of transcendental oneness, with all, and everything. In the Aces, one has the potential for vast perceptions and understandings, which transcend the ordinary human condition. But remember, this does not happen automatically, nor will it happen instantly. Ouspensky said that our efforts are our money; with regards experiencing higher states.

When one gradually activates and accesses the Aces, one may receive impressions, which are not normally available in our ordinary consciousness. Yet, these rarefied impressions are glimpses into the highest potential for human awareness. Envision living in harmonious equipoise, and receiving lucid impressions, without words, and without descriptions or explanations. Of course, these flashes of insight and limitless comprehension are inexplicable in our ordinary language. And, while words are rather clumsy to describe the higher centers, words are all I have at present for this book.

An elevated state of pure perception, lucid understanding and direct knowing, would be properties of the higher centers. Aces, as higher centers, process rarefied perceptions of very fine impressions. Refined impressions would only be received with the finely tuned antennae of acute perceptiveness. This is not a reference to extrasensory perceptions, which may be a property of the King of Clubs. The Aces are highly refined centers which function as organs of acute sensitivity, but, do not fall under the many dense laws which govern the ordinary five senses. It is said that the Aces have much higher capabilities, which are not limited by our ordinary senses. We can begin to grasp these rarefied organs of perception when we realize that life is not only restricted to that which governs the five basic senses, from which we normally live.

As you develop your personal understanding, and gain greater command over the primary centers, you will begin to recognize your limitless potential. One can begin to attain higher levels of awareness by first observing the primary centers within oneself. One must make conscientious efforts in order to take greater command of one's personal awareness with sincere self-observation. Balancing the four primary centers, will ultimately serve to elevate your level of consciousness.

Remember, we can become more than we are at the present. We can rouse our primary centers to awaken from our ordinary states of awareness, and activate our dormant potential by employing consistent intentional self-observation. We can gain greater self-awareness to reach self-realization.

Einstein said that we only use a fraction of our intellectual powers. Therefore, it is reasonable to assume that we use only a fraction of our higher center's potentiality as well. We can be much more than we are at present, and with sincere consistent efforts we can awaken and activate our own higher centers

Regarding the Jokers

The Jokers represent the highest potential for human consciousness, complete self-realization, permanent consciousness and self-awareness. The Jokers are in a category of their own. It is said, the heightened level of awareness which these two cards represent, implies the highest state of consciousness possible for a human being, a level quite rare in the realm of ordinary human awareness. The two Joker cards represent the state of permanent consciousness of a fully realized being who has achieved total self-mastery. These are the higher levels of mankind which are reverently referred to in sacred, mystical, and esoteric wisdom traditions. Different traditions have different names, titles and distinctions for these higher beings, to denote their uniquely elevated, perhaps God-like status.

Oddly, the Jokers in a deck of playing cards are generally regarded as unnecessary, and, as a result, are discarded. They are not used in most card games, and are therefore assumed to be disposable. It is ironic that the highest cards in a deck are considered unnecessary and useless. Perhaps, as in life, we assume we are already conscious, hence we do not seek higher states of consciousness. This correlates with the dismissal of the Joker cards, as unnecessary. It seems the Jokers are not necessary to participate and function in the ordinary states of human awareness. However, with the goal of self-awareness comes the added impetus to reach these rare centers, as they represent the highest state of consciousness possible.

It is odd they are called Jokers if these are the highest centers. Great beings throughout history have been called foolish, and were often persecuted during their lifetime. Subsequently, they were recognized as true masters who made substantial contributions to benefit humanity, and who left a massive body of wisdom knowledge preserved in art, literature, mathematics, and science as their legacy. The Jokers were those who sought true wisdom despite personal peril, who succeeded in attaining their highest consciousness.

It is said, the Jokers imply permanent higher consciousness, with the potential to enhance, or change one's destiny. Such a being would in not be limited by the ordinary influences of life. At present, we can only speculate the possibilities this state may imply. This heightened level of consciousness would allow one to be under less internal, and external influences, and would give one conscious control over one's emotions, thoughts, actions and inclinations. Although we may not be at this level of conscious awareness, we can certainly aspire to attain it. Those who work on them self with attention and intentionality, may occasionally have fleeting glimpses of the Jokers. Although this heightened level of awareness takes effort to achieve, it will serve as inspiration to strive for a world quite different from the ordinary world one usually habituates.

The Jokers represent self-mastery and true will power which is achieved with consistent efforts. To attain the consciousness of the Jokers requires unrelenting perseverance, whilst making consistent efforts to work on oneself with mindful self-observation while eliminating negative self-defeating elements within oneself. Remember, the Jokers represent the ultimate enlightenment which we human beings can attain.

By balancing the four primary lower centers, developing harmony and greater equilibrium within, you will gradually elevate your level of consciousness, and your level of being. The Jokers represent the highest potential for human consciousness. It may be rare to experience the Jokers in our everyday life, but, it is not impossible and is within our realm of possibilities. We only need to remember the Buddha and countless others who have achieved enlightenment for our inspiration and reassurance. Illumination, Satori, Nirvana, Samadhi, Samyama, and all the other names for awakening affirm that we too can each individually achieve this heightened state of consciousness with and by our own consistent sincere efforts.

Please know, achieving higher consciousness is your birthright.

Your path is within you.

CHAPTER 10

PRACTICAL APPLICATION ~ EVALUATING YOUR PERSONAL CENTER OF GRAVITY

As we learn about the unique characteristics of the different centers within we begin to witness how they continuously exert their influences on us in every moment. By practicing mindful self-observation, you will recognize the varying nuances of the primary centers. These ideas might be quite new to you, and initially it will take intentional effort to assimilate how the various centers function, influence and manifest. As you practice mindful self-observation you will gradually be able to determine which of the centers functions most frequently in your life. Employing sincere mindful self-observation, allows one to gain vital insight and self-knowledge with increased self-awareness. Using these practical tools with ongoing right effort, helps one to achieve personal growth in a gradually increasing manner. Working on oneself to acquire, and enhance self-awareness, helps to circulate energy in an ascending direction, not unlike an ascending musical octave. The ancient Greek mathematician Pythagoras observed the law of octaves at work in all of nature, and each one of us is part of this magnificent natural world.

Mindful self-observation brings attention to your life, assisting you to be self-aware in the present moment. This lends powerful energy to your work on yourself as you learn about the centers of influence within. As you gain understanding of distinctive traits and functions of the primary centers, you will recognize how distinctly they manifest in your life. You may not immediately recognize the variances of each center, but continue observing. With patience and practice their shades of difference will become more apparent. As you continue to practice mindful self-observation, you will see habitual patterns emerging from certain centers. At this point, it would be helpful to make notes of any patterns you observe to help you formulate which center is manifesting repeatedly. Your notes will be useful in helping you make comparisons between the centers, and in determining your own personal center of gravity. Employing consistent mindful self-observation, you will begin to recognize which of the four primary centers manifests most regularly as you go through your day. Keep in mind, your center of gravity influences and determines the majority of your experiences and manifestations, as you live your life

As one particular center is typically dominant, as your personal center of gravity, it is beneficial to know how this specific influence is guiding your life experiences, and directing or limiting your potential. By learning about these ideas, and incorporating them into your life, you are taking a major step in developing enhanced self-awareness. It is helpful to think of the wisdom of centers as a psychological science which can help you gain self-knowledge. This unique science will help lay the foundation for truly knowing one self, which can be a powerful transformational experience. In the beginning, simply observe your natural inclinations impartially, without favoring one suit, card, or center over another. Allow yourself sufficient time to truly understand how all the centers, and their parts, function and manifest. This requires consistent efforts with self-observation, and it may take practice before you can make an accurate assessment of which particular suit, and card, has the most influence in your life. Again, as you become acquainted with the centers it will help to take notes of what you observe in yourself, to compare with the different card descriptions. Some centers may feel familiar to you, while others may be unfamiliar, or they may function in a manner different from your own experience. As you begin to understand the inclinations and tendencies of each suit and card, you will start to see more clearly what influences you most in your own life.

It will be beneficial to read the descriptions of all the centers in order to get a clearer idea which card feels most natural to your own essential nature. Refer back to the descriptions to maintain an overview of your understanding. Continue to mindfully self-observe as you monitor your feelings, thoughts and actions. This will help you develop greater insight into your essential natural. You will soon begin to recognize which iconic royal suit and card seems to resonate with your inner being. Be attentive to distinctive nuances of each center to determine which feels most familiar to you, and which predominates as a primary influence in your life. Be patient and allow yourself time to evaluate which might be your dominant center. Whichever suit you determine you are centered in, will be affected by other factors, such as which part of the suit. But, in the beginning, it is not necessary to be overly concerned with which part of the suit you are centered in. Your primary center of influence will gradually become more apparent as you continue to practice mindful self-observation. However, it is a remarkable achievement to simply recognize that you are emotionally centered, intellectually centered, moving centered, or instinctively centered. This discovery in itself explains a great deal about why each one of us is the way we are because of influences from within. The suit that resonates most strongly with you is a clue to help you to recognize your personal center of gravity. You may not recognize your personal center of gravity immediately, but do not worry. Often, people decide upon one center, and then later, they realize that they are centered elsewhere. This is because, certain parts of centers have similarities to other parts of centers. For example, someone centered in the Queen of Diamonds may initially suspect they are centered in the King of Hearts, which is because of the intellectual and the emotional element that is present and influencing their life. This can occur with different centers which share similar elements, though they manifest differently. You will gradually determine whether you are centered in the Kings, Queens, or the Jacks, of the Hearts, Diamonds, Clubs or Spades suits.

As you observe yourself and review how each center functions, you will become more familiar with the quite different distinctions within the four primary centers. Your efforts will give you a solid foundation, and enhanced comprehension of the centers to help you determine which suit exerts the primary influence over you in your life. Practice consistent self-observation, and record your personal discoveries and findings. Taking notes will help you to see your repetitive patterns more clearly. Your notes will help you arrive at a more objective assessment of what your personal center of gravity might be. Remember, it takes consistent observation and sincerity to isolate the one particular center which is the main influence over your entire life. By incorporating the information about centers into your normal daily life, you will understand why you feel, think, behave, sense, and generally manifest as you do. Consistent mindful self-observation will help you recognize if your essential nature is emotional, intellectual, moving or instinctive.

With enriched self-understanding, you will develop a clearer perception of how to improve your life, and also, to seek what you truly yearn for deep within. Your self-knowledge will become the directive for your life, guiding you as you evolve and transform. Ask yourself some simple, honest and basic questions that can help you see yourself more authentically as you really are. Do you experience feelings of sentimentality, melancholy, happiness, or other emotions about people? Are you interested in art and literature? Are you a mathematics whiz, a science buff, a geeky nerd, or a crossword puzzle aficionado? Or, are you motivated and activated by physical movement, dance, athletics and sports? Do you intuit and sense your way through life with the subtle psychic impressions you pick up on? Try to notice which center seems to influence and stimulate you most often, whether it is emotions, thinking, moving or the physical senses. Recognizing this will be extremely useful in helping you determine which card is your personal center of gravity.

Developing a clear understanding of your internal influences and motivators allows you to gain much greater control over your life. Knowing which influences from within motivate, define and activate your life, has great practical value for your personal growth. Making consistent efforts with self-observation will be instrumental in allowing you to see yourself with clarity, which increases your self-awareness, and will enhance the smooth functioning of all your centers. Our dominant center of gravity is where we generally emanate from and also, where we habitually make decisions from. Overall, our center of gravity affects and influences everything that we feel, think, do, and experience in our normal daily life, throughout our entire life. This center is also the key influence and stimulus from where you derive your personal perceptions of reality. Everything in your life is affected by it. Initially, simply observe to determine your primary influencing suit. Investigate all the suits, and observe how they manifest in your normal daily life. After you have decided upon your primary influencing suit, you can move on to the more advanced work of discovering which numeric part of the suit you emanate from as your center of gravity.

It is also helpful to realize that there are numerous external influences that intervene in our life, which affect our choices, our relationships, and so on. These external influences may not always permit us to exercise our authentic inner predisposition, so we often make personal adjustments, whether we wish to, or not. However, with mindful self-observation, you can achieve more personal effectiveness, without modifying your true self unnecessarily. When you are present in the moment, it slows down reactions and responses, allowing you to make more selective decisions and choices which are in line with your true needs. Being present with mindful self-observation helps to minimize negative energies which may be circulating in your thought processes, particularly about what other people think about you which might affect your decisions.

The force from external influences can sometimes lead us astray, and away from our true essential nature. Studying centers will help you evaluate your center of gravity, so you will recognize your true needs, your natural talents, abilities, tendencies and inclinations. This knowledge will give you strength to create more positive outcomes for yourself. Our center of gravity affects virtually everything we do for our entire life. Consistent efforts to observe yourself with the aim to gain self-knowledge and self-awareness will help lead you away from harmful and habitual behaviors that might limit you in your life.

Though we have all the centers within us, only a few are ever fully accessed, or linked together in a balanced manner. All the centers are rarely utilized to their highest capacity. Our center of gravity steers the course of our life, but a higher aim is to balance our centers for more harmony. As a result, we may function less than optimal. We are capable of so much more than we usually experience in our daily life, as we perform our habitual routines, and activities. Despite the influence of our center of gravity, we may also fluctuate from one center to another, depending on the external circumstances and the people we are with. When we are hungry we may basically become our instinctive center in that moment. The instinctive center will ascend so that we provide it with the nourishment it requires. However, this does not necessarily imply you are instinctively centered. Likewise, if you run to catch a bus, or enjoy throwing a Frisbee on the beach, this also does not necessarily imply you are moving centered. It may simply be that in these moments you access your moving center to get somewhere, and it feels good to exercise your body.

Find what you personally gravitate toward naturally to help narrow it down. Use the descriptions about each center as you practice mindful self-observation. If your relationships with friends, family, and other people tend to dominate your feelings, interests, and fills your schedule, this might be an indication that you are emotionally centered. If you are keenly interested in studying to develop your academic knowledge, this may indicate you are intellectually centered. If you are physically coordinated, agile, excel at sports, and actively participate in athletics, it is quite likely that you are moving centered. If your life revolves around your physical wellbeing, gratifying your physical senses, and you have strong intuition, or even psychic abilities, this may suggest you are instinctively centered. Make notes of all the different character traits you experience within yourself. Pay attention to your feelings, thoughts, actions and your senses. Try to be impartial and completely honest, as this will assist you in determining which suit predominates most naturally within your life. This will help you to discover your personal center of gravity.

Please do not to judge yourself when you make an observation. Simply be impartial about what you see. We each have all the centers within us, but, the center that tends to predominate is generally our center of gravity. Occasionally, we recognize that certain feelings or activities do not come easy to us, because they do not naturally occur, or manifest in our essential nature. For example, it may appeal to someone to become an Olympic athlete; but, not everyone is a natural born athlete. If this person has never excelled at sports, or moving centered activities it may not be a realistic goal. Of course, this is a very broad example, but it illustrates how we may have goals which are inconsistent with our essential nature, and our personal reality. Continue to observe yourself as much as possible to increase your self-awareness. Record your observations to use as your own personal research database to refer back to. It is reasonably likely that you may make a few wrong guesses, or minor errors at the inception of your study, but do not be concerned. Just keep observing yourself and with continued self-observation you will discover your personal center of gravity.

The key is to unlock the mysteries of yourself within your true essential nature. We have all the centers within us, and they will all probably manifest at various times. We have an emotional center that may sometimes cry at a sad movie and remembers a friend's birthday. We have an intellectual center that takes in information, processes the data and has the ability to remember and utilize details we have learned. We have a moving center to move the physical body in our activities and towards our various destinations. The instinctive center alerts us when it is time to eat or sleep, and, can also sense danger to alert us to protect our self. You have all the centers within you to experience. Knowing this provides you with the opportunity to experience them all with objectivity and increased intentionality. For example, it can be advantageous to call upon the diplomacy of the King of Hearts to make emotional decisions, or, to compassionately understand and help others. You can learn to access all of the other centers to benefit yourself, and others. Continue to self-observe as you go through your day to see the different centers arise and function.

As you gain self-knowledge, you will naturally gravitate to live more within your essential nature. Our energy emanations shift as we become more naturally who we really are. But, these changes do not occur overnight. Studying the centers within your self will naturally enhance your personal awareness. You may discover that certain habits which seem difficult for you to control, or even observe for that matter, may be imbedded within a mechanical tendency which is programmed into a certain center. With consistent mindful self-observation, you can break free from habitual behaviors and mechanical tendencies. Once you begin to see yourself more clearly you can begin to make necessary adjustments, perhaps incrementally, but we each must begin where we are right now. And, from where we are now, we can begin to advance forward with mindful self-observation to make improvements and changes to our life. Blending and fusing the knowledge of centers with the powerful tool of mindful self-observation will reveal deeper aspects of your life that may have mystified or confused you. Employing sincere self-observation as you monitor the centers as they function, helps you see your true nature with enhanced clarity. As you increasingly experience and live from your true essential nature regularly, your life will consequently attract more natural energy from external sources as well. As you acquire a deeper understanding of how the centers influence everything that you feel, think and do in life, it will help you to function more naturally from your own center of gravity. As we become more comfortable within, our life begins to feel more comfortable overall.

Your efforts to gain self-knowledge, and understand the centers, while practicing mindful self-observation, will open up possibilities that may have seemed unattainable before. As you study and integrate these practical esoteric ideas into your life perhaps you will discover new interests, or undeveloped talents which have lain dormant until now. Truly understanding your predominant center of gravity allows you to explore avenues that may have previously felt closed off to you, perhaps because of self-doubt. As you self-observe, you will start to recognize your inherent talents and natural abilities, which will allow you to fully access them with greater ease and self-confidence. It can be as simple as just recognizing what you are naturally drawn to, whether it is art, literature, science, sports and physical movement, or the world of the senses. At the core of your being there is an essential blueprint for what you are best suited. Acknowledging your fundamental inner core blueprint will help you gain more confidence to achieve your goals.

For example, an old friend really loved to bake since she was a young girl. It seemed as if she could almost magically intuit her delicious recipes. She worked as a secretary, but was not genuinely satisfied at her job. However, she simply did not feel confident enough to open her own bakery. When she began to study the wisdom of the centers, she soon realized that she was instinctively centered in the Seven of Clubs, as the intellectual part of the Queen of Clubs. It became clear that she had a natural affinity for cooking, and a highly discerning palate, able to create delicious recipes that everyone enjoyed. Eventually she opened a small, but, charming bakery that was quite successful. This is an example of how you can utilize your personal center of gravity for your own best and highest interests.

Keep in mind, your aim to gain enhanced self-knowledge lays the foundation for gaining greater personal self-awareness. As we raise our level of self-knowledge we inevitably bring a higher level of understanding to what we truly value in our life and in others. One begins to live from this heightened understanding which benefits all aspects of one's life. Comprehending the simple reality that you can develop you highest potential by becoming more self-aware, will help propel you forward to achieve the higher levels in your personal growth. Keep in mind that without a solid foundation of self-knowledge we are like an unfinished work of art still in the process of being created. In this case, you are the artist and the creation is your inner world of self-awareness. Consciousness itself becomes the art form one which is aspiring to master.

Self-knowledge is pivotal to enhance your grasp of life and your role in creating the reality you live. You can certainly increase your self-knowledge which is vital to gaining conscious self-awareness. As you study the manifestations, qualities and tendencies of each suit, the Hearts Diamonds, Spades and Clubs, you will gain an overview of the centers to help you to determine your personal center of gravity. Observing the details in your life will help you recognize which of the centers feels most natural and familiar to you. As you observe and evaluate your personal manifestations and tendencies it will gradually become apparent which iconic suit feels most comfortable to you, and which card has the greatest influence in your life. With consistent mindful self-observation, you will witness your personal center of gravity as it is manifesting.

Determining your center of gravity by employing consistent self-observation, will serve you well to develop and enhance your self-awareness. This will lead you forward and assist you to experience the higher levels of consciousness. Remember, it is vital to be impartial about what you see in yourself, and how you manifest in your life. While our personal interests may vary over time, our natural essential tendencies remain fairly consistent. When you consistently witness your personal center of gravity with clarity, you will begin to understand how it's distinctive influence has shaped, developed and directed nearly everything in your life. However, this shaping and directing may be somewhat lopsided if other parts of other centers have remained unexplored and undeveloped. This is precisely where the knowledge of the centers can help you to enter uncharted realms within yourself, by intentionally accessing and experiencing all of the centers. Getting acquainted with your center of gravity will be of great assistance as you move forward toward increased self-awareness, and self-knowledge. However, it is vital to also monitor the other centers to see where any imbalances might be occurring and causing disharmony in your life. While we are shaped by our center of gravity, we need to work intentionally to bring balance to all of our centers.

Developing our abilities, tendencies and natural talents to the highest level is where we can really excel. Yet, we may become a bit confused while trying to determine our natural inherent talents, abilities and our true inner potential. It is beneficial to develop personal inner guidance, by learning about centers to discover and unlock your true essential nature, and to work with your natural abilities, talents, and authentic potential. Discovering your personal center of gravity will help pave the way to living in your true essential nature.

Balancing Centers:

Understanding how your center of gravity has shaped your decisions, your personal preferences, your aims and goals, will help bring more balance into your life. As you self-observe you will begin to see areas of your life that are neglected. This system of knowledge suggests that we tend to have lopsided development, which is often due to our unmonitored habitual behaviors. While this lopsidedness is unconscious in its manifestation, we can minimize imbalances by bringing more attention and intentionality into the moment, to help activate other centers with conscious awareness. We all tend to naturally favor certain areas of life which are most important to us, but we also tend to habitually ignore, and neglect other areas of life that are less interesting, and perhaps less important to us. Try to be honest and impartial as you consider this. If there are specific issues in your life that are not running smoothly, this may indicate an area which you neglect or ignore. Other areas of your life may thrive, simply because this is where you put most of your energy. As you think about your personal priorities, you may begin to see which center seems to command most of your attention. This center may dominate your life, at the risk of causing imbalance in other centers.

We each have our natural predispositions, which focuses most of our life energy to, and from our personal center of gravity. This may seem to be correct on the surface; however, we can look at a simple example to gain a more comprehensive grasp of how things work. An automobile requires the participation of all of its parts, and components in order to function properly, so we can drive from point A, to point B. Obviously, our car's engine must work in harmony to cooperate with the wheels, the gears, the brakes, and so forth. In reality, we are not so different from our automobile in this regard. We have parts, and components in our centers that need to be exercised in harmony. Every organ of our body must work with and cooperate with all other organs for optimal health. And, our centers must also work together harmoniously, so we can achieve our maximum potential. The idea of regarding one self and one's centers as comparable to an automobile may seem rather odd to you; however, Gurdjieff and Ouspensky both referred to humans as machines. So, if you consider our functions and different organs, it is not so peculiar. This comparison helps illustrate disparities, as neglect in our centers, which cause imbalances. Imbalances reveal where we do not address our emotions, thoughts, physical activities, and physical needs and senses equally. It is beneficial to be aware of and exercise all centers with balance and harmony to function optimally.

It should be fairly apparent that to achieve more harmony and balance within, one needs to pay attention to all of one's centers. The most difficult part is learning that we are composed of many different centers, each with their own unique functions, which you are learning by reading this book. To become balanced, healthy and whole, we need to harmonize our centers. This helps us get to the core of our being as our true essential nature, which needs to be recognized, understood and expressed. We can accomplish this effectively with mindful self-observation, and by paying attention with intentionality, to access and activate all centers more naturally in our life. This very simple holistic plan to become self-aware with self-knowledge, is not difficult or mysterious. With the aim to develop one's awareness and consciousness, the holistic approach is most helpful. You begin your journey to arrive at higher states of conscious awareness, with self-knowledge as your foundation. You alone must become the expert on you, by learning about your centers with a holistic approach to gain understanding and balance within. In the contemporary popular culture, the concept of developing a holistic approach to living one's life for optimal health, is clearly part of its mass appeal. We can frequently see people jogging and bicycling along pathways, dressed in athletic or yoga garb, armed with hefty bottles of water. Living and being holistic is quite trendy, and implies treating and exercising the whole body. Thus, it seems quite evident that in developing self-awareness to reach higher states of consciousness, we must likewise employ the holistic approach to balance all of our centers.

Depending upon your personal center of gravity, you may discover that you have been relatively inattentive, or unaware of the other centers. For example, your emotional center may be neglected as you pursue your intellectual endeavors. Or, you may discover that your instinctive center tends to govern and dominate most of your life, but you neglect your moving center's needs. In addition to our centers being out of balance, wrong work can also occur. For example, the emotional center cannot efficiently, or safely drive your car. The moving center cannot make appropriate emotional decisions, and so forth. Accessing all centers helps you achieve and maintain balance in your life. Mindful self-observation and enhanced self-awareness will naturally help to bring vital attention and balance to your centers. Certainly, as you begin to recognize your own personal center of gravity, and how it manifests, this will help you to understand why you feel and think as you do, and why you are interested in, or attracted to particular people, ideas, activities, and so on.

The elements which comprise your life will become more comprehensible, as you consistently observe yourself to help make sense of your life. You will see why and how your personal interests, tendencies, natural talents and abilities manifest as they do. As you begin to witness your center of gravity it becomes imperative to pay close attention to the aspects of your life which you habitually neglect. For example, an emotionally centered person may not give thought to physical exercise, or eating healthy foods. But, when the emotional center ignores exercise, and eats unhealthy foods, the instinctive center suffers, and one becomes ill, or gains excess weight. The moving centered individual may be so involved in physical activities, that he does not pay enough attention to his personal relationships. Eventually his emotional center suffers, as he has forgotten his girlfriend's birthday. Misunderstandings with other people often occur because we are out of balance within our self. These simple examples illustrate the need to balance one's centers to achieve peaceful equilibrium. Consider the consequences of a lifetime spent out of balance. If one center has totally governed you, and dominated your life at the expense of all the other centers, a general lack of balance occurs. Certainly, one's center of gravity will always be the primary influence over the other centers. However, to neglect the needs, or development of every other center creates an inharmonious state. It is helpful to be aware that different centers have quite different needs, with different ideas and opinions about what is important in a given moment.

Making sincere intentional efforts to be more self-aware will help bring balance to your centers, and your life will function more efficiently, and become more harmonious, overall. Working together harmoniously with attention, the centers can perform with an enhanced ability to achieve optimal results. Instead of living one's life in a lopsided manner one can consciously direct attention and energy to all the centers and to their parts. Maximizing the power of all the centers working together, brings enhanced balance and equilibrium to how we function in our life. Instead of living automatically from our habitual mechanical routines, we can consciously change our patterns. Bringing mindful self-observation and attention to all the centers helps circulate energy to achieve balance. Rather than working against each other, the centers can work together to create more harmony in your life overall. For example, the intellectual center can intervene during heated emotional arguments, which helps to slow down the energy to prevent the situation from escalating. The intellectual center has the remarkable ability to slow energy down, by thinking things over to minimize harsh reactions. From a broader perspective, we can more accurately evaluate situations with the help of the intellectual center, to achieve greater clarity. This simple example illustrates how the centers can work better simply by working together.

Just as with any program to heal the individual, whether from illness or psychological issues, we need a practical program to bring attention to each center to correct our personal imbalances. To address our inner imbalances, this holistic approach for self-care with self-study, helps us develop a consistent practice to be more aware of all our centers. Having a compassionate attitude about oneself, can help infuse energy into the centers which one has neglected throughout one's life. Implementing these ideas as a holistic practice to attain inner balance, helps demystify and clarify confusing areas of life, and highlights centers which are out of balance from neglect. Maintaining a nurturing attitude to heal imbalances in your life self, helps you to gain deeper insight and objectivity to achieve more balance in your centers. Regardless of your personal center of gravity, is it is beneficial to be aware of, engage and activate all of your centers. Typically, our center of gravity dictates the routine and pattern of our daily life. But, bringing balance to your centers can be implemented in simple ways that are easy and practical. For example, an emotionally centered person can benefit from increased physical exercise, more intellectual stimulation, and, by paying attention to dietary needs, while also getting adequate restful sleep at night, rather than partying all night with friends.

These basic suggestions may seem obvious on the surface, but take a few moments to make an impartial survey of your life. Do you see harmony and balance in your emotional attitudes and in your relationships? Or, your intellectual interests, physical activities, or with your eating habits and sleep patterns? Are all your centers regularly addressed and activated to keep them in balance? Or, do you recognize discrepancies in specific centers that could benefit from more attention and activation? Generally, people unconsciously ignore some centers which are not immediately connected to their dominant center of gravity. If you are emotionally centered it is beneficial to engage your body in moderate physical exercise to activate your moving and instinctive centers, and find interesting ways to stimulate and activate your intellectual center also. For example, you could study some new intellectual ideas and concepts. Read the biography of Albert Einstein, to activate your intellectual center while keeping your emotional center engaged. You might enroll in yoga classes, or join a gym, to simultaneously activate the moving center and help maintain your instinctive center, for your health and well-being. If you are intellectually centered, it is helpful to activate your emotional center, engage in moderate physical activity, and pay more attention to your physical health. These generalized examples naturally apply to the moving center and the instinctive center as well.

Remember, the centers are connected directly across all the iconic royal suits depending upon the main predominating influence, whether it is from the King, the Queen, or the Jack. Thus, all the Kings of centers are connected across the four different suits. All the Queens of centers are likewise connected, and, all the Jacks of centers are also connected. Therefore, the most efficient and expedient method to create enhanced balance in your centers is to strive to make intentional efforts to access the centers that connect to your personal royal predomination, whether it is he King, the Queen, or the Jack. The key to bring enhanced balance to centers, is to focus your attention with intentionality, rather than allowing mechanical tendencies, or habitual patterns of behavior to control you. For example, if you are centered in the King of Spades, you have an inherent ability to access and connect to the Kings of the emotional, intellectual and instinctive centers. The King of Spades predisposes one to naturally give forethought to movements and spatial relationships. The King of Spades engages in thinking and analytical processes, which can bring a higher level of attention and intentionality to the moment in order to access the other intellectual parts of centers.

All the Queens of centers are connected across the royal suits; thus, if one Queen is activated, the other Queens will also be activated. An example is when the Queen of Clubs becomes hungry. It is quite likely that the Queen of Hearts will also become distressed, if nourishment is not readily available. This occurs automatically and habitually unless one mindfully self observes to bring attention to the present moment. When we are behaving unintentionally, the connection across suits can also evoke unconscious weaknesses. Using self-observation to bring intentionality to the Queen of Clubs, will focus attention to effectively address her hunger pangs. She can intentionally engage the Queen of Diamonds to research the situation to locate the nearest food source, and, she can engage the Queen of Spades to prepare food, or drive to a restaurant. When the Queen of Clubs makes an intentional effort, it will help prevent her Queen of Hearts from becoming agitated or distraught. This relatively simple process of making intentional efforts may seem obvious; however, when we are hungry we may begin to feel moody or distressed due to low blood sugar. A hypoglycemic Queen is not a happy Queen, but, employing mindful intentionality will mitigate distress.

Consider another common occurrence, when we misplace our keys. Suddenly one is immersed in a frenzied whirlwind of anxiety, searching to find the lost keys. Usually, in these moments any thoughts of calmness or intentionality completely evade us. But, this is precisely when one needs to exercise intentionality, and make efforts to bring one's attention to the moment by being still, focusing the mind and quieting the emotions, to engage and balance all centers calmly. I have verified the best method to find my lost keys, is to simply stop moving. Then, I engage my intellectual center to review my thoughts to envision my previous movements. After this, normally I can simply engage my moving center and almost always go directly to where I have placed my keys. This simple procedure, can be beneficial in many situations.

Using the elemental quality of our personal center of gravity to directly access the other centers across the iconic royal suits, can help us achieve more balance to harmonize our centers. This applies to all the centers, and whatever your center gravity may be.

The qualities and inherent abilities of your dominant center of gravity can be developed across the suits with intentionality. The strength of your dominant center of gravity, will evoke a similar strength in the corresponding centers across the royal suits. Your personal center of gravity gives you the ability to intentionally access these other centers to gain enhanced balance within. When we employ this natural holistic approach to connect our centers across the suits, we can greatly empower our personal abilities to achieve our goals. We can enhance our internal balance, and we can effectively empower our self. Connecting the centers intentionally, across the royal suits, enhances your abilities and exponentially expands your potential for personal self-empowerment.

Ultimately it is beneficial to balance all aspects of our life to the best of our ability. Certainly, it is vital to develop and maintain balance within our physical body, which serves all the other centers. One need not be instinctively centered to be more aware of and take care of one's physical body. Strive to self-nurture and work to maintain a healthy life style that fosters your personal growth. Please remember, physical suffering is not necessary, as this is not the path of the fakir. It is helpful to be mindfully respectful of your physical needs, and get sufficient sleep and adequate rest. We are extremely fortunate to have our physical body which allows us the opportunity to develop our deep inner being, and become enlightened. Treat your physical body with respect and gratitude with healthy doses of food, sleep and exercise. Also, it is best to avoid extremes in these areas, and strive to maintain a healthy balance. Develop good eating habits with a healthy diet to get the proper nutrients to maintain good health. While we do not need to obsess over food or diet, it is important to respect our physical body and take excellent care of our self for optimal health. The incentive for maintaining a healthy body is that it can encourage our essential nature to flourish.

Continued self-observation lends valuable insight to your awareness, with greater control over your habitual patterns, and imbalances. But, it requires your willingness to honestly observe, record, and, to be receptive to seeing yourself as you are naturally, in your true essential nature. By observing your habitual behaviors, you will begin to recognize which center generally ascends to take control. You may also begin to see certain incongruities, which cause imbalances to occur. Over time, with consistent efforts, we can gain control over our imbalances by bringing attention to the centers which are not elementally connected to our natural center of gravity. Insightful glimpses into oneself can help serve as an incentive to make necessary shifts to establish and maintain greater internal harmony. Naturally, it is beneficial to access all your centers; encouraging energy circulation between centers which helps establish, and maintain balance and harmony. Mindful self-observation brings attention to the imbalances within, and ultimately will help you to restore balance as you activate your other centers, to intentionally develop your self-knowledge and self-awareness.

As learn about the centers of influence within, you will begin to understand yourself more. While employing mindful self-observation, you will make discoveries about yourself, which you have not noticed before. You may be rather surprised at what you see in yourself, but please understand, this provides vital insights and revelations for your personal foundation of self-knowledge. Many of your deep personal mysteries will become more understandable as they come into sharper focus. When you eventually determine your true center of gravity, it will provide valuable information for deeper comprehension into your personal mystery. For example, if you determine that you are emotionally centered, you will begin to realize that your emotions have probably governed and dominated your entire life. This may also be an indication that the other centers have not been exercised with active participation, except when absolutely necessary. Knowing this, can help you to integrate the other centers more fully into your life with attention and intentionality. This helps create balance within. Whatever your center of gravity, it is beneficial to attain balance within. Your intentional efforts will enhance your internal harmony, and every aspect of your life. Strive to develop different skills by accessing all the diverse characteristics inherent within each center's unique potential.

Achieving harmony despite conflicts of interest within:
It is helpful to understand that on the occasions when we experience a conflict of interest within our self, or when we experience inner turmoil, it may simply arise from the different suits and centers opposing one another without our conscious awareness. Within the same suit there may be varying ideas, or opinions, which are not in exactly in agreement with one another, despite the fact that they exist within a single individual. This is often the root cause of inner conflict, especially when we have many opposing thoughts. It will be helpful for you to become well acquainted with all of the centers, so you can begin to understand yourself better. There are 52 cards in a regular deck of playing cards, so perhaps you can understand the many potential internal influences we live under from these 52 different centers. While our personal center of gravity serves as our main internal center of influence, all the other centers certainly play their part in our overall existence, every day, in every moment. As you mindfully self-observe, you will begin to recognize some of the conflicting and alternating influences as they arise in your daily life.

A very rudimentary example is when the moving center needs to do housework, but, another part of the moving center decides to go play tennis instead. Yet, returning home to a dirty house is quite unpleasant. Or, the emotional center might get annoyed with friends, and decides to break free of these relationships to become more self-reliant. But, soon one feels lonely and decides to forgive insensitive friends, so as not to feel alone or isolated. These simple examples illustrate how within one center we have different ideas which are within the same suit. And, there can also be inner conflict when two, or more centers have differing opinions about a certain matter. For example, the emotional center may wish to quit smoking cigarettes, but, the instinctive center and the moving center absolutely refuse to cooperate. The instinctive center is addicted to nicotine, and the moving center enjoys the habit of lighting a cigarette and holding it, while doing other things. Or, the intellectual center may make a decision to lose the 20 pounds that one gained over the holidays; however, at the same time the instinctive center absolutely revolts, disagrees and tries to sabotage any threat of dieting for fear of a food shortage. It is as if these disputes arise as competition between centers, despite being on the exact same team, and despite being in one single individual person! In reality, the different centers may not necessarily know each other, so they do not recognize the absolutely vital necessity to cooperate with each other. This is due to their different functions and processes, as they perform their tasks differently from one another within us. Thus, it is quite likely they may disagree with certain decisions we make in one center, and then, other parts of centers refuse to agree. One center can be a saboteur of another center, which is simply trying to make efforts to improve one's life overall. Remember, this occurs quite mechanically within us, without our attention, so it is vital to become more cognitive of our internal influences, functions and processes to gain more control of them. This will help mitigate conflicting inner confusion, and internal disputes which cause discordant imbalances.

Several years ago, I had a dear friend who was emotionally centered in the Queen of Hearts. She had endless social engagements, frequently dined out, and drank quite a lot of alcohol socially. It seemed that she always focused on relationships and socializing. She preferred going out with friends, over all other activities. She was fifty-pounds overweight, but refused to diet or exercise, and she ignored her moving center. She rarely read or studied new ideas, and neglected her intellectual center. One day she told me she had decided to quit her computer classes at a vocational college. I encouraged her to reconsider, for her future, but, she refused. She said she was satisfied working at the dairy office, and she got free food, primarily cheese and dairy products. However, this only added to her weight issue, creating physical imbalances as she suffered from frequent chronic illnesses. The focus of her life was her emotional center at the expense of all the other centers. She was the quintessential party girl, but, her lively social life eventually created major imbalances in her life. She continued to party, and continued to suffer from extreme bouts of illness. There was no way she could achieve harmonious balance in all her centers. I was deeply saddened to hear that she died suddenly. Excessive emphasis on one center, at the expense of all the other centers, can create severe imbalances which may seriously impair our health and wellbeing. While it is not necessary to negate one's center of gravity, one must bring attention to all the centers actively to help assuage and diminish imbalances before they get completely out of control.

We need to bring consistent conscious attention to our inner world to gain more control over our routines, habitual behaviors and mechanical manifestations. Automatic behaviors are programmed into our centers, and can steer our life off course and sabotage our sincere efforts. Think of something you attempted, but, it failed before you could reach any real success. It does not matter what it is, small or large, whether it is going on a diet, starting a workout regime, learning to knit, quitting smoking, playing an instrument, taking tennis lessons, or getting up earlier in the morning. Try this simple experiment, set your alarm clock one hour earlier than normal, so you can arise early to do one small task that needs your attention, such as balancing your checkbook. Observe what occurs in the morning when your alarm clock rings. Do you get up out of bed, or, do you re-set the alarm and go right back to sleep? This may seem rather insignificant, but ultimately these neglected moments compose our entire life. Try to remember other occasions when you wanted to try something new, but you got frightened, and simply gave up. These are the moments that create our life, and this is where we can make bigger efforts to take more control over our feelings, thoughts, actions, and senses. We can do anything we want to do, but we must ignore the fleeting opposition from other centers that are not allowing us to succeed in new, or different situations. We can forge new paths for our self, in new directions to develop healthy habits or hobbies which we can succeed at. You gain success by maintaining conscious control over conflicting thoughts that arise within yourself from different centers. You can succeed at almost anything if you make attentive, intentional conscious efforts.

Many people habitually suffer from negative self-doubt, simply because it is what they are accustomed to. Self-doubt arises mechanically in negative imagination to sabotage one self. As you gain comprehension of the different centers, you will begin to recognize the habitual behaviors from certain centers which undermine your true possibilities and potential achievements. Mindful self-observation encourages attempts to improve our life, while increasing our personal awareness. Your habitual pattern of sabotaging behavior can be changed, bad habits can be broken and unhealthy habits can be conquered. By developing new habits with enhanced awareness, you can denounce your old habits and conquer them. We all start by developing the beneficial habit of mindful self-observation to achieve conscientious control over everything in our life. Start small by observing yourself in this moment.

The Fourth Way esoteric system points out the conflicting emotions, thoughts, opinions and desires which arise within us, and refers to them as the many "I's." These multiple different "I's" are often from different centers manifesting habitually, which challenge and compromise our inner balance causing disharmony and discord. We are not one single unified "I" within; we are many different "I's" and each "I" has its own preferences. If you do not understand this concept, refer back to the suggestion to set your alarm clock an hour earlier to complete a task. Or, commit to a program of exercise, sign up for a college class, quit smoking, or any other challenge which has been difficult to accomplish. This is why large groups of people get together to support one another in order to successfully quit unhealthy habits such as over eating, drinking alcohol, or other unhealthy habits. We can build our own support group within our self, by uniting our different "I's" with consistent mindful self-observation to develop self-awareness. Unifying our emotions, thoughts, actions, and senses helps to build healthy self-support. Rather than being divided by our plurality within, we can gain unity within, to support our self. Unifying our many different "I's," within enhances inner harmony.

In Buddhism the concept regarding duality within, is said to be a cause of our inner disharmony. Buddhist teachings encourage one to develop non-duality. When we begin to observe, and understand the different centers within us, we can more readily grasp the many internal sources which cause not only duality, but perhaps more accurately, our plurality within. As one becomes more aware of the many different centers within, it can certainly shed light on the divisions and origins of our inner plurality. Keep in mind, that each center has different functions, diverse needs and multiple desires. The different centers tend to cause many of our internal contradictions, which creates the state of plurality within, and causes personal inner conflict. Thus, our personal internal mechanisms are the origin of much inner confusion and discontent. Understanding the multiplicity within us which can emanate from the many different centers, will help us to gain much more control over our plurality.

We have the potential to become more harmonious within, and to live a more fulfilling life. All the centers exist within you, but some may be relatively dormant. Others may function incorrectly, as perhaps they have been relegated to habitual functions or routine mechanical behaviors, which do not require our conscious attention. Observe yourself honestly and impartially to witness which habits are not serving your best interests, your well-being, or your conscious evolution. The most important factor in developing self-awareness is to be aware of yourself by observing yourself as you live your life. This includes looking into neglected patterns which have become habitual behaviors, and do not serve your best interests emotionally, physically or psychologically. We need to practice mindful self-observation as we bring attention, and awareness to all the centers to create a harmonious inner state. With self-observation, you gain a more lucid understanding of the centers functioning within yourself. You will begin to recognize the differing opinions which cause conflict within, when centers compete and work against your interests. You will see yourself and your life with greater clarity. Mindful self-observation allows you to consciously direct your life with attention while it is happening, rather than merely allowing your life to happen automatically, resulting in ungoverned habitual behaviors. By being attentive and intentional you will experience the higher levels of awareness necessary to direct your life more consciously. You will begin to go in the direction you wish, to succeed and accomplish your deepest yearnings and aspirations.

Self-esteem and self-worth:

Genuine self-esteem and authentic self-worth will develop naturally as you increase your awareness. Seeing yourself as you are in your true essential nature, will assist you in determining your innate talents and uniqueness. It is important to distinguish, this is not a reference to arrogance, vanity or other self-defeating attitudes of self-absorption. It is absolutely vital to gain a clear perception of yourself to properly evaluate your natural tendencies and true abilities. Enhanced self-knowledge allows us to more accurately recognize our personal virtues, talents, strengths, and our natural inherent abilities. Using sincere scale and relativity also allows us to accept our flaws. In this manner, we can begin to recognize and distinguish what has real merit and value within our self. We develop and enhance our self-valuation by making consistent efforts with mindful self-observation.

Remember, all the centers exist within us, and no center is better, worse. or more advantageous than another. All the centers have relative equality with regard to one's potential to become self-aware and awaken. Our center of gravity does not limit us, and does not affect our potential to gain enhanced self-awareness. However, it does not enhance our possibilities if we continue to habitually manifest with lack of attention. People often make the mistake of thinking that being centered in a certain card is more advantageous, better, or perhaps, more glamorous; however, this is completely untrue. Remember it is vital to observe yourself with sincere honesty and complete impartiality to truly discover your natural essential center of gravity. Regardless of which center one may consider to be potentially more attractive, or more desirable, is simply an illusion of self-deception. It is only by being true to our inner essence that we gain real self-knowledge. Realistically, one cannot possibly become that which is not within one's true essential nature. It is unrealistic and self-defeating to try to be something which is inconsistent with your natural essence.

Sometimes, we may put forth an outward appearance that emanates from false personality, or from a center that does not occur naturally within us. This forced behavior appears awkward, and tends to manifest to others as a falsified character portrayal, or an unnatural projection. It will also be rather uncomfortable for others to be around you, especially those who are striving to live more naturally in their own true essence. Please understand, it is unnatural to try to force oneself to be something other than what one truly is within one's essential nature. Trying to be something which you are not, or pretending to be anything other than what you are, is an artificial illusion. Artificial illusions defeat self-esteem, undermine confidence, and sabotage higher consciousness. Self-deception is the antithesis of self-confidence. One cannot build strength of character on an illusion. Being true to your essential nature is the only way to honestly build your self-esteem. Depending on your center of gravity, you will be more naturally inclined toward certain elements of life. For example, if you are emotionally centered, yours is the way of the heart. If you are intellectually centered, yours is the way of the mind. If you are moving centered, yours is the way of motion. If you are instinctively centered, yours is the way of the physical senses. Your personal center of gravity influences your natural inclinations and talents. It is the foundation upon which you can direct positive energy to build genuine self-esteem and authentic self-confidence. It is from your personal center of gravity that you can balance the other centers to gain harmony within which enhances self-esteem.

One's center of gravity is simply how one is born in life. All centers are necessary, and all enters perform vital functions in our life. Learning about centers while employing consistent mindful self-observation, will help you gain true self understanding. Please remember we cannot become anything other than what we are naturally within our true essential nature. We need to eliminate self-deception, and vanquish the imaginary picture we have of our self. By developing your self-knowledge, you will begin to understand your true essential nature within. Being true to your natural essential self, enhances your self-acceptance. This helps in developing sincere self-appreciation, glowing self-confidence and naturally healthy self-esteem.

Moving forward in your life on your path to awaken:
In our personal self-development, it is vital to our progress to have sincere humility as we live, and journey on our path. Always keep in mind, it is our true essential nature which we are encouraging to blossom and grow within. Whenever possible, it is beneficial for you to spend quality time in healthy environments which are conducive to being as natural as possible to experience your essential nature, for yourself, and also, for others. The need to be respectful toward others is paramount to avoid causing unnecessary pain to anyone. Respectful behavior helps to minimize negativity, and other unnecessary manifestations, and helps us achieve balance within, plus enhanced harmony with other individuals. Use the knowledge of centers to observe yourself and others. Strive to maintain a compassionate attitude to be more accepting and respectful of the people around you. Treat others in a manner that addresses their higher potential as well as your own higher potential. Continue to self-observe, and practice these simple virtues to enhance your life experience. It serves you well to be a model of compassion and humility as you live your life with self-awareness.

Ultimately, everything you do affects your life. So, it is highly advantageous to recognize your true essential nature, and become self-aware as you experience each moment of your life. Simply open your eyes and observe the world you inhabit. You will see an abundance of miraculous reality surrounding you. Practice looking for the miraculous in life regularly; it is all around us, and everywhere we look. Witness the centers come alive in yourself and others. Unlocking the mystery of the centers of influence within you, will begin to change every aspect of your life, and you will benefit immeasurably. You will gain deeper understanding of every element of your life, how and why you are the way you are. You will develop greater control over your emotions, your relationships, your thoughts, your personal psychology, your actions and reactions, and your own personal life destiny. Perhaps most importantly, you will understand yourself with infinitely increased clarity.

As you continue to practice mindful self-observation, you will be taking vital steps toward gaining increased self-awareness, self-understanding, enhanced self-esteem, and self-confidence. With consistent mindful self-observation, you will begin to recognize your innate inner being as your true essential nature. Observing the self is the beginning of personal growth. Remember, your essential nature is what you are at the very core of your being, and has a well-deserved and rightful place in the universe which we all share. We each have our part to play in this magnificent universe, and. we must play our part as naturally as possible. Welcome to the miraculous wonderland of your true self.

Remember, knowledge is power, and self-knowledge is transformational personal empowerment.

CHAPTER 11

OTHER ESSENTIAL ESOTERIC CONCEPTS AND WISDOM FROM THE FOURTH WAY

The following segment includes other essential esoteric concepts from the Fourth Way system, which will assist as you study the centers of influence within, and begin to practice mindful self-observation. These additional ideas include helpful terminology to enhance your knowledge base as you work to develop your self-awareness. Initially gaining understanding of the centers will pave your way. A working knowledge of these essential esoteric concepts will help to expand your potential for greater self-awareness and personal transformation. While the Fourth Way ideas form an extraordinary system of esoteric knowledge, it also makes one quite aware of one's inner personal solitude in this vast universe; hence, the necessity for self-study, self-sufficiency and personal self-development based in self-awareness. Keep in mind, there are no shortcuts to awakening, other than being present in the moment with mindful self-observation. This will encourage you to build a true reality based on the foundation of your essential nature. Practicing mindful self-observation and intentional presence are key methods.

There are various factors and influences which affect your personal internal world, and how you live your life. We all experience personal internal influences from our own centers, but it is helpful to realize we live with numerous external and superficial influences as well. Some influences are relatively insignificant and we can control them; however, there are other influences over which we have minimal control, or none at all. There are general external influences which all of us experience daily, such as the weather, the economy, and political issues. Other types of personal external influences which affect us include our job, our family, our friends, relationships, where we live, and other normal day to day issues and events. In certain situations, we may be able to select the influences which affect us. But, everything outside of us can potentially have an influence over us in a positive, neutral, or a negative manner, and also, in varying degrees.

You can gain greater control over certain influences by knowing how they affect you personally so you are prepared when they arise. The most important control you exercise is your own well governed self-control over your responses and reactions to multitudinous issues and situations which routinely occur every day. In some instances, we can minimize potentially negative external influences by making informed decisions on a moment to moment basis. Life provides us with ongoing opportunities and unlimited events, which we can use to develop and strengthen our personal resolve and self-control. I am referring to our responses to all issues and all situations in life, regardless of their significance. We habitually respond to virtually everything that occurs around us, and we react to everyone we encounter. Our habitual automatic responses represent a constant energy drain on our life energies. But, how exactly do we begin to stop our unnecessary reflex responses and energy losses?

It is helpful to realize that we live with an ongoing flow of impressions as influences, some of which are beneficial, some neutral, while other impressions are negative and potentially harmful. However, it is not necessary to react to, or respond to every impression or external influence. Some of these influences are momentary impressions which pass quickly and are forgotten. Yet, many influences linger, provoking unnecessary reactions within us which can cause exorbitant emotional energy drains and loss of attention. We can begin to conserve our energy by closely monitoring our habitual tendencies which manifest routinely, automatically, and continuously in every moment. There are some insignificant issues of little consequence, such as noticing different foods and products on the shelves at the market. In every moment, we have the opportunity to observe our personal internal reactions and responses to everything and everyone around us. However, you can be more selective about which impressions you choose to take in, and also, which people you allow to enter your life. You have the option of limiting some influences, such as certain people who may be potential energy drains in your life. You can begin to mindfully observe yourself right now, to monitor and minimize your energy losses and conserve your energy for the efficient development of self-knowledge for conscious self-awareness. The following segment covers essential esoteric concepts that will assist you as you begin to incorporate and experience these methods. Understanding these various concepts can put certain elements of your life into perspective which assists to conserving your life energy. Knowing what is actually occurring within you will help you to address your obstacles to higher awareness. Incorporating these ideas as personal guidance can enhance and empower your process of self-discovery to reach insightful self-knowledge with heightened self-awareness. Gaining self-knowledge with increased control over your personal internal world is your most powerful resource and transformative discipline. Everything you need to begin is already within you.

Self-Remembering and Mindfulness:
The Fourth Way system uses the terminology, "remember yourself," and, "self-remembering," as a task to remind one to be aware of oneself in the moment. Yet, the Buddhist term, "mindfulness," is essentially synonymous with self-remembering, and is quite likely the origin of Gurdjieff's terminology. When researching the history of the term mindfulness, one is referred back to the ancient Hindu and Buddhist wisdom traditions. The term mindfulness is derived from the Pali term *sati,* and the Sanskrit term *smrti,* both of which translate as, "to remember," or, "to recollect." Pali and Sanskrit are the languages that were prevalent in the ancient Hindu and Buddhist literature. It seems apparent that Gurdjieff appropriated these ideas and began using the Pali-Sanskrit terms as the basis for his terminology, "self-remembering." It is evident that the term, "self-remembering," is a direct reference to, "mindfulness," as they represent the exact same state of being present in the moment while living your life. I have not heard this direct parallel before; yet it is my personal deduction as it is quite obvious.

It is most helpful to realize that the Fourth Way system was originally translated from other languages, including Russian, Armenian, Greek, Turkish, Sanskrit, and perhaps Tibetan. Gurdjieff traveled extensively throughout Asia and India, and it is said he lived and studied in Tibet. There are vague suggestions that Gurdjieff may have also used a different name, which was that of a Tibetan Lama. While this is speculative, it is apparent that his system was derived from the other systems which Gurdjieff had studied in depth while on his search for higher knowledge. One must keep in mind that translations are quite often approximations, as certain terminologies may not be translated exactly, thus, are translated approximately. Gurdjieff spoke several languages, and he certainly appropriated ideas and terms from his studies, translating them to work effectively within the system which he began to teach and promote. He presented his teachings as fragments which were derived from other systems of knowledge he had previously studied while on his quest for truth.

By paying attention with intentionality while observing yourself, you are indeed remembering yourself with mindful presence. One must be mindfully present to oneself to observe one's ongoing different thoughts and imagination, to minimize identification, loosen the bonds of habitual behaviors, mitigate negativity, lessen one's features and false personality. It is helpful to acknowledge that with the myriad distractions of life, we generally do not remember our self in every moment. With consistent mindful self- observation, you can truly experience your life on a moment to moment basis as it is actually happening. With consistent self-observation, you will be remembering yourself with mindful presence.

Self-Observation:

Throughout this book, I have repeatedly referred to self-observation as a key practice to gain self-awareness. It is an essential element of the Fourth Way system, and serves as a practical method for self-development. Though I have referred to this method throughout the text, I wish to provide more information for clarity. With self-observation, one becomes both the watcher and what is being watched. The art of self-observation is simply being present to one self in the moment while self-observing with attentiveness and intentionality. Self-observation is a powerful transformational tool which you can begin to use right now in this moment. The practice of mindful self-observation is consistent with most systems which strive for self-awareness, and this is strikingly true with Buddhism. In the Buddhist tradition, one is encouraged to be mindful, and to live with mindful presence. Mindfulness is synonymous with the Fourth Way term, self-remembering, which is used with self-observation. You can observe yourself in any moment you remember yourself.

As you practice mindful self-observation you become present to the moment as it is happening. When you begin self-observation, you may notice you only remember for short periods of time; this is normal. As you continue to make efforts to be present and mindfully self-observe you will develop more of an aptitude for it. Then you will experience longer sessions observing yourself as you live your life. Remember, you are both the observer and that which is being observed. To improve your life, you must be aware of what you are actually creating or manifesting with habitual behaviors and actions. This requires mindful presence with self-observation. Mindful self-observation is the practice of maintaining your awareness as you watch yourself whilst being aware that you are watching and monitoring yourself intentionally with objectivity. Self-observation occurs when you are present in the moment while witnessing yourself without judgment, deprecation, analysis or comparison. You become the observer, and that which is being observed. Consistent mindful self-observation can help you to change what you observe. It helps to make conscious efforts and economize your energy to gain more control over your centers. Mindful self-observation has been employed for thousands of years in psychological wisdom traditions as a practical method to increase self-awareness. It is an essential component of the great psychological systems, particularly Buddhism where mindful self-observation becomes the starting point for stilling the mind during meditation. The venerable historic Buddha practiced mindful meditation self-observation to attain enlightenment.

One must observe oneself impartially to witness the authentic truth about one's life, rather than what one simply imagines about one self and one's life. Keep in mind, self-observation is not the activity of being in imagination. It is not habitual thinking about one self, or one's personal problems. Rather it is when you are mindfully observing yourself with the aim to honestly learn about and understand your personal feelings, thoughts, motivations, behaviors, and sensitivities. Self-observation gives you more control of your life, with enhanced attention and intentionality. Self-observation shines a light on energy losses and imbalances, which we may not normally notice. Observing your personal habitual patterns allows you to make manageable incremental adjustments on a moment to moment basis. We cannot stop all energy losses immediately, but we can begin to make small investments to conserve our own personal energy supply. Consistent self-observation will help you take control over your habitual patterns to conserve energy.

As you develop greater self-awareness with consistent self-observation, certain elements of your life may begin to change. Self-knowledge helps you gain a clearer picture of who you truly are in your essential nature. Enhanced self-knowledge imparts natural assurance to build self confidence in your innate abilities, talents and affinities. This tends to refine your aims, and you may attract different circumstances. You might be drawn to new environments which nurture your true essence, and perhaps you will manifest different opportunities. As we begin to grow and change, our life also grows and changes. To be impartial, it can be helpful to look at your life as if it is a "movie," and to regard yourself as the lead actor. As an actor, you must play your role as conscientiously as possible. In this experiment, you can multi-task as the creator, writer, producer and director of your personal life movie. Treat this idea as an experimental concept to help you be more self-observant of different occurrences as you go through your day. As your life movie, how you play your personal role will determine your potential for success, triumph, or failure. But, remember, it is your movie, and as the lead you can decide affirmatively that failure is not an option.

As you practice mindful self-observation and participate more consciously in your life, you will notice the different centers manifesting with their different functions and processes. Each center has its own distinct nuances which are observable when we pay attention. Although we have all the centers within us, our personal center of gravity will have the most influence over our life. But, with consistent practice you will be able to observe the other centers as they function in your life as well. Keep in mind, it will be relatively easy to observe your personal routines and preferences, such as how you wear your hair, which magazines you read, which foods you like, and other habits which are part of your normal daily life. We tend to develop preferences and mannerisms based upon the predisposition of our dominant center of gravity. Therefore, it may be that some habitual patterns reside within a specific center, rather than in your conscious awareness.

Here are some simple examples of how the different centers might influence the tone, or theme of your life. If you are emotionally centered, your life may sometimes feel like you are living in a situation comedy, a tragedy, or a melodrama. You may feel transcendent serenity when you choose events to fulfill your emotions, such as going to a fine art museum. If you are intellectually centered, your life may be more like the slow, methodical process of assessing and evaluating matters with deep thought and rationale. You enjoy doing crossword puzzles with your encyclopedic knowledge, reading scientific theory, studying mathematical equations, or playing masterful games of chess using strategic calculation. If you are moving centered your life may flow like an elegant ballet, a landscape painting, rush like an action-packed theme park, speed like a race car, glide like a tennis tournament, or perhaps, rise like an architecturally engineered city skyline. If you are instinctively centered your senses may lead you to intoxicating fragrances, delicious foods and luscious beverages to satisfy your sensitive taste buds.

You feel enlivened by gourmet foods, fragrant perfumes and aromatherapy, relaxing massages and spa treatments, rejuvenating juice cleansing, and perhaps, the mysterious realm of psychic impressions, intuition, and extrasensory perceptions.

To observe your habitual patterns of behavior, employ consistent mindful self-observation. This practical exercise brings your habits and patterns to the forefront of your attention, which will greatly assist you in gaining clarity. Sincere self-observation can help you gain greater control over habits, or patterns which may be controlling you. Observing yourself honestly, without judgment allows you to learn which particular center dominates in your life. Remember, self-transformation is a timeless endeavor and as with any worthy goal, the path may be pebbled with patches of rough terrain. It is wise to avoid making harsh judgments about yourself. Strive to set aside feelings of vanity or pride as you begin to witness yourself, as you are. Being impartial and nonjudgmental about what you see in your self will help dispel and diffuse unnecessary self-criticism, self-blame, and self-doubt; which are not conducive to achieving of self-awareness and higher states of consciousness. Keep a clear open mind and a compassionate open heart for yourself. Mindful self-observation helps you gain compassionate self-understanding which is vital to achieve balance within. Your goal is to gain true understanding of yourself, and your essential nature.

To awaken, we must look at our behavior, our feelings, our likes and dislikes, examine our thoughts and actions, the people we are drawn to or are repelled by, and observe our interactions with others. Practicing mindful self-observation is the most effective method to witness, and understand how our centers work and manifest within us. It is beneficial to recognize the practicality of mindful self-observation as an important step towards gaining self-knowledge. As you begin to understand how your centers function, manifest, and tend to create your life, you gain more self-control. Without self-knowledge and lucid self-perception, an individual may lack the necessary elements to achieve natural harmony within. Self-knowledge, internal harmony and balance can be achieved by practicing consistent mindful self-observation; that is, watching yourself live your life, while simply being present in the moment. Gaining awareness and more command over our habitual tendencies is eminently beneficial. Observe your imagination, identifications, false personality, buffers, and all your chronic automatic habitual behaviors. Everyone has habits, but we must observe these patterns honestly and impartially, before we can gain control of them. As we gain more control over our habitual manifestations and behaviors, we also begin to take command over the endless cycle of recurring feelings, thoughts, desires, cravings, and tendencies that drive our life on auto pilot, leading us away from our essential nature.

Remember, we each individually experience our personal role in life with a range of possibilities, depending upon our dominant center of gravity. Our primary center of influence determines why we do not agree with others, especially those who try to force their ideas or opinions upon us. But, they are functioning habitually from their own specific center of gravity, along with their chief feature, which is their particular weakness in their life. Note: I will address chief feature in a subsequent segment. Each center contributes certain elements which create the different experiences we have in our life as they influence us and cause our manifestations. Ultimately, it is up to you to determine, select, direct, and decide the potential outcome of the influences and events in your life. No one can do this for you, although they may try.

As you mindfully self-observe, you will begin to have more awareness of, and control of the manifestations of your dominant center of gravity. Becoming more self-aware, will help you to be better equipped to monitor, manage, control, and direct your feelings, thoughts, actions, sensory impulses, and all other manifestations as they occur. Again, with mindful self-observation, you are both the observer and what is being observed. If at any point, you feel confused, please do not despair. Simply return to the moment with mindful self-observation and begin again. Remember, each moment is a new opportunity. Continue with this simple, beneficial practice to become more present to the moments of your life, as you develop enhanced self-awareness and higher consciousness. Also, please understand, your personal practice of mindful self-observation will not be visible to others, and no one can possibly judge your efforts.

Throughout the ages people have awakened to their true nature to become enlightened simply by being present in the moment to their life, while they are living it. The historic Buddha became enlightened after enduring extreme personal struggles, and many fruitless efforts while on his personal path to awaken. Then, he sat under a tree, while being present in the moment with mindful self-observation meditation, he became self-aware and awakened to his true essential nature. There is a charming story about the Buddha which illustrates the fundamental simplicity of the goal to become self-aware. After his enlightenment, the Buddha was out walking and he encountered a man who became intrigued by his presence and tranquility. The man asked the Buddha a series of questions, as he was curious about who this serene person might be. He inquired if he was "a god, a magician, or an angel?", to which the Buddha replied, "no." Then the fellow asked him outright, "are you man?" And again, the Buddha replied, "no." Very puzzled, the man then asked, "well, what are you?" And the Buddha replied, "I am awake."

To attain perfection in our life, we must become aware of what we are creating and manifesting with our feelings, thoughts, behaviors, actions, attitudes and sensitivities. Mindful self-observation is the starting point and begins anew with each moment. You can achieve more balance by simply observing yourself. If you notice that you have forgotten to observe yourself in a moment, simply begin again in the next moment.

Essential Nature:
Throughout this book, I have used the term, "essential nature" in reference to ones "essence." I have chosen to use this term rather than the word essence, as I discovered over the years that the term essential nature helps people to understand that it is simply what is naturally within one self, which is part of one's natural being. In the past, I also realized that some individuals were confused by the word, essence. They asked if essence was their intelligence, their thinking processes, their health, their relationships, their jobs, their belief system, or even, their personality. Essence was often mistaken for their body, spirit, soul, and so on. Using the term essential nature proved to be a simpler way of introducing the word essence to them, and certainly facilitated their comprehension. One's essence or essential nature is one's natural being within. For this reason, I use the term essential nature as it elucidates that which is naturally within oneself, and has nothing to do with external influences. Your essential nature is your true self within, unencumbered by acquired traits or false personality, and it is what you are naturally, within yourself. Essential nature is what one is without superficialities of false personality, negative emotions, unnecessary contrivances or acquired traits. Your essential nature is within you, but it may be rather subdued for protection, and, submerged beneath false personality. As one begins to peel off the many layers of false personality, one will begin to see one's essential nature more clearly. Living in one's essential nature and respecting its needs is an ideal which one can strive for with consistent mindful self-observation, intentionality, and by paying attention to one's life

as it is actually occurring in the moment, rather than reviewing it in retrospect.

Developing enhanced self-awareness to arrive at your most natural self in your essential nature will help harmonize your centers. This allows you to be true to your natural inner being, which is a positive step to achieve your personal self-transformation. And, as we interact with the world it is beneficial to intentionally develop a true personality, which is more in harmony with our essential nature and our inherent inner being.

Understanding your personal essential nature brings you closer to realizing your true purpose in life. People are often confused about what to do, and how to attain their goals and desires. This occurs because we do not truly know our self. We understand the purpose of devices we use, such as our telephone and our computer, but, we may not actually know our own purpose. Your purpose originates in your essential nature, from what is most natural within you. The Fourth Way employs the term, essence, similar to how it is used in Buddhism. Ouspensky described essence as what you are born with. Essential nature expresses more clearly what essence is. Discovering your own essential nature will guide you to what is most natural for you in your life, in all matters.

Imagination:

The aim of using our imagination with attention to create literary works such as poetry, or, to compute a magnificent equation like Einstein, or, to strategize effective athletic maneuvers in sports, or to concoct a tasty recipe for a healthy lifestyle, are examples of using creative imagination with intentionality. However, quite often we drift off into our imagination without consciously being aware of our lapse in attention. Our unmonitored thoughts shift into uncontrolled mental activity, which works habitually and automatically, and does not require our conscious participation.

As we are not being present in these moments we are not fully aware of what we are actually doing. When we are in imagination we are not being present to our life. We are not aware of our self, others, or, of what is occurring around us. Being in imagination renders us less receptive to what others are saying, which may be the cause of the confusion and disagreements which arise between people.

Each one of us has habitual patterns of behavior and acquired traits that do not serve our best interests, particularly the lazy mental habit of being in imagination. Mindful self-observation is helpful for gaining more control over your imagination, which is vital for developing self-awareness. This allows us to gain conscious control over the chronic energy draining pattern of habitual imagination, which only takes us away from reality. For example, you may be driving along the freeway on your way to an event, but are lost in your imaginary world, completely oblivious to the highway you are on. As you ponder rambling scenarios in your head, you cruise right past your freeway exit, having forgotten about where you are going. Suddenly you come to attention, and are quite surprised to discover that you have driven past your freeway off-ramp. This is a typical description of how imagination manipulates our attention, and diverts our thoughts into fantasies about anything and everything. And, this happens to everyone. We may be driving 60 miles per hour on the freeway, but we are thinking about our dinner, our friends, dreaming about a vacation, or worrying about our mortgage, our job, or anything other than what we are actually doing. This is imagination and we are functioning automatically and habitually without conscious attention or intentionality. In reality, we are actually asleep to our life when we indulge in habitual states of imagination.

A very common cause of misunderstandings between people while conversing, is lack of attention. This inattentiveness is typically caused by mental drifting, which occurs whilst in one's imagination. Someone might suddenly interrupt our imagination, and abruptly ask, "Are you even listening?!" This can be quite unpleasant; however, not giving someone your attention while conversing is disrespectful. Their question is a clear indication that they are aware your attention is elsewhere. Uncontrolled imagination functions habitually, and occurs without our conscious participation. The major issue is that imagination is simply not real, but it takes us away from reality in every moment. When we indulge in habitual imagination we miss what is actually occurring in our life.

A common scenario is attending a lecture, but you absent-mindedly drift off into habitual imagination. Thus, you do not really hear what the lecturer is saying. If you apply this scenario to your spouse, your friends, your family, your job, your education, and to other situations, you will begin to comprehend why mistakes, mishaps, accidents, errors of judgment and misunderstandings occur. We tend to spend much of our lives indulging in our imaginary fantasy worlds, which may be quite far from our actual reality. As you practice mindful self-observation you will begin to recognize when habitual imagination takes over. You will also understand why habitual lack of attention causes malfunctions in our centers. Typically, we are immersed in activities, but suddenly wake up to realize that we have not paid attention whilst doing these tasks; hence, we make mistakes. At these times, the brain is working habitually on automatic pilot without any real conscious effort or participation. This becomes an automatic mechanical pattern which takes us away from moments of reality. Many accidents are simply a result of being in imagination.

Please understand, our memory banks are vital and serve an important purpose to facilitate our life on a moment to moment basis. However, we often lazily drift into our imagination while our real life is running on automatic pilot. Imagination takes over as our mind unconsciously drifts over endless subjects, ideas and issues. Keep in mind, imagination requires no effort and it is not a conscious state of self-awareness. Our habitual patterns of imagination function as the path of least resistance which prevent us from actively participating in our life as it is actually happening. Being self-aware necessitates that we make intentional efforts to escape the habitual mechanical patterns of our life. This requires that we make consistent efforts to be mindfully present to observe our self in the moment. For example, if you are not intentionally using your imagination to write poetry, calculate an equation, create a symphony, write a letter, paint a picture, design a dress, strategize a chess move, create a healthy new recipe, or do any other useful mental work with attention, then it is quite possible you are in imagination and functioning on automatic pilot. With consistent mindful self-observation, you will begin to notice when you are in your imagination.

Paying attention while being mindfully present to the moment as it is occurring requires intentional effort. Regardless of which center is dominant in us, we need to make efforts to be more intentional by paying more attention on a moment by moment basis. Although we have all the centers within us, one center will be dominant, and our imagination is often propelled by our personal center of gravity. An emotionally centered individual's imagination will quite likely revolve around people and relationships. Whereas the imagination of one who is moving centered may revolve around sports and moving activities in general. Our center of gravity serves as the primary influence over all that we feel, think, do and sense in our life, therefore, it is typically the primary influence over our imagination. Our center of gravity tends to serve as the wheel around which our imagination churns habitual thought patterns. Recognizing the patterns of your own imagination will help you to see your center of gravity more clearly. This can ultimately help you to monitor your thoughts to gain more control over whatever causes you to lapse into habitual imagination.

A greater concern with habitual imagination is that we create unrealistic scenarios, or fantasies which can result in unnecessary suffering. Worry, anxiety, depression, unrealistic expectations, fear, resentment and stress are some potential negative results of excessive habitual imagination. Chronic negative imagination causes distractions and deviations which distort our reality, and clouds our ability to make well informed decisions. Uncontrolled imagination is energy draining. As we mindfully self-observe, it becomes apparent we are not consciously monitoring the control panels of our life. Without mindful self-observation and being present in the moment, our centers tend to function automatically without our conscious participation. Monitor your thoughts with mindful self-observation to minimize habitual imagination.

Using creative imagination is a wonderful practice to help focus your mental discipline. But, it is important to distinguish the difference between creative imagination and uncontrolled habitual imagination which is aimless mental activity, hence counterproductive and energy draining. Creative imagination is productive and enriches life, whereas the repetitive habitual, automatic grind of imagination has no qualitative value. Creativity helps us harness and discipline our imagination. Gaining more control over habitual imagination requires intentional efforts with mindful self-observation to bring attention to the moment. Practicing meditation regularly can also help to bring attention to lingering habits of uncontrolled mental activity. By employing consistent mindful self-observation, you will soon begin to notice how often you drift off into habitual uncontrolled imagination. Mindful self-observation brings vital attention to all areas of your life, and will improve your communication skills and enhance your creativity while conserving your energy. To do things well, it is eminently beneficial to be mindfully present in the moment and not dwell in imagination.

You may think this does not apply to you as you might not be an artistic, or creative type. But, please understand, we each individually create our personal life with our thoughts. Being present in the moment with mindful self-observation will help create the life you truly desire. Rather than allowing imagination to run habitually, focus your thoughts attentively and intentionally to create what you yearn for in your life. Uncontrolled imagination takes us away from reality, and may lead to undesirable outcomes. If you are not monitoring your imagination, it may be undermining your life and your potential. Imagination is an obstacle to self-awareness. We must make consistent efforts to be present to each moment as it occurs.

Mindful self-observation is the best method to minimize habitual imagination. There are traces of this methodology in virtually all meditative and contemplative practices. Certainly, one can see the value of meditation and tranquil contemplation as beneficial practices to help quiet the mind. Employing a simple mantra while in meditation is an effective tool to gently train the mind to focus. If you consider the mind to be your mental muscle, you will readily grasp the necessity to train and develop this miraculous muscle with consistent mental exercises. Utilizing intentional mental exercises, such as mindfulness meditation enhanced with self-observation, helps you to have more control over your mind and your imagination. These practices are consistent with most esoteric, metaphysical and spiritual doctrines. We can train our mind to focus by regularly practicing mental exercises to develop the skill to be aware and mitigate chronic habitual imagination.

Using mindful self-observation as a practical method to monitor thoughts will help you gain control of imagination. Self-awareness is developed through our consistent efforts to practice self-observation in each moment. Just as we exercise our body to gain strength, flexibility, and endurance to maximize mobility, we must likewise exercise our mind with attention and intentionality to maximize its brilliant potential to become aware, awake and enlightened. Continue to mindfully observe yourself.

Identification:

The psychological concept of identification is discussed in many philosophical and psychological systems, but is referred to by different terminologies. Identification can be regarded as one's attachment to any, and all illusions relative to one self, which includes other people and all facets of life. Identification exhibits as personal psychological attachment to everything in one's life. Identification generally revolves around certain habitual areas which we become focused upon, generally in an unproductive manner. Identification can arise with almost anything, such as being identified with another person, an ideology, an object, a desire, or, a subject one is attached to. While identification manifests somewhat differently within each center, identification itself has distinct characteristics which cause one to be focused with tunnel vision on the subject of one's identification. The range of one's identification may exhibit as interest, fascination, intrigue to extreme obsession that can lead to compulsive behaviors. One can become identified with anything.

Identification is similar to the Buddhist concept of attachment. Identification implies that one has become dependent upon, or transfixed by something, whether it is a person, an idea or an object. Regardless of whether it is internal or external, one tends to lose oneself, one's personal identity, and one's objectivity when one becomes lost in identification. Identification is the habitual clinging to people, ideas and things in such a manner that one loses one's personal sense of identity. If one is identified with something one cannot really understand or appreciate it objectively.

When one is identified one becomes psychologically trapped by the object of identification. The more identified one is the more trapped one becomes. Thus, identification tends to create chronic dependency on an external or internal subject, object, idea, opinion, or a person. What one is identified with can be as simple as a personal preference, or as strict as one's rigid adherence to routine. This also includes chronic addictions and habitual patterns of behavior. We each go through our life with our own particular areas of identification. Some people define their lives by what they are identified with. For some people, it may be their career, for others it may be their relationships, and for others it may be the food they eat, or even the car they drive. One can become identified with virtually anything. And while some types of identification may seem relatively harmless, other types of identification can cause severe suffering, or extreme adversity.

Identification is often a particularly gripping type of imagination that revolves around certain fixed ideas or things, which may not necessarily be fixed in reality. This can involve one's imaginary unrealistic attachment to anything, large or small, real or unreal. Also, an idea or a belief does not need to be true for someone to become identified with it. When one is identified with an idea one may become obsessed with it. One can also become identified with nonexistent subjects, imaginary objects, or imaginary people. What one identifies with tends to become what one considers to be true, whether or not it actually is true. When one is identified with another person one tends to think about that person quite a lot, and often in rather unrealistic terms. The other person may not be aware of it; such as when a fan is identified with a celebrity. The individual who is identified may feel deep longing for the other, but it may be unrealistic imagination.

While the Fourth Way encourages one to monitor identification with mindful self-observation, Buddhism advises to decrease dependency on the external world, to detach from personal attachments to attain self-realization. Attachment is the same as identification; one must detach from attachments, and simply let go of the objects or subjects which one is identified with to gain self-control. Identification tends to distort our emotional perceptions, while it undermines our understanding in our personal interactions and relationships with others. We may have unrealistic expectations of others in our relationships when we are identified. Identification is fed by imagination, and the more we think about a person the more identified we become. However, identification creates separation between our self and others, and we may experience a negative sense of personal isolation. Please keep in mind, when one is trapped in identification over another person one may not be able to interact with them in a realistic or balanced manner that is conducive to a healthy relationship. Relationships which are primarily based on identification with another person tend to become obsessive. Ouspensky gave an example of a cat being identified with a mouse, which is single minded focus, or tunnel vision. Obviously, a cat and mouse cannot possibly ever have an equitable relationship.

The problems with identification tend to multiply as it distorts and diminishes the present moment of reality, as we relinquish our personal identity to the subject, object, or person. When we are identified we are not being present to our real life, thus we lose our awareness, energy, and identity to the subject of identification. What we are identified with is what we lose our identity to. The problem of identification is that it creates limiting and self-defeating tunnel vision and obsession, wherein one cannot experience truth directly, or accurately. Truth become distinctly obscured while one is in identification, lost in one's own subjectivity. Illusions and self-delusions cloud one's perceptions.

Identification creates internal negativity which permeates our thoughts and actions while coloring our decisions. Identification creates misunderstandings and limits the actions that we take, or do not take.

A common area of identification for many people is weight loss and dieting. Perhaps one needs to shed a few pounds, and thus, begins a restricted calorie regime, all the while thinking about food, and thinking about being on a diet. The incessant thinking about food and diet is identification and one tends to lose oneself in the process, rather than merely losing weight. This is merely one example, but there are endless types of identification. While we are in identification we lose our sense of our self and our personal identity, usually without realizing it. Identification is contradictory to self-awareness. Our self seems to completely disappear as we become psychologically dependent on and anchored to whatever it is that we are identified with. Identification is often rooted in habitual patterns of behavior which sabotage our self-confidence, our self-esteem, and our self-awareness, while limiting our freedom. Identification puts our focus on tangible and intangible things, ideas and people. One pours one's attention into one's identifications, typically without taking reality or facts into consideration.

Please know, to be impartial, detached and unidentified does not mean one is being passive toward one's life. Passivity may lack the interest or energy to bring presence to the moments of reality. Passiveness also implies inaction, when what is needed is right action. Right action is intentional energy directed toward one's sincere aim to be more self-aware and to be present in the moment. Identification perpetuates illusions in our perceptions, and distorts what we believe to be reality. This results in energy losses, loss of quality in one's life and creates distance from what one truly desires. By developing a healthy attitude of impartial detachment, one can more readily accept the truth of a situation.

This helps one understand why events, issues and relationships manifest as they do.

For example, I knew a woman who was so completely identified with being a good mother to her children that her entire personal identity was completely wrapped up in them. When her children went to college and eventually left home, she said that she felt her identity was completely negated, so she began to slip into depression and despair. She had been a wife and mother for so long that she was unable to think of herself as an independent person. She had no individual sense of herself, and felt her life no longer had meaning. She telephoned her children several times a day, but they began avoiding her incessant calls as she was interrupting their studies or their work. She could not understand that she simply needed to adjust, adapt and relinquish her obsessive identification with motherhood as she had previously experienced it. In truth, she had not actually lost anything at all, but her identification convinced her she had lost everything.

Some types of identification create conflicts in life, such as a person entrenched in fanatical belief systems. Heated arguments often arise, but nothing will sway their extreme opinions while they are identified. We can get a glimpse of our own personal identifications by looking at issues which we have strong feelings or opinions about, including politics or religion, for example. The ideas, things or people that we are sensitive about may point to a particular area of identification. The degree to which we are identified with something determines the power it has over us. We tend to lose our true essential self in our identifications, whether they are positive, negative or neutral. To some degree, all identification is potentially negative, even if we think it is good for us. As you begin to mindfully self-observe you will notice your personal sensitivities more clearly and can determine whether they are serving your best interests. With sincere self-observation, you can subdue your personal identifications and loosen the strong hold they have on you and on your life. In his writings Ouspensky repeatedly advises to practice self-observation, but not identify with anything. The Buddhist path encourages one to minimize one's dependency on the external world, and to detach from personal attachments to increase one's potential to attain enlightenment. An impartial attitude can certainly help you detach from your identifications and experience increased self-awareness.

When we live our lives in a more detached manner, without being trapped in the identifications of our inner psychological world, we experience reality as a timeless presence in a state of pure conscious awareness. Mindful self-awareness and self-presence in the moment is devoid of qualifying judgments, good or bad. Neutrality with enhanced self-awareness lends objectivity which is essential in eliminating identification, while helping one experience higher states of conscious awareness. Lack of identification will propel you to attain higher levels of your personal potential with self-knowledge and enhanced self-awareness. When you consistently practice mindful self-observation, identifications will gradually decrease and diminish naturally, and you will experience higher levels of consciousness.

Negative emotions and negativity:

At this point it is imperative to discuss the habitual traits of negative imagination and the expression of negative emotions. Chronic habitual negative tendencies infringe on our personal wellbeing and drain our precious life energy. It is vital to gain control over our negative thoughts, negative emotions, and their negative manifestations. Nothing is gained from negative thoughts or emotions. Expressing negativity drains excessive amounts of energy, and depletes emotional, mental and physical resources. In the process of developing self-awareness, one must develop an alert attitude, to guard against negativity, and to assuage negative thoughts or emotions from arising, or escalating.

Negative emotions are habitual weaknesses which prevent us from experiencing self-awareness and higher states of consciousness. It is a habitual process of feeling, thinking, expressing and manifesting negative emotions and negative attitudes. Persistent negative habits may take many forms in our life, but these toxic habits tend to control a great deal of what we feel, think and do, thus preventing us from having a happy and positive living experience. Habitual patterns of negative behavior become one's automatic response mechanisms to almost any stimulus. Unfortunately, we do not even realize we have programmed our self with repetitive negative reactive responses that become automatically ingrained within us. Negativity necessitates our consistent intentional conscious efforts to minimize. Centers do not automatically eliminate negativity as they process. But, our centers do not manifest with self-awareness, unless we mindfully direct our attention to them with intentionality.

Everyone experiences difficult situations, and difficult people from time to time throughout their life. However, when we feel negative about something or someone, we tend to spend a great deal of mental energy thinking about the issue or person in question. Repetitious negative imagination builds a momentum within which creates unnecessary anxiety and tension. Negative imagination and negative emotions trigger other difficult psychological tendencies such as aggressiveness, intolerance, bigotry, and the habitual pattern of losing one's temper. These negative habits and patterns cause stress for everyone involved, and are contradictory to achieving peaceful solutions. People often blurt out whatever they are feeling with the justification that expressing negativity is normal, or that letting off steam is healthy. However, quite the opposite is true. The expression of negative emotions releases excessive adrenaline and other glandular secretions which create extreme pressures in the body. This is not healthy for our emotions, our mind, our physical body or senses. After venting anger or expressing negative emotions one generally feels drained and depleted from the excessive expenditure of energy, and its consequential hormonal imbalance.

We all seem to have our own endless reasons, rationale and excuses as to why we get angry or upset, but, in many cases it is usually the direct result of someone else having been negative to us. Negativity tends to breed more negativity, and in a rather peculiar manner, it is contagious. Our lingering discontent may be a result of disappointment from not getting what we want from another person. This may occur despite our attempt to please them, or quite possibly to manipulate them. This type of interpersonal negativity is usually embedded within our acquired personality traits, which are inconsistent with our true essential nature. It is imperative to recognize and understand that our false personality, and all of our acquired traits and attitudes, often work at cross purposes to our goals and stand in the way of actually getting our genuine needs met and our wishes fulfilled.

There are harmful consequences to harsh negative outbursts, such as the detrimental effect we have on another person's well-being, who may simply be an innocent victim of our undeserved wrath. No one wants to be the recipient of someone's toxic negative emotions, and no one will ever benefit from the expression of negativity. We may not consciously intend to become negative, or get into heated disputes; but, we can plan ahead to consciously minimize potentially negative issues. Simply knowing that one can activate the intellectual center during a heated argument, can help bring calmness to the emotional center, primarily due to the slower paced element of intentional thinking. Thinking slows down the momentum of anger; thus, your emotions can be effectively quieted, and your responses can be subdued. If you begin to feel negative emotions arising, try to slow the energy down with the intellectual center's slower thinking processes.

Most events that occur daily are rarely the fight or flight situations which result in sudden bursts of adrenalin as a survival mechanism; however, people often treat very minor issues as if they are. As you practice mindful self-observation, you will become more aware of habitual negative tendencies. We are not typically aware of our habitual reactions, but negative patterns may reside in a specific center rather than in our conscious awareness. To change habitual negative patterns, requires consistent mindful self-observation to assuage and mitigate negativity. Patterns of negativity are not hopeless and can be minimized with attention and intentionality. Remember, adding the intellectual element helps inhibit the development of negativity and prevents it from escalating. Rather than working against each other, the centers can work together more harmoniously with mindful self-observation, which helps to create balance. No one gains from negative emotions or angry disputes which cause our centers to malfunction. When centers work improperly they become out of balance. Bringing your attention to the moment with mindful self-observation, will restore balance to the moment, allowing centers to regain proper functioning. Again, intellectual rationale lends reasoning power to angry situations. Instead of a heated argument, matters can be discussed with understanding, lending necessary objectivity which helps restore balance to the centers.

The presence of negativity in our emotional and psychological states, disable our ability to see things as they truly are. From one perspective, many things are what they are, neither good nor bad. In our ordinary states of awareness, we often lack clear objectivity, so we attach a subjective negative factor to subjects, objects and people, which in reality are neutral of them self. This does not help us achieve understanding, and certainly curtails our comprehension. Our negative attitudes diminish our grasp of reality in a situation. Yet, if we can be impartial, we might not prejudge or qualify our concept of a subject, person, or a situation. Ordinary uncontrolled negative emotional responses, reactions, and attitudes are generally habitual, and, ungoverned reactions are the path of least resistance. It is valuable to understand that much of our inner conflict and strife is caused by our own internal habitual negative emotions.

As you pay more attention, you will notice that people complain about events, issues, or situations in their life which are actually well within their power to change. Yet, people remain in unhappy situations, often out of habit, and they continue to feel powerless despite having other powerful options. Habitual negative emotions and pessimistic attitudes lack the neutrality that is essential to experience reality, self-awareness, and to achieve self-empowered higher consciousness. The emotional, intellectual, moving and instinctive centers often function from learned, or programmed negative habits as an automatic mechanical response. These negative habits curtail our potential to see our own life clearly, or the miraculous world around us with the objective perception necessary to gain understanding. Often, people simply do not realize that they have the power to make changes that will effectively improve their life in a positive manner.

By intentionally deterring indulgences in negative imagination, you minimize distortions and prevent minor problems from blowing out of proportion. This helps conserve your emotional and physical energy, by not allowing negative thoughts to get out of control. Energy losses tend to accrue as a deficit, so this is precisely where we need to economize. If habitual negativity is dominating your life, perhaps it is time to gain more control over these harmful patterns of behavior. By intentionally monitoring negative thoughts which habitually fester in imagination one can gain more conscious control, so the negative thoughts do not escalate. Gaining control over all negativity, allows us to have more energy to make positive efforts for the necessary changes to improve our life.

Each one of us has a complex nervous system that works most efficiently and harmoniously, when we are experiencing composure. Of course, each one of us becomes confused from time to time in our life, but this does not need be a bad negative experience. It is fairly normal to occasionally get a bit flustered or confused during moments of difficulty. Confusion can be a point from which we can gain more control by simply acknowledging the confusion in the moment. When this occurs, it is eminently helpful to try to be more present with mindful self-observation. Meditation can be beneficial to calm the mind and diffuse negativity which one may feel during times of difficulty and confusion. Afterwards, when you feel calmer and your mind is less confused, things will become clearer and you will be better equipped to make more appropriate choices. Mindful self-observation will assist you to make conscientious efforts to economize and gain more control over your centers. When observing yourself, you bring mindful attention to unnecessary energy drains caused by negative imbalances. Deter habitual inclinations to think or express negativity in any form.

We each have issues which we can work on intentionally by bringing attention and self-awareness into the moment. This will help you achieve more positive and peaceful resolutions. Self-observation is essential to gain self-knowledge in order to have balanced harmony in your life. This is life energy conservation at the source. Instead of allowing one center to dominate your life with negativity, you can utilize the power of all the centers to help dismiss negative energy and regain your balance. With enhanced balance, our centers function more efficiently and more effectively. When you are more balanced within you have greater clarity to correctly evaluate personal issues, other people and the events in your life. As you bring your awareness to all the centers, even if only momentarily, you will be more aware of everything else in your life, as you naturally access your inherent talents and innate abilities. Do not let chronic habitual patterns of negativity minimize your potential for happiness. It is your life to live harmoniously, with balance in your centers.

False personality acquired traits:
False personality is an artificial persona, the mask through which we live and experience life. It is the imaginary picture we have of ourselves which we project to the world as a barrier to reality. It is how people wish to be perceived rather than how they truly are. False personality develops as an individual adopts traits and attributes which may be quite inconsistent with their true essential nature. False personality is created from the numerous acquired traits we pick up, which are copied from external influences. These acquired traits exhibit when we speak in common clichés, mannerisms, gestures, postures, caricatures, and attitudes we have accumulated since childhood. False personality traits are imitated from the influences of family, friends, education, the media, social pressures, fashions, styles, and are all based on gestures, thoughts, ideas, opinions and actions of other people. The different attributes we acquire over time create an artificial persona, or mask, through which we interact with the world. However, these various attributes, identities and behaviors are unnatural to our true essential nature. They are merely falsely acquired impersonations.

The person we present to others may not be who we truly are within, but is instead an artificial concoction of elements that do not blend well together. Ultimately, false personality leads us away from understanding our true essential nature. Acquired traits which are inconsistent with our authentic inner essence are certainly not harmonious to our true nature. False personality is a barrier to having meaningful exchanges and creates a wall between people. Thus, not being true to one self can prevent one from having rewarding relationships. Remember, this artificial persona is created from acquired, imitated traits, rather than one's natural inherent traits and abilities. An accumulation of acquired notions about oneself, creates unnatural and unhealthy imbalances. These unnatural acquisitions trigger identity problems, wherein a person does not really know who they are, what they want, or what they truly need. This imaginary picture of oneself is false personality. We become quite lost in this illusion, but, the illusion is unconsciously encouraged and perpetuated by the ordinary world.

We may pick up certain traits we see in others in order to feel as though we fit in. For many, it is easier to imitate and blend in, than to be an original version of oneself, which may attract criticism. Often, when people want to be accepted by the social order, they adopt artificial traits, which may not be in total harmony with their true inner essence. The basic need and desire to fit in causes one to develop a false persona which mimics and imitates the world that one wishes to be a part of. In the process of creating this new persona, one's true inner needs and desires are negated, neglected or possibly, vanquished. The fear of not fitting in, and the dread of being different, outweighs the need to express one's uniqueness. But, acquired traits which are not natural to us, create inner turmoil, which strains our essential nature. As our true inner nature is subdued, sublimated, dismissed, or negated, we develop stressful tensions within which are not easily resolved. Our true identity becomes lost in false ideals which confuse and mislead us. Complex issues arise from acquired false personality traits which fuse with negative emotions and attitudes. This is certainly not conducive to gaining real happiness, harmony or self-awareness. Despite trying to fit in, false personality is an artificial, illusionary barrier which may keep real friends and like-minded individuals away from us.

False personality is an amorphous construct which we build around our self, but it is an illusion which requires enormous energy to perpetuate. Trying to be something other than your true self, cannot possibly fulfill your honest needs and sincere wishes, nor will it help your life in the long term. Ultimately, our fleeting impersonations are not beneficial for anyone. Acquired personality traits which are not in harmony with one's true nature eventually cause one suffering and identity issues, such as low self-esteem and lack of self-confidence. It is impossible to have confidence in a false identity that does not truly exist in our essential nature. False personality is self-sabotage which wastes precious life energy to maintain, and ultimately hinders conscious evolution. Nevertheless, people create a shell around them self as a shield from life for self-protection. Everyone does this to some extent, whether we mimic others or have unconscious motivations. We unconsciously feel the need to hide our essential nature from the harshness of life. Given the chaos and confusion in the world, one can understand that false personality is pervasive.

As you practice consistent sincere mindful self-observation, you will recognize traits in yourself that are at odds with your true essential nature. False personality is an illusion which is unnatural, but requires efforts and energy to maintain. This artificial persona is a boundary we create, by trying to be different than we are naturally. Most people spend their lives building and fortifying their false personality without even being aware of it. False personality may be created almost unintentionally, as a survival mechanism for self-protection and to fit in with society, friends, one's job, and the culture in general. But in creating this false personality, one hides their true inner self from the world; thus, one's true inner self diminishes. In reality, our illusionary persona becomes a burden, while some acquired false personality traits become habits which require extreme efforts to relinquish. Habits acquired in false personality may also be fueled by the demands of particular centers, particularly the Queens of centers. For example, smoking cigarettes, alcoholism, drug addiction, over eating and other harmful physical habits may be the habituated demands of an indulgent center, such as the Queen of Clubs. But, these harmful habitual patterns of behavior which are acquired in false personality, can become highly detrimental to one's health. Often unhealthy physical habits originate from false personality impulses which become lodged in the negative half of a center. These habitual behaviors are difficult to break from, unless one works to develop enhanced self-discipline with increased self-knowledge, diligence and determination.

Keep in mind, people tend to fuel one another's imaginary illusions to help them feel more secure in their life, with the prevailing culture and the society. Again, this is a completely false sense of security as it is as though one is wearing a costume, or a mask simply to fit in with the world. The authentic version of you is hidden, submerged beneath a disguise of false personality, which shields your true identity. False personality is promoted by the mainstream culture in television shows, the cinema and in the pervasive cult of celebrity worship. These are not accurate depictions of reality. It is quite odd that almost no one notices that nearly everyone is hiding their true nature behind an imaginary façade. In many philosophical doctrines, this is known as the great illusion. False personality causes distortions which can eventually harm one's essential nature and prevent healthy self-assurance. One cannot build healthy self-esteem or self-confidence on a false premise.

If one lives in an identified state of imagination while emanating from false personality, one is not likely to experience objective reality, or to have a positive influence on one's life as it is occurring. False personality also attracts people or relationships that are inconsistent with our natural needs. Due to distortions in false personality, many relationships lack a fundamental natural basis. As you learn about the centers, observe yourself. and become more self-aware you will begin to understand that it is vital to allow your true essential nature to emerge. With mindful self-observation, one can intentionally discard the mask of false personality. Practicing mindful self-observation will help you to become comfortable with yourself to encourage your essential nature to flourish, which is conducive to enhanced self-awareness and personal transformation.

Please understand I am not suggesting we reveal our shortcomings for others to judge, but that we learn to interact with others in a more natural manner, which is less of an energy drain. Being who we really are within our true essential nature may encourage others to respond more naturally as well. At first this may feel somewhat awkward, but with sincere consistent mindful self-observation you will begin to feel more comfortable with yourself as you truly are naturally. Also, do not confuse polite etiquette, or good manners with false personality. The social graces encourage harmonious interactions with others, and certainly help to create an atmosphere of good will. Employing polite behavior with awareness helps one bring attention and intentionality to the moment, and enhances healthy communication in our interactions. Diplomacy and tact are valuable social skills which honor the needs of others and help to generate trust and compassion.

With mindful self-observation, we begin to realize that the characteristics we had once been attracted to in others, or which we have developed in ourselves, we now recognize as weaknesses. These particular weaknesses require enormous amounts of energy to interact with, and to maintain in ourselves. This drains our natural essential resources. Habits which originate in false personality also contribute to unrealistic expectations, which generate negative parasitic attitudes that drain energy. False personality is an unnatural energy depleting habit perpetuated by mechanical parts of centers. False personality can be quite flimsy, which often leads to self-doubt and personal insecurities. It is truly helpful to honestly ask yourself, what exactly is it that you like, or, do not like about the people you spend your time with. Keep in mind, false personality is not a good judge of character and can mislead one into difficult relationships. It is vital to have a clear understanding of your relationships so that each person benefits and has their needs met in a healthy and harmonious manner. Yet, often our social mannerisms are rooted in our habitual false personality mechanisms. Over the years, we develop certain habitual behaviors in our centers, which manifest automatically and mechanically, depending on the circumstances we find ourselves in. Although people may prefer to veil their true nature behind acquired traits of false personality or other psychological devices, certain fundamental underlying characteristics remain. Being untrue to one self in hopes of pleasing others is an obstacle to self-awareness, and creates a barrier to harmonious relationships. When we dismiss our acquired traits and attitudes in favor of those that are more agreeable to our nature we begin feel more in tune with our life. When we drop false personality, we begin to emanate a more harmonious natural energy that is conducive to healthy, balanced realistic interactions with others.

Harmony with another is based on mutual respect, acceptance and understanding. That is, by accepting a person for who they are, rather than how, or what we want, or expect them to be. Often, we think our role is to change someone, but this is quite wrong. Understanding centers and eliminating false personality will help you see others with more clarity. Manifestations and motivations become less obscured as you look beneath surface appearances of false personality. But, it is essential to make intentional efforts to eliminate your own false personality weaknesses. With enhanced sincerity and clarity, we can see, and accept others with greater compassion, which encourages natural responses. This allows greater self-expression and creates a harmonious environment for relationships to evolve. As we strengthen our will with consistent mindful self-observation, and sincerity, we can eliminate the illusion of false personality.

Discovering who you really are in your essential nature is one of the most rewarding tasks in life, and the key to your personal self-development. As you practice mindful self-observation you will recognize how false personality fortifies weaknesses of negative features, and you will gain much greater insight into your true inner self. This allows you to observe artificialities with more clarity, impartiality and transparency in yourself and in others. Observing influences of centers, will help you see what is a natural function of centers and what is artificial. Penetrating the walls of false personality, helps diminish its dominance in your life. Realizing false personality is an illusion will help you to minimize and relinquish it. Just as we have built a wall of false personality around ourselves, we can also create a sincere true personality within ourselves. When we drop the mask of persona as false personality, we are naturally more in our true nature and more authentic. With consistent and sincere practice, this exercise can encourage your essential nature to emerge. If we strive to live our life from our true essential nature, rather than living from false personality, we can minimize unnecessary and excessive energy drains. Economizing our energy helps balance our centers and assists us in reaching higher states of consciousness as a natural progression.

With consistent sincere self-observation, you can gain a clearer and more lucid understanding of yourself, your friends, your family, and other people in your life. Gaining control over habitual patterns and falsely acquired traits, which do not truly serve your life, will open more doors on your journey of self-discovery. We all begin the journey of self-knowledge with mindful self-observation to gain self-knowledge, and by looking deep within our self to discover our true essential nature.

Remember, knowledge is power. Self-knowledge is empowering and transformational.

Buffers:

Buffers are the habitual psychological and physical devices which people employ to hide from, mitigate, deflect, avoid, ignore, or deny the reality of life. Buffers block acknowledgment of what one does not want to know, or deal with. Buffers basically act as false cushioning to soften the blows of life, fate, facts, or other people, even if they exist only in one's imagination. Buffers frequently become part of one's habitual patterns of behavior and take the form of a response mechanism that immediately rejects or negates anything or anyone that is disagreeable or threatening to one's false personality. Generally, buffers are nothing more than flimsy imaginary excuses we employ to negate what we do not want to deal with, whether it is a person, a situation, an idea, or whatever else we cannot cope with in a given moment. Buffers can also manifest in harmful instinctive center habits such as alcohol dependence, cigarette smoking and drug addiction. Frequently when a person feels a threat, real or imagined, they defer to their addiction; perhaps they light a cigarette. Buffers cannot and will not improve your life in any real way. Ultimately buffers only cause harm.

Buffers also may take the form of little white lies which people consider harmless and which they employ when attempting to block reality in a particular moment. Buffers often manifest when a person is caught off guard, and most significantly when they are guilty of some type of action, or offense. These automatic habitual lies are typically a defense mechanism to protect oneself in some manner, but especially one's imaginary picture of one self in false personality. People feel they must protect and perpetuate their false personality which is their alter-ego. However, buffers can also be harmful lies used to manipulate people or reality, and to prevent the truth from being known. Buffers heap habitual lies on top of other lies to block, distort, or cover the real truth in what may be perceived as an inconvenient, or an uncomfortable moment. Buffers typically take the form of an illusionary cover up employed to disguise another illusion.

There are many common buffers which are often utilized when a person is trying to minimize the impact of a negative activity, especially their own unhealthy physical habits. The following are basic examples to give you a general idea of how buffers might sound as they manifest. An overweight person may insist that a few chocolate chip cookies will not hurt their diet at all. Or, a smoker who is trying to quit may say, "Oh well, a few cigarettes a day are fairly harmless." An alcoholic who wants another drink may argue, "But, it's just a tiny shot glass of tequila!" Buffers frequently take their form in substance abuse which people are trying to hide from others. These types of harmful buffers can become habitual patterns of behavior which may lodge in specific parts of centers. Buffers can especially become imbedded in the Queens of centers, which renders them even more extreme, and where they can become obsessive and compulsive.

Another form buffers take is personal declarations about one self which are inaccurate, or simply just untrue. These personal declarations are usually based in one's fictional false personality as part of one's imaginary self-portrait within. This nonexistent device is an attempt to conceal one's flaws in outward expressions, which further obscure reality, but typically only conceal reality from one self. For example, a person who complains about everything, from the weather to the stock market may declare that he, "never complains." Of course, this is simply his personal buffer which allows him to believe that he is a delightful person. However, those around him do not believe his fictional declaration as they have repeatedly witnessed his incessant complaining. Yet, people have different buffers which require other false personality declarations. Buffers all tend to serve the same purpose, to conceal the truth of one self to one self, and if possible to deceive others into believing your personal lies about yourself. Examples of other declarative buffers are, "I am always punctual!" Or, "I am always polite to everyone." Or, "I am always helpful!" and so on. The person who repeatedly makes these personal statements probably believes them; however, other people who are more observant can often see through these fictional façades. Remember, this type of declarative buffer is only relevant to the person who is stating it.

Buffers in any form are typically lies we fabricate to protect our imaginary self-portrait. Buffers also manifest as lies we tell about others, typically by gossiping, but which ultimately cause harm to all involved. There are other types of buffers which take the form of certain physical behaviors that people employ when they feel threatened or socially inadequate. These habitual behaviors may take the form of verbal comments, physical postures, gestures, and other automatic habits which manifest without attention or intentionality. The behaviors can range from sudden bursts of giggling when one is embarrassed, or wringing one's hands when one is nervous. Other examples may be how we arrange our body when speaking with others, based on the person, or the subject. You may automatically fold your arms over your chest defensively when speaking about emotional subjects. Another person may take a wide physical stance to maximize their size to intimidate someone. All of these physical mannerisms are buffers which we habitually employ to protect ourselves, or soften the blow of anything that life throws us, which we are not equipped to manage sensibly.

For example, recently I hired a fellow to clear the weeds along the narrow borders of my garden. Later, he knocked on my door, saying he needed to leave, but assured me he would return the following day to finish. He asked for payment and I gave him the agreed amount in cash. But, over the next three days he did not return to finish clearing the weeds. Then I saw him in the neighborhood and asked him to please come over and finish my weed clearing. But, he gave me excuses why he could not finish my yard. His arms were crossed over his chest and he acted very nervous. And then he lit a cigarette and told me he could not complete it as his hourly rate had gone up and other people paid him more. He also insisted I had only asked for one border to be cleared, and so on. I remained quiet as he gave me one flimsy buffered excuse after the other, and then he left. Afterwards I realized what the real problem was; I had told him he could not smoke cigarettes while he worked in my garden, as I am allergic. But, without his cigarette habit smoking buffer he became angry, willful, and basically refused to finish the work in my garden. While we may not always understand people's buffers, sometimes it is helpful to try. Simply acknowledging their buffers can help to minimize confusion or any lingering resentment we may feel toward them.

Buffers also arise out of sheer boredom with life. People often indulge in excessive unnecessary talk, repetitive movements, and an endless circle of activities in order to buffer reality. There are those who get nervous in certain situations and they begin to shift about quite visibly, repetitively tapping their fingers, the toes, or rocking their foot as they twitch about. Other people may take up extraneous activities to avoid experiencing a moment of stillness in their life because they are terrified of boredom. I knew a woman who went to any event that was available just to stay busy, including a dry-wall repair demonstration at a hardware store as she desperately needed to stay busy. She was also unable to remain quiet, and rattled off a stream of empty idle chatter about running around town doing endless meaningless tasks. Her children were grown which also made her feel completely lost, and it was clear that she was bored with her life. She was unable to ever be by herself, even for a moment, so she buffered her empty nest with constant incessant activities to fritter away time.

Some people buffer reality by speaking non-stop with uncontrolled chatter. However, they fail to take in information about others, or events occurring around them. Their lives are filtered through the miasmatic fog of their own incessant narratives which habitually emanate from overactive imaginations. I had tea with friends recently, but left early because one woman dominated the group with a narration of her trip to Washington D.C. The group had met to discuss a specific film, but she ignored the agenda and carried on her peculiar monologue. She punctuated her chatter with random comments, carelessly insulting a few people. It was apparent that she could not endure silence or anyone else speaking. Afterwards, the hostess sent an email apologizing for the woman's rude behavior to everyone. She added that she was totally unable to comprehend the woman's insensitive, aggressive and incessant talking.

Buffers become a habitual cycle of lies that manifest automatically without any attention. The fact that they manifest habitually is an indication of how mindless buffers truly are. Buffers are ongoing habitual lies and false thinking which keep people asleep to the truth of reality. Throughout life we come up against issues, ideas, opinions, topics, situations or people that are uncomfortable for us, or that we disagree with, or which we prefer to ignore, or that we wish would go away, or perhaps would just disappear. This is a rudimentary description of any scenario wherein a buffer might be employed almost instantaneously to try to stop or cushion whatever it is that one objects to, or is afraid of, regardless of whether it is true or false, real or unreal. Ultimately buffers are extremely counterproductive to living a healthy balanced life, and are counter intuitive to attaining true self-awareness. Using mindful self-observation, you will begin to notice your own buffers, which will certainly help you see yourself more clearly and accurately. Minimizing and eliminating buffers can help you to create a more meaningful existence for yourself, and for other people in your life. Monitor buffers with mindful self-observation by paying attention to yourself with intentionality.

Lying:
Throughout our life, we are prone to speaking about things which we honestly know nothing about, and cannot possibly really understand. People commonly chat about topics which they do not truly know about. For example, certain groups speak quite descriptively about life on other planets; however, they have not personally been to another planet, so whatever they say about it is merely speculative casual chatting, or simply lying. While chatting about the subject of life, on whichever planet they choose to speak about, they may embellish their story or theory with all sorts of strange descriptions, such as "little green men." Virtually everything they say is based on their imagination, science fiction, simple conjecture, or just random thoughts. However, as they have not personally verified the alien life form which they are describing, they are actually indulging in a form of lying. The concept of lying is really quite basic, very common, and is just this simplistic.

In our lifetime, we have witnessed increased exploration of outer space. NASA and other space agencies around the world have successfully sent rocket ships to explore other planets in our solar system. The brilliant scientists, physicists, engineers and extraordinarily brave astronauts who travel into space actually do know something real and quite important about life on other planets. However, these individuals do not appear to indulge in random discussions speaking about their experiences with casual rhetoric, or in farfetched speculative hypothetical terms. Their knowledge is based on their practical experiences, scientific investigations and verifications. And each person involved in the space program has spent many years acquiring a highly trained, specialized education, doing practical applications, while developing their own empirical knowledge. Their exploration of space is based in truth and scientific reality, and certainly not idle chatter or casual lying.

Certainly, most of us do not go through life researching everything we encounter with scientific precision and accuracy. Yet we often speak about subjects, ideas and people as if we know them intimately. People commonly speak about famous celebrities as if they know them well, although they have never met them. Their discussions and opinions are based solely on that which the celebrity's press agent, and publicity representative has given for publication to various media outlets. This information about the celebrity may be exaggerated to generate interest or create more popularity. So, while people cannot really know what a celebrity is like personally, they speak about them as if they know them. This is a fairly common form of lying. Typically, when we have not personally verified information we may tend to resort to casual forms of lying, without even realizing it. When we notice that we are speaking randomly about a subject, it is best to just stop speaking, or change the subject to something we do know about.

Certainly, we each have a vast storehouse of personal experiences from which we can draw true information. Before you speak, you can make a conscious decision to evaluate what you are about to say to see if it is true, or whether it is really necessary to mention it. Ask yourself a few questions, "Will this help anyone?" or, "Is this important?" and also, "Is this true?" You can also assuage casual lying by not indulging in endless streams of imagination about everything and everyone. It is vital to realize that when we engage in rambling imaginary scenarios we are only lying to our self.

Many of the conversations we have on a daily basis are harmless, and usually somewhat superficial. Generally, when we go to the market, or to our local coffee shop, or to the newspaper stand we probably do not engage in deep lengthy discussions. But, when people get together socially with friends, colleagues, paramours or partners, generally quite a lot of discussion takes place. Without realizing it we may quite innocently pepper our dialogues and conversations with various forms of gossip and speculation, such as, "I just heard this juicy tidbit about so and so." While these comments may not have a serious personal impact, it is prudent to avoid indulging in idle chatter or gossip, both of which lean toward lying in various degrees. Gossip about anyone at any time is harmful to everyone who speaks it, or hears it. Do not indulge in speculative gossip. Remember, only harm is borne of gossip.

Mindful self-observation is beneficial to mitigate excessive or unnecessary talking overall, and it can certainly help one to minimize, and eventually put an end to the incessant habit of lying. In many spiritual and philosophical systems, the concept of "silence" is considered highly valuable, and is employed as a disciplined method to assist one to become more aware. Those who are striving for increased self-awareness and self-knowledge, often practice the art of silence at various points in their personal work. Perhaps you can begin to practice the gentle quiet art of silence for 15 to 30 minutes a day. With a bit of practice, you may be able to extend your period of silence to 1 hour or more each day. While you are in silence observe yourself as you monitor and control your imagination, so you do not engage in internal monologues, dialogues, or unnecessary internal talking. Make a conscious decision to maintain quiet silence in your mind to avoid indulging in random imagination, which only perpetuates unnecessary talk and lying. Silence will help you see yourself and others more truthfully, and with much greater depth and enhanced sincerity.

Internal considering and external considering:
The importance we place on the opinions of others can affect how we live our life, and how we function in our world. This is simply identification with other people. We tend to care too much about how others perceive us, and what they may think about us. This habitual projection of what others might think, expect or want from us, drains our precious life energy and is an underlying cause of social phobias. Thoughts and concerns of what others might think can severely inhibit our natural responses and essential manifestations. This type of negative imagination is the antithesis of compassion, as it creates deep seated self-doubts which ultimately erode and stifle healthy self-development. Rather than being concerned about what people think of us it is healthier to dismiss these thoughts when they arise. In truth, what other people think of us is irrelevant for our personal growth. Worrying about what class mates, friends, strangers, or what the neighbors think, is counterproductive to our efforts to become self-aware.

When we are overly concerned with what others think of us, we may be indulging in a form of unnecessary self-criticism. If we stop worrying about what other people think, we might have a more meaningful exchange with them. It is vital to observe the people in our life impartially, without preconceived notions, without attaching unreal expectations to them, but especially not giving their thoughts or opinions more value than they are worth. When we are impartial we have an opportunity to be more objective about others. With enhanced objectivity, we begin to see that they may actually be in need of help, or may be suffering in some manner. Often what another person needs in a moment, is kindness and unbiased understanding, not our projected false fears of inadequacy. Compassion tends to arise naturally from consciously caring about other people. and having their best interests at heart. While the idea of developing compassion may seem to be an obvious mindset, compassion requires one's intentional effort. Our compassion manifests in the outer world as "external consideration" of another person. This type of thinking in a positive manner about and for the welfare of others, necessitates our conscious participation. The Fourth Way system advises one to engage in the practice of external consideration which is compassionate. Compassion is the practice of being aware in the moment to externally consider another's needs and wellbeing.

The opposite of compassion is "internal considering," which manifests in habitual self-absorption which makes us care too much, or worry excessively about what other people think of us; whether they like us, approve of us, disapprove of us, and so on. Internal considering is simply identification with other people, which manifests in negative imagination and attachment, thus one becomes overly concerned about what other people think. Internal considering inhibits us from feeling comfortable, or behaving naturally in their presence, because of our imaginary personal insecurities. Internal considering creates unnecessary tensions as we worry or become anxious about other people's opinions. This unnecessary suffering is simply one's personal negative imagination. What others think of us may not actually have any direct effect on us, unless we believe it does. Internally considering is habitual negative imagination and identification, which is the polar opposite of compassion.

Most people are conditioned by the world media to care too much about what others think of them. The negative identification of our internal considering can be about anything; what we are wearing, how we look, whether we are too thin or too fat, whether our hair is the right color or style, whether we are too short or too tall, what type of car we drive, what foods we eat, what newspaper we read, what television shows we watch or do not watch, how old we are, how attractive or unattractive we feel, whether we vote for a certain politician, whether we believe in the same god, or believe in any god for that matter, and so it goes on infinitely as we habitually worry. But, these variable mindsets or situations really have nothing to do with our true essential nature. Quite often we may not know exactly what we are feeling in a situation, but we may feel somewhat uneasy or uncomfortable being around certain people. We may feel shy, awkward, embarrassed or ashamed, and we may not truly know why this is happening. But, it is simply identification and negative imagination.

Internal considering arises from the habitual conditioning of our unintentional thoughts and conflicting ideas or opinions about what is important, either to ourselves, or to other people. Without knowing why, we may feel inferior, or that we are not good enough, which manifests as self-doubt and other negative behavior. But, the more we give in to our negative internal considering, the more likely it is that others will perceive us in a negative manner. If you feel inadequate in a situation, people may take advantage of you. Most of us have experienced internal considering at some point in our life. In order to mitigate internal considering and overcome our habitual worry and concern about what others think of us, it is helpful to put our attention into more beneficial patterns of thought, which are more conducive to our self-awareness and personal growth, rather than negative identification.

People are often influenced by the dictates of fashion and trends. The television and movie industry may promote certain images as being better than what we personally prefer. Fashions are constantly changing, but it is impossible to keep buying new things to achieve genuine happiness. It is highly beneficial to use scale and relativity to gain a deeper understanding of what your needs truly are in your life. Your hair style, or the clothes you wear are not connected to, or even remotely relevant to your sincere conscious evolution. Though I spent many years of my life in careers directly related to advertising and fashion, I understand the role they play in our society. However, I am also well aware of what is of importance to me in my own life. How you choose to dress is your personal choice, and it is fine to be different from others. With regard to developing self-awareness you are fully encouraged to be true to your unique essential nature. Begin with mindful self-observation and bring your conscious attention to the present moment.

When we recognize internal considering as habitual identification and negative imagination, we can gain more control over its manifestation. But, we must also understand that we cannot truly know what others think of us, nor can we have any control over their thoughts or opinions. Keep in mind, if someone is not working intentionally to develop enhanced self-awareness, it is fairly likely that they are operating from their own automatic habitual patterns of behavior. They might not even really notice you, because of their own self-absorption. Knowing this provides valuable relativity about your own perceptions of others. As you practice mindful self-observation, you will see more clearly that many exchanges with others happen almost automatically, with little conscious participation, or awareness. You will begin to see through the veneer of false personality, identification, and negative imagination, to witness your personal interactions with greater transparency. It is helpful to understand that each person is experiencing their own life at their personal level of awareness, and we must learn to respect and honor this in everyone. It is beneficial to externally consider others, and make intentional efforts to eliminate our own habitual internal consideration.

Many years ago, a teacher I studied with said, we can accomplish goals we aspire toward with enhanced ease, if we do not internally consider. This simple advice can give us freedom from our self-doubts, if we understand and embrace it. We can begin to loosen the grip of negative imagination, and stop worrying anxiously about what other people think of us. In truth, we cannot know what others think of us, and it is not relevant to our personal self-awareness and higher consciousness.

As you monitor your internal world with consistent mindful self-observation, you will be able to minimize internal considering, and its negative side effects. As this element of your inner life begins to evolve and change, quite naturally many other areas of your life will also transform. You will begin to notice the needs of other people, which gives you an opportunity to exercise external consideration towards them. This can manifest as compassion, sympathy, empathy, gentleness, acceptance, tolerance, generosity, and other forms of sincere human kindness. As we focus our attention to the real needs of others we can more readily dismiss our own lingering self-doubts and other self-defeating concerns. External consideration puts the emphasis on being compassionately aware of others. You will elevate your consciousness while behaving with conscientious goodness.

Scale and Relativity:

Another valuable concept is the practical application of scale and relativity, which helps one gain a higher level of understanding and comprehension in situations. Peter Ouspensky spoke about scale and relativity with regard to understanding the universe and our rather unique position in it. He spoke of using scale and relativity to determine the exact mathematic relationship of one thing to another, such as the micro-cosmos to the macro-cosmos, and their relationship to one another as an exact mathematical equation within the laws of the universe. However, for the purpose of this book these references may be a bit too theoretical for practical use in your daily life. Some abstract theories, though immensely interesting, may not necessarily advance your personal self-knowledge. Yet understanding the correlation of one thing to another in your own life by employing scale and relativity is eminently practical. It is a beneficial means whereby you can introduce and incorporate more common sense in situations; in your relationships with others, and to everything else in your life.

Scale and relativity will help you to determine and to separate minor issues from major issues in your daily life. This can help you monitor and manage your emotional energy, thoughts, actions and your senses. Certainly, monitoring the optimal functioning of our centers helps conserve energy. But typically, we make proverbial mountains out of molehills during daily events, owing to a lack of scale and relativity. This can happen even with minor occurrences in everyday life. Scale and relativity can be a powerful tool to regain balance and harmony with a more precise view of issues and people in our lives. Thinking with scale and relativity helps to minimize the enormity of what we believe to be a crisis. Viewed from this perspective we can experience less stress, make better decisions and more accurate assessments of matters, even under duress. By introducing relativity and scale, we can bring problems to a more manageable level sooner, and with more control. This helps one to attain greater clarity, comprehension and balance during a difficult ordeal. For example, when we are over reacting in a situation, we can try to freeze the moment with a mental pause, to implement relativity and scale with the intellectual center. Taking a mental pause slows things down to allow you to gain greater control. This enhances your ability to correctly understand what is required in a situation, regardless of what it might be.

Consider for a moment the extreme volatility of the Queen of Hearts in Alice in Wonderland. She went absolutely berserk simply because the roses were the wrong color. Her display of outrage and excessive anger is an extreme energy drain and throws everything and everyone else out of balance. The Queen of Hearts is a vivid example of how centers can become out of balance; hence, emotions lack relativity and scale. She was consumed by a small matter, and completely lost all sense of reason and rationale. Using scale and relativity, we recognize that negative outbursts are useless and counterproductive. When extreme emotions arise, excessive life energy is depleted.

To gain more self-control it is helpful to practice with scale and relativity in calmer moments. Use this to gain experience to enable you to see all sides of a situation, as this will help later with more serious concerns. Try to observe yourself in a clear impartial manner throughout your day. Then, if heated issues arise, or the atmosphere becomes agitated, you will be better equipped to deal with it. Scale and relativity help one to resolve matters, and to introduce practical common-sense solutions. It may simply be matter of adjusting your viewpoint to see the bigger picture in the details which are occurring. Monitor situations as calmly as possible as you strive to gain understanding using scale and relativity, especially in heated situations. Introducing the element of scale and relativity into the moment will bring more attention and awareness to whatever is occurring.

Using this concept in a practical manner will enhance your decisions and choices, to help you know what is the best option, and the higher right in a given situation. Compassionate action is always right action and an excellent medium in which to use scale and relativity. It helpful to try to recognize what might be more beneficial for another person in the moment, and perhaps you can assist then in some way. Employing scale and relativity with mindful self-observation helps you to make better choices which are harmonious for yourself and others. Creating a pleasant psychological environment while implementing scale and relativity in situations can help you to experience healthier interactions with others. Also, attitudes of self-importance or arrogance are often misplaced in our personal interactions. These attitudes typically manifest as habitual behaviors which interrupt the flow of right action in a moment and discourage positive outcomes.

It is vital to become more self-aware to experience one's life as it is actually happening. Using scale and relativity as you learn how your centers function will help you identify more accurately what feels most natural to your essential nature. Observe your life with as much clarity, simplicity and honesty as possible to gain enhanced understanding of yourself in your most natural manner, and without judgment. Strive to be intentional, mindful, objective, impartial, and tolerant as you begin to employ scale and relativity in your interactions on a daily basis. This will help you to develop right attitude so you know what is the best thing to say, or do in a moment, for yourself and for others. Certainly, using scale and relativity will assist in developing better communication skills to achieve greater harmony and balance with others. Observing what resonates with your inner being allows you to make positive changes which are in tune with your true essential nature. Employing scale and relativity will help you to weigh the pros and cons of a situation, and will help you gain enhanced objectivity with self-awareness to think things through clearly to make informed decisions. The key to making positive changes is knowing what needs to change. Scale and relativity can bring you a step closer to understanding precisely what changes would be beneficial in your life, and also, what might be helpful for another person in a situation.

Of course, you can also use scale and relativity to understand the bigger picture, the universe and all things in relation to their place in the micro-cosmos and the macro-cosmos. Regardless of whether you are an astrophysicist, an artist, a teacher or a farmer, the concept of scale and relativity can be applied to your practical reality on a moment to moment basis. With consistent mindful self-observation, you will begin to notice what has greater or lesser importance for the essential smooth functioning of your life.

The law of Octaves:

In nature, we can witness the continuous ebb and flow of patterns which repeat over and over again with reliable regularity. By observing these ongoing patterns, the Greek mathematician Pythagoras formulated his masterful theory about the law of octaves. This mathematical theory is apparent in the musical octave. However, we can also observe the law of octaves at work in our own daily life. There is always a definitive beginning, and an end with everything. Between the beginning point and the end, there are high points, low points, points where we falter, and points where we must exert more energy or it will end. Consider that each point of any activity is a note, not unlike a musical note, and forms a precise pattern. This is essentially the law of octaves at work in our life.

Certainly, there are moments in our day when we get tired, need a break, or require nourishment, and this is perfectly natural. And, it is helpful to observe that these patterns occur repeatedly with regularity in your daily routine, and in all your personal experiences. We tend to be creatures of habit, but natural habits form distinct patterns in life, and these patterns form a distinctive rhythm. With observation, you will recognize different points, where you start something, digress, lose interest, come to a standstill, or change course. Ask yourself, are you proceeding in a specific direction, gaining or losing interest, succeeding or failing? Consider your current situation, your goals, your job or career, your projects, your relationships and simply observe to see if there is a rhythmic pattern unfolding of how events are playing out, whether proceeding, progressing, or stalling at a standstill, or ending.

As you begin to observe your personal patterns you will see a repetitive schematic, perhaps energetic beginnings, alternating with high and low points, points where you get tired, get hungry, get distracted, take action, lose interest, give up, or other possibilities in between. Everything we do has a beginning and an end. However, it is what happens between the beginning point and the end point, that we must learn to work with, in order to actually realize and manifest our most cherished goals. By gaining a basic understanding of the law of octaves theory, you can apply it to your own life. You can observe the octave of your day, your job, your relationships, and all the various events of your life. Being aware of a pattern of the law of octaves in our life, allows us to see clearly where we are at a given moment of time. The law of octaves is naturally at work in everything we do. Every day we experience the law of octaves in all that transpires.

When we feel that life is at a standstill or going nowhere, most likely we are in an interval in our personal life octave. We may need to pay more attention in these particular moments, to add more energy to move forward in a positive direction, and move out of our temporary state of stagnation. A stagnant pond holds still lifeless water, but an increase in circulation will help to introduce new life to the pond. It may be that events in our life or our relationships are in a state of stagnation. Recognizing that one is at a standstill in life is the first step to getting out of stagnation. Remember the metaphor of the stagnant pond; as circulation is increased it will regain its flowing equilibrium. We must also increase circulation in our life, by adding fresh energy to increase balance and attain harmony and equilibrium. Being aware of how the octave functions will help you understand your life better, and the need to introduce energy to overcome inertia. Also, knowing that there are two intervals in every octave, prepares one for moments when new energy must be added to continue. At these points, one must add energy by making conscious efforts to bridge the gap of the interval. For the octave to continue and progress, we must recognize the intervals as points where we must make efforts to add energy, in order to succeed or ascend. Our success or failure in whatever we attempt is tied to our ability to bridge the intervals in octaves. When we make a conscious decision to add energy at the interval exactly when it is needed we will be able to continue, and hopefully to succeed.

Throughout our day, we experience moments where we feel we have lost our focus. At this point you may simply be in an interval and need to add energy to be able to complete what you are doing. Taking a coffee break, or having lunch, are both examples of how you might gain the requisite energy to continue your day. As we consistently observe these patterns, we can begin to recognize when we are in an interval in our life. The interval is the point at which we must add more energy to help the activity to continue, or it might just suddenly end. These intervals can be looked at as points where things will change in some manner; things may get better, get worse, or simply end.

The law of octaves is an interesting concept that can be utilized in a helpful manner to get clarity in the moment and to see precisely where one is. Whether it is your career, relationships, or your personal growth hoping to achieve a more conscious evolution, it is not difficult to observe the simple rhythmic pattern of the law of octaves in your life. Continue to observe and you will recognize intervals as moments of fatigue, points where you lose interest, or moments of indecision. It is at these points that you must intentionally do something more for the octave to continue. Analyze the situation, whatever it may be, and ask yourself if you truly want to keep putting energy into this octave? Although we may not realize it, the outcome of many events and situations in our life are totally up to us. It may be our sole responsibility, whether we succeed or fail. In order to succeed we must add the vital energy at the intervals to fulfill our goals and to propel the octave in an ascending manner to completion.

By utilizing the idea of the law of octaves in your daily life you will gain a better grasp of many situations. As you learn to refine, discern, and recognize what is valuable in your life, you can make more informed decisions and elective choices about what stays in your life, and what is no longer beneficial to continue with. Perhaps the octave with a relationship, with your job, or whatever you feel blocked about, is in an interval that cannot be bridged with any amount of additional time or energy. Sometimes we simply need to let go of events, issues, or people who are not a positive influence in our life. We can understand that by letting go, we also allow others to move forward on their own personal evolutionary path. Ultimately this becomes the fuel of personal growth for everyone involved.

This brief discussion about the law of octaves is an overview to provide you with a few basic ideas about this remarkable concept. Understanding octaves can assist you on your personal journey to gain enhanced self-awareness. It may be helpful to do additional reading to gain a deeper comprehension of the law of octaves and how it manifests. Peter Ouspensky has written substantial passages which elucidate the law of octaves in the insightful book, "The Fourth Way."

Alchemy ~ the Process of Self Refinement:
Alchemy is the process of personal self-refinement through the purification of one's internal being. Intentionally working on oneself to be present in the moment with the aim to elevate one's self-awareness, creates a shift within which assists in the transformation of one's alchemy. Self-development requires the process of intentional self-study to purify oneself, evolve, and to activate and access one's essential nature. The acquisition of self-knowledge with an aim to experience higher states of conscious self-awareness, initiates personal transformation as an alchemical process. Alchemy requires consistent personal efforts to refine the elements of one's life with the transformative power of self-knowledge through self-awareness.

Alchemy is personal self-transformation to achieve higher levels of awareness and elevated consciousness.

Historically, the science of alchemical chemistry was believed to be a mythical, or mystical process for turning base metals into pure gold. In medieval times, it was believed that alchemy was not only the transmutation of base metals into gold, but was also thought to be a magical elixir of longevity, perhaps comparable to the legendary fountain of youth. Alchemy is an ancient philosophical and psychological practice, or science, which has always been associated with magic, the use of magic, or the attainment of magical powers. The church treated the study and practice of alchemy as heresy. Dabbling or experimenting with alchemical chemistry was heretical. Quite literally the practice of alchemy as magic was forbidden and highly illegal.

Certainly, we can apply the same conceptual associations to the transmutation process of one's personal alchemy. The same ancient ideas about alchemy, such as turning common base metals to gold, also describe the transformational process in the acquisition of self-knowledge and the process of self-refinement. One works to achieve enhanced self-awareness through one's personal efforts. Self-study with the aim to become more aware, elevates and refines one's personal alchemy. This personal aim necessitates consistent mindful self-observation, not indulging in imagination, not identifying, not expressing negative emotions, not buffering, not lying, and eliminating false personality. Self-development for the acquisition of higher states of conscious awareness is a process which is no less golden or magical than the alchemist. It is one self which one is transmuting into gold.

Keep in mind, often when an individual embarks on a personal quest for self-development, they tend to step away from the standard, or established belief systems which are in place. This may be rather uncomfortable for others, and might possibly feel threatening to them. While others may feel excluded, they may also suspect or believe the individual is going against the safe, or accepted standardized belief systems. This is fairly common. In ancient times those who were different from the ordinary, who did not follow regulations set forth in customs of the day, were often persecuted in some manner. Remnants of this intolerant attitude holds true for those who are different, even today in our theoretically modern world. As you gain greater self-awareness many of the standardized customs, systems or patterns of belief, and the general social conditions of life may lose their appeal. Thus, their hold over you may diminish. This can be quite liberating.

Minimizing and eliminating false personality already begins to change your personal alchemy by changing how you present yourself in the world, and also, how you interact with others. As you make consistent efforts to stop energy draining habits, such as negative emotions, imagination, and identification you begin to transform your personal alchemy. Self-transformation is the process of making efforts to attain higher states of self-awareness, while simultaneously refining one's personal internal alchemy. The primary method to begin your process of refinement is mindful self-observation.

An important point about transforming one's alchemy, is that one cannot mechanically, or automatically elevate or refine one's alchemy simply by changing one's outward appearance. Wearing expensive clothing, or driving a Rolls Royce, has nothing to do with one's internal essential alchemy. Appearances are deceptive in this regard. Exhibiting arrogant lofty airs is merely false personality behaving badly, which is not conducive to refinement. Artificial devices and pretentious outward manifestations, are part of one's imaginary picture of oneself in false personality traits and have no beneficial effect on one's alchemy. Exchanging the mask, one is wearing for another mask will not help. External contrivances have no merit in purifying oneself, or in elevating one's alchemy.

The more refined and purified one becomes within oneself, the less one would wish to flaunt artificialities. However, being intentionally polite with sincerity, attentively well mannered, and immaculately groomed may help one to become more aware of oneself. Becoming more aware begins to change your internal processes, which helps facilitate your personal alchemical processes. Our internal alchemy affects our ability to receive and perceive impressions. The more rarified and refined the impression, the more refined one's internal alchemy must be to receive, and to perceive these finer impressions. One's personal alchemy is reflected in how one feels, emotes, thinks, speaks, behaves, reacts, responds, and certainly with how one manifests in the world. Our personal alchemy affects what energies we attract from others, and also, how others perceive us. We can purify our alchemical properties through our consistent sincere efforts to monitor and transform our personal feelings, thoughts, words, actions, deeds, senses, and our physical presence with increased awareness, attention and intentionality. The refinement of one's personal alchemy is an essential component in the process of one's self development.

For our personal reality to become more refined we must strive to gain enhanced self-awareness by making consistent efforts to be present in the moment. We can create a more refined reality by employing mindful self-observation with attention and intentionality. We must shed habitual identifications, curb unmonitored imagination, minimize unnecessary talk, dismiss internal consideration, and strive to eliminate artificially acquired traits in false personality. The cessation of these unnatural habitual behaviors will improve your life immeasurably and will help you to experience a more refined, pure and objective conscious alchemical reality.

We are composed of many different I's:

As you read these concepts regarding our general human condition, it may become apparent that we are not unified, but are composed of many different parts. As you recognize the numerous obstacles to awareness that each of us face with habitual imagination, identification, buffers, false personality, features, and so on, you will appreciate the simplicity of the practical tools which can help enhance your self-awareness. Mindful self-observation helps one see the many different components and inconsistencies with enhanced clarity. In his writings, Ouspensky encourages us to verify we are not unified, but are composed of many different parts, each expressing their own needs. The idea that one is not a unified being may sound strange, but, as you examine your feelings, thoughts, opinions, actions and sensory desires, you will notice you have many different ideas about everything, perhaps even about your self-awareness.

For example, at this moment you may have different thoughts about certain matters which are quite different from what you thought last night, or last week. These different thoughts, feelings, ideas, and opinions are magnified and multiplied by the different centers as they function and manifest, but, also according to diverse situations we may be experiencing from external influences. Typically, in one moment you may be thinking, or feeling one way, but certain new information, or contradicting influences and opinions enter, which creates self-doubts, or opposition within. You may make a decision to do something new or to try a different regimen, but then you realize that you feel quite conflicted about it, despite your original impulse.

To illustrate this point, here is a simple example. You read a trendy magazine and see a coat that you really like, and are also inspired by an article on healthy eating. You decide to go shopping for the new coat, but you look out the window and it is pouring with rain. You abandon your shopping trip and go online to buy the coat on the internet. But, you discover the coat got terrible fashion reviews and one fashion blogger said it is hideous! You suddenly feel rather silly about admiring the coat, and then begin to question your fashion sense and doubt your personal taste level. But, in the next moment you remember your decision to try the healthy eating regime in the magazine. You make a long shopping list to take to the health food store as soon as it stops raining. But, when it finally stops raining you have completely forgotten about healthy food, and go to a café to treat yourself to chocolate chip ice cream with whipped cream.

This simple scenario is merely an illustration of how we might decide one thing, then change our mind and make very different choices. And, it is also an example of how the many different I's within us can manifest. You might be thinking, well we all just change our mind from time to time. Yet, if it was truly this simplistic we could manage all the various different I's quite efficiently. In reality, we have numerous different I's on virtually every subject, person, object, situation, event, or issue, whether it is an opinion, notion, idea, belief, superstition, or just a hunch.

We are all constantly in flux internally, churning inside with our many different I's struggling, competing, or fighting to micro-manage our life. While you may dismiss this as simply changing one's mind, remember, we do this constantly, hundreds of times a day, about everything on a moment to moment basis. So, it is vital to begin to observe the many different I's within one self.

These conflicting different I's emanate from our desires, thoughts, imagination, interests, likes, dislikes, senses, our programming, and so forth. The many I's manifest habitually, without attention or intentionality, so we do not notice the shift. One minute one "I" may want something, and the next minute another "I" wants something different. We are composed of so many different "I's" that we do not really know which "I" will arise, or when. As you practice mindful self-observation you will notice when different I's manifest, and perhaps what triggers them. This gives you an insightful overview of yourself in each moment which grants you more control as you develop the ability to see yourself as you truly are. To become more aware of yourself you simply need to be mindfully present in the moment to observe yourself as you live your life. Self-observation brings you to the moment with presence, giving you more command over the different I's to assist your internal unification. To create more unity within is really just this simple and basic.

Although we might not gain complete control over every different "I" immediately, we can certainly make incremental adjustments on a moment to moment basis by increasing our attention and intentionality. Making sincere efforts with mindful self-observation helps one to gain more self-control over automatic habitual behaviors. Thus, we become less subject to the endless meanderings of life as we become more objective and increase our potential to raise our self above the mundane. We must make consistent efforts to be present to our life. Mindful self-observation is the key to becoming self-aware, and living life consciously in your essential nature.

CHAPTER 12

CHIEF FEATURES ~ CHIEF WEAKNESSES WITHIN OUR SELF AND IN OTHERS

Chief features are additional characteristics which manifest habitually, and become our primary weaknesses in life, despite the great value we tend to place on them. They can exert a powerful influence over us, and over other whom people we interact with. While chief features arise from our general tendencies, they develop in false personality and fuse with our artificially acquired behavioral traits. Our chief features manifest in our words, actions, postures, and gestures as we habitually and unconsciously behave, function and interact in the world. All chief features are negative and manifest mechanically from false personality. Thus, features work against our essential nature and hinder the development of genuine self-awareness. Our personal chief features represent our primary chief weaknesses, although we may not necessarily regard them as such. Quite often people regard their chief feature as an asset, such as having a forceful or dominant personality and exerting power over people. However, these and all chief features are negative weaknesses. Each person has a primary chief feature which manifests frequently and habitually throughout their life. Chief feature is fed by false personality, causing it to grow with that which is false.

The development of certain chief features is somewhat dependent on one's physical characteristics, and glandular predomination. Physically active types tend to have active chief features, while physically passive types may have the more passive chief features. For example, tall people often have dominant chief features, which manifests as dominance over other people. They can work to more effectively utilize the chief feature of dominance in managerial and executive type careers. But, in their personal life, they exert a domineering presence over people, which can be intimidating. Active, aggressive individuals tend to have a chief feature of power, and they generally exert their forceful disposition over everyone they interact with. Power and dominance are both active chief features and manifest precisely as their name implies, with assertiveness, aggressiveness, force and domination as controlling behavioral traits. Others may unwittingly disappear into the more passive chief features while they are in the presence of those who exhibit the strong feature of dominance, or the forceful feature of power. Common chief features you can begin to watch for are power, dominance, tramp, lunatic, naïveté, nonexistence, fear, periodicity, and willfulness. Each particular chief feature manifests as its name implies. Active chief features such as dominance, power, and lunatic, are quite apparent and emphasized by false personality. The passive chief features may be less noticeable, as they are not typically accentuated overtly by outward gestures or mannerisms.

For example, the chief feature of naïveté is rather passive as it does not clearly recognize the potential for negativity, either in a person or a situation. Their good nature may be too trusting, as they are not typically suspicious of others; however, this can be much to their detriment. Nonexistence is passive to the point of being submissive, and the person may withdraw inward, away from people and social activities. They may passively become meek, allowing others to have control, perhaps over them, or situations which involve them. Fear is also passive, and becomes easily threatened by situations or people, particularly those with more active chief features, such as power or dominance. Tramp feature lacks valuation for everything and everyone, and appears quite casual, careless, reckless, and negligent about important issues and people. The hippie generation is characterized by chief feature of tramp. The feature of periodicity is someone in continual flux, alighting briefly upon ideas, situations, or people, fluctuating as they change course. Willfulness is obstinate and contrary, opposing virtually everyone and everything. They function with chronic habitual opposition, even before they know the facts or truth of what is occurring; thus, they typically disagree. Lunatic is the extreme chief feature of those who think in radical terms and act irrationally, generally quite abruptly, harshly and often uncontrollably.

These are some of the main chief features and hopefully, they can serve as examples to look for. Remember, most people are typically quite unaware of their own chief feature, that it is their primary habitual weakness. Yet, chief feature exerts an influence over them and other people. With mindful self-observation, you will become more aware of your chief feature as it arises. When an individual's chief feature manifests they tend to attract, and interact with the opposite feature in another person. For example, chief feature of power tends to elicit passive features such as fear, naïveté, or nonexistence. Power feature manifests as force as it tries to exert control over people and situations. Keep in mind that features feed features; hence one's own weakness fuels the weakness in another. It is helpful to monitor chief feature, as it habitually attracts and interacts with others, rather than having conscious exchanges. Chief feature can interfere with our interactions, causing imbalances in relationships, or inhibiting our ability to develop lasting friendships and meaningful exchanges. Typically, we are unaware of our features, as chief feature manifests habitually as we interact with others, unless we become consciously aware of it.

Chief features are a very specific element of our life which mindful self-observation can help us monitor more effectively. Chief features are active or passive, thus they manifest accordingly. It may take time to recognize your personal chief feature, but it helps to know that it tends to manifest habitually. As you consistently employ mindful self-observation, you will begin to recognize your chief feature. It is helpful to realize that your chief feature is your personal weakness in life, primarily because it occurs without attention. But, interacting from chief feature may create barriers between people, rather than create intimate bonds of trust and friendship. Chief feature can also manifest from other imbalances, which may include various forms of mental illness, depression, psychosis, narcissism and other psychological impairments. For example, the chief feature of lunatic, is an extreme person who follows false ideals without regard for other people, or the negative results of their actions. Lunatic chief feature may be unable to discriminate between right and wrong. This is psychological impairment to the point of malevolence, violence, and dysfunctionality. There may be combinations of chief features which contribute to extreme imbalance.

Many years ago, I knew a person with combined chief features of willfulness and vanity. This person was extremely arrogant, and always believed she was right, but particularly when she was completely wrong. She had a willful tendency to interpret words quite opposite to what a person had actually said. One time I asked her to take care of my new kitten while I was out of town. I carefully instructed her to leave soft classical music playing on the stereo to keep the kitten calmly pacified during my absence. When I returned home, I was dismayed to hear inordinately loud rock and roll music blasting from the stereo. The kitten was so traumatized that he attacked me and everyone who tried to comfort him, so I had no choice but to take him to the animal shelter. This person eventually revealed herself to be the proverbial, "Calamity Jane." Wherever she went, and, whatever she did, odd calamitous events transpired, much to the dismay of others, myself included. Yet, she was oblivious to her peculiarities, and boldly defended her actions, no matter how peculiar or disagreeable they were to everyone else. To my chagrin, I later discovered that she was acutely addicted to marijuana, cigarettes and various stimulants, and realized she was too unreliable to trust.

Understanding the idea of chief feature and how it manifests in yourself and in others can be an insightful guide to help you gain more clarity about your interactions. It is useful to try to observe and discover your own chief feature to gain more self-control, although you might not recognize it right away. Be patient as you continue to practice mindful self-observation and eventually you will start to notice habitual patterns and symptoms of your chief feature. Think about what is important to you, what you feel most vulnerable about, or what you defend the most in your life. This may be a clue that will point to your chief feature. In time, you will begin to sense a familiarity in situations, and this can help you to witness your chief feature as it is manifesting. Consistent mindful self-observation will help you gain control over your chief feature.

As you begin your journey of self-discovery you may feel as though you already have self-control and see yourself clearly. However, truly seeing oneself in the moment takes practice with consistent efforts. And, remember, you cannot change other people; you can only work on yourself. Simply observe what you see in others, as best you can. Do not make excuses for other people, as this will only buffer what you see in them. Try to keep your expectations to a minimum. Also, quite often what you see in others may be their best behavior, which they exhibit as part of false personality. Yet, this is precisely what they want you to see. False personality works just like a mask which a person wears to conceal their identity, and perhaps to cloak their hidden intentions. What you know of an individual may only be their superficial appearance. This is primarily what they allow you to see, and interact with. One day it may surprise you to discover you do not really know this person, and, perhaps other people with whom you interact, as well as you thought. Try to look beneath surface appearances in order to see their chief features beyond false personality.

Remember, trust is an essential component in all of our relationships with others, but trust must be earned. Even those who appear to be valiant pillars of society may ultimately reveal something about them self, or their life that might severely alter your impression of them. Peter Ouspensky cautions us to verify everything, and this includes what people tell you about themselves. Hidden motives may reveal something quite different. I mention these words of advice as a cautionary measure at this point as I genuinely and sincerely hope you will benefit from this book. Perhaps, our wisest words of wisdom are learned from our own personal experiences. However, those whom we trust may not actually be trustworthy in reality. Long ago, a wonderful friend wisely reminded me, "Trust must be earned."

Watching out for the most negative chief feature, the Hasnamuss:

It is helpful to become aware of your own chief feature, but it is also important to be aware of chief feature in others. By observing people carefully, you gain a better understanding of their general tendencies. You may not always get an accurate glimpse of their true nature, but it is important to try. The following segment describes an inordinately difficult type of person who Ouspensky referred to as "Hasnamuss." These are unscrupulous people, who may also be criminals, unbeknownst to you. They conceal their devious intent with false personality, which may appear quite friendly and pleasant. They are adept at hiding their selfish motivation, as they are chameleons, making them very difficult to know. You may not suspect a hidden agenda when you meet these Dr. Jekyll /Mr. Hyde types as they present a charming façade to disguise their ulterior motives. They cloak selfish aims with false personality fortified by lies, and they have no regard for others. Ouspensky said the root word for Hasnamuss is Turkish, but, I have found it in other traditions. It may also be derived from Sanskrit particles, which loosely translated expresses sorrow, pain, dejection, and thief. But, this describes the end goal and the tragic results of meeting the Hasnamuss.

I have given much thought about whether to include details of the Hasnamuss, uncertain if this book needed it. But, owing to constant injustices in the news, especially against women, all minorities, immigrants, plus many others, and because of pervasive corrupt political problems, climate change and environmental issues, I realize this information is necessary. I have rarely watched television during the course of my life, but now the need to be informed is eminently vital. Having become more aware of global issues and disturbing current events, I feel it is critical to include information about the devious Hasnamuss to protect innocent people from the potential harm they cause. It is essential to be aware, self-protective and vigilant as the Hasnamuss acts without conscience or remorse. They take advantage of innocent people so they alone profit, despite it being undeserved, unearned, and unnatural. Initially they will flatter you, or shower you with attention, but they will betray you if and when an opportunity arises.

These are narcissistic egomaniacs who rob the innocent, and enjoy basking in the glory of another person's wealth or accomplishments. In psychology, Hasnamuss are sociopaths and psychopaths. Though they may seem pleasant, a dark agenda will eventually reveal them as deceptive, unethical, and self-serving especially to those of us who are sane and unsuspecting. Ouspensky said they have combined features of tramp and lunatic, functioning from false personality and mechanical parts of centers. He said we usually only see the tragic results of their existence. Some examples are, Hitler, Mussolini, and con men, such as Bernie Madoff, who exemplify the worst types of Hasnamuss in politics and business. These thieves of virtue present themselves in various ways, but typically act as if they have your best interests at heart, which is not true. They may convince you they are an esteemed entrepreneur, an altruistic humanitarian, a wealthy benefactor, a successful business person, or a benevolent leader; and perhaps a portion of this is true; however, whatever their occupation or vocation, it usually serves their agenda and veils their devious intentions. Many years ago, I had unfortunate encounters with two different people who I later came to recognize as the Hasnamuss. Perhaps my bad experiences can inform others of the need for increased self-protection.

The first incident occurred long ago, when I was doing research for a successful real estate broker. We had worked on various real estate research projects, and she asked me to help her develop information databases. I thought I knew her well, as she seemed straight forward and honest. But, one day I received a telephone call from an attorney, who represented her boss. He was suing her for business theft and fraud. She had stolen his client files and took them to a large corporation which secured her a powerful new job there. I was stunned by this news, as she always acted so cheerful and upbeat. I knew nothing of her deceptions, and was unable to provide any information to help her boss whom she bankrupted for millions of dollars. When I asked her about it, she shrugged it off and showed no remorse. Thus, I ended all our projects.

While I believed I had learned a major life lesson in who not to trust, I was mistaken. Some years later, I was in car accident in Southern California and needed to remain there indefinitely due to my injuries. I rented out my home which was several hundred miles away to someone whom I thought I knew well, but again I was mistaken. Later, I decided to sell that home, but my realtor telephoned in distress, aghast to see her living there. He said she was a local criminal, guilty of many fraudulent crimes, and illegally squatting in rental properties. Afterwards, I discovered this tenant never paid her rent into my bank mortgage account, which caused me massive financial losses. Sadly, her direct access to my bank mortgage account culminated in identity theft, which tragically implicated me in her chaotic business fiascos. I was absolutely blindsided and swindled out of a great deal of money while recuperating from several surgeries from the car accident. Like many innocent people, I had never heard of identity theft, but now I pay for identity theft protection.

Not everyone is working on them self to gain self-knowledge to live a pure life with conscious awareness. Neither of these two people who I naively believed were my friends, would ever be interested in awakening. Both of these people executed complex, devious, disruptive plans, but kept it all hidden until it was too late.

Betrayal is a painful shock to the innocent emotional center, so we must do the best we can to make better decisions about people we allow in our life. One must examine one's friendships and personal relationships to gain greater understanding about the individuals one is involved with. Are people in our life for the right reasons, and is there a genuine foundation of trust? While I had no reason to suspect that either of these people could be so dishonest, devious, malicious and deceitful, I was mistaken. It is very painful to witness incidents such as this, but it is unbearable to experience them. While these incidents occurred many years ago, they illustrate how unscrupulous people can deceive the innocent, unsuspecting normal person. Neither of these two people, showed any remorse, shame or conscience when I asked them about what they had done. The Hasnamuss is immune to the enormous suffering they cause to others.

I cannot underscore enough the potentially hazardous consequences of dealing with the evil Hasnamuss. Owing to the current political climate and unethical behavior of certain people who are in positions of power, I have determined this difficult segment is necessary. Perhaps my rather unfortunate experiences with the Hasnamuss can serve as a warning to other innocent people. From my perspective, it is vital to be cautious. Strive to see beyond superficial appearances, and become more aware of others. Observe their attitudes, actions, habitual behaviors, and chief features, in order to protect yourself from those who might cause you harm. I hope you never meet a Hasnamuss, and perhaps this information will help to avoid them.

Learn to trust your intuition and your instincts about others to help protect yourself. Always remember, you are a valuable human being and you deserve respect. Protect yourself.

CHAPTER 13

OTHER PEOPLE IN OUR LIFE

Learning about centers, mindful self-observation, imagination, identification, chief features, buffers, and other essential esoteric ideas, provides us with self-empowering tools to gain enhanced knowledge of our personal dynamic and to understand other people. Observing centers functioning in others will help you gain insight into their manifestations. Perhaps you will begin to understand better why they feel, think, act and behave as they do. Gaining a comprehensive overview of the different influences, manifestations and motivations of each center allows one to glimpse beneath the façade of surface appearances with enhanced perception. Those who intrigue, puzzle or perplex us may become easier to understand. Perhaps you will begin to understand why certain relationships in your past were not appropriate for you, and also, why they did not work out well. With increased understanding, we can more effectively and accurately evaluate our personal relationships. We can begin to understand the real reasons why they work, or do not work, and how they affect our life favorably, or otherwise. Observing centers as they function and manifest within yourself and others is a highly practical method for understanding yourself and your relationships.

Mindful self-observation shifts your internal awareness, so it is quite possible you will experience changes in the external world you inhabit, as you begin to emanate your transforming internal energies. Changing our self from within can alter the way we generate our energies, which may affect how others perceive us. With enhanced self-awareness, our energies become more refined, and we may attract different energies from others. As you work to develop self-awareness with ongoing self-observation and intentionality, it is possible you will attract people and social situations which are more in tune with your essential nature. You may also experience changes in your own personal understandings which spark a need for change in other areas of your life. As you develop interests which are better suited to you, and more in tune with your essential nature, you may gravitate toward relationships which will be more conducive to your personal growth. Remain focused as you mindfully self-observe to monitor centers as they function to see how they influence you, how they affect your personal life and your choices about other people.

By observing centers within yourself, you will also begin to notice the various centers manifesting in others. It will be informative to recognize centers in other people, particularly individuals whom you know well. It is helpful to be aware of energies emanating from others. Some centers manifest with subtle energy, but other centers are more intense. As you observe others, be mindful not to make them feel uncomfortable. While you may simply be observing the outward characteristics of their centers manifesting, they may feel intruded upon. It is paramount to be respectful of other people. As you observe, always be impartial, and do not judge what you see in anyone. We are all equally mechanical, unless we are working with sincere intentionality to gain enhanced self-awareness and consciousness. It is vital to be conscientiously aware of others, and to act with compassion. We are each quite different for many reasons.

For example, if you determine you are emotionally centered and your boyfriend is moving centered, you will begin to understand why your individual approaches to certain situations are quite different. While emotionally centered types wish to spend social time with friends, the moving centered types may prefer to go surfing, play a game of tennis, or play golf. It is important to understand that not everyone is a social butterfly, nor should everyone be. Recognizing and understanding our natural inherent differences helps to conserve your life energy. By economizing our personal energy expenditures, we have more energy to put into beneficial pursuits to improve our life. We will also begin to minimize negative energy drains. Becoming more self-aware helps you see others in a more realistic light. Mindful self-observation can shift your perceptions, and help you to put other people and events into proper perspective. Rather than being dominated by other people and external influences, you will feel more self-reliant and self-empowered.

As you self-observe you will become more aware of the external influences which enter your life directly from the people with whom you interact. Be aware that external energy influences can affect, alter, or distort your self-perceptions, your disposition, and your responses to life. As we develop enhanced self-awareness we begin to intentionally moderate and control these external influences. We become better equipped to make more informed decisions about the immediate external influences that surround us, which includes choices about friends. As you develop increased self-awareness you may also develop a better sense of which individuals contribute meaningful healthy energy, and which individuals seem to drain your energy for various reasons. We must be prudent to avoid becoming victims of those with power driven motives, negative false personality traits, and harmful toxic habits. As you develop your self-awareness you will become more sensitive to the energy emanations from others. You will be better equipped to monitor your relationships to determine whether they are healthy or harmful to your wellbeing. You cannot control other people; however, you can begin to control who you allow into your life.

Learning about the centers of influence within while practicing mindful self-observation will open a vast universe of new understandings about yourself, and about others. When you recognize a particular center manifesting in another person, take note of it. Quite often we see something in another individual that feels quite familiar to us. It may be that we also have that particular element within our self. Sometimes, these same people irritate us, which may be caused by similar traits which compete, rivaling for dominance. Seeing this is a helpful lesson in humility. Observe manifestations of yourself and others without judgment. Each one of us has various imperfections which we can learn to accept, or we can work to heal, repair, or change. Some of our imperfections cause our imbalances, and mindful self-observation can be eminently healing. Addressing our personal imbalances helps us to develop more humility with a greater sense of compassion, and takes us a step closer to truly knowing others.

Gaining greater self-awareness improves the quality of our life and our relationships. Understanding how the centers manifest, helps demystify our relationships as we gain valuable insight into our needs, as well as the needs of others. An easy way to begin to recognize how different centers function and influence us, is to simply observe the people you spend your time with. Being with friends and family gives you with a wonderful opportunity to observe the centers at work as they come alive in others right before your eyes. Watch for the art loving King of Hearts, an intellectually reserved King of Diamonds, a sporty Jack of Spades, a trivial pursuit whiz-kid Jack of Diamonds, or, a gourmet Queen of Clubs. When you recognize someone is emotionally centered, intellectually centered, moving centered, or instinctively centered, it will help you to understand them in greater depth. This will also help you see your differences more distinctly. Remember, those who have a direct influence on us may not be necessarily centered in the same iconic royal suit, or center as our self. Within our own family, we may discover that a sister is moving centered, a brother is intellectually centered, and our parents might be emotionally centered, and so on. We are each different because of our center of gravity, but we can begin to truly understand these differences.

Also, it is imperative to avoid making automatic superficial judgments about others. Quite often, we tend to prejudge, or classify others, based on our own preconceived notions and mental constructs, in an attempt to define them. This occurs due to our habitual thinking processes in the Jacks of centers. They might be quite different than how we judge them to be from our narrow tunnel vision. Also, another person's false personality will often shield their true inner nature. This gives us a limited perspective, which can make it rather difficult to truly understand them in depth. So, we need more and better information to make accurate assessments. Learning about centers will expand your knowledge of others in an objective manner, which will help you to see beneath their surface appearances. Also, having an objective point of view is conducive to developing more sincere compassion for others.

Keep in mind, the various centers function at different speeds, with different needs, which affects how they interact, react, respond, and coexist with other people. The different centers may not interact harmoniously, particularly between diversely different parts. For example, the methodical Kings of the centers may become rather uncomfortable with the extreme emotional volatility emanating from the Queens. And, the Kings may feel a bit irritated by the repetitive habitual behavior of the Jacks. Queens may be fascinated by the pensive Kings, who prefer to proceed quite slowly and think things through, but she may lose patience. Queens can exert power over the Jacks of centers with her insistent demands. The Jacks might regard the Kings as slow and perhaps, a bit boring, but may think the Queens are too excessive, moody and intense. Unless it is a substantially meaningful relationship, such as parents, spouse, or your boss at work, it may be best to minimize interactions with others whose centers are incompatible with yours. This is not always possible, and there are times when we must make efforts to work with and harmonize with those around us. However, do not negate your needs, or dismiss your essential nature. Sometimes people make demands of us which are inappropriate to our nature. No one should force their opinions, or demands on another, but, it happens all the time. If possible, with very difficult cases, it may be best to remove yourself from those who are too incompatible or contrary to your essential nature, to mitigate excessive energy drains.

Many people have family members who irritate, agitate, annoy, overwhelm, or sadly, abuse and victimize them. I have counseled several people who had experienced rather serious and traumatic events caused by someone in their own family, whose centers they were completely incompatible with. Although these events may have happened a very long time ago, one can begin to heal from past painful experiences. Utilizing information gained from studying the centers of influence, can help you to process hurtful issues caused by people in your past. Understanding the centers can help one to heal, by putting the family member and the bad experiences into context. This does not negate, or deny the bad experiences, but it may help you to understand and process your family member's negative behavior and your experience. You can begin to heal by putting old problems into proper perspective, while practicing self-nurturing in this moment.

For example, a common family problem is bullying. One rather quiet King of Hearts friend of mine grew up with two aggressive, bullying Queen of Spades and Queen of Clubs siblings, and suffered cruel injustices at home. The Queen siblings were unable to understand why the shy quiet King of Hearts preferred to be alone, or to spend his time with calmer people. The quiet King retreated from the noisy rambunctious siblings, but the Queen siblings bullied him even more. Remember, the Queens thrive on getting attention and refuse to be ignored! When he grew up he moved far away from his family to minimize interactions with them. We spoke about this on many occasions when he shared his childhood issues. It was apparent that the Queen siblings were jealous of the intelligent King of Hearts child, who got more approval from parents for doing well in school. But, the adult King of Hearts has chosen to have minimal interaction with the adult siblings, because of his incompatibility with their respective Queen centers. Although his suffering was real, the King of Hearts finally understood the bullying problems arose because of their conflicting and competing centers. The siblings continue to be quite bossy and aggressive, but the quiet King of Hearts has intentionally elected to live a more subdued, harmonious life. Incorporating the knowledge of centers allows us to comprehend others and their behavior better, and to detach or disengage when necessary.

Please know it is always right action to be true to your essential nature and to aspire to your own highest potential, regardless of what is going on around you. As we continue to mindfully self-observe we gradually begin to see our own weaknesses and the weaknesses of others, which helps us to develop compassion. Balancing the emotional center with the thoughtful pace of the intellectual center helps one slow the energies to develop conscientious compassion for others, and for one self. Our relationships with others may still occasionally manifest in ways that are not positive, but we will begin to understand why this occurs. It is vital to acknowledge problematic relationships, so that you can make better decisions and make informed changes when it is truly the best option for all involved. This may not happen instantly, but you will gain greater insight by observing the centers in others and monitoring reactions in yourself.

Enhanced awareness will assist you to understand why certain situations and people do not fulfill your needs. You may also see more clearly why you do not fulfill the needs of others, despite trying. Having a clear perception of others, allows you to make informed decisions about their role in your life. And, truly comprehending this is a big step in developing greater compassion for yourself and others. Making use of the knowledge of centers in your personal interactions will help you gain more understanding of how, and why people manifest as they do. As you observe others you will gradually recognize their dominant center in the patterns of their general behavior. This will increase your comprehension of their psychological predispositions, their habits and tendencies, their talents and abilities. As we gain knowledge and insight, ultimately our friends and family become easier to understand and appreciate.

As you increase your efforts with mindful self-observation, you will gradually become more aware of how you manifest in situations with others. For each of us, our experiences studying centers will differ based on our personal life experiences. Mindful self-observation helps you adjust your focus to see your part in the bigger picture. Observe with an impartial attitude to get a clear perspective. You may also see distinctive traits and patterns in others that eluded you prior. Behaviors which you have been unable to appreciate or comprehend in others, may make more sense as you recognize a certain center's influence manifesting. It is not that you will like a person any more, or less; but, you will understand their behavior with increased objectivity. As we witness the visible manifestations of centers at work in another person, we can begin to understand why they feel, think, behave, or act as they do. With consistent efforts, it is possible to gain a much more objective view with greater insight into another person's traits, behavior and manifestations. This can potentially lead you to have more refined, qualitative, and rewarding relationships, in addition to developing greater self-awareness.

As we adjust our personal perspective we perceive and appreciate others with enhanced comprehension. You will also understand that you cannot change another person, and perhaps more importantly, why you should not even try to change anyone else. When we finally realize that we cannot change others, we conserve a great deal of our own life energy. Simply respecting someone as their natural self, functioning from their center of gravity, allows us to be less attached to what we expect of them. It also affords them the unique opportunity to feel, live and be more comfortable with who they truly are in their essential nature. Also, while you may wish to share the ideas in this book with people you care about, please be respectful of the possibility that they may not be interested. We cannot give new ideas to those who do want them, or have no interest. Everyone hears their own truth at their personal level of interest and understanding. Observe this important element to increase your ability to discern what is actually in the best interests of everyone, which will help maintain harmony in your relationships.

The best we can offer others is a more balanced self, while being a positive influence with a healthy attitude of acceptance. Gaining increased self-knowledge can enhance your development toward sincere growth oriented friendships and relationships. As you observe others, with their unique characteristics, you will begin to understand why you cherish certain relationships, and, why some relationships feel anxious and stressful. You will realize why some relationships simply take too much energy and hard work to maintain. This will also help you to have a clear picture of the unsuitable traits which you may encounter in others. But, please keep in mind, a person is not bad, or unworthy simply because their centers are incompatible with our own center of gravity. We really must refrain from judging, classifying, or discriminating against a person because of their center of gravity. Every center is part of the natural order of life, and each person has their own natural predisposition from influences in their essential nature. Everyone evolves as they can

We each play a part in our magnificent universe, though in the present moment we may not know what our part might be in the grand scheme. However, we can maintain a firm grasp on reality in each moment with consistent mindful self-observation. Self-knowledge infused with healthy self-respect is the greatest teacher in recognizing what you need or want, and what your truly deserve in life. And, your life is enriched simply by being true to yourself. Paying attention to inherent tendencies of your centers and your essential nature will certainly help you to learn about yourself with greater honesty. Emanating from your authentic self may open new pathways to fulfillment in your relationships. But, being true to your essential nature is imperative. Living in harmony with your own essential nature, is naturally conducive to having healthier interchanges. Being true to your essential nature as you aspire to your higher potential is right action.

Keep in mind, while you are observing yourself to become more self-aware, it is unlikely that there will be obvious visible changes which others might notice. Working on one self is a quiet personal endeavor which is best done without attracting attention to oneself. Moreover, it is in your best interests to mitigate any desire to point out to others that you are working on yourself to become more aware, awake, or enlightened. These personal proclamations are generally not well received, as they can sound rather condescending, demeaning, or simply preposterous to others. Most people in the world consider themselves to be aware and conscious already, and it is highly inappropriate to suggest otherwise. You might cause uneasiness, or discomfort by speaking about your personal efforts with mindful self-observation. Those who are working on them self with the aim to become aware, to evolve and transform may recognize your efforts; but, it may be best to remain silent and invisible about your work on yourself, unless someone asks you about it.

As you develop your self-awareness it is possible you will attract more like-minded companions, who share your goals and ideals. Keep in mind, the most important relationship you have is with your own true self. As you develop self-knowledge you will gain an enhanced ability to see the compatible traits in others who you can connect with. Perhaps you will be able to see another's qualities better, and recognize how they enrich your life, and how you might enhance their life. It is rewarding when we feel a connection with others, but more so when we are inspired by the qualities we recognize and hold in high regard. Whatever their talents and abilities, we can aspire to be more like those whom we admire and look up to, especially those who radiate their pure presence and generate positive energy. And we can inspire others as well.

Understanding our self and others:

Employing mindful self-observation with the knowledge of centers, are vital tools which will shed light on your relationships as you gain greater self-knowledge and enhanced self-awareness. Learning about and understanding the centers within oneself and in others, allows for deeper understanding of our differences, as well as our shared mutual similarities. Using the centers as a psychological program to observe one self and other people, assists one in gaining more meaningful insights into our relationships and interactions. When you have gained sufficient understanding about the centers and have made consistent observations, you will begin to clearly witness the different centers as they manifest in yourself, and in other people in your life. And it is vital for those who wish to live a more self-aware life, to have harmony with others in relationships, especially as we achieve more balance within.

However, people often find it rather difficult to understand one another. To understand one another it is helpful to share a common ideal or mutual reference point for objectivity. For example, someone living in Europe during the Renaissance could not possibly comprehend someone in our modern era walking around while speaking to another person on their mobile cellular phone. There would be no reference point for them to formulate an understanding of what is occurring. While this example may seem a bit farfetched, we continue to expect others to understand us, despite the fact that we do not share common references to put matters into context, or with proper perspective in order to understand. This is a common occurrence, particularly with different generations, even those separated by as little as 10 years. Each individual understands others only from their own personal life experiences, and perhaps limited references.

It is imperative to be mindfully aware that each one of us experiences our life in our own personal way through our centers, chief features, false personality, identifications, imagination, and every influence we have experienced since birth. Hence, we do not all experience reality in the same manner, with the same perceptions, emotions, understandings, sensitivities, and so on. Consequently, we each experience reality, and our personal comprehensions of life quite differently. In this sense, our perceptions of others may also be rather subjective. Keep in mind, reality is neither uniform nor static, which contributes to our different subjective experiences and personal perceptions. Accordingly, we may not easily understand one another, and we may not grasp the reasons why we do not understand one another. Learning about the centers within, as well as other essential esoteric wisdom included in this book, will help you gain more enlightening understanding about yourself and about other people. You may also become more sensitive to those who tend to manifest in an unnatural manner from false personality. Enhanced self-knowledge and awareness can help you recognize when a person is behaving falsely, and when they are emanating from chief features. As you continue to observe others you will gradually begin to recognize people's tendencies, behaviors and habitual patterns with greater clarity. This takes consistent sincere practice, but it will enhance your understanding as you become more aware of others, their centers and influences.

There are many clues which people provide us if we simply watch their behavior. How a person behaves, or performs in the world can reveal what they are really like. Despite the strong force which false personality exerts, ultimately each person tends to revert to their most basic internal influences, motivations and tendencies. These actions can reveal their truer nature, which is usually hidden behind false personality traits. People reveal who they truly are, if you simply observe their behavior and listen to what they say. Even though false personality hides many facets of their identity, you can begin to recognize potentially discordant elements that would not work out well for a friendship. However, this requires absolute honesty about your own needs. Remember, a person's habitual behavior in the everyday world is basically who they are. How they act, the things they do, what they say, and how they say it, will tell you a great deal about them. As you observe others they will tell you who they are with their actions, words, deeds and behaviors.

Observing centers, habitual patterns of behavior, chief features, and false personality in others will help you make better choices about the people you invite into your life. You can be more selective as you choose alliances and friends, and make more well-informed decisions about who you spend time with, and also, who you are most compatible with. The primary point in observing others is to learn about them and determine compatibility. You alone must come to terms with what you are truly comfortable with, and what you will accept from others. But, please be aware that we do not share compatible energies with everyone we meet. It is imperative for you to have realistic expectations, which are based on what you honestly want and need from others. It is essential to comprehend this point to assuage the potential for misunderstandings and unnecessary difficulties with others. When you are more discerning about who you spend time with, it can slow the pace of your interactions. Careful discernment with lucid observation lends an intellectual element to help guide you. This increases your objectivity about the people you choose to spend time with. However, life is not always so simple, and each one of us has flaws. We can certainly be more flexible with people whom we know and truly care about. Over time you will become more in tune with your deepest essential needs, desires and expectations and will understand better what you need from your relationships. As you practice mindful self-observation you will develop more clarity and understanding in this regard.

When you observe others, it is helpful to determine whether they are emotionally centered, intellectually centered, moving centered, or instinctively centered. For example, if someone excels at sports and athletics, it is reasonable to assume that they are moving centered. If someone gives lectures on particle physics, quantum mechanics, or string theory, it is fairly obvious that they are intellectually centered. Remember to observe their features as well. Active chief features, such as power and dominance, are fairly apparent and easily recognized. But, passive features, such as naïveté, fear, and non-existence are less obvious. As you practice observing others, you will become more skillful about determining their centers and their features. Learning about others by observing them impartially, will give you vital information to help you understand them in greater depth. Having harmonious relationships which are nurturing, respectful, fulfilling and meet both individual's needs, is a healthy realizable goal you can strive for in your life.

Yet, quite often, despite vast differences, we try to change our self in order to fit in, or, we try change others. Remember, it is unwise to conform, or to force your opinion on others. It is beneficial to respond with compassion towards everyone, as we cannot know their life experiences. But, it is vital to realize that we can only ever work on our self, which is a sufficient task unto itself. We cannot possibly do the internal transformational work for another person, ever! Each person individually must make their own efforts to work for their personal self-knowledge. And, it is helpful to realize that not everyone is ready or willing to look more deeply within. For many it might be too painful to see themselves as they truly are. This is why buffers become a habit. Strive to be respectful, compassionate, and remember, it is not your place to point out anyone's flaws. We each certainly have enough of our own flaws to attend to. Each person must work on their own issues, and develop their own personal awareness with their own consistent sincere efforts

Life is a rather complex, mysterious experience for nearly everyone. But, we are not all working with the aim to become self-aware, or to experience higher states of consciousness in our life. The concept of someone living with increased self-awareness, who can see through the illusion of the ordinary world, might be terribly confusing for other people. It is helpful to remember this if you wish to speak about your personal consciousness studies and self-observations. Moreover, most people believe they are already fully conscious. Be mindful to never criticize anyone about their level of awareness, consciousness or their personal beliefs. You can only ever raise your own self-awareness; never that of anyone else. While our personal inner work amplifies the necessity to be aware of others, we simply cannot change another person. With this in mind, it is also beneficial to break the habit of seeking your answers from other people. While others may occasionally try to convince you otherwise, please remember no one is an authority on your inner world, your feelings or thoughts. You alone are responsible for answering your own questions.

As we continue to observe our self and others, we begin to recognize certain repetitive patterns of behavior. Some patterns we observe may reveal our habitual attractions, or repulsions to others. Often this is a result of our centers mechanically reacting to their centers, harmoniously or discordantly. Our centers emanate energies that magnetically attract people to us, or repel and push them away. Therefore, many people seek psychological counseling if they suffer from complex relationship issues. They may even come to realize, they are unable to naturally interact socially with others, and are uncomfortable with people they encounter. Generally, people do not know how to change this, other than merely coping with their personal problems, or reacting against these problems. Learning about the centers in yourself and in others, gives you valuable holistic tools that will help you understand the dynamic of your personal relationships with greater clarity, as to why they are harmonious, disharmonious, non-existent, or simply too complicated.

I have counselled many people over the years, and have come to realize that they believe they are doing the best they can in their life, regarding friendships and personal relationships. Yet, they continue to endure strained personal interactions, as misunderstandings continue to occur. At these times, negativity may feel like the only response to a particular person, problem or situation. But, it is beneficial to take more conscious command of our reactions to adverse people, or difficult situations to assuage anger, and gain control over the expression of negative emotions. It is helpful to realize that most people act, or react, from their habitual patterns of behavior. If someone is not working to gain increased self-awareness for personal growth, it is reasonable to assume that they are unaware of the negative effect they are having on others. Most people in the world go through life believing they are the center of their own universe, as they continue to function in the same repetitive habitual patterns. But, no one can truly see them self objectively until they make a conscious decision to become more self-ware. Mindful self-observation will help you see when your own centers are manifesting habitually, or mechanically, particularly when you are interacting with others.

At these moments, you can strive to be more intentional, to shift or change your habitual tendency, and, to be more present in the moment as it is occurring. Remember, heightened levels of awareness are not about self-aggrandizement. An outward display, egocentric behaviors, or attitudes of arrogance are inconsistent with higher states of conscious awareness. Self-aggrandizing behavior is inappropriate for an individual who is working to gain self-knowledge and self-awareness. We have all met people who acquire a little bit of new information, yet they act and speak about it as if they are the world's leading expert. This type of behavior is vanity and arrogance combined with ignorance. There may be situations like this which arise when we are personally involved with someone who is behaving arrogantly. It can be beneficial for the relationship to speak to them with sincere honesty about how they are manifesting. Tell them impartially they are behaving with vanity. Others often need a gentle reminder to help awaken them to the moment. Those who have gained a certain amount of self-knowledge, and have worked intentionally to elevate their own awareness, will appreciate your need for sincerity and humility. But, do not attempt to force your own views or opinions on another, even with the best of intentions for their wellbeing. It may simply backfire, particularly if they are not interested.

It is far better for you to do your own personal inner work in silence than to promote ideas which you may not have fully assimilated into your being as yet. Respect others when they say they are not interested, regardless of how much you think it will help them. Do not promote. or project your personal opinions, or beliefs onto others. Keep in mind, many people are on rather shaky ground with their own beliefs, and they may feel very threatened by your ideas and opinions. We cannot possibly know exactly what others have experienced in their life on their personal path. The aim to be more self-aware on a moment to moment basis with conscious objectivity requires a humble demeanor. Those who are striving to become self-aware understand the vital need for sincerity, humility and compassion under all circumstances.

Keep in mind, people are often confused by life, and they may be disappointed about where they are, what they have achieved, and how events have turned out. They may be unhappy or depressed, but are trying to cope with their issues. Thus, it might not be the best time for them to be receptive to hearing new ideas. Everyone has issues, regrets and fears in life, but it is not your place to tell them how to live. If you come along and enthusiastically start telling someone how marvelous their life could be if they would only learn about these esoteric ideas, or some other philosophy, they may feel you are invalidating their life and their personal beliefs. At these times, it is best to be respectful, compassionate, and silent to avoid hurting someone who is probably doing the best they can in a difficult moment. When I speak of having compassion for others I do not mean having pity for them. Elevated self-awareness emanates with sincere compassion toward others. We each have our own difficulties, so please strive to be kind to others. Sometimes, it is best to keep your personal ideas and your own inner truth to yourself. Others may become confused, feel insulted, threatened or angered by these new ideas which they are not familiar with. Remaining quiet about one self also helps protect your virtue and discourages criticism, negative attention or negative energy. In some esoteric philosophical and psychological doctrines, the concept of being invisible is wisely encouraged. This implies that one is deliberately working with intentionality to be aware of one's outward gestures and behaviors which may attract unnecessary attention, or negativity to one self. Most people have their own beliefs, interests and preferences, and may have absolutely no interest in yours. The term, flying below the radar, may facilitate and enhance the lifestyle of the individual who wishes to live their life with enhanced self-knowledge and conscious self-awareness.

However, if you are interacting with others who are also working to gain self-awareness it is also helpful to remember that they are only human. I have frequently observed people in esoteric schools, and other similar environments, who were struggling with their problems and personal issues. Although we might expect people who are working for self-knowledge to be perfect, in truth many are just doing the best that they can, while dealing with their problems. They may be trying hold onto their personal work, while striving to vanquish their own inner demons, illusions, fears and self-doubts. Often, the very best we can do for another person is to simply remain silent, be compassionate and let them get on with their personal efforts. Higher knowledge advises that one respect others and not interfere with, or harm another person. We each have enough to do while making our own efforts to awaken. Many times, it is right action to simply be kind, and leave others alone to work out their difficulties. There may be a time in the future, when you hope they will do the same for you. Remember, you can only work on yourself; you cannot work for another. But, if someone asks for your help, perhaps you can assist them by responding with compassion.

Continue to practice mindful self-observation, be attentive, intentional, do not identify, avoid imagination, eliminate negativity, dismiss illusions, drop false personality, and, always externally consider others with sincere heartfelt compassion. Be gentle. People often turn to ideas of self-development after other methods have failed them, when the ordinary world has frightened or disappointed them, when their religion did not fulfill their prayers, and so on. I have met people in esoteric schools, and in spiritual environments, who were from unhappy homes and dysfunctional families. Some had been bullied as a child; often at home from sibling rivalry, in school, or at work. So, they searched for a more peaceful path, and sought a peaceful haven for their more sensitive inner nature. It was quite common to meet people who had failed marriages or unsuccessful relationships. While not everyone had endured harsh suffering, many had, and this served as an incentive to explore esoteric ideas and metaphysical concepts of self-awareness and personal growth. Quite often it is our painful personal problems or other adverse situations which trigger the quest to find a more meaningful way in life, and to live in more harmonious environments. Those who wish to live in tune with their essential nature prefer to be where they do not feel threatened by false illusions, which is natural. Being different from the norm may have had ramifications for many of us as individuals, but we must earnestly strive to be true to our essential nature.

With mindful self-observation, your self-awareness will increase. Objectivity and conscience also increase. Conscience guides us to thoughtful behavior towards others as we see them with enhanced insight. Our conscience helps us to make informed choices in our relationships. As we develop conscience the seeds of compassion germinate. Compassion evokes a humble demeanor which generates understanding and more appropriate responses to people we encounter, because we see them with increased clarity. Respect each individual's belief system and do not force your ideas, beliefs, or concepts on them, especially if they are not interested. Be externally considerate and do not try to tell anyone how to live their life. You cannot possibly know someone's deep inner needs and you cannot magically fix another person's problems. Strive to remain impartial. Learning about centers and incorporating these ideas with practical application will help you to determine what is right action in a given moment; for yourself, and for others. The ability to understand yourself and others will prove to be an asset in your life.

Trust:

Beyond centers, identification, imagination, false personality, negativity and chief features, there are other influences to be aware of which may emanate from people we interact with. It is imperative to establish a foundation of trust as a component to gain understanding of others, especially when developing new friendships and relationships. Certainly, technology and the internet has changed the way we meet people, and the pace of life has quickened exponentially. This intensifies the need to be more observant, and cautious about whom you elect to spend your time with, when, where and how. Trust is an essential element as a cautionary measure when interacting with others. Developing sincere bonds of genuine trust with others is vital in our relationships. Yet, we cannot trust people initially or believe everything they say, as it may be their false personality speaking, or their chief features, or a random "I", or the positive or negative half of a center, or they may be exaggerating, or they may be lying. Trust must first be established and earned.

Trust is an essential component in all of our relationships with others, but trust with others must be earned. We often trust people based upon what they tell us, and from what they reveal about them self. However, from personal experience I have verified at great personal expense, that this is absolutely inadequate as some people simply lie. It is wise to examine your relationships carefully, as we often overlook issues that seem inconsequential in the beginning. Those of us who are working to develop self-awareness and enhanced self-knowledge, are often a bit naïve, so we especially need to be mindfully aware of duplicitous types. On our adventure to gain enhanced self-awareness and self-knowledge, we may wish to meet others who are also exploring consciousness, but it is wise to be cautious, perhaps even more so. As we go forth in search of miraculous heightened awareness, it is wise to prepare for some potential detours we may encounter on our path. And it is vital to be aware of those who may mislead us. Gurdjieff told a tale of a man who had squandered all his money in his search for mystical knowledge. Later, he realized he had not acquired the precious knowledge, which he had so desperately sought from people he studied with. Perhaps he was naïve, unrealistic, or, he may have trusted the wrong people. It is common for naïve people who seek higher consciousness teachings, to be innocently duped by charlatans selling questionable ideas. Clearly, not all metaphysical, mystical or spiritual teachers are sincere, and one must proceed with caution. Peculiar practices, strange behaviors, extreme addictions, lavish indulgences, weird people, and excessive demands for money are critical red flags which you need to pay attention to. Do your own research to verify teachers, as one does not always get what one pays for, particularly from those selling mysterious powers. The miraculous voyage into one's own consciousness is a bit like an adventure into wonderland. People we meet may seem like harmless smiling cats, or silly mad hatters, but look for what is not clearly visible on the surface. And, while you may arrive at a charming tea party, always know what is in the tea pot, and know where the exits are. Although some people may promote higher consciousness, please be aware that others may have very different opinions on how to reach this higher realm. One must be true to oneself, regardless of what others think, say or do. Empty promises are empty. Always be true to yourself, and trust your emotional sensing abilities, intuition and instincts when they are trying to caution you.

Keep in mind that people are often not what they say they are, or even what they appear to be. Remember the adage, "Appearances can be deceiving." The manner in which someone presents them self to the world may not represent their hidden inner nature, or their real motivations. While we can observe centers as they manifest in others, it may be more difficult to see their negative weaknesses which they may be hiding, but which can manifest later in very harmful traits. Initially, it is impossible to truly know new people, to see their true motivations, potentially hidden agendas, or their ulterior motives. It can take many years before we really know someone for who they truly are. Naturally we all seek to share meaningful exchanges with others, but we often open our self to those who would exploit the sincere individual. We all wish to have companions and like-minded friends, but it is prudent to be aware of potential charlatans who want to enrich their bank account at your expense. I addressed this issue in depth in the segment about a negative chief feature called, "Hasnamuss." This particularly applies to metaphysical teachers in the new age market place.

As you become more sincere and eager about your personal work, please remember there are people who are looking to take advantage of precisely this quality within you. And, just as it is wise to be cautious of charlatans in the often pseudo new-age marketplace, it is also important to be cautious of charlatans who might already be involved in your life. Many people are not what they seem and they may not have your best interests at heart. Innocent people are often duped by people they believe they can trust, such as new age leaders, spiritual teachers, gurus, and metaphysical preachers. This is a common occurrence. There are situations in life which appear fine on the outside, but for those of us who wish to live a more conscious life, it is absolutely essential to look more closely. People who work in the new age or metaphysical markets, may claim to be enlightened and to have all the answers you seek; and, perhaps they do have some answers which you seek, but, it is wise to be cautious and proceed slowly. If these people act superior or arrogant, be aware, this is a manipulative business strategy. Arrogant behavior is the antithesis of true awareness and higher consciousness. Arrogance emanates from the realms of vanity, pride, self-love, ignorance and deception. You will not benefit from anyone's arrogance. The best action is to ignore them, and distance yourself as soon as possible. It is prudent to be wary of anyone who expounds their lofty abilities or invisible higher powers. To paraphrase the poet Rumi, do not follow others as they might be blind.

Gaining self-awareness is your personal responsibility. Following another may not be the most direct way, or the shortest path to higher consciousness. It is essential to be diligent and selective in the metaphysical marketplace, as there is an abundance of unverifiable ideas that can certainly confuse the unsuspecting. I have met people who were terribly disoriented and felt overwhelmed by all the controversial information. Whatever you decide, my best advice is to trust your own sincere instincts. Again, it is solely up to you to awaken by your own consistent personal efforts. Trust your own natural potential within. One has only to think about the Buddha, who after years of personal efforts and austerities, eventually sat beneath a tree, and quietly in solitude, gained enlightenment. His personal journey took him on many paths while making many difficult efforts he thought would help. Then he began to practice mindful detachment as he relinquished all worldly distractions, illusions and delusions to attain his enlightenment. The Buddha became enlightened by his own consistent sincere personal efforts, just as we each can. Please be assured, we can each individually awaken by our own personal efforts. Trust your true essential needs.

Finding quiet and developing balance within:
Throughout history, sages in the various wisdom traditions have gone off alone to meditate, or they went into seclusion to attain self-awareness and enlightenment. Quieting the mind is essential to your awakening; but, you do not necessarily need to go into seclusion. Conversely, one does not need to live with groups of people in order to work on one self. While no one is an island, we do need islands of solitude, in peaceful environments with tranquility. Spending some quality time alone while practicing mindful self-observation, is beneficial as you gain self-knowledge and connect to your essential nature. It can be most helpful to set aside small periods of time simply to be alone, as you practice mindful self-observation. This method will assist you in arriving at higher states of awareness to ultimately realize your own enlightened potential. Only you can personally awaken yourself; no one can ever do it for you. With mindful self-observation, one commences the journey to gain enhanced self-awareness and higher consciousness. Balance is the key.

It is essential to begin to work on yourself in the ordinary conditions of life. You can begin right now where you are in this moment with mindful self-observation. You do not need to live in an artificial environment to become self-aware. If we elect to live in extraordinary artificial environments separated from our normal reality, we may not be able to function well in the ordinary world. If one can only function in an artificial environment, one will not be able to function in a normal environment. What is gained in the artificial environment may not apply to one's normal life. What you gain in these artificial situations must translate into the practical reality of living your life. Practice mindful self-observation wherever you are as you work to develop your self-awareness. One must honor one's true essential nature while living in the ordinary conditions of life. However, choosing to become self-aware in the ordinary conditions of life does not imply that one behave as if one is ordinary. You are a powerful, valuable person and you have many options.

Work against obstacles to awareness such as imagination, identification, unnecessary talk, false personality and so on. It is best not to attract undue attention to yourself, or to your efforts. One must live in the world, but one does not need to indulge in the world. You can participate in what is necessary to maintain your life while working to become self-aware. This process has been described as walking the razor's edge. Having cherished role models like Peter Ouspensky encourages our personal potential to reach higher and farther. It is these unique individuals who personify our own aspirations, and whose example we can follow, to help dispel our personal cloud of self-doubt and uncertainty. True conscious beings inspire us to manifest from higher parts of centers with refined energies. When one has verified the masterful possibilities inherent with self-awareness and higher consciousness, one's life advances with enhanced momentum to achieve this pure and lucid state permanently. You will realize that being alive gives you ample opportunities to become self-aware, to awaken and to become enlightened.

While it may be your preference to live in a quiet, peaceful environment which is conducive to harmonious inner balance, it is necessary to exist and function in the world. One must learn to function normally, and invisibly in the ordinary world without losing the connection to one's essential nature. Self-observation is the magic key to open the door to your own awareness. Finding quiet within with balance will help.

Recognizing disharmonious energy and knowing when to disengage from others:
As you work on yourself to develop enhanced self-awareness it is particularly wise to be mindful of others. Not everyone you meet is interested in experiencing higher states of awareness. There will be times when you feel out of your element when you are with people. Perhaps it is an unfamiliar place, or a new situation, which may compound your discomfort. In certain instances, when this occurs we need to pay close attention to the energies that are surrounding us. We might be in an environment that is not appropriate for us, and the people may not be the best choice to socialize with. We need to be cognizant of the company we keep in all circumstances, and to monitor the energies that are being directed at us. When we sense or perceive uncomfortable exchanges, or inappropriate behavior, we need to make a conscious informed decision to disengage from these particular people. Yet, we are often blindsided by people, events, or sudden situations that arise and we may have difficulty knowing precisely what is the right thing to do at these times. These moments can test of our own internal fortitude. But, the consistent efforts we have made to prepare our self with increased self-knowledge will help us to overcome the awkward social challenges in life.

It is vital to strive for balance in relationships. As you loosen the grip that false personality has on your life, you can respond more from your true inner self to attract more suitable friends and companions. You have the right to experience harmonious interactions which nurture your essence, and do not subdue, limit or endanger your wellbeing. While we cannot know exactly what is going on in someone's mind, with careful discernment we can begin to sense their energy. We can certainly make more informed decisions about who we allow into our life. It is wise to develop conscious discernment to avoid habitually responding to illusions and appearances. We cannot blindly trust someone because of their pleasant characteristics, as these may be emanating from their false personality. Quite often, we give our personal power away to the very people who do not have any interest in our wellbeing. Understanding how false personality tends to veil another person's hidden nature, allows you to peak beneath their veneer, in order to get a clearer, more accurate assessment of them. This will help you to recognize people with whom you will be more compatible. As you continue to observe centers and features manifesting in others, you will become more aware of their true nature, inclinations, predispositions and general tendencies.

A common mistake we might make, is to trust people who spew forth ideas from their memorized data banks, the Jacks. Although they may seem charming, their memorized data may not be sincere, and might not apply to us in a practical manner, or to our situation. I have a friend who gets overwhelmed by the polite, but aggressive sales people in department stores, who seem so wonderfully interested with helping her. She comes home very unhappy, armed with shopping bags of expensive garments, which are quite impractical in her normal life. She complains about being in debt, but sales people continue to charm her into making more purchases. With self-observation, we can begin to minimize our reliance on the thoughts and opinions of others that can mislead us, or steer us away from our own true needs. While it may be quite innocent, our own misplaced trust might result in errors of judgment, unnecessary expenditures, and disappointments. It is wise to be cautious, as one can also be deceived, or misled by exterior appearances, which may be based on another person's mechanical traits. For example, this can occur with people who are tall, who tend to be assertive, domineering, forceful, or powerful. Appearances can manipulate us to respond mechanically to a person's center of gravity, their false personality, their chief feature, and also, their body type. Our own mechanical response to these superficial illusions, can cause a considerable amount of wrong thinking about our personal relationships with others.

You have probably experienced energy drains at certain times, from making too big of an effort to fit in with a certain social group, or certain types of people. When we spend time with people whose ideals clash with ours, we often compromise our personal needs or preferences to fit in. When you are influenced by people who do not truly resonate with you, it tends to feed false personality and creates wrong work within yourself. For example, if your Queen of Hearts friend has the habit of drinking alcohol to excess, and you decide to join her, this may not be a healthy choice, or alliance. Developing unhealthy habits because you wish to fit in with people is contraindicated for genuine lasting friendship. We have all the centers within; however, we do not need to allow a center to ascend, or, to take over our life to our detriment. Indulging in addictive substances does not nurture your true essential nature in any healthy manner whatsoever. Hence, if certain people are too demanding or difficult for you to be with, observe which center is manifesting and acknowledge your sensitivities. All centers do not necessarily agree, nor do they complement one another. There are centers in others which are completely incompatible with ours. Do not ignore your center of gravity, your personal needs, your essential nature, or anything which you are personally sensitive to.

Circumstances can sometimes feel out of your control for various reasons. This might seem to dictate the people you meet in your daily life; but, this may simply be a temporary setback. These setbacks can occur because we have unintentionally selected the wrong social pursuits, which do not serve our highest interests. As we begin to live with more objective awareness, we gain the power to change our reality, especially the external influences which we live with. We may not have a major effect on the outer world in which we must function, but we can certainly have an effect on our internal world, and thus, enhance our immediate experience, and how we perceive or respond to others. From this perspective, we can strive to place our self in more balanced and harmonious positions, to make more objective choices and healthy decisions. As we work on our internal harmony, it can help to change or minimize unfavorable external influences around us, which includes the people we interact with. Remember, it is always in your best interest to disengage from people and social groups who do not share your ideals and preferences, and whose centers and features are not compatible with your own. It may take a bit of time and practice to develop your self-confidence as you gain greater self-awareness, but with enhanced inner fortitude you will make better decisions. Ultimately you will benefit greatly from being selective about your interactions. I have verified many times that it is best to disengage from disharmonious people as quickly as possible.

Often the best we can do in certain situations is to simply distance our self, walk away and leave. For your security, remove yourself from the presence of people who exhibit stressful conflicting energies in the safest manner possible. There is no need to subject yourself to people who are functioning from their unbalanced centers, and which are not in harmony with yours. Do not make excuses for yourself, or your needs, and, do not internally consider. You do not need to endure unnecessary conflict, toxic energy, or negative people who do not have your best interests at heart, and who may harm your essential nature. Sometimes we are blindsided by people, but with mindful presence we can begin to minimize this. You have many options.

Using self-observation to develop discernment:
Mindful self-observation can help you to discern other people's behavior, actions, disposition, and attitudes.

We can create options to heal ourselves and grow from our experiences in life, good and bad. Increasing our self-awareness helps us develop discernment, and is beneficial for our healing process, especially after we have endured difficult, painful experiences. Practicing mindful self-observation, we can begin to loosen the grip of psychological pain, sorrow, identification, and, people or situations which are unhealthy for us. With consistent mindful self-observation, we can work to develop clear discernment to make more informed decisions about people, or situations that might arise, and perhaps in a more expedient manner. Remember, if someone makes you feel uncomfortable, it may be due to conflicting interests from their center of gravity, or from their negative chief features in false personality. For your personal wellbeing and protection, it may be best to leave their presence, or tell them to leave yours. It is not necessary to suffer from others who are not in control of their centers, their habits, or their life. Avoid internally considering what they may think or say. If you are in the company of people whose centers or false personality traits and chief features are not in harmony with you, it is best to acknowledge your differences and minimize, or cease interactions. Again, when you sense negativity from someone, it is wise to disengage to prevent losing precious energy. If you are uncomfortable with someone's energy, please always respect your personal needs and remove yourself from their unhealthy presence. Setting your boundaries is a healthy self-protective methodology.

As you make efforts to compose yourself with mindful self-observation, your interactions with others can become easier to understand, and you will recognize what is occurring sooner. This is highly beneficial discernment. Remember, others manifest from their own centers and chief features, and this might simply be incompatible with yours. It is helpful to monitor a person's words and observe their actions to assess their center of gravity, and to gauge potential incompatibility to avoid conflict. If you sense negativity, it is best to distance yourself from discordant people, energies, and situations to mitigate problems. Protect yourself and your essential nature to avoid losing precious energy. I encourage you to avoid wasting your time with those who do not meet your own ethical standards of behavior in a harmonious manner. This is discernment.

Maintaining your true individuality:
Developing self-awareness with consistent mindful self-observation will help you become in tune with your essential nature and your own unique individuality. Yet, we are often brought to attention by contradictory people and opposing forces, which clash with our personal beliefs, our rights, our sense of order and our wellbeing. It may seem difficult at these times to maintain your personal individuality, your beliefs, your integrity, or your sense of what is best for you in your life. However, mindful self-observation will help you put things into proper perspective. It is common sense to carefully choose one's friends and associates, but we often try to fit in with people who are not compatible with our essential nature. We can become confused in the process and our own false personality, which we are striving to subdue, may reemerge. When this happens, we have drifted away from our personal aim to be self-aware. Remember, we do not become enlightened by trying to fit in with people who we are incompatible with. It always best to maintain your personal individuality, even if it puts you at odds with what is considered popular, or trendy. Conforming to the demands of society diminishes your own uniqueness, and creates more artificial barriers to surmount. When we alter our behavior to fit in with others, it is at

the expense of our individuality and conflicts with our essential nature. Conforming to society is not helpful to an enlightened aim. At these times, we need to increase efforts to mindfully self-observe.

Everything in life is always changing and transforming. What does not work for you in this moment, will most likely change. Life is about transformation. This includes your life as you transform to your natural essential needs. As mentioned earlier, spending quality time alone helps to clarify what you truly need. Rather than being with people who do not share your ethical standards and values, experiment with being alone. While this level of confidence may take practice to develop, ultimately you will make more accurate assessments of your true needs. Those of us who work with the aim to become more self-aware, willingly elect to spend time alone to help harmonize our internal energies as we strive to truly know our self within. This is an important part of the process for self-study and self-development. Spending time alone has a quieting, calming effect that helps one to see oneself more clearly, while lessening false personality and diminishing pressure to perform in the world, or to fit in, which only drains energy. Quality alone time will help you to determine, define and refine your true needs, which is much more economical energetically. Rather than performing in life, you can interact more naturally with others, especially those who are also evolving and transforming their lives. You have choices and options regards who you spend time with.

It is helpful to understand that if you spend your time with energy draining people, you are doing an injustice to your true essential nature. Gurdjieff mentioned that when we spend time with lowly, or undesirable people, we tend to become like them. Remember, it is always appropriate action to intentionally disengage from people, or situations that do not feed your highest needs or your essential nature. You gain nothing by clinging to illusionary identifications and unhealthy attachments to others. What you willingly relinquish, frees you from painful psychological burdens and helps restore your internal equilibrium. Then you are much more likely to encounter kindred souls who share your values, and who respond to and nurture your essential nature. Being with likeminded people helps eliminate unnecessary energy expenditures. It is healing to spend your time with people you are naturally comfortable with and who inspire you.

Learning about centers as they manifest in our natural inclinations and predispositions helps us make better choices as to how we spend our time. Understanding your personal center of gravity will help you become more aware of your essential needs. As you become increasingly self-aware you may create opportunities to attract, and interact with people and social situations which nurture your essential nature in a positive holistic manner. Self-knowledge will guide you to consciously select activities and people who are more suitable to your true needs and essential nature. By observing the centers in yourself, and in others, you will be more capable of selecting more rewarding social scenarios for yourself with enhanced self-confidence. You will benefit immeasurably from your personal efforts to understand your unique individuality with mindful presence, conscientiousness, consciousness and compassion for yourself.

CHAPTER 14

BEGINNING TO KNOW YOUR SELF AS YOUR TRUE ESSENTIAL NATURE

At the heart of all the wisdom traditions lays the most important task of developing one's self-awareness. To develop your awareness, try using the ideas and practical methods in this book to commence work on yourself. As you learn about your innate influences from within, your inherent tendencies and your natural motivations, you begin your personal journey to gain enhanced self-knowledge. Developing self-awareness is a transformational art form to learn about and truly know oneself. As one embarks on this quest for higher self-awareness and consciousness, one may also encounter one's own inner demons, fears and insecurities. We must proceed courageously to penetrate through the accumulated layers of false personality to see our true inner essential self. Using these practical methods for self-development, can help you to recognize and resolve deep inner conflicts. In the process of working for enhanced self-knowledge you can begin to heal your personal issues with gentle understanding, enhanced self-esteem and greater self-respect.

One begins the most basic first steps, by observing oneself in a new way without old labels. This requires honesty, impartiality, sincerity and gentle kindness to one self. As you begin to look beneath the layers of your accumulated traits, you will observe a more authentic version of yourself. As you begin to develop self-knowledge, you will also see yourself with more clarity, and with greater compassion. Self-knowledge develops and proceeds in stages, but slowly, and quite miraculously, you will begin to recognize your true essential nature. You will realize that acquired traits, and artifices, are simply no longer sustainable in your life. You can gradually shed the mask of false personality and other artificial encumbrances, which have limited your potential, and prevented you from experiencing your true self.

Learning about the centers of influence within will greatly assist you on your path to gain self-knowledge. Remember, your personal center of gravity affects virtually everything as the primary influence over your emotions, thinking, physical actions and sensory responses to life. This knowledge must be put into practical application in your life for real growth to occur. Merely acquiring information does not create change of itself. Work on oneself has to be practical in your daily life. Sometimes people seek mystical ideas which they cannot apply in their normal life. Impractical information might serve as a band-aid, which when removed can leave one with a sense of disenchantment, betrayal and confusion. If an individual remains unchanged or unhappy, it may indicate they have not applied the wisdom as a practical method to gain self-knowledge. One must genuinely observe oneself to begin to truly know oneself. As you gain a more comprehensive knowledge of the centers within, it will help you identify your personal natural influences in your life. By implementing the concepts about the centers of influence while utilizing the practical method of mindful self-observation, you will begin to see yourself, the people around you, and the world of life in a new way. The wisdom of centers is eminently verifiable and will assist you as you consistently observe yourself and continue to make sincere efforts.

Mindful self-observation is pivotal for working on yourself with the aim to evolve. It is up to you to become your own well informed personal expert on yourself. The absolute best you can do is work with what you are born with, and accept yourself as you truly are naturally and essentially. With ongoing self-observation, you will gain an enhanced understanding of who you are deep within yourself. As you gradually become self-aware you will also begin to elevate and transform your personal alchemy. You will begin to recognize what you genuinely want with authentic need in your life, which helps nurture and protect your essential nature. Your personal influences within will guide you on your journey to develop enhanced self-knowledge for transformation, and higher consciousness. Always remember, your true inner self is your best guide, teacher and counselor for living your life attuned in harmony with your essential nature. We must each look deeply, and truthfully within, to gaze at the miraculous universe of our own essential nature.

Your path is within you.

CHAPTER 15

ORIGINS OF THE FOURTH WAY

Over the many years that have elapsed years since I initially began formal study of the Fourth Way in 1975, several people have asked me one rather simple question: where did this system originate? I do not have a definitive answer to this question, and Gurdjieff did not provide one. Ouspensky indicated this was a common question, but answers remained vague. Esoteric knowledge and wisdom have been transmitted and preserved throughout the ages in different forms. From my own studies of various wisdom traditions, I have verified there is a significant similarity between the Fourth Way and other psychological knowledge systems used to enhance self-awareness and elevate consciousness. Though it has been attributed to Georges Gurdjieff, the exact origin of the Fourth Way remains vague; however, he said he had not invented it. Peter Ouspensky is the brilliant scholar who studied the Fourth Way with Gurdjieff in Russia, and later systematically organized and documented the system into a cohesive body of practical knowledge. He also skillfully interpreted the mathematical diagrams which are included in his precise Fourth Way writings.

The Fourth Way system of esoteric psychology is quite thorough, as well as highly practical. It has proven eminently insightful in helping me understand other ancient wisdom traditions which I studied previously. Many ideas and concepts which had seemed too exotic to grasp, became more comprehensible. When I first began reading Ouspensky's books, which detail the Fourth Way's comprehensive ideas and methods, I recognized certain basic similarities to Buddhist, Taoist, Sanskrit and Hindu doctrines. While Ouspensky may caution against comparing different psychological systems initially, clearly it is evident that some ideas of the Fourth Way have their roots in other, and perhaps much older systems of knowledge. For example, the Sutras of Patanjali, which detail different levels of awareness, are similar to the Fourth Way ideas regarding the different levels of conscious awareness. The distinctive Fourth Way ideas about the different states of consciousness, are also quite similar to Buddhist concepts regarding the levels of delusion which one must overcome to become self-aware, to ultimately become enlightened. Certainly, the similarity between these different teachings cannot merely be arbitrary random coincidences.

As I studied Ouspensky's articulate account of Gurdjieff's fragmentary teachings, I realized that certain philosophical concepts which eluded me prior, became more comprehensible. Also, my feelings about my spiritual beliefs were enhanced, and deepened. But, keep in mind, the Fourth Way is not religion, nor is it necessary to relinquish your religious or spiritual beliefs. The Fourth Way may enhance your spirituality, but it is not a religion, nor religious doctrine. However, I have observed that some teachers tend to stamp their personal spiritual beliefs onto this system. Ultimately, this has proved to be a difficult hurdle, and an unnecessary encumbrance for many students. In essence, the Fourth Way system is a practical methodology, based upon one's own personal verification of the ideas, concepts, and practices.

The Fourth Way has no exact religious affiliation, as it is not a faith based system. It is a practical psychological system which focuses upon one's own personal verifications of everything, in one's normal daily life. Certainly, there is no requirement to withdraw into a monastery, or an esoteric school.

While, the Fourth Way is a unique psychological system for self-development, its precise origins remain veiled, perhaps due to its esoteric nature. In his autobiographical book, "Meetings with Remarkable Men," Gurdjieff writes of his extensive travels with his comrades, the Seekers of Truth. They journeyed throughout Asia, Central Asia, China, the Gobi Desert, Tibet, Egypt, the Hindu Kush, Iran, and other remote areas to find hidden knowledge. They journeyed to far flung exotic regions delving into ancient psychological and philosophical systems, hoping to find hidden esoteric wisdom. Gurdjieff wrote of an encounter with the Sarmoung Brotherhood; however, despite theories, there is no easily verifiable evidence of its existence, except in ancient Babylonia. Perhaps he was referring to studies with Sufi dervishes. Gurdjieff journeyed extensively throughout Asia and China, so it is possible he was referencing the Surmang Tibetan Buddhist Monastery in Eastern Tibet, which is now part of China. The Surmang Monastery is formed by a complex of several monasteries which are located in the nomadic farming region of Kham in eastern Tibet. This ancient Tibetan Buddhist lineage dates back many centuries, and may have been the inspiration and source for some of Gurdjieff's basic Fourth Way concepts, which are comparable to Buddhist teachings.

From my own lengthy personal studies, I find Buddhism to be strikingly similar to most of the psychological ideas, methods and principles which Gurdjieff put forth, although they are presented in a different context. Also, Gurdjieff's Fourth Way system does not mention nor include meditation practice as Buddhism does. In his various writings, Peter Ouspensky admits of the similarities in the Fourth Way to other wisdom traditions and psychological systems, which may be much older methodologies. But, when he was specifically asked about the comparison of the Fourth Way to Buddhism, Ouspensky revealed he was not very familiar with the Buddhist teachings. This would have included its distinctive disciplines, concepts, methods and practices for personal self-development. Thus, at that particular time and as a highly cultivated, well informed scholar, seeker and teacher of esoteric knowledge, Ouspensky himself was not fully aware of the massive teachings for personal growth embedded within the ancient Buddhist legacy of wisdom.

While Buddhism has existed for over 2,500 years, it had only become more known to the Western world in comparatively recent times. So, Ouspensky's lack of knowledge regarding Buddhism, would have been consistent with the world's scant knowledge of Buddhist thought and its profound psychology, at that time. Buddhism had not been fully revealed, nor elaborated to Westerners, until the early 20th century. However, Gurdjieff had traveled throughout the exotic Eastern world, and is said to have lived and studied in Tibet, and other countries steeped in Buddhist tradition and wisdom. It is quite reasonable to assume that Gurdjieff may have borrowed various Buddhist concepts to embellish his own system at a time when most people were still relatively unaware of Buddhism, and the profundity of Eastern philosophy and psychology. This seems apparent in his presentation about the levels of consciousness and awakening. Ouspensky agreed that comparisons can be made to other esoteric and philosophical systems, particularly if one is already familiar with the characteristics of distinctive systems and teachings. And, comparisons are inevitable, because of the Fourth Way's uncanny resemblance to older established systems, concepts, and methods.

From my perspective, some of the most distinctive elements are the Fourth Way's similarities to the historic Buddha's "Four

Noble Truths," and also, to the particles of his "Eightfold Path." We can see a very clear connection to the ideals, methods, disciplines and the practices which the Buddha taught. For example, the Buddha's Four Noble Truths are based on the cessation of suffering, which the Fourth Way also teaches as the elimination of negativity, which includes the cessation of negative emotions and negative imagination, which cause our unnecessary suffering. Also, the Buddhist path is based upon the ideal that one takes refuge in the Buddha, the Sangha and the Dharma. In this manner, the disciple of Buddhism essentially pledges to study in the manner of the Buddha, to cooperate with other disciples, and to work for the benefit of mankind. This is nearly identical to the three lines of work as referenced by Gurdjieff in his Fourth Way teachings. However, Gurdjieff also stated that one can work independently without a school, as one's objective path.

The Fourth Way proposes to function as a highly organized efficient methodology for the development and attainment of enhanced self-knowledge and consciousness. It focuses on personal self-study, implemented with mindful self-observation, as its practical method to gain understanding of one's essential nature. Yet, this methodology is consistent with most wisdom traditions. Nonetheless, the Fourth Way is configured into various components for effective self-study, which work well to achieve optimal results. The core elements form a cohesive body of practical methods that one can utilize to commence self-study to attain enhanced self-awareness. This system is designated for practical work on oneself, with the aim to achieve higher states of consciousness. One must make consistent efforts with mindful self-observation, while eliminating negative habits and false traits. The Fourth Way system serves as a practical psychological method to gain self-knowledge, and in this sense, is consistent with other philosophical and psychological systems, whose primary focus is self-knowledge. Whatever its origin, Fourth Way concepts and practical methods help answer the deeper questions we have about our life and human existence. Its vast wisdom base lends support as one practices mindful self-observation to harmonize one's internal world to gain balance within, without being dependent upon external resources. Remember, owing to the practical nature of self-study, there is no rigid rule that you must join a monastery or school.

Gurdjieff referred to this method of self-study and development as the, "objective way," as one works on oneself in one's normal daily life. I reiterate this to assure you that you can most definitely begin to work on yourself right now, where you are now, and exactly as you are right now. Mindful self-observation is the key starting point to gain self-knowledge which is consistent with the majority of wisdom traditions and practices. The remarkably striking similarities to other systems, is what primarily led me to realize that the Fourth Way is quite likely a combination of various esoteric teachings. Gurdjieff characteristically made the point of claiming his method was, "the way of the sly man." Perhaps he intended to camouflage its origins, but he emphasized the Fourth Way is not the way of the monk, the yogi, or the fakir. Yet, it is reasonable to assume it is a combination of these three ways. Embellished with components from other wisdom traditions, the ideas work well together because they do not contradict one another, and promote compatible ideals. Ouspensky indicated that Gurdjieff had said that Fourth Way schools typically manifest in a distinctive outer form with the primary intention to preserve and perpetuate knowledge, after which the school may completely disappear.

The Fourth Way's similarity to other traditions seems particularly evident with the Buddhist teachings. Most apparent is the employment of mindful self-observation, which is a key essential starting point in Buddhism, and through which the historic Buddha attained his enlightenment. Buddhism teaches about the concept of identification, which manifests as attachments and illusions, which cause our personal sense of separateness and isolation from others. As mentioned, the striking similarity to Buddhism is also apparent with the proviso for three lines of work. The Fourth Way presents the concept that, one must work on one self, which is ones first line of work; one must work with fellow students, which is ones second line of work; and, one must contribute to maintain and support the school, as ones third line of work. An interesting note regards the third line of work, Ouspensky clearly stipulated that he would not contribute financially, and instead, as his personal third line of work, he helped Gurdjieff to acquire new students. In the Buddhist tradition, this concept is presented with simplicity, and is less rigid and demanding. One takes refuge in the Buddha, the Sangha, and the Dharma; thus, one works for one's enlightenment, one is compassionate and helpful to fellow students and others, and one works for the benefit of humanity. While Buddhism is often regarded as a religion, the Buddha did not claim to be a god, and did not require others to worship him. He merely claimed he was awake, and taught others his methods to reach their own awakening and enlightenment. It seems fairly evident that certain Fourth Way concepts and methods may have their origins in Buddhism, which has existed since the time of the historic Buddha, circa 500 BCE. While I have no wish to dress the Fourth Way in Buddhist, Hindu or Asian garb, it is apparent that its source is related to these other, much older wisdom traditions whose inner esoteric meaning is timeless.

Upon close examination, the Fourth Way appears to be somewhat of a collective body of wisdom, possibly from multiple sources, including its similarities to Buddhism. Again, please keep in mind, Buddhism and its concepts were relatively unknown in the western world in the early 20th century. Yet, Gurdjieff had traveled and studied extensively throughout the various Buddhist regions of Asia with his friends, the Seekers of Truth. Up to this particular point, the fundamental ideals of Buddhism were not commonly known when Gurdjieff brought his teachings to Russia, in the years preceding the turbulent Russian Revolution. Gurdjieff and Ouspensky were both world travelers who had searched for miraculous esoteric knowledge, and had explored the exotic Eastern world, including India where Buddhism originated, as well as other remote lands, rich with myth and mystery. Gurdjieff's travels in these ancient lands may have inspired the inclusion of Buddhist and Sanskrit ideas into his Fourth Way system. Also, in his travels to Egypt, Gurdjieff may have found fragments of other wisdom traditions. Regardless of its exact origin the massive body of esoteric knowledge within the Fourth Way system imbues it with the unique ability to help one become self-aware with objective guidance, practical methodologies and clarity. Overall, the Fourth Way's methods to attain self-knowledge seem most complimentary to, and similarly consistent with the historic Buddha's own highly evolved awakening methods and practices. But, the Buddhist practice of meditation was not emphasized by Gurdjieff. Also, at that time, the Buddhist philosophical ideals and psychology concepts would have been relatively unavailable to westerners. However, in the early twentieth century, there was an explosion of mystical ideas, which included Asian philosophies and other profound psychologies, along with previously unknown metaphysical esoteric doctrines. The time was ripe with opportunity to advance mystical philosophical teachings and esoteric concepts. Those who brought forth ancient ideas in new ways, were pioneers of the emerging new age philosophy, psychology and spirituality. Gurdjieff was a master of self-promotion, and he advanced himself and his teachings, perhaps as the Gurdjieff brand of exotic esotericism. But, he was not the only one.

There were a significant number of explorers and philosophers, traveling through Asia, the Himalayas and Tibet including the Russian artist, Nicholas Roerich and the French female scholar, Alexandra David Neel. At a time when Buddhism was almost completely unknown outside of the Asian world, she eloquently documented her massive Buddhist knowledge base, making vast contributions to its world legacy. She traveled to regions throughout Asia and the Himalayas from 1911 through to 1946, and had her first meeting with the Dalai Lama in 1912. Thereafter she continuously traveled throughout Asia, and studied in China, Tibet and Japan. She was one of the first to introduce the mystical teachings of Buddhism to the West, with its tapestry of enlightening ideals, saturated in its ancient history. However, prior to Alexandra David Neel's extensive journeys and studies throughout Asia, the doctrines of Buddhism were still rather obscure and relatively unknown in the western world. Certainly, intellectuals such as Schopenhauer, were aware of Asian thought and philosophy, yet it was not commonly known to most westerners. Traditionally, esoteric wisdom was preserved in different capacities within monasteries and by various methods, and in mediums, such as art, poetry, mathematics, architecture, philosophy, and literature. But, very few individuals would have been on familiar terms with Buddhist philosophy, psychology and its profoundly enlightening thought outside of Asia, except perhaps in the aforementioned intellectual philosophical circles.

Contemporaries of Gurdjieff and Ouspensky, including the charismatic Russian mystic author and teacher, Madame Helena Blavatsky, taught and wrote about the Ray of Creation, as a component of her acclaimed writings, entitled, The Secret Doctrine. Ouspensky and Gurdjieff were independently drawn to Blavatsky's work, as well as to the Theosophical Society. While Ouspensky said, the Theosophical Society led him to a certain point, clearly it had an enormous impact and influence on his work, as he began to enter esoteric realms of thought and profundity. The Theosophical Society is still in existence today, due to its timeless relevance. Additionally, the concept of the Ray of Creation is not unique to the Fourth Way, as it was taught by Madame Blavatsky, the Theosophical Society, and other metaphysical teachers. Madame Blavatsky's mystical literature is said to have intrigued another contemporary genius of the time, Albert Einstein.

Ouspensky was rather clear that Gurdjieff had introduced and taught the Fourth Way ideas and methods as fragments of knowledge. After studying with Gurdjieff, he took it upon himself to teach, organize, and document the Fourth Way as a cohesive system of esoteric wisdom, not only to preserve it, but to elevate and exalt its massive vault of knowledge. The diagrams, which Ouspensky calculated and devised, are utilized in the Fourth Way system as a mathematical component to illustrate the relationships between worlds, space and time. But, also, to illustrate the system's practical psychological concepts for purity of understanding. There is a precise elegance with mathematics which demonstrates that which words may not easily convey. Certainly, Ouspensky's initial focus and inspiration was mathematics, as is evidenced by his prior studies of physics, and the different dimensions. Ouspensky writes of the need to make super efforts to become self-aware to develop higher states of consciousness. Again, the references to the different states of consciousness are similar to the teachings of Patanjali. In the sutras, Patanjali teaches of the three levels of awareness which one must develop intentionally to overcome one's ignorance to achieve super normal mind. He refers to the first level as Dharana, the second level as Dhyana, and the third level as Samadhi. Patanjali encourages one to combine all three levels of awareness to achieve Samyama, or liberation. These stages are identical to the Fourth Way idea of states of consciousness which detail states of consciousness as ascending in numeric sequence. With self-observation, one begins to realize one's different states, as levels of conscious awareness.

I have also recognized similarities within the Fourth Way, which almost exactly parallel esoteric astrology. This includes planetary influences on the physical body through its complex endocrine system and glands. In western Astrology, one can study the planetary influences on the endocrine system, depending upon which planet is in a particular constellation within one's natal astrological chart. This precise astrological system is comparable to the Fourth Way's system of body types, which states that planets influence our specific glandular predisposition, thus determining our particular body type. The Ayurvedic, or Vedic astrological tradition suggests three primary body types, depending on physical traits, and other types are a blend of these traits. Western Astrology and the Vedic wisdom of body types, are both vast sciences, far too extensive to cover in this volume; however, it is apparent that our magnificent starry universe has provided mankind with eternal inspiration to aspire to learn and understand the reality of life.

Yet, regardless of its exact origins, the Fourth Way system has proven to be a highly beneficial source of knowledge. As a systematic resource of unique esoteric importance, and psychological relevance, it addresses virtually all human experiences ranging from our deepest feelings and most abstract thoughts, to our most basic physical sensory impulses and instinctive physical needs. Within its vast body of knowledge, one can find many answers that address our basic, yet puzzling human concerns. The most essential desire to understand oneself within the context of ones living experience, becomes more manageably attainable as one grasps a bigger picture which is distinctively presented. As a microcosm within the vast body of the universal macrocosm, we are no less significant. In the larger scheme of life and our personal reality we are each individually of equal and immeasurable importance. The Fourth Way deftly addresses many of the most fundamental questions about human life, as well as the more abstract and theoretical concepts. As physicists extrapolate meaning from complex mathematical formulas, quotients and equations as they probe the nature of life, the Fourth Way points out that, what is above is also what is below. This is consistent with the ancient Hermetic formula of the Emerald Tablets, "As above, so below." Thus, we are part of the infinite expanding body of the Universe within the vast and perhaps seemingly infinite, Absolute.

Thinking with scale and relativity we begin to understand how an atom of living matter is virtually identical to our own solar system. An atom is comprised of particles, known as protons and neutrons within its nucleus, and has electrons spinning around this nucleus in an orbital path. Yet, as we gaze into the starry magnificence of our own solar system, we see this same basic structure consistent with the humble atom. Our solar system is part of one galaxy amongst billions of other galaxies, all of which are filled with stars, planets, moons, and asteroids. These billions of galaxies comprise our massive universe, of which we are part. Stars, or suns seem to function as the nucleus, with planets and moons as the protons and neutrons, while the asteroids may function as the electrons. Another compelling thought, the satellites which we send into space to orbit around our own dear planet, may begin to function as electrons which may be changing our atomic structure and perhaps speeding up, or hastening planetary evolution. Regardless, within our own solar system we have the same precise model as that of the tiny, but powerful magnificent atom. We are part of the life of the larger body of the universe, expanding into what some call, the Absolute.

Despite the obvious comparisons and visible similarities to many other psychological systems, the Fourth Way stands on its own merit as a practical body of esoteric wisdom. Its eminently practical application for the attainment of self-awareness can be implemented by each individual who intentionally elects to pursue their enhancement of self-awareness and higher consciousness. Gurdjieff advises, "remember yourself," which is synonymous with the Buddhist practice of, "mindfulness." Mindfulness is derived from Pali and Sanskrit words, "to remember," and has been embraced by millions of people to achieve self-awareness, inner peace, balance and harmony. Just as mindfulness encourages one to be aware and present in the moment, Gurdjieff's system advises one the same. Perhaps there is nothing as simple, nor as profoundly beneficial than to simply remember to be present in the moment while mindfully observing oneself. I encourage you to remember, your path is within you.

CHAPTER 16

THE ROLES OF GURDJIEFF AND OUSPENSKY IN THE FOURTH WAY

Those of us who encounter this miraculous system quite naturally tend to be drawn in by the enigmatic magnetism of the two men who are the foundation of the teachings and whose lives have immortalized it. They are the eminent Russian scholar, theoretician and author, Peter D. Ouspensky; and, the Armenian Greek teacher, Georges I. Gurdjieff. The fragmentary teachings which Gurdjieff presented in his Fourth Way system, seem to function as a collection of esoteric methods and concepts, which have been culled from various sources. It is reasonable to assume that the ideas are derived from different wisdom traditions, but, it is clear the ideas included blend seamlessly and harmoniously together. Though it is not always possible, it may be beneficial to know where certain ideas originated from, as the source material may be helpful for further study. In his relentless extensive searching and travels, Gurdjieff seemed to have gained access to a significant body of mystical, metaphysical, esoteric psychological and philosophical ideologies. But, it seems quite probable that Gurdjieff utilized knowledge he found in Asia and India to supplement and enhance his own Fourth Way system.

While Gurdjieff said he had not invented these ideas, he also does not attribute this system to a particular teacher, country, or, a specific school of thought. However, in his own teachings, Ouspensky spoke of the need for real esoteric teachings to share a common truth at their core. He suggests that if ideologies which espouse esoteric truths are in conflict, or disagree in their central teachings, that they are not esoteric in origin, but are simply man-made inventions. Ouspensky had travelled throughout Asia and India, and he must have become aware of the similarities to other philosophical and esoteric psychological systems. Subsequent to his departure from Gurdjieff, Ouspensky makes references to Buddhism, yoga, meditation and other systems of knowledge. These references illustrate specific points regarding other comparable methods for gaining self-knowledge and enhanced awareness.

I feel it is important to mention that Gurdjieff was known to be a chameleon whose appearance even seemed to change on occasion. Previously, he had worked as a hypnotist, a jack of all trades, and later, as a carpet trader, musician and mystic choreographer. It would not seem to be out of his character to assume, or appropriate ideas and concepts from other wisdom traditions, such as Buddhism, Hinduism, Sanskrit, or the Theosophical Society, to embellish his own system and methods. This would have allowed him to unify these various fragments of knowledge and take command as the preeminent scholar and teacher at that particular time in history. He spent many years travelling in search of truth, and it is evident that he found components of knowledge which he later taught as fragments of teachings. Clearly, Gurdjieff was motivated to establish his own brand of metaphysical teachings at a time when he could gain a foothold in the emerging mystical spiritual business culture which was beginning to thrive throughout the world. And, he targeted Ouspensky to help him. Ouspensky had also sought sacred knowledge before he encountered Gurdjieff. Significantly, Ouspensky later admitted that Gurdjieff did not possess what he had attributed to him.

Ouspensky was candid about his difficult decision to stop working with Gurdjieff. Ouspensky clearly stated in a commentary that he, and most of Gurdjieff's students, left him in 1918 because he had abruptly altered core concepts of the system. Gurdjieff suddenly demanded students must believe everything he told them. This implies that students were ordered to accept what he said on faith without personal verification, which contradicts the system, negating its primary directive to verify everything. Ouspensky saw this departure from the original direction as quite unacceptable. As an intellectually centered individual, Ouspensky felt that Gurdjieff's abrupt change from the Fourth Way core tenets began to border on religious faith, which he could not endorse. Keep in mind, Ouspensky was responsible for bringing students to Gurdjieff to expand his circle and enlarge the scope of his teachings. Ouspensky introduced many people to Gurdjieff, who were successful and educated, as his personal third line of work. Apparently, Gurdjieff gave him this task to expand his teachings to people in St. Petersburg and Moscow, just prior to the Russian Revolution. Yet, one can understand Ouspensky's reluctance to continue with Gurdjieff after he dispensed with vital elements which keep the Fourth Way esoterically unique, and verifiably honest for each individual.

There are many clues that Ouspensky had his own rationale for diminishing his connection to Gurdjieff. He may have had boundaries as to what he said about Gurdjieff, yet he made insightful comments which reveal his disappointment and disenchantment. While I would not characterize Gurdjieff as a charlatan, it is apparent he was a bold opportunist. It is obvious that Gurdjieff specifically targeted Ouspensky to enlist his help to promote himself, his teachings, and to propel the Fourth Way into more elevated realms. Ouspensky was a successful author and highly regarded theoretician, at the time when he first met Gurdjieff. Ouspensky must have been pleased to meet Gurdjieff in the early days, but this eventually dissipated. Initially Gurdjieff appeared to embody exactly what Ouspensky referred to as the miraculous, yet clearly this original magic evaporated as they worked together. When Gurdjieff abruptly changed core ideas of the system and the outward form of the teaching to a faith-based way, Ouspensky realized he simply could not continue with him. Yet, he also reveals that his decision to leave Gurdjieff was very difficult for him.

Also, it is apparent that Gurdjieff had a tendency to be manipulative. Ouspensky wrote of an event where he invited a friend to have dinner with him and Gurdjieff, which descended into an uncomfortable situation. Gurdjieff and his group remained resolutely silent during dinner, encouraging only the guest to speak. This awkward experiment was to demonstrate how ordinary people function habitually like automatons. Yet, any guest in a strange situation might speak because of their unfamiliarity with the environment and the people. Gurdjieff may have manipulated innocent people to use as teaching devices for his students, but his behavior feels quite unsympathetic, rather than kind sincere compassion one associates with a teacher. It is understandable that Ouspensky, a refined intellectual suffered from Gurdjieff's peculiar social behaviors.

My personal preference has always been Peter Ouspensky. He consistently reveals integrity and emotional restraint. Of course, it is possible that Gurdjieff simply did anything, and everything that was necessary, to get his teachings across to the people who were interested. Clearly, both Gurdjieff and Ouspensky each manifested from their quite different respective centers of gravity. Gurdjieff was said to be instinctively centered, and it is quite obvious that Ouspensky was intellectually centered.

After various odd incidents, Ouspensky began to distance himself from Gurdjieff, especially when he changed core elements. Perhaps their parting was also due to their vastly different centers of gravity. While both men seem to have exhibited inordinately high levels of consciousness, it is reasonable to assume they had each acquired what they set out to acquire from one another, and moved on out of necessity for their own work. However, after they separated, Ouspensky continued to help Gurdjieff recruit new students to support his teachings.

Both of these remarkable men remained true to their distinctive essential natures. Ultimately, Gurdjieff's teachings, particularly at his institute in France, took an outer form which seemed to be influenced by his early studies with the Dervish orders he encountered in the Middle East. This included various movements, dances, postures, gymnastics, and other physical exercises. Certainly, Ouspensky remained quite true to his intellectual essential nature as he plumbed the depths of the Fourth Way while teaching in England, and later in America. He continued to present the ideas by giving public lectures in London, while working closely and in greater depth with his private students at his school in Surrey, England. Both Gurdjieff and Ouspensky travelled independently to America to teach, particularly during the second world war, when Europe was embroiled in chaos. Ouspensky settled in New York with his students to wait out the war, and Gurdjieff spent time possibly courting potential supportive donors, including the great American architect, Frank Lloyd Wright, who was married to one of Gurdjieff's former pupils.

In my heart, I, have always felt Ouspensky was the true great master of the Fourth Way. It is my sincere belief that Gurdjieff had intentionally targeted Ouspensky to help promote, systematize and deliver these ideas to a larger audience which he would never have been able to reach on his own. When Ouspensky first met Gurdjieff, he was certainly in a position to help him. He had the world at his fingertips with his brilliant mind and acclaimed writing skills as a successful author. At that time, Ouspensky was an internationally recognized writer, journalist, scholar and theoretician. Ultimately, Ouspensky translated and presented Gurdjieff's fragmentary teachings in his refined, articulate, intelligent, cohesive manner which elevated the system to the rarified realms of intellectual esotericism. He imbues the Fourth Way with literary prowess, endowing it with his distinctive voice, which deserves our unified attention and wins our deepest respect.

We can understand Ouspensky because he understood his students needs for an articulate transmission of knowledge. He leads us straight to the point without unnecessary elaborations, or tangential digressions which might confuse us. He recognized the need to help others awaken through his own enlightened view, and with an intellectual focus. It is also interesting to note, that while Ouspensky and Gurdjieff taught in Russia, England, France and America, neither man spoke English as their original native language. Ouspensky was Russian, and Gurdjieff was Armenian and Greek. These remarkable ideas and concepts were interpreted and translated from various diverse foreign languages including Russian, Turkish, Greek, Armenian, Sanskrit, and possibly Chinese and Tibetan, amongst many other original languages.

Ouspensky interpreted the fragmentary Fourth Way ideas and methods Gurdjieff taught, but in a manner which renders them elegant, accessible and understandable, while also granting one entrance into the esoteric realm. Ouspensky did not publish his Fourth Way writings in his own lifetime. His monumental works, In Search of the Miraculous, and the Fourth Way, which is a compilation of his lectures over an extended period of time, were not published until after his death. Significantly, it was Gurdjieff who moved forward to help arrange the publishing of these great works after Ouspensky died. This may clarify any confusion about whether Gurdjieff knew of Ouspensky's extensive Fourth Way writings. Gurdjieff might have been the active force in perpetuating Ouspensky's vast literary legacy, while perhaps also promoting his own massive personal mythology as well. It is written that Gurdjieff approved the writings and set about to have the books published after Ouspensky's death in 1947.

Peter Ouspensky was specific about his personal mission to teach and document the Fourth Way system, maintaining its purity and contributing to the preservation of its timeless legacy. He took it upon himself to make the teachings available to as many people as possible in his lectures in England and America, and in his writings, to perpetuate the system so it would not disappear completely after he and Gurdjieff died. This was a major undertaking, but he was clear about his need to do this as part of his personal third line of work. He observed how art, literature and other humanizing systems were supported and perpetuated by the masses. Thus, he realized he had to do the same to keep the Fourth Way system and its massive body of knowledge alive for the people not yet born, who would want it, need it, use it and would truly value it.

In his master work, "In Search of the Miraculous," Peter Ouspensky writes with clear objectivity in his characteristic pristine delivery. He conveys his experiences and vast knowledge of the teachings without artifice or speculative invention. This encourages us to align our self with the ideas of this system as we begin to experience our personal potential to elevate our life and consciousness with and by our own miraculous efforts. Ouspensky teaches with a purity of intellect fueled by his compassion to inspire others to become self-aware and awaken. We can trust Ouspensky's unambiguous presentation of the concepts and methods of the Fourth Way. He is insistent of what is possible, because he is there beckoning us to join him and lift ourselves out of our own unconscious lethargy. He finesses his intelligence within precise presentations, to help us understand in order to connect with our own essential higher potential, as he urges us further than we ever thought, or dreamt, was possible for us to go.

Ouspensky's encyclopedic work, The Fourth Way, is a verbatim record of his teachings from the period when he resided and taught, in England and New York. These well documented teachings, discussions and dialogues reveal not only his distinct intellectual qualities and vast comprehension of the Fourth Way system, but also his subtly nuanced and refined emotionality. Through dialogues with students and others, including Aldous Huxley and T.S. Eliot, we hear his distinctive voice. From these revealing question and answer sessions we gain unequivocal insight into the depth and magnitude of his remarkable psyche. Responses to his student's questions are direct, elegant, precise, calm and economical. He is concise and eminently eloquent without arrogance. Ouspensky was intellectually centered, which gave him the power to impart knowledge with precision and skill. He says what is necessary, while avoiding digressions.

The quintessential Fourth Way teachings of P.D. Ouspensky are remarkable. He compares the human being to an airplane that does not know it can fly. He elucidates while directly addressing the needs of each student. In this sense Ouspensky taught the miraculous, without putting himself on an elevated pedestal. His unpretentious humility comes through rather clearly. Ouspensky seems to modestly place himself on the same level as his students, and uses phrases which are inclusive, employing the word we, rather than pointing out any particular student's flaws, or lack of awareness. He speaks skillfully in exact terms to assuage misunderstandings. Throughout his teachings, he impresses upon his students the possibility to experience their own higher centers with, and by their consistent efforts to be present and to self-observe. He tells us that we manifest from the lower centers habitually, which is the path of least resistance for almost everyone. He assures us that we already have the higher centers available within ourselves to access. To reach the higher centers we must remember to be present in the moment to become aware of the potential within us. His lucid explanations of these massive esoteric ideas demystify the mysterious, and render the obscure knowable.

Ouspensky calmly asks us to understand, and then he tells us how. He taught the Fourth Way with a steady articulate voice which never strays from his intentional objective. He repeatedly insists that one must verify everything, and that one must work to make this knowledge one's own. Ouspensky preserves the essential ideas of the Fourth Way, reconstructing the system which he also instructs his students to do.

Peter Ouspensky delivers the miraculous with lucid brilliance, as he consistently encourages us to follow his lead so we may reach our own highest potential to awaken.

Your path in within you.

CHAPTER 17

YOUR PERSONAL EVOLUTION AND AWAKENING ARE YOUR NATURAL BIRTHRIGHT

The concepts and methods of the Fourth Way have been an illuminating resource that have enriched my life in countless ways. But, these ideas at their core are practical and must be put into practical use to be effective. All the ideas in this book can be used immediately and efficiently for your personal benefit, and without making any drastic changes to your life. The magical driving force of these ideas are that they are intended for use in your normal daily life experience. You do not need to go anywhere or find anything. Your own life is the foundation for your personal practice to awaken and you can begin right now in this moment to improve, heal, and transform your life into the miraculous living experience you truly deserve. You are your own miracle and you deserve the most rewarding life possible by awakening to your essential nature. Understanding how centers function within you, and in others, will help you gain a firm grasp on your life experiences with greater depth. This lends vital insight into making better choices in every area of your life. Employing these essential esoteric concepts will expedite your growth to help you reach your goals for enhanced self-knowledge. Knowledge is power, but self-knowledge is personal empowerment.

My pure intention for this book is to help you gain greater understanding of these valuable ideas for your personal benefit. Learning about the different centers of influence within, as well as other essential esoteric concepts which I have included, will help you build a firm foundation for your path of self-study. As one works on oneself, one becomes more receptive, more open, and more sensitive. This heightened sensitivity can help you to develop better discernment about others. It is vital to select the right people to spend one's time with, and the most appropriate environments where one's essential nature is nurtured. This is especially important if one seeks involvement with groups which promote higher consciousness. While one can most certainly gain self-knowledge, and develop greater self-awareness by oneself, as your objective path to your own higher consciousness, there may be some who wish to find a teacher or a school. For this reason, I am including this chapter with the intention to assist you in being well prepared, and also, well informed. Again, my aim with this book is to inform, empower and encourage you in your personal growth.

Using the ideas in this book in a practical manner in your normal daily life can begin to generate and create new energies within you. These new energies may attract what is more appropriate for your life purpose. Naturally it is wonderful to have like-minded companions, friends and confidantes who share your emerging desire to live in your essential nature and have a more fulfilling honest life experience. Yet, not everyone will be interested in these particular ideas, so do not take offense. Keep in mind, you may occasionally feel somewhat detached from everyday events or occurrences. And this is perfectly normal. There are times when you may feel as though you are an observer on a sweeping wave of reality, a wave that churns some people under, but also allows one to ride the crest of the wave to reach higher understanding for real growth.

Awakening is your personal journey to your true self, and is generated by your consistent sincere efforts. However, I feel it is important to mention additional information regarding unforeseen issues that can arise. As with any endeavor, there might be some stumbling blocks, or obstacles. Thus, it is prudent to mention potential issues to caution you regards these factors. Those of us who wish to develop our self-awareness and gain self-knowledge generally tend to hope for the best, and to look for the good in others. Yet, we must also be aware of traits in others which are less than ideal, and may be detrimental to our goals. Personal growth opens one up to new experiences and to new people. But, one must guard against the unexpected which can manifest from others who may be on a very different path from you. It is wise to be aware that there are people who would lead you off your path, so you must be vigilant. It is possible that one may be enticed or misled into circuitous distractions, or onto journeys with less than scrupulous people who tell you they are a "teacher." However, they might not have your best interests at heart. There are always people who are selling their wares to the unsuspecting, so it is prudent for the innocent buyer to beware. Awakening is your natural birthright, and no one can sell you anything that will automatically awaken you. Your personal awakening is your task alone. Please remember, no one can awaken you, but you yourself. You are responsible for your own awakening. However, others may try to convince you otherwise.

Peter Ouspensky wrote about his experiences, interactions, and difficulties in groups with other students, but especially his difficulty with Georges Gurdjieff. I have always found his honesty in this regard helpful, as it made my own studies and interactions more relatable and therefore, more understandable. He wrote about stressful conditions with Gurdjieff, and the hardships of working in close proximity with others. This part of his writing is quite revealing as it gives one a glimpse into the atmosphere of an esoteric school as a rather stressful environment. Circumstances working closely with others in these environments push one past one's limits in every way. In reality, the outer form of a teaching situation which pressures people to extremes is not necessarily helpful, and it is not required. No one needs to suffer unnecessarily simply to exist in a painfully pressurized teaching situation. Even the historic Buddha said that discomfort was not conducive to personal growth. He taught and exemplified moderation, compassion and human kindness.

Yet, it seems that certain groups emulate Gurdjieff's pressurized conditions to imitate the outer form alone. However, during Gurdjieff's era, they were forced to flee the ravages of war torn Russia, and later, Europe. So, the conditions were already deplorable and everyone was thrown up against the chaos of a world at war. But, certain groups which came later, appropriated the harsh duress of Gurdjieff's style by implementing difficult circumstances while making extreme demands on sincere students. This exemplifies imitation, and is indicative of pseudo-schools and pseudo-teachers. Artificial demands and peculiar difficulties are devised as distractions for obfuscation. Life provides sufficient material to cope with in our normal daily existence.

Please know, my intention with this book is to inform, enrich and empower you to transform and awaken. Thus, I feel obligated to clarify certain situations in order to give you clear insight for your own direction.

If you feel the need for a teacher, or a school, I suggest that you do your own research and be cautious. Rather than recommend a facility, my advice is, seek what you think you need by your own efforts. One must be well prepared and informed, as Fourth Way schools demand a great deal from one. Commitment is required; emotionally, intellectually, physically, and financially. One must be willing to relinquish one's personal way of life to study in some schools. Yet, ideally, the true purpose of an esoteric school would be to create a living teaching where sincere students can get the necessary assistance and encouragement they need to work on them self. Despite my own experiences in these rather secluded environments, I encourage you to be absolutely certain you need a school for your personal work. In these schools, you must relinquish your normal life, despite Ouspensky's clear directive that one must do the work in the ordinary conditions of one's normal daily life. Remember, Ouspensky was specific when he said the Fourth Way occurs in the ordinary world, in one's normal daily life. One must apply these practical methods in the ordinary world in which one actually lives on a daily basis, and in a normal manner that is neither contrived, nor artificial. Thus, joining an esoteric school can be a contradictory conundrum. Remember, an esoteric school is not necessary for your awakening. Only you can awaken yourself by your own consistent sincere efforts.

Before you consider a school or organization, it is vital to verify the history and legacy of their teaching. You must be certain it is the right environment for your pure essential needs. Also, it is wise to be cautious of teachers who put themselves on a pedestal above students, and who ascribe to themselves supernormal powers that are impossible to verify. If a teacher is too remote from students, or seems to have lost touch with reality and the essence of the teaching, then he is not a real teacher. The historic Buddha was humble and his teachings were based on his personal experience of awakening. He worked with his students, and did not place himself above them, as that would have been inconsistent with his honorable noble truths.

Esoteric systems, at their core are intended to function in a manner which allows the sincere student freedom to fully embrace the living tradition, and make it their own. This would be the ideal situation to serve your efforts to awaken to your essential nature. One would be encouraged to achieve harmonious internal equilibrium to live in one's natural inner being. But, this precious ideal is not necessarily the reality of life in esoteric schools. Plus, there are obstacles to finding an authentic esoteric teaching environment, as there are questionable schools and teachers, who do not have every single student's best highest interests at heart. The driving force of some schools is strictly making money. These issues are endemic in the metaphysical and new-age marketplace, so I would be remiss if I did not address the obstacles which can befall one who might seek a school. It is inappropriate for me to endorse any school, organization or foundation, but I feel obligated to provide you fair warning of potential problems, as no one is likely to advise you otherwise.

Treating the Fourth Way system as a practical, efficient method to gain self-knowledge, should serve to dispel its propensity towards rigid exclusivity and nouveau spiritualism. People who are interested in this system may be spiritually inclined; however, your spirituality is personal to you and separate from this system. Thus, there is no need to neglect or abandon your personal spiritual or religious beliefs. At its core, the Fourth Way makes no promise of spiritual fulfillment and does not present its ideas, concepts or practical methods as faith based ideologies, nor as religious disciplines. Ouspensky was quite specific about this, and repeatedly advised his students that faith and religion have nothing to do with the precise orderly methodologies which constitute the Fourth Way. Religion and spirituality are quite distinct and separate from the Fourth Way's practical methods for self-study. However, this does not prevent certain teachers from making lofty unverifiable spiritual or mystical claims that border on cultish exploitation. Sincere students may be blindsided by a teacher's claims about their invisible connections to spiritual realms, beings, powers, or forces. This is simply manipulative unverifiable nonsense to confuse and control you.

Those of us who have studied in Fourth Way schools are familiar with their artificial hierarchical structure. Rigid artificial hierarchies are counterproductive to personal growth, as they impose a wall of conflicting challenges around a brilliant esoteric system, which in essence is free of artificially imposed limitations. This hierarchical construct creates an artificial class system which consequently drains the life out of the living practice of personal growth. People who comprise the hierarchy are not enlightened, but are chosen for their active chief features, such as power and dominance to enforce the rigid rules and strict exercises. Inappropriate demands may be made on you by people placed in positions of authority who exert artificially acquired power. While rules and regulations can provide guidelines for how to behave, some students were pushed far beyond their limits. This approach to governing students can also have the unfortunate side effect of turning them into co-dependent followers or powerless devotees, a typical by-product of cults. This odd approach to governing students, seemed to have the strong energy of the Queens of centers, which have a tendency to be controlling. Controlling people does not function as well as an "ethical code of conduct" which would apply to everyone. Instead of intense power struggles, it is more effective to implement an honorable code of ethics which everyone would follow. And, I do mean everyone, including the teacher.

Order and decorum are a necessary component of any organization, but in an esoteric school there may be the unintended consequences of giving power to those who cannot handle it appropriately. Artificial class systems are unhealthy, unnatural and mechanical; precisely that which esotericism aims to work against. Thus, it does not function as a healthy, sustainable model for sincere individuals who seek their own true miraculous potential for higher consciousness. In one school, I witnessed weird behavior from some people in positions of authority, who lacked basic interpersonal skills such as good manners and compassion, which are essential. We can easily observe this unnatural behavior in politics when unsuitable people who have no political experience or legislative expertise are elected to political office. America is currently a nation in chaotic turmoil owing to the arrogance and smug power of a questionable elected official who vents hatred, fear, racism and discrimination on social networks causing disharmony, discord and divisiveness.

In writing this book I feel an enormous responsibility in presenting these valuable ideas carefully and clearly to help people. However, I also believe it is imperative to caution you to be self-protective and alert to avoid being duped by charlatans, and cultish schools that may not have your best interests at heart. It is essential to verify these groups to be assured there is not a history of problems, or misrepresentation. Keep in mind, most organizations have plentiful resources to maintain appearances and public relations. Please be aware of lofty unverifiable claims which groups may put forth. Be prepared, as no one can tell you where to study, or with whom. If you genuinely believe that you need an esoteric school, your task is to find it for yourself.

Please remember, no one can awaken you but you, yourself. Awakening is solely your own personal work. However, I feel the need to inspire you to recognize what you genuinely need, and, what you do not need. It is best to address these matters in a forthright direct manner to protect those who seek a true school. My conscience urges me to elucidate issues which I witnessed in schools. In one particular situation, many students appeared to worship the teacher. As a result, they seemed to lose interest in achieving their own enlightened self-awareness. Perhaps they felt that worshipping the teacher would automatically connect them to higher centers, or to the mysterious higher powers he spoke of. This is impossible. Blindly following anyone only creates unnecessary obstacles, which prevent you from benefiting. Following a teacher does not guarantee you will gain self-awareness, higher consciousness, or awaken. The Fourth Way is not spiritualism or religion, and blind faith simply has no part in it. You must empirically verify everything. You can only become self-aware by your own consistent personal efforts. No one can awaken you, but you.

An esoteric school must serve every student with integrity, dignity, truth and ethical behavior conducive to each individual student's wellbeing. A teacher must serve each student who wishes to learn these methods. Yet this rarely occurred in one school, which was set up as a corporation, and operated various businesses under its corporate non-profit status. It is best to avoid the schools which function primarily as corporate businesses. In these organizations, you will not have any quality contact with, or direct access to the teacher, who merely serves as a figure head, and remains distant from most students. If you have no direct contact with the teacher is impossible to verify his merits in a realistic capacity. It may be that schools and teachers such as this have become obsolete and have lost any usefulness for sincere seekers in our modern times.

Other Fourth Ways schools and groups I studied with, were arranged in a more holistic manner to facilitate and accommodate each student directly, and individually in a qualitative manner. They served solely as schools for the development of awareness and higher consciousness, rather than as business corporations. This ensured that one would receive direct transmission of knowledge from a verifiable source. One distinctive school I studied with was comprised primarily of artists who worked in various mediums, such as music, literature, fashion and fine art. There was direct contact with a teacher and no artificial hierarchy, so it was democratic and beneficial for everyone. In real esoteric schools, each student must spend quality time with a teacher to have their needs addressed. For example, in Taoist and Buddhist traditions, one works closely with one's teacher, which encourages one's personal growth, and enhances one's true potential for awakening. A genuine school will be verifiable, and one will have direct contact with one's teacher. Without this solid foundation of a healthy wholesome connection to one's teacher there is no teaching, as there is no legitimate compassionate mentor to guide one. In truth, it is best to follow Ouspensky's vital directive to verify the teaching situations which you may encounter, and particularly to verify schools and teachers.

An esoteric school does not need to be harsh, but sometimes working with others can feel rather harsh. A sincere student may feel confused, uncertain, or discouraged, rather than feeling mentored and guided in their aim to reach their highest potential in their essential nature. It is imperative to be self-protective if you wish to find an authentic school or teacher to work with. You must feel free to express your submerged essential nature to develop your true potential and enhance your self-awareness. But, you must also be free to leave a school at any time for your own reasons, without any peculiar comments or veiled threats. If you find an esoteric school that is inclusive, free of dogmatized cultism and which functions in a naturally occurring wholesome nurturing manner, you will be quite fortunate indeed.

Several years ago, I contacted an interesting fellow whom I had known in a particular Fourth Way school, which we had both departed from. He had been a staff member there, and had always been helpful and kind. I went to see him to discuss certain matters which had surfaced. During our discussion, I asked him why he left the school and his answer was revealing. He said he had never been able to verify the incessant spiritual references which became pervasive. I clearly understood his reasoning. He was intellectually centered, and this school had become riddled with weird spiritualism. Without verification, one cannot build a foundation for awakening. My personal reason for leaving was that I had gotten all that was possible from that school.

Please know, you are a valuable human being. Self-knowledge, enhanced self-awareness and awakening are your natural birthright. You have options and personal rights to protect yourself if unethical situations arise. Your personal wellbeing and protection is the most important factor. It is essential to clarify any confusing matters that might arise, and always protect your precious true self. For example, one school claimed that gaining self-awareness was impossible without them. They insisted students be dependent on their help for personal growth. This was a blatantly false doctrine, used as a manipulative tactic to intimidate sincere individuals. Schools that try to convince you that you cannot awaken without their instruction are not real schools. The teacher in this school put forth dogmatic rhetoric riddled with contradictions, and was revealed to be embroiled in pervasive sexual abuse scandals. Charlatans are rampant in commercial venues of consciousness which plague the world of nouveau spiritualism in the new-age market place.

If you are cautiously mindful, you will minimize the risks of falling under the spell of those who claim to have super-conscious powers. One must be vigilant, as unethical charlatans never have your best interests at heart. These pseudo-teachers are unsuitable for sincere students who are seeking wholesome nurturance and pure mentoring with ethical integrity. There is a history of pseudo-teachers who have caused innocent students horrific harm. Appearances can be deceiving. Perhaps it is useful to remember the fairy tale about the emperor's new clothes, as it may help protect you and guide you to verify any questionable teachers you might meet on your path. Although many of us as young sincere seekers, thought we needed a school or teacher, we were merely naïve. In this modern era, it is wise common sense to protect yourself.

Like Ouspensky's realization that Gurdjieff did not possess what he had attributed to him, I also realized that some teachers did not possess what they claimed to possess. They revealed they did not have heightened levels of consciousness which they claimed, nor a high degree of conscience or compassion. Having met some of these pseudo-teachers, I feel it prudent to caution you on your path to enlightenment. I place great value on these brilliant esoteric concepts and practical methods. My sincere wish it that their pure wisdom will assist you. Remember, those who live in truth and have attained the higher levels of consciousness, will not make boastful arrogant claims about lofty super achievements, nor flaunt artificial powers of mysterious spirituality that are simply unverifiable. Rather, they would fly quietly below the radar of life, without attracting too much attention to themselves. This is the essence of esotericism and all truly authentic esoteric teachings. Quiet dignity and truth prevails.

I wish to emphasize, there is no need to depart from your normal daily life to experience the wealth of wisdom which these essential esoteric ideas and practical methods can bring to your life. Although we may tend to think that what we need is, "out there, somewhere," in reality what we need is already within us. Going away to some remote location is not necessary. You only need to go in search of your true inner self. Be mindfully present in this moment and observe yourself impartially as you are, without any judgments or criticisms. Continue to mindfully observe yourself to gain command of your fears, negative emotions, identifications, attachments, self-doubts, illusions, delusions and to relinquish false personality. You become self-aware by eliminating what is false, negative, and unnatural to your essential nature. This work requires your ongoing honest efforts to discover who you truly are within. Your awakening is your personal responsibility. Only you can awaken yourself by your own sincere efforts. With mindful self-observation, you will gradually recognize your personal centers of influence and understand yourself with greater clarity.

Remember, knowledge is power, and self-knowledge is personal empowerment. Gaining self-knowledge gives you greater power over your fears, identifications, self-doubts and your life choices. We may not live in a fully enlightened society which truly nurtures the sincere individual aspiring to enlightenment, but we can achieve our own awakening to contribute to and create a more enlightened world.

You are the most miraculous element in your awakening.

Your path is within you.

CHAPTER 18

ABUNDANT OPPORTUNITIES FOR PERSONAL GROWTH AND TRANSFORMATION

Your awakening is a natural holistic experience which occurs in your normal daily life on a moment to moment basis, and it is your personal choice. You can begin right now by being mindfully present in this moment while observing yourself impartially without illusions, negativity, or self-doubts. The practical reality is, we can awaken and experience our personal enlightenment as we live our normal life. There are abundant opportunities for sincere individuals to develop enhanced self-awareness and to discover their essential nature in the ordinary conditions of daily life. Awakening begins in oneself by recognizing what is most authentic within. There is no need to abandon your life to retreat to a secluded esoteric school or a hidden monastery. Awakening is not an isolated event that can only occur on a remote mountain top, or in a walled forest retreat. There is certainly a massive legacy of wisdom and guidance available to help you. You can study independently or with credible organizations and groups around the world, from accredited universities and colleges, to small local meditation groups. The University of San Diego Center for Mindfulness in Southern California, and the Oxford

Mindfulness Center in England are two examples of accredited world class universities offering this valuable resource. There are countless more beneficial resources available in towns and cities around the world. Be assured, there are abundant opportunities and credible resources available for you to investigate to explore higher consciousness wherever you may live.

The Buddhist term "mindfulness," is synonymous with the Fourth Way term, "self-remembering." They are essentially the exact same concept. Mindfulness is derived from the Pali term, *sati,* and the Sanskrit term, *smrti,* which both translate as, "to remember," just as Gurdjieff's term, "self-remembering," indicates. It is apparent Gurdjieff studied various wisdom traditions in his quest, including Hinduism, Buddhism and Sanskrit. Mindfulness and meditation are traditional methods that you can easily implement into your life, on your own, or with others. There is truly no need to disavow your normal life for a hidden esoteric school. Again, there are plentiful opportunities to practice locally wherever you live in towns and cities worldwide. If you feel the need for a study group, you can locate credible mindfulness and meditation resources online, which you can research before attending. There are abundant supportive resources to assist you in a natural, wholesome, holistic manner which can be found nearly everywhere. Enlightenment is not an obscure exotic mysteriously unattainable destination. It is a practical reality we can experience in our normal daily life.

Even pure wisdom tradition teachers, such as the honorable Dalai Lama of Tibet, have made their teachings available around the world, so we may treasure their precious wisdom. But, we must not discount the tragic events which transpired in the 1940's, when China invaded Tibet and decimated their peaceful culture, to understand the dramatic impact of negative circumstances on authentic esoteric teachings, from foreign invasion and war. Some of the true teachers who I had the good fortune to learn from have died. One unique Armenian teacher I studied with, told me about his personal experiences when he studied with Gurdjieff in his younger life. As a result of studying with this teacher many years ago, I was given a rare opportunity to ask him my personal questions about Gurdjieff, the Fourth Way and other esoteric concepts which were important for me to verify in my early studies. When I learned of his death, I realized how very fortunate I was to have had that quality time with him to ask my sincere questions.

Many of the wisdom traditions share a common core of truth and are quite complimentary to one another. In this regard, one can avail oneself of the honorable wisdom teachings in local holistic groups which offer wholesome nurturing, and are readily available in towns and cities around the world. These provide an excellent opportunity for you to receive sincere assistance as you begin to work on yourself. For example, the timeless teachings of Taoism, Buddhism, Zen, mindfulness, meditation and yoga are all living wisdom traditions which are available to study in a beneficial, practical and ethical manner. For more than 40 years studying and utilizing the Fourth Way esoteric ideas in my life, I have repeatedly verified its striking similarities to Taoism and Buddhism, in all their forms and practices, but particularly with Buddhism. Millions of people around the world have discovered the simple holistic practices of mindfulness and meditation which can be easily incorporated into one's normal daily life.

There are authentic honorable teachings which are widely available for you to study their perennial wisdom. You can locate and research viable resources online to learn more about mindfulness and meditation. Certainly, there are wonderful teachers in these wholesome living wisdom traditions whom you may wish to spend some quality time with. Perhaps they will inspire you gain greater insight into your personal reality. For example, I discovered Taoism in the 1960's and felt a natural affinity for its sensible psychology and treasured tenets. Fortunately, it came to my assistance in 1985 when I was studying in a Fourth Way school which I had become skeptical of. At that time, I felt a need to develop myself along pure humble lines consistent with the sincere wisdom of Taoism, and was grateful to find a compassionate Taoist priest who taught principles and methods of the Tao near my home. He met with students in his modest sanctuary, and was also available for individual guidance. His sanctuary was a welcome haven, and provided a respite from the restrictive limitations and harsh rules of the school which was making inordinate financial demands on students. The humble Taoist priest created a nurturing environment, which gave me an opportunity to ask my vital questions. He was a King of Diamonds who responded with deep thoughtful logical answers based in lucid reality. He assured me that my decision to leave that particular school was right action. But, if I had not been prepared by having previously studied Lao Tzu, the Tao Te Ching, and other Taoist literature, this unique opportunity for healing growth may not have arisen when I needed it.

In addition to Taoism, I had wonderfully fortunate opportunities to meet and study with Tibetan Buddhist monks and lamas. One Tibetan lama was a compassionate King of Hearts who gave helpful advice about my art projects. This period of study reinforced my personal understanding of the connectedness between the ancient wisdom traditions. I recognized precise parallels between the Fourth Way and different forms of Buddhism, which were absolutely clear and unmistakable. This illuminating period was followed by two years studying at a humble Zen Buddhist temple with a Japanese Soto Zen priest. He was a King of Spades who taught Zen meditation and yoga with his serene Zen monks. Other insightful transformational trainings also came my way. When I availed myself of these studies, it was as if one opportunity after the other arose. In these wonderful learning experiences, I verified a nearly identical core of truth within each wise teaching. The remarkable and prevalent availability of honorable wisdom traditions has provided me with consistent potential for self-study and self-discovery. Certainly, the most sustainable renewable energy, is one's own personal desire to fuel one's journey to self-knowledge, enhanced self-awareness and enlightenment.

The key factor is one's willingness to be receptive to what is readily available to one, with a keen eye of discernment. We must each avail ourselves of the opportunities that arise to lift ourselves out of our own complacency. Mindfulness and self-observation are our practical methods. Awakening and enlightenment is certainly possible for individuals who make consistent sincere efforts. One must seize this moment, and each moment that follows, with mindful self-observation and one's own pure presence. You can begin right now, in this moment. To paraphrase the philosopher, Johann Goethe, whatever you can do, or think that you can do, begin it now, as this moment has power.

My personal aim and responsibility:

I feel a strong sense of responsibility, and commitment in writing this book about our centers of influence within, and other essential concepts and methods from the Fourth Way. My primary objective is to present these ideas and practices as I have studied and lived them, in an easy to understand concise manner. I feel humbly obliged to elucidate this unique system, and hope to bring these ideas to life for a new audience. Individuals who may not approach Ouspensky's massive intellectual writings, or who might find Gurdjieff a bit unwieldly, may find this book easier to understand. I have worked to keep the essential elements as pure as possible without distortion, but also, with the aim to enliven the ideas, concepts and methods clearly and objectively. My personal work necessitates that I fulfill my obligation to write this book to move forward on my own path of self-discovery and enlightenment. Much time has elapsed since I initially began my personal studies over 40 years ago. Since then, and throughout this incredible journey through time my inner work has evolved propelling me onto parallel pathways for other miraculous journeys which have been vital to my personal growth and awakening. And, my journey continues.

There are many paths which you can follow to reach your own self-knowledge and personal enlightenment. The Fourth Way is one path you can employ to develop self-awareness with practical ideas and methods. These are universal concepts to help you achieve self-knowledge, self-awareness, greater self-confidence and self-reliance, while allaying your fears and your self-doubts. As you awaken, you contribute more meaningful energy to the world with your pure presence. Raising your personal level of being, radiates higher influences to the world you inhabit. I wish to assure you that becoming enlightened is your natural birthright, but you alone are responsible for your awakening. The task begins with the simplicity of being present in the moment as you mindfully observe yourself with impartiality, but also with wonder. Awakening is a pure human miracle.

Remember, there is no need to withdraw from the world, from your life, or from your normal daily activities. There are no extreme rules, nor severe austerities you must endure. Practice mindful self-observation and incorporate it into your daily routine to enhance and enrich your life. Perhaps the only real requirement is that you possess a sufficient desire to gain self-awareness. You must make consistent efforts to be present to your life in the moment. Employ mindful self-observation, be attentive and intentional, limit habitual negative thoughts, minimize aimless imagination, eliminate unnecessary identifications, and drop the mask of false personality so you may awaken to your highest potential. You can begin where you are right now, with pure mindful self-observation in this moment and in the moments to follow. Enlightenment is certainly possible for you when you live your life in the moment guided by your true essential nature.

This book represents my personal lines of work and reflects my deep sense of purpose and appreciation for this wisdom. To enliven the practicality of these ideas, I have added supplemental esoteric concepts to assist you. These ideas and methods are all user friendly and highly practical. There are other elements of this system I have not mentioned, as this book is primarily focused on the centers of influence within which play a key role in shaping our life. I wish to acknowledge that I have opted out of using a manuscript editor, simply to preserve the meaning of the ideas without misconstrued interpretations. This is to avoid the possibility that someone might alter words, or phrases which are specific to this system, the language and history of these ideas. In the past, some of my art projects were altered by editing changes which other people made. Unbeknownst to me, one fellow made changes prior to printing that vastly altered the appearance of one project. His boss apologized for the unauthorized changes, and the fellow lost his job as the damage was irreversible. To preserve and protect the essential meaning of this work, I have edited it myself. Although I have spent much time reviewing for errors, there may be some which have been missed. It is my hope the deeper meaning will come through to inform, empower and encourage you on your path. My humble aim is to inspire you. I feel that those of us who have studied these majestic concepts in depth can serve as guides and messengers to help uplift others to their own inherent higher possibilities.

Remember, these concepts can be implemented simply and seamlessly into your normal daily life. You do not need to go anywhere or change the circumstances of your normal daily life to benefit from these enlightening ideas. These practical methods are a natural progression of beneficial modalities which can be incorporated into your life right now, as you are in this moment. All you need is already within you as your true self in your essential nature. As you begin to see through the layers and accumulations of negativity, imagination, false personality, self-doubt, fear, habitual behaviors and identifications which weigh you down, you will gradually shed and eliminate that which is unnecessary. Artificial encumbrances prevent you from experiencing your true self in an authentic holistic manner. With sincere mindful self-observation, you can consciously and willingly let go of artificial burdens, which do not serve your highest potential or your essential nature.

The eminent Fourth Way master teacher, Peter Ouspensky, advises that we must each reconstruct the system for our self. This book has been written with my purest intentions, to reconstruct my personal knowledge from my own lengthy experiences of the Fourth Way, with its massive wisdom, as I have lived it. My hope is that it will help sincere seekers on their path to gain self-knowledge, enhanced self-awareness and higher consciousness. This book is my humble contribution to perpetuate the Fourth Way legacy of great wisdom. It is also my tribute to honor the esteemed P. D. Ouspensky who masterfully preserved these precious ideas.

My personal aim is to inform, empower and encourage others to reach their authentic awakened potential. As you practice mindful self-observation you will gain increased harmony in your emotions, your intellect, your physical actions and your sensitivities to bring healing to our world. As you become more self-aware, conscious, compassionate, and conscientious on your path to enlightenment you create vital energy to heal, and transform the negative effects of social injustice, and political turbulence. Those of us who strive to become conscious must play a more conscious role in helping the world eliminate that which does not serve the highest good of everyone, for the environment and for our dear planet

Please know, your awakening contributes enhanced awareness and illumination to our society, our culture, and our world. As we each individually awaken to our highest potential to become enlightened, we emit our own radiant inner light of consciousness to brighten the path and light the way for others to follow. Like a newborn star, your personal enlightenment shines a beacon of hope where there was darkness. Awakening and enlightenment are your natural birthright to claim for yourself and for the world which you are such an important part of. You are much more valuable and powerful than you might realize at present.

In closing, I wish to emphasize, only you can enhance your self-knowledge with your own personal efforts. No one can awaken you, but you yourself. To attain enhanced self-awareness, you must build a firm foundation based upon your personal self-knowledge. You begin your journey to reach self-discovery with mindful self-observation. Understanding the wisdom of centers will help unlock the door to your essential nature. Being present in each moment with mindful self-observation is the master key to open the door to your own unlimited personal universe.

May your journey lead you directly to the source of the miraculous within your true essential natural self.

Your path is within you.

ABOUT THE AUTHOR

Cheryl Shrode-Noble graduated high school with a drama scholarship and studied theater. She began modeling as a teenager and later spent eight years working as a model in Paris, Milan, and London. While living in London, she was introduced to the Fourth Way and recognized similarities to both Taoist and Buddhist philosophies. She decided to explore these new esoteric ideas in depth and studied in various Fourth Way schools for ten years.

After Shrode-Noble retired from her modeling career, she worked as an account executive for Ralph Lauren fragrances. Subsequent to her studies in Fourth Way schools, she studied Tibetan Buddhism with humble Tibetan monks, Zen Buddhism in a Soto Zen temple, and Taoism with a Taoist priest. Shrode-Noble, once an active member of the Sierra Club, is passionate about environmental protection. She appreciates fine art and antiques, spending time in nature, and inspiring others to follow their personal paths.

39934883R00263

Made in the USA
Columbia, SC
11 December 2018